SWANSEA UNIVERSITY COLLEGE
LIBRARY

Classmark: DA 600 B9 2

Location: Miners' Library

Accession No:

100387878

WITHDRAWN FROM STOCK

Approaches to local history

This book must be returned immed-
ately it is asked for by the

D1556631

285186

To my students

And even I can remember
A day when the historians left blanks
        in their writings
I mean for things they didn't know

Ezra Pound
Cantos XIII

Approaches to local history

Alan Rogers, M.A., Ph.D., F.R.Hist.S., F.S.A.
Senior Lecturer in History
Department of Adult Education
University of Nottingham

Preface by W. G. Hoskins

Longman
London and New York

SOUTH WALES
MINERS LIBRARY 280

Longman Group Limited London

*Associated companies, branches and representatives
throughout the world*

*Published in the United States of America
by Longman Inc., New York*

© First edition (*This Was Their World*) Alan Rogers 1972
© Second edition Longman Group Limited 1977

All rights reserved. No part of this publication may be
reproduced, stored in a retrieval system, or transmitted
in any form or by any means, electronic, mechanical,
photocopying, recording, or otherwise, without the
prior permission of the Copyright owner.

First published as This Was Their World *1972*
Second edition 1977

Library of Congress Cataloging in Publication Data

Rogers, Alan
  Approaches to local history.

  First ed. published in 1972 under title: This was their world.
  Includes bibliographical references and index.
  1. Great Britain—Historiography.   2. Great Britain—History,
Local. I. Title.
DA1.R65 1977   942.081'07'2   76—54265
ISBN 0 582 48508 8
ISBN 0 582 48509 6 pbk.

Set in IBM Journal 10 on 11pt
and printed in Great Britain by
Richard Clay (The Chaucer Press) Ltd,
Bungay, Suffolk

UNIVERSITY COLLEGE
LIBRARY
SWANSEA

Contents

List of figures

List of plates

Preface

As long ago as 1885 Bishop Creighton remarked in the *Archaeological Journal* for that year that 'English history is at bottom a provincial history, but the vigorous undercurrent of a strong provincial life in different parts of England is seldom seriously considered by historians'. Few universities if any took notice of this profound piece of sense, though there was the occasional eminent scholar like A. Hamilton Thompson (affectionately known as 'Ham Tom' to many of us in our young days) producing what was fundamentally local history for decade after decade, lecturing to local antiquarian and historical societies all over England and writing almost innumerable learned articles. Few parts of England escaped his eye.

But it took a long time to get the pursuit of local history 'organised' in classes (and some old-fashioned local antiquarians seem to deplore the new discipline); and here a handful of adult education tutors during the 1930s and afterwards (of whom I was but one) laid the foundations slowly and methodically. They were the real growing-point of a wide new field of historical knowledge, and I tried to systematise the approach in my *Local History in England*, first published in 1959 and revised in 1972. But even so it was not possible in that revision to take account of all the new work which has been done by amateur groups and professional students – work which has been blazing new trails as well as consolidating the findings of those of us who were pioneers in this field of scholarship.

It is thus fitting that some twenty years of real progress in local history should be marked by a revised edition of Dr Alan Rogers' book now entitled *Approaches to Local History*. Few people have done more than he to promote local history throughout England – whether by his own studies on Lincolnshire and especially medieval Stamford, or by teaching and lecturing widely throughout the country, or by helping other students of local history with advice and information. In this book originally published by the BBC under the title of *This Was Their World* (incidentally, a more imaginative title than the newer one), he has brought together a great deal of his accumulated knowledge and insights, and offers them to the local historian. It is a practical book outlining both the questions which can be asked of the local community and the sources from which they may be answered. It maintains a judicial balance between the documentary and the material evidence from buildings and landscape which I personally find most gratifying. It takes account of much recent work over a very wide field indeed. If perhaps its interests are more urban than rural, more in the nineteenth century than earlier, in this it complements my own studies; and the earlier centuries and rural communities are by no means neglected.

This is a book which should be read by all who are engaged in any form of local history, for it deals with the local community in the round. Every local historian will find some new information, some new insight in these far-reaching pages. It is a book addressed to practitioners, written by one who is himself a practitioner; and I am most pleased to associate myself with it, in its new form.

W. G. Hoskins
Exeter

October 1976

Acknowledgements

Acknowledgement is due to the following
Faber & Faber Ltd for extract from 'Cantos XIII' from *The Cantos of Ezra Pound.*

Acknowledgement is due to the following for permission to reproduce illustrations
Aerofilms Ltd, Plate 19
Banbury Public Library, Plates 40(c) and (d)
Birmingham Reference Library (Local History Department), Plate 30(a)
Curators of the Bodleian Library, Plate 39
B.T.C. archives, Plate 20
Derby Borough Library, Plates 8(a) and 9
Professor Dyos, Plate 13
Exeter City Library, Plates 30(b) and 32(b)
P. M. Goodchild and Son, Plate 25
Greater London Council Print Collection, Plate 22(b)
Controller, HMSO, Plates 2, 6, 8(b), 26 and 35
House of Lords Record Office, Plate 21
Kent County Council, Plate 33 (original document in Kent County Archives Office)
King's Lynn Museum, Plate 23
Leeds City Corporation, Plates 4 and 5
Leicester Museums, Plates 11 and 12
Manchester Public Libraries, Plate 18
Dr Helen Meller, Plate 40(a)
National Monuments Record, Plates 22(a) and 32(a)
Newham Borough Libraries, Plates 14, 15, 16 and 17
Norfolk and Norwich Record Office, Plate 27(a)
University of Nottingham (Department of Photography), Plates 1, 3, 7, 10, 24, 29(b), 34 and 36
Nottingham Public Libraries, Plates 37, 38, 40(b)
Radio Times Hulton Picture Library, Plate 29(a)
Sheffield City Libraries, Plate 28
Wymondham Methodist Church, Plate 27(b)
Plate 31 was specially photographed by John Topham with permission of Farnborough Hospital.

Acknowledgement is due to the following for sources of the figures
M. W. Beresford, Professor of Economic History, The University of Leeds, Figs 14(a), (b), (c) and (d) and 15(a), material based on redrawing of unpublished manuscript maps from the Leeds Civic Hall, Town Clerk's conveyances.

xii   *Acknowledgements*

Burton Joyce Local History Group, Fig. 13.

Chester Record Office, Fig. 6, based on Hunter-Weston Map of Chester 1789 and DeLavaux's Map of Chester 1745.

David and Charles, Newton Abbott, Fig. 18, based on a diagram by R. Lawton in *Geographical Interpretations of Historical Sources* edited by Alan R. Baker, John D. Hamshere and John Langton.

R. L. Greenall, Department of Adult Education, University of Leicester, Fig. 12.

Harrogate Public Library, Fig. 18, based on a diagram by J. Patmore showing distribution of occupations in the towns of Harrogate and Knaresborough in 1851 reproduced from *An Atlas of Harrogate*.

Adrian Henstock and The Ashbourne Local History Group, Fig. 17, based on a map drawn by Peter Fletcher.

Controller, HMSO, Fig. 15(c), from Schedule to LGP G39, Leeds Housing Confirmation Order 1951.

J. R. Lowerson, University of Sussex, Figs 24 and 25.

All drawings by Constance and Brian Dear.

Foreword

This book in itself demonstrates something of the difficulties which face the average local historian. His subject is a very wide one indeed, ranging over the whole field of human activity in the past. And yet he must attempt to write within a limited space. There is thus always the danger that his statements may become misleading generalisations, not applicable to all parts of the country or to all periods. The amount of material to be covered may lead to the tendency to put into the story a long, meaningless catalogue of events or sources. At the same time, the themes of the local historian are not always clearly distinguished and the sources he must use may well refer to more than one of them, a fact which can result in some tedious repetition. I am very conscious that this book reflects all these problems.

Nevertheless, the book will, I hope, have some value both to those who are about to start the process of local historical study and to those who are already engaged in it, whether individually or in groups. Originally, the book accompanied a series of broadcasts on local history on BBC Radio 3, and each of its chapters corresponds with one of the programmes. These pages thus contain much of the material referred to by the contributors to the broadcasts; indeed much that is in this book has been written by these contributors.

But the book ranges rather more widely than the programmes and should therefore be of more permanent use. For instance, it aims to paint in something of the general background to the subject under discussion — although in covering so much this part of each chapter has had to be very much condensed. This is particularly true of the background earlier than about 1800 which has received very summary treatment. Most of the emphasis in this book, as in the programmes, has been placed on the nineteenth century. Even here, the background section is only intended as a general guide to trends. The local historian must turn to more detailed accounts of his period, such as Professor Best's survey of *Mid-Victorian Britain, 1850–1875*, which for many purposes may be regarded as a 'set text' to go with much that is written in this book.

Again, this book discusses source material for local history for the periods before as well as during the nineteenth century. The programmes confined their attention to the later period. But both range widely in their use of examples. I have been most conscious that I know most about the East Midlands and Norfolk, and I have tried as far as possible to take my examples from work I have done myself. I can only hope that I have been able to fill out the gaps in my knowledge by drawing on the willing help and great experience of other local historians in other parts of England.

This has left me with enormous debts. How great they are may be seen in the notes. Several scholars (and not only those who took part in the series) have given me time as well as unpublished material, together with permission to quote from it.

Others have read parts of the manuscript and commented freely on them. To try to name them all would be hazardous; to name a few invidious. But three in particular stand out — R. L. Greenall of Leicester University who wrote and presented the radio series; Roger Fieldhouse of Leeds University who spent a great deal of time on this book; and Robert Fleetwood of Nottingham University Library who dug out the most unlikely books from the most unpromising places in the shortest of times. They are responsible for making this book possible, but cannot be blamed in any way for anything said within its pages. Mrs Margaret Gosling who typed the manuscript and Mrs S. Davies who helped with the proofs and index have eased my burdens enormously. To them and all the others, I say a very sincere thank you.

Burnham Market,
Norfolk

October 1971

That a new edition of this book is called for is most encouraging; it has provided me with the opportunity to correct those errors which reviewers have pointed out in the first edition and to take note of the very significant advances in local studies which have marked the last few years. While the text has been amended very slightly, the notes and references have been entirely rewritten and expanded.

A.R.

August 1975

Introduction

This is a book of questions. It deals with the approaches to his subject that a local historian can adopt. It does not provide the answers to these questions, for such answers will be different for each local community studied. Rather it sets out to isolate some of the most usual questions which can be asked in the study of the past of any group of people. Local history concerns the search for answers, but in order that the answers may be meaningful, the questions themselves must be well framed in the first place. It is to this end that this book has been written.

These questions cannot however be treated in isolation. They depend for their validity upon the overall framework in which the history of each town and village is set. An outline of such a framework is thus given. But it must be remembered that the brevity necessary to do this within such a short compass in many cases leads to generalisations which more detailed local studies would deny. Nor is the framework important by itself for, as Professor Finberg has reminded us, each of the units of local history has its own timescale, which may or may not be related to the overall national framework.[1] Rather, it is intended to do two things only – to establish whether the local answer is or is not in line with the general pattern, and in its turn to lead on to further questions.

Questions not only need a framework; they also need answers. And answers depend upon raw material being available to provide the necessary information. There is thus provided here a brief description of the most common types of source material used to answer these questions. Clearly space does not allow a full treatment of all the sources for English local history; rather only the most useful and most common are given and their uses discussed. But not all of these will exist for each locality, and on occasion gaps in the records relating to some specific local community will have to be filled in, in outline, by assumptions drawn from the general framework. Nevertheless a great deal of material for local history does survive, and with the posing of the question goes the need to expound the techniques to find out the answer.

But such a general approach, by itself, may well prove rather unsatisfying. Detailed examples, illustrating such techniques, are necessary. There is, however, an embarrassingly large number of such examples, both published and unpublished, ranging widely both in time and in place. In order to achieve some measure of coherence, all those chosen here relate to what has been called 'the mid-Victorian period', the England of about one hundred years ago. No restriction has been made in regard to place. No one specific community has been selected; rather the illustrations have been drawn from all over the country (as far as possible), and what is said about them is relevant to virtually every place in England. But they are connected in that they are almost all concentrated in period in the second half of the nineteenth century.

There are several reasons for choosing such a period. The most important is, I suppose, that the period is not so far away as to have lost contemporary social significance. There is a great deal of interest in the not-so-distant past, and the opening of the 1871 census in January 1972 will have focused attention once more upon a period which in some families will be well within family memory at least.

The 'coming-out' of the 1871 census returns is indeed an event of importance in this context. For the censuses are one of the great advantages which this period has for the local historian over all other periods. The nineteenth century is the only period when one can guarantee a universal coverage of the whole of England in certain record material (Wales, Scotland and Ireland have very distinct local history problems, even in that period).[2] Several of the basic sources are comprehensive, especially what may be regarded as the staple diet for local history in the late nineteenth century, the records of the census and the Ordnance Survey maps. The first was collected locally but preserved centrally,[3] and both the printed statistical summaries for all the censuses from 1801 onwards and the unprinted enumerators' books, which from 1851 to the last available returns of 1871 contain a great deal of local information, cover every region of England, every town and village. The second, the maps of the O.S., began very early in the century on a scale of one inch to the mile, and this was completed in 1873; meanwhile new, larger scale surveys, at 6 inches and 25 inches to the mile, had been begun and by the end of the century almost the whole of England and Wales had been covered.[4] Thus for every place in the mid-nineteenth century, there are three detailed social surveys at ten-yearly intervals (1851–71) and at least one detailed topographical survey,[5] and from them a great deal can be learnt about the local community as it then existed.

These are not of course the only sources for local history at this date. Indeed, the nineteenth century is the richest period for the study of English local history. There is a whole range of material not available at earlier periods, such as government reports and the so-called parliamentary 'blue books', and increasingly as the century went on new legislation (especially in the years about 1870), such as Forster's Education Act of 1870 and the Public Health Acts of 1866 and 1872, created new sources. Much locally produced material has survived as well, the most important and universal of which are the newspapers. These are almost as comprehensive as the census and the O.S. maps, for the events of virtually every village and certainly of every town were diligently recorded and circulated for their neighbours to read about. The local newspaper (of which there will usually be more than one for each locality) provides the third staple diet of the nineteenth-century local historian. Similarly, the non-written sources for the nineteenth century, the buildings and the village and town-scapes, are prolific, despite considerable depletion during and after the last war, and these once again call for a full examination by the local historian. At the same time, the memories of the older members of society are often still fresh. It is thus possible to draw upon living tradition (or 'oral history' as it has come to be called) for this study.[6] From all of these and of course other sources, a good deal can be learned of the history of any English local community in the 1870s, whether it is a big city or small village.

Not only are the sources of local history for this period plentiful, but they are often more easily available. Many of them are printed, and even those which are hand written do not require the skill of palaeography to read them as do sixteenth century documents. And they can be readily understood; they do not call for an extensive knowledge of legal history like early deeds, nor a proficiency in bastard

Latin like most medieval records. They are normally straightforward in their interpretation.

What is more, the background for this period is perhaps by now the best charted territory of all English history, and thus the local historian has an adequate framework within which to place his own studies. The analysis by Professor Best, in his *Mid-Victorian Britain, 1850—1875* (1971) is only the most recent (though from the local historian's point of view, probably the most valuable) of many descriptions of the social trends of the Victorian period. Professor Best's book is indeed an important work in this connection. It clearly illustrates the interaction between the national framework and the various localities, each of which had a separate identity and often divergent development. Further, it asks the sort of questions which especially interest the local historian as we shall see, and it becomes clear that a good deal more is known for this period (at least in these terms) than for many earlier periods of English history.

It is for these reasons that the various detailed illustrations, taken as they are from many different parts of England, have been limited in time to the later nineteenth century. It must however be stressed that they are simply examples, and as such have much wider application than just to the history of the local community in that period. The questions that we shall pose about them can be asked of the same community (or others) at earlier periods of their existence. The sources from which these questions can be answered may not always be universally valid; they will of course vary from period to period. They may exist for some places and not for others. But it is along the line of these and other similar questions that the truest approach to local history would seem to lie.

In what follows then, the chapters are divided into four sections. The first, the analysis of the questions, is followed by an outline of the framework, and by discussions of the sources of local history, both before 1800 and in the nineteenth century. Of the four elements it is the first which is the most important. This is not a general history of English local society, though such a book is very much needed.[7] It is not a book primarily about sources, although a good deal of space is devoted to this.[8] Nor is it a study of the English local community in the 1870s.[9] It is basically a study of how to approach local history; an agenda for local historians.

Chapter 1

Local history and its approaches

Any discussion of the approaches to local history must be preceded by a definition of the subject itself. What is local history?

It is not difficult to define 'history', although a good deal of discussion still surrounds the word. Partly this is caused by ambiguity in the use of the term 'history'; it frequently appears in two quite distinct, though related, senses. On the one hand, it is often employed to mean 'the past'. Whatever happened in days gone by is history. Thus the historian studies history, in this sense. On the other hand, it also means the reconstruction that any historian makes from his study of the past. In this sense, the historian writes history. The difference is a marginal one, but nevertheless can lead to some uncertainties and confusions. For the purposes of this enquiry, however, the word history may be defined as 'the study of man's past'.[1]

It is not so easy to define the word 'local', in this context. So much goes under this term. The study of a family or of a village at a certain date; the narrative of a business firm or a canal; the account of a county or region; the study of an estate or a house — all this is embraced within the term 'local history'. Clearly the words and the subject need to be defined more carefully.

One may start from the premise that there is only one real subject for any historian, man in the past. Man's past as a whole needs to be investigated, recorded and understood. Man is a complicated being, whether taken as an individual or in groups, and he defies full analysis. We can dissect him, study his psychology or his social relationships, and still not have explained him fully.

Similarly, those who examine man's past find it easiest to divide the subject up in order to comprehend it. And this division may take one of two main forms. On the one hand, the historian can attempt to isolate *themes* of study, to unravel the intellectual or economic or literary or military or constitutional or political or other strand of man's past. Such an unravelling is most difficult, for the strands keep running from one theme into another; but nevertheless much of the present study of the past is based on such a division. On the other hand, the historian can attempt to isolate a *unit* and try to understand that unit in full — a task just as complicated, for 'no man is an island' and the units are as interrelated in man's past as the themes are. The number of such units is very large indeed. Thus the biographer chooses an individual, the genealogist a family. There are groups of families making settlements; groups of groups making regional entities and nations; groups of nations making cultural entities like western Europe or the Americas, and so on, until we embrace world history.

Local history occupies that stratum in historical studies below the national level but above the level of family and individual. In this sense it is no different from any other branch of the study of the past. It draws on different sources from national history, it is true, but then so does business history or biography. And although it forms a microcosm of wider trends, it is not for this that it becomes worth studying. It is not just an example of national history; it has its own significance.

It is for this reason that a closer definition of the unit of study is necessary. For the units of local history are not artificial ones, created by the scholar; rather they are organic units. Men have organised themselves in many ways below the national level; they have formed different and often overlapping communities. Sometimes it has been a number of families forming a village or a religious group; at other times, a few individuals forming a commercial or industrial concern or a society. Whenever an identifiable community can be isolated, possessing a coherence and identity of its own, that community is a subject worthy of the attention of the historian. It is a 'significant unit', the members of which clearly had an identity of interests, a unity in some common purpose. In this sense, the communities of the historian are very varied indeed.

For most local historians, the normal unit has been the township or settlement. Here is a community easily identified and with a life of its own, 'local' in the sense that it is formed by a group of people living together in one place. It has marked topographical limits and its members are bound together by many more than solely economic interests. The reason for this is that for most of the previous ten or fifteen centuries or more, the inhabitants of England have had to live almost the whole of their lives within the narrow bounds of these local communities; here they found their spiritual satisfaction and recreation and formed their own systems of government. And at the same time, most of these communities have had a more or less continuous development since their establishment in the post-Roman days (or even earlier) until today. Some have died, it is true; some have moved. Most however have grown and exist in some form today. Some have become so large that smaller, sub-communities have developed within them. And it is this continuity which causes so many people today to be interested in these past communities. The craving for identity in today's huge urban crowds leads to the search for smaller groups, for the identifiable community of interests.

Such local communities may however not always be easily identified. Areas such as the moorlands of Derbyshire or the woodlands of Kent or Shropshire may be characterised by dispersed, non-nucleated settlement, so that the boundaries of significant communities are often not clear; thus Myddle (Salop) consisted of several small hamlets loosely tied to each other and indeed to neighbouring townships. Further, it is impossible on occasion to distinguish the communities from those administrative units (such as the parish) that created the sources which the local historian must use. Gedling parish (Notts), for instance, housed within its boundaries three quite different social units, Carlton (an 'open' and industrial village), Stoke Bardolph (a 'closed' riverside village) and Gedling itself, and on some aspects of our study it is rare that we can say anything significant about these separate communities[2]. Nevertheless, it must surely be with the social realities rather than the administrative units that the historian must deal, and his search is for real bonds of common interest.

But such units, the early towns and villages of England, are not the only communities to occupy the attention of the local historian. Other groupings, like gilds and businesses and social or economic classes like the gentry within an area, are also legitimate fields of study. Nor were the village or town groupings ever completely self-contained; they frequently overlapped with each other or with larger communities. At any one time, some inhabitant of a town or village may have been in addition a member of a religious grouping which lay outside that settlement; of a local government pattern which grouped together several settlements; and of an economic complex, the centre of which might lie far from his place of residence.

Nor were the units static; they do not remain fixed for all purposes. For the study of pre-history, the unit must be Britain as a whole, or at least cultural areas, as in an account of the megalithic builders of the western half of these islands. For the immediate pre-Roman period, it would be tribal areas, often transcending later county divisions, like the Parisi of South Yorkshire and Humberside, and these units continued into the Roman period. For the early Anglo-Saxon period and the Danish colonisation, the identifiable unit would be settlement areas of Angles, Saxons, Danes and Norse rather than the kingdoms or even their subdivisions, like Northumbria and its parts of Deira and Bernicia. During the Middle Ages, the units may at one and the same time consist of village, manor or estate (which may be administered from some *caput* near at hand or far away), parish (by no means always coterminous with the village), diocese, hundred and county for different aspects of the life of the local inhabitants. Not all of these were of course of equal significance at any time. The county was most clearly a unit, it would seem, in the seventeenth century; it is unlikely that it ever before or since achieved such a strong common identity as at that time. The parish really emerged as significant in the fifteenth and sixteenth centuries, at the same time as the manor declined in importance. Newer groupings were created, with a strong sense of identity, such as the colonising villages of the Fens or the Quaker societies, while others like the hundreds faded away. And again, for different aspects of the study different units will be studied. Thus for the development of local government in the community it may well be necessary to take a group of parishes such as poor law unions or school board areas or parliamentary constituencies. The units into which human beings have organised themselves have never been static; they have been constantly changing and are always closely interwoven with each other, just as life itself is complex.

An example may be taken from the town of Lincoln to illustrate this. To study the pre-history of that place, the significant unit in the immediate pre-Roman period was the territory of the Coritani centred on Leicester. During the Anglo-Saxon invasions, the small kingdom of Lindsey in its relations with the larger neighbouring kingdoms of Mercia and Northumbria is the significant unit. The medieval history of the town is only understandable in terms of the diocese originally settled at Dorchester-on-Thames and of the duchy of Lancaster which held the castle. For later periods, the parishes were of small significance except for early poor relief; rather the town was divided between social groupings established on the top of the hill and in the valley. Only as local government developed a real coherence within the town does the community of interest become clear, and the town's history stand on its own.[3]

The units of local history are thus neither uniform nor static. They will vary according to circumstances in different localities and for different purposes. The arbitrary choice of one unit as the basis of a continuous local history is unjustified.

This perhaps applies most frequently to regional history — the study of a county or even wider region. This often imports into the past concepts which had no place there, chosen because of their modern implications or the convenience of record material. There are, it is true, genuine historical regions — geographical settings which created or helped in the development of a corporate identity. Some areas, like the Mendips, created significant common social patterns among the inhabitants at many points in their past; others did so rarely, if ever. The men of the Isle of Axholme, within their separate communities of Haxey, Epworth, Belton and the others, could on occasion act in concert;[4] but it is doubtful whether some other regions (especially the larger ones, like East Anglia) ever produced such common self-consciousness. To take a region or a county for a local history study covering the whole of the past would seem to be stretching the community of interests of its members too far. At any rate, such a study should incorporate an attempt to identify precisely what it was that made such a region into a community.

The definition of local history may thus be given as 'the study of the past of some significant local unit, developing as a community, in its context and compared with other such units'. The subject chosen may be a village or it may be some other unit, such as an estate or a firm. Any association of men, whether undertaken voluntarily or compulsorily, with common interests, concerns the historian, and where these fall below the national level, they are properly the concern of the local historian.[5]

Approaches: place or . . .

There are almost as many different approaches to the study of local history as there are local historians. Each person comes to the subject with his own interests and experiences, and seeks for his own satisfaction in it. One may look for the explanation of some particular feature in the locality; for another there is the discovery of unknown facts concerning a place already having many personal associations.

In general, however, all such varied approaches start from one or other of two points. Either the historian is more concerned with the *place* that he is studying or with the *people* who formerly lived there. And springing from this basic divergence in interest are a number of other major differences in attitude, which are reflected in the type of local history produced.

All history, and local history more obviously than many other branches of that study, concerns the interrelation of people and place. The two have interacted on each other in a manner which is often hard to disentangle.

There are several ways in which 'the place' has influenced man's historical development in terms of small localised communities. First, of course, there is the topography of his settlement. The lie of the land, the shape of the hills and river courses, help to determine the way people have lived together. In some places this fact is clearly evident. Thus, for example, Bath is largely shaped by the configuration of the river Avon and the steep downs through which it flows; similarly Durham and York have been affected by their respective rivers in their topographical growth. Too much stress must not be laid on this. Just as frequently, if not indeed more so, the shape of a village or town has been determined by human decisions. Thus at Lincoln, the town grew to the south-west largely because the owners of the neighbouring parishes of Burton and Canwick refused to allow settlement on their land. Late enclosure of common fields, delayed often for similar personal reasons, could affect the shape of settlements, as at Nottingham and Stamford.[6] At the same time, geographical factors themselves soon came to be little bar to settlement. At Bristol, for instance, as early as the thirteenth century, the river Frome was diverted and drained to provide better docks and more land for development, and there are other examples (like Exeter) of natural features providing no real bar to the growth and shape of the town. Nevertheless it is still true that the geographical features of the locality greatly influenced both the original siting of the settlement and its later topographical development.

There is a second way in which 'the place' affected the history of any group of people; it played an important part in what they did for a living. The overall situation of a settlement helped to create markets or major meeting places. London itself is the clearest example of this, the focus for routes from north and south, at the lowest crossing point of the great river Thames. Fishing and coastal trade developed at smaller seaside settlements, shipbuilding on the larger inlets. The nature of the soils and the physical characteristics of the land influenced the type of agriculture and its associated industries — like the bulb growing and the canning industries in the Fens, cheesemaking in Derbyshire or sheep walking on the Cotswolds. The industry engaged in was largely determined by the natural resources immediately available (as for instance the water power of the West Riding, the iron and coal of Birmingham, or the alabaster of Derbyshire) or by the ease of communications.

All of this is well known and frequently explored. But there is another side to the coin. Nothing is simple in history, and certainly it is clear that geographical determinism just does not work in every case. The agricultural development of much of lowland England in the later Middle Ages was determined by man's decisions to take advantage of the profits of wool production. The iron and coal needed to keep Scunthorpe and Corby alive come from afar. The development of the hosiery industry in and around Nottingham does not seem to owe a great deal to geographical factors but rather to the growth of a specific local tradition and social structure.[7] In some cases, an individual's inventiveness or initiative laid the basis for local development, while in other cases influential persons might refuse to allow potential industries to grow. In the economic history of mankind, as much as in the topographical history of his settlement, the countless decisions of individuals have played as significant a part as the forces of geography.

It is thus clear that, in history in general and in local history in particular, there is a dualism of people and place, and the relative strength of each factor is perhaps as indeterminate as in that other controversy over 'nature and nurture' in the development of the individual. What is clear is that every local historian must at some stage thoroughly examine the setting of his chosen subject. Its immediate topography — the soils, the physical features and the resources of the locality — as well as its wider context in the surrounding countryside must form part of his brief. An approach to local history through 'the place' is thus a valid one, but if pursued on its own it will have considerable limitations.

Some of these limitations become clearer when the types of history written with the emphasis upon 'the place' are examined. These frequently take the form of enquiries into 'what happened here?' or 'who was associated with this place?' The local history which consists of a series of unconnected incidents relating to eminent persons and great events is not confined to guides of historic houses — 'Queen Elizabeth slept here', 'Charles I passed through here after the battle of . . .', or '. . . was born here in . . .', or 'there were Chartist riots here in 1840', and so on. For many people, this is the stuff of local history, and no place which cannot produce its line of worthies or happenings has a history worth talking about.

There are others who conceive of local history in terms of what they can see in the place around them. Thus to them Cirencester is an historic place, full of interesting remains, which must therefore have an interesting history, whereas Coventry or Plymouth have not got such interest. Indeed, we speak of 'historic towns', meaning the same by it as we do when we say 'historic (or old) building'. York, Chester, Bath, King's Lynn and Chichester are officially 'historic towns', while their near neighbours of Leeds, Liverpool, Bristol, Peterborough and Portsmouth are not; similarly Edinburgh is, while Glasgow is not. The history of the place is determined by its more obvious visual remains, according to many persons.

These are views which it is hard to dispel, precisely because they contain some element of truth. Great events and great persons do have some significance in the story of any locality. It is important for the history of any community that some royal visitor passed through the place, that some notable person originated there, that some people in the neighbourhood were involved in wider national events of the past. But the task of the local historian is to go further than just the chronicling of events; he has to explain just what is the significance of these events in the context in which they took place. Why are they important? What do they mean? These are questions he constantly has to ask. And even when all the great events which touched any particular locality have been thoroughly examined, there is still a great deal more which can be learned about the history of that place, a great deal which would not otherwise be covered. An approach to local history which deals only with important happenings is a very partial one indeed.

A somewhat different approach to local history, but one still related to 'the place', lies through the collection of source material relating to the locality. In this, the student begins by asking 'what can I find out about Little Piddington' (or wherever the place may be)? This leads to an exploration of the records and to the amassing of data, usually in some chronological order. Such an activity is of course essential as part of the task of the local historian, for the sources are always very scattered and often hidden in less obvious places. Further, the records themselves prompt questions, such as why a long series of court rolls should survive or why there were so few terriers and no vestry minutes. But as with the approach through 'the place', so there are limitations here. For one thing, for some communities, especially towns, there is an excessive wealth of material, and the indiscriminate compilation of factual material adds nothing to what is already known. But more seriously, such an approach does not lead the historian to assess the significance of what he has collected. Not all of the events of the past had equally significant results. The death of one of the leaders of the community will have far greater consequences for that community than the death of one pauper. Writing a local history is a bigger task than just collecting the facts. A story has to be made from them, some connected tale about the people of the past.

. . . people

A better approach would seem to come from one which started from 'the people' rather than with the sources or the place. The historian is different from the historical geographer. The latter is more concerned with the study of the land and its effect on people; the historian is concerned with the story of *man*, man's past. And thus his approach to local history is a radically different one, however much he may need to use some of the geographer's tools.

For the local historian, his subject is not a place, a village, parish or town, but a group of people. Northampton, Nantwich and Nynehead (to take but three random examples) are not places, they are congregations of people, communities of varying sizes. Anyone studying the history of Northampton (or any other group of persons) will need to be aware of this. From the time when, in the far-off post-Roman confusion, a group of Anglo-Saxon invaders settled beside the river,[8] there has been a group of people there with a continuous development all of its own. At times this community has grown in size, at other times it has declined; it has changed its character, sometimes radically, sometimes subtly, but there has never been a complete break. There has always been a continuity in the flow of people, and it is with this group of people that any history of Northampton must be concerned.

An approach to local history based on these premises has several important results in the way in which the subject is studied. For one thing, the historian realises the continuity of the past into the present. Those who today live in Northampton are part of that continuous tide of people who have occupied the site for some 1,400 years at least. And that applies as much to those who have moved into the town as to those who were born there, for at every stage in the community's history there have been living there those who have moved into the group, having been born elsewhere. An awareness of how the present community has become what it is, as well as how different it has been at various times in the past, helps to create a sense of identity with the community being studied.

On the other hand, the historian is not just interested in communities which still exist. Those which have vanished are as much his concern, and in this study the attitude to local history which begins with people is just as necessary, if not indeed more so. A deserted village like Wharram Percy in South Yorkshire is now just a site;[9] but it was once a community of people which came to an end, probably in the late fifteenth century, and it is with these people that any history of Wharram Percy must be concerned.

It is this which distinguishes local history from the related aspect of the subject, 'local studies'. This latter, which may for example consist of surveys of buildings or industrial archaeology or the like, is properly an aid towards local history, the exploitation of some of the source material eventually to be used in the reconstruction of the past of the community. Local studies are of value primarily in what they tell us about the people of the past.

A series of questions
It is in the approach to his subject which the student is forced to adopt that the most important result of this concept of local history lies. Instead of asking 'what can I find out about the history of such-and-such a place?', he finds himself faced with a quite different series of questions about a group of people. And it is in this attitude of asking questions about people of the past that the truest way forward in local history would seem to be found. It was Marc Bloch, the great French medieval historian, who conceived of history as the answer to 'a series of intelligently posed questions'.[10]

Many such questions immediately spring to mind. How big was the community? How has its size fluctuated, and why? How did its members earn their living? Where did they live (in the sense of topographical development)? How were they governed? How far were they bound together and on what issues were they divided? There is probably no end to the questions which can be asked. They will clearly vary with the interests of the individual local historian. Thus questions of social structure and industrial relations will seem more important to some than questions relating to religion or leisure activities. Nor must the historian close his mind to further questions. There is no God-given questionnaire in community studies; the material for the answers to these questions may well throw up extra problems to pose, additional themes to study. But the approach to local history would seem to be soundest when one thinks of the subject chosen for study as a community of people, and asks a series of questions about it.

Once again, of course, there are limitations in this approach. Very real danger for the historian lies in this use of the machinery of the sociologist. For history is not a laboratory in which the social scientist of today can try out his techniques of analysis and find the answers to preconceived problems. A series of arbitrary, narrowly-defined questions imposed on the local history of the community will not produce either a true or satisfying description of the past. Whole aspects may well be overlooked because the categories devised did not fit them. The picture drawn from the answers to these questions can result in the loss of the dynamic element in the local community's history, in too static an account of the past. Particularly, the involvement of the local community in great national events like the Civil Wars may tend to be omitted. Further, the evidence itself can be distorted to fit the problems. The very questions may suggest the answers. A great deal depends upon how narrowly the questions are drawn. A more open approach, one which merely pre-supposes an enquiring disposition, is clearly better than the questionnaire enquiry. For the local historian is dealing with men, and human beings have the knack of defying categories. Answers are never simple when it comes to analysing human behaviour.

But with all these limitations, it is clear that the social scientist and anthropologist have a good deal to teach the local historian; and the attitude to local history which bears in mind all three factors, of place, sources and people, is likely to be the most fruitful one. For all three have contributions to make, and they each help to overcome the limitations and distortions inherent within any single approach. Nevertheless the most important would seem to be that approach through questions related to persons. For one thing, the sheer weight of the source material can be overwhelming, without some more or less clear idea of what one is looking for. A systematic enquiry to answer specific problems will prevent the indiscriminate collection of merely random material and add coherence to the study. But above all, it will direct us to the real subject of study, the people. For both the place and the sources merely provide evidence for the study of the history of mankind. They are subordinate to the true aim of the local historian which is 'to make sense of the dead', to tell the story of past men. It is in the process of enquiry and search for the past that true history is written.

What follows thus is an attempt to isolate some of the most common questions which can be asked in the study of any local community. It is of course always easier to ask than to answer. Not all of them can be examined for every town and village in every period. For the material with which they can be answered survives only partially. Some places have plenty of one or other kind of evidence from the past. The so-called historic towns have plenty of visual material like buildings and street plans, but some of them have little in the way of written records. Other places, sometimes apparently unprepossessing ones like Grimsby,[11] have plentiful records and plans, while a few of course, like King's Lynn or Winchester, have both[12]. There are some communities however which have little of any sort of evidence from the past, although that past is just as long as that of their more fortunate neighbours. The survival of evidence from the past is in general more sparse for the earlier than for the later periods; indeed for the Middle Ages, some of the questions can be discussed only tentatively and, for many communities, a good deal of their medieval past has gone beyond recall. Nevertheless, the search for answers to these questions may lead to a re-assessment of what clues do survive and their significance, and will lead to a fuller and more satisfying type of local history.

Chapter 2

The size of the community

1

An approach to local history which consists of enquiries concerning the group of people who lived in any given place provokes as a first question what the size of the community at any time might be. How many people were there in the locality? And since in any historical approach we cannot adopt a static attitude, we shall not be content with a mere figure, for there is a flow in history which must be traced. What then is happening to the community? Is it growing or declining? And further, since we cannot study our community in isolation, nor indeed assess the significance of our findings except against a general framework, a further question arises; is this consistent with what is known of other similar communities and indeed of the wider community of which our chosen subject is but one small part?

These are essentially simple questions, but they are the first basic steps in the enquiry into the history of a local community. Indeed, they may seem so obvious as not to need asking. And yet there are still large numbers of local histories being produced which never give any idea as to how large a community is being discussed, nor whether it is a growing or declining community. And in turn the answers to these questions lead on to what are perhaps more important and certainly far more complex questions, the reasons behind the pattern of increase or decrease which emerges. It is in the answers to these further questions that much of what is most significant in local history can be discovered. A discussion of why any particular place was attracting a growing number of settlers or failing to prevent them from leaving may throw light on many aspects of the history of that local community.

The first step in local history is thus to establish the size of the local community and whether it was growing or declining. But such an analysis achieves greater significance when placed against an overall framework of population trends. Such trends are, it is true, an aggregate of the many local movements, but nevertheless any variant from the norm requires further examination and explanation.

2

Background: population growth
The general trends of population growth in England are of course well known, but it must always be remembered that very large local fluctuations limit the value of any overall approach. It is indeed easier to arrive at agreed national totals than at any, even rough, local estimates. Nevertheless the outline itself provides a useful framework, although it is often only partial.

All medieval figures are of course very vague approximations and vary greatly from assessment to assessment, for scholars differ over such subjects as what the average size of family was and whether a taxpayer was a head of a household or not. Population estimates therefore vary widely. Some archaeologists now think that population densities in some parts of England were as great in the first thousand years B.C. as they were in the sixteenth and seventeenth centuries, and such views will affect greatly later estimates based on documentary evidence. In general, however, it is assumed that the population of England and Wales at the taking of the Domesday Survey was somewhere in the region of 1¼−2 million, rather more of it in eastern England than elsewhere. It rose (or, probably, continued to rise), perhaps more sharply in the thirteenth century than in the twelfth century, until in the early fourteenth century it stood at some 4¼ million (although estimates vary from 6 million to 2½ million). The so-called Great Famine of the early fourteenth century and the Black Death of 1349−50 reduced it to something between 3½ and 2½ million and it may have fallen in subsequent outbreaks of plague as low as 1½ or 2 million by the middle of the fifteenth century. Thereafter it rose (although clearly not evenly) until in 1600 it had recovered most of what had been lost since 1349.[1]

The picture from 1600 is both more certain and more detailed. Starting from rather more than 4 million there was an overall increase for the first part of the century, but the middle of the century seems to have been a period of stagnation, perhaps even some decline. By 1700, the growth had been resumed and the population of England had reached some 5¼ million, by 1750 some 6 or 6½ million.[2] Thereafter the rate of growth sharply increased. By 1801, when the first national census was taken, the overall total was 9 million; by 1850 it was 18 million. Not only was the rate of growth achieved in the early nineteenth century very high (although probably not in fact unprecedented), but it was maintained for a long period. By 1910 the 18 million had become 36 million in a period of some sixty years, but thereafter the rate of increase slowed until the population reached 41½ million by 1939 and nearly 46 million by 1971[3] (Fig. 1).

Migration
The reasons for this overall growth in the total population of England throughout the last thousand years are not without dispute, but the fact of the increase is clear. Not all local history studies however will deal with an equal rate of increasing population, for the growth has not been felt evenly throughout the country. Some areas indeed had lengthy periods of falling population, a result of some massive redistributions of people. On the whole such redistributions have taken two main forms, changes in the balance between the different regions of the country and between town and countryside within those regions. It is true that these two factors have not been the only ones at work to create mobility. Varying social and tenurial conditions have helped to stimulate inter-rural movement from one village to another on the part of all classes, the labouring, the professional and the landholding. Throughout the whole of English history, the population of the country has been on the move, drifting over the countryside like slowly moving clouds. Communities have formed, grown in numbers, moved (sometimes a few hundred yards, sometimes miles) or dispersed, for a large number of reasons. Some were artificially created or fostered, others grew or declined according to changes in geographical or climatic conditions, or changing patterns of economy or social life or transport. The picture has never been static. Even during the Middle Ages, when

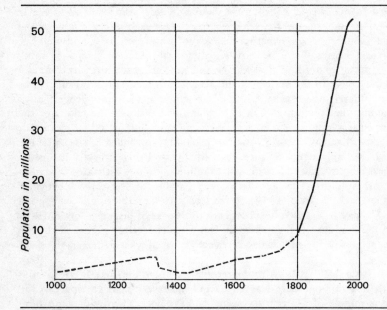

Fig. 1   Approximate overall rise in population in England and Wales 1000–1950. It must be stressed that this shows totals, not rate of growth. To show this would need the use of logarithmic graphs.

historians tend to assume a greater measure of uniformity in the distribution of population, it is clear that settlements came and went with bewildering speed.

The overall trends of these redistributions are not always clear. It would seem that until the late thirteenth century, the towns probably attracted persons from the countryside, itself suffering from a fast-rising population; thereafter, there was a drift away from the towns, while in regional terms, the clear predominance of the eastern counties which the Domesday survey revealed gave way in favour of other areas, notably the south-west and the north. Such major disturbances as the Reformation, the early enclosure movement and the Civil Wars all helped in a localised way to keep the population of England on the move. But apart from such changes for a multitude of personal reasons, the movement from region to region and a resumed movement from the countryside into the town, probably beginning in the late sixteenth or early seventeenth centuries, can be seen to have caused the later large-scale changes in population centres[4].

Some of these redistributions have been only temporary in their effects. Population north of a line from the Humber to the Severn was in the seventeenth century only some 40% of the country's total. By the end of the first quarter of the nineteenth century it had risen to 50%, but by 1900 it was just over 40% again.[5] But perhaps more significant has been the trend from rural areas into urban areas. In 1700 there were few large towns in England, London with its half-million, and only Bristol and Norwich above 20,000. Thereafter they grew rapidly, both in numbers and in size. Up to about 1830, it would seem that the towns grew only slightly more rapidly than the total population. It was in the north-west that they first began to outstrip the general level of population increase; in the south they kept pace with the rising tide of people. From 1830, however, urban increase

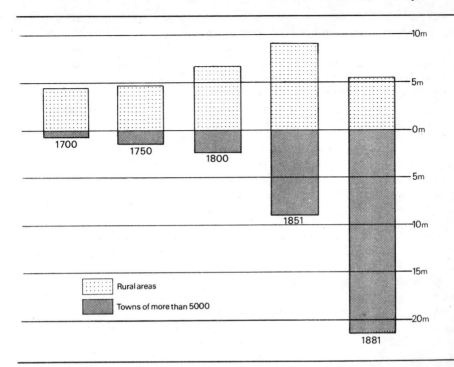

Fig. 2 The population of England 1700—1900 in (a) rural areas and (b) towns of more than 5,000.

exceeded the national growth rate. Once again, the reasons for this trend are obscure; it is not clear whether the immigrants were driven from the countryside or drawn into the towns, whether economic, social or psychological factors predominated. But it certainly happened. In 1700, some 13% of the population were in towns of more than 5,000; indeed, only 4%, if London is discounted. By 1800, the proportion had risen to a quarter, by 1850, to a half, and by 1880, to some 80% (Fig. 2). In fact between 1800 and 1850, urban population increased from 2¼ million to 9 million, while the rural population only grew from 6¾ million to 9 million. Some of this urban increase is of course accounted for by changing boundaries. Settlements previously regarded as rural were now included in the urban categories. Thus not all of this increase represents migration from the countryside to the towns. Nevertheless, this too happened. Rural population continued to grow until the late 1840s when, despite the enormous total national increase, it began to show an overall decrease, the result of emigration, not of falling birthrates.[6] A slight but purely temporary halt in the 1860s was followed by a persistent fall in rural areas, only offset today by dormitory development near to the larger cities or in holiday areas.

The later nineteenth century

The picture thus of England in the 1870s is one of rapidly increasing population growth. The total rate of growth was, it is true, just beginning to decline. In 1851, there was a 48% increase over the population of the preceding thirty years; by 1881, this had fallen to 43% and thereafter it fell, to 37% in 1911 and to 21% in

1931. Nevertheless, the *growth* was still there, and it was a much more obvious fact to contemporaries than the fall in the *rate* of growth.

What was also obvious to contemporaries was that there was a great deal of migration. Some of it of course was purely local and circular in nature. Nevertheless there was a distinct drift into the towns. It has been estimated that many parts of London were, by the second half of the nineteenth century, more than half non-native.[7] Thus in total the rural areas were losing their population to the towns, although there appears to have been a slight and temporary gain in the decade 1861–71.[8] But such a picture, of growing towns and declining villages, is much too simple (see Fig. 9, p. 26). Some villages were still growing, on a basis of industrial activity (like Buxton in Derbyshire) or dormitory suburbs near to large towns (like the Essex villages of Wanstead and Loughton or Camberwell in Surrey, near London) or changing patterns of holidays (like Seaford in Sussex). On the other hand parts of some towns (like St Laurence's parish in Southampton) were beginning to lose their population; while a number of completely new settlements, in the nature of suburban development or 'urban scatter', were being created within every large town and in some rural areas like Staffordshire, Derbyshire and County Durham. The overall framework, for the local historian, hides something of the total complexity of population movements within any given area. But at least the two major factors emerge — total population growth, and a good deal of mobility, both from region to region and from countryside to town.

3

Early sources: population size

It is against this national and regional background that each particular local study must be set. The history of some areas will help to reinforce the national pattern, that of others will vary significantly from it. It is in this relationship with the framework that local population studies acquire much of their significance.

The first task of the local historian in the study of his community is one of static analysis, that is to determine the size of the community at any one time. The process by which this may be achieved will vary from period to period. The most marked difference lies between the years before the nineteenth century and the period after 1801 when the first official and universal census was taken in England. Before 1801 the local historian has to rely on a range of miscellaneous occasional sources; after that date, there is a regular sequence of records, specifically demographic and in a format which in many respects invites comparison. A pattern of development is thus easier to acquire for the later period than for the earlier. This means that the approach to local population for many places before 1801 can hardly be any other than a static survey of the community. Even when the historian can accumulate a number of more or less firm figures for his community from different periods, it is not always easy or safe to establish a relationship between them.

The records from which population figures for any local community can be drawn for the years before 1801 will also vary from place to place. There are, it is true, a few records which were drawn up centrally and thus were intended to cover most towns and villages in the country. Such are the most useful of the medieval records, Domesday Book[9] and those returns relating to the lay subsidies of the early fourteenth century and the early sixteenth century and the poll taxes of 1377—81.[10] The commonest and most helpful later records of the same class are the hearth taxes from 1662 to 1685[11] but there are also the rarer returns for the 1660 poll tax or the slightly later tax on births, marriages and burials (1695—1705).[12] The compilation of other local surveys, like those which produced the sixteenth century chantry certificates or the muster surveys, or (in the early seventeenth century) the protestation returns of 1642 (covering all males in the parish or township over eighteen years of age), were also authorised centrally and the returns themselves retained by the government.[13] Some other sources from which total figures of population size may be drawn for many places are the ecclesiastical surveys, a few (like those of 1563, 1603 and 1676) national in character, but most of them diocesan, which may record an approximate number of families within the parish.[14]

The records vary in their reliability and usefulness. On the whole the government-sponsored enquiries tend to distinguish between townships, while the ecclesiastical surveys more frequently hide the local communities within the parish totals. But not even these wide-ranging records are complete; the surveys may never have been taken or the returns, if made, may not have survived. The more occasional and specifically local records which may provide such figures, like medieval manorial surveys[15] or later estate surveys or the ecclesiastical enquiries conducted during the Interregnum[16] or the censuses taken by local incumbents or by interested antiquarians[17], are clearly a matter of chance. There will however be few local communities without any such record, and further allusive evidence of population size will be available for most places, if examined in detail.

There are many problems in the use of these records[18] for they were rarely drawn up for demographic purposes, and thus they pose difficulties in terms of reliability and interpretation. Nevertheless, such figures have their uses, despite their limitations. Their value is greatly increased where a number of totals can be obtained, for in these circumstances, it may be possible to move from static analysis to an assessment of some pattern of growth or decline.[19] This process, which involves the establishment of a relationship between the figures obtained from disparate sources in order to discern trends, is one fraught with dangers, for many of these records use different categories — families, houses, communicants, taxpayers, etc. — but in most cases some overall picture will appear.

A specific example may throw some light on these problems. The town of Stamford consisted of two parts, Stamford Within (the part lying to the north of the River Welland in Lincolnshire, within the medieval town walls) and Stamford Without or Stamford Baron, lying in Northamptonshire to the south of the river. A number of population figures can be obtained from the late sixteenth century onwards.[20] In 1563, a total of 213 families were recorded for Stamford Within in a diocesan survey; in 1603, there were 746 communicants given in another survey.[21] The hearth taxes record two different totals, amounting to nearly 400 houses in 1674. A survey of nonconformists (the Compton return) in 1676 gave a total of 1,594 communicant or noncommunicant adults. Early in the eighteenth century, these were 470 families in another diocesan survey. At the end of the century a local writer gave a calculated total of 3,937 persons, while a fourth diocesan survey gave 856 families.

One problem clearly from all of this is to reconcile families, communicants, taxable houses and individuals. These sources were compiled for different reasons, not for purposes of comparison with each other. It is very difficult indeed to make one coherent story out of the figures. Nevertheless,

- if a family in 1563 was on average 4½, we get a total of about 958 heads
- if communicants comprised two-thirds of the population[22] (children under twelve being omitted), we get a total in 1603 of just under 1,000 heads
- if an average taxable house contained some five persons (rather more than a family), we get a total in 1671 of just under 2,000 persons
- using the communicant formula, we get a total in 1676 of 2,125 persons
- in 1705–23, the 470 families at 4½ heads give a total of 2,115 heads[23]
- by the end of the eighteenth century, the estimate of 3,937 heads and the total of 3,952 which a family of 4½ gives tally very well indeed.

Such figures give too solid a feeling of accuracy; in fact, in details they are very unreliable. Nevertheless, the outline is clear: about 1,000 people at the beginning of the seventeenth century became just over 2,000 at the beginning of the eighteenth century and nearly 4,000 at the end of the eighteenth century (in 1801, there were 4,022 persons in Stamford Within) (Fig. 3).

This pattern may be compared with two other Lincolnshire settlements. Bourne was a large parish, comprising three separate townships, Bourne itself and the two disparate hamlets of Dyke (a relatively large community) and Cawthorpe (which was very small indeed). Together, the three places in 1563 had a population of about 1,000, about the same size as Stamford; this remained at just over the 1,000 throughout the seventeenth century, when Stamford was growing, and indeed may

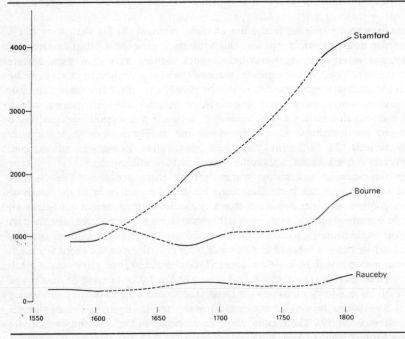

Fig. 3   The story of population changes 1550–1800 in Bourne, Stamford and Rauceby, Lincolnshire. Although the material is thin, the differences are very clear. The trends in Rauceby on the same scale somewhat distort the smaller fluctuations. It must be stressed that the dotted lines are sheer speculation.

even have fallen slightly (from 223 families in 1563 to 217 families in 1704–22);[24] and its rate of growth during the eighteenth century was very low, so that by the end of that century, the three townships held a total population of about one-third of Stamford (see Fig. 3). Rauceby similarly was a parish with two villages, North and South Rauceby. Together, the two communities only slightly increased their size from 1563 to 1801[25] (Fig. 3). These patterns thus differ in outline from each other and indeed from the national pattern.

It must be stressed that it is not possible to do this for all places in England; those parishes which lay within dioceses like Lincoln are fortunate in the administrative machinery which existed and in the energetic and efficient officials who ran it, thus ensuring that frequent and on the whole reliable surveys were both made and preserved. Some other areas are however not so fortunate. But even in the favourable areas, the figures are not without their problems. Thus a number of different communities may lie hidden under blanket totals, as at Rauceby and Bourne. It is true that there are many single villages for which such figures may be compiled, but the historian must always be alive to the unit for which they were compiled. In the towns, it may be best to obtain figures for each separate parish or ward, if possible, rather than for the town as a whole. In this way, areas of growth may be identified. But here there is the problem of changes of boundary, a problem which becomes even more acute with the census returns of the nineteenth century.

Population changes

The biggest difficulty with these figures is the movement from a comparative static analysis to a dynamic analysis of population growth. It is not at all clear when the significant changes in the population actually occurred. For this, more detailed and regular information is required.

In many places this can be acquired from the parish registers.[26] The survival of parish registers varies greatly, some places having complete sets from their beginning in 1536 (or 1558 or 1598), others having many missing. Some were carelessly written up or neglected for long periods, or are illegible and untrustworthy, especially from about 1780 onwards. Before any work is done on them, an assessment must be made of their value to the local historian.[27] On occasions deficiencies can be made up by using the transcripts which the incumbent was obliged to send in to his diocesan registry.[28] Not all of these transcripts survive, however – indeed, some may never have been made. Sometimes where they have been carelessly copied up, they are more unreliable than the registers themselves. In any case, they suffer from the same disability as the registers: they were neither of them strictly maintained for demographic purposes. They record religious services, baptisms, marriages and burials, not demographic events such as births, conceptions and deaths. This fact can distort their findings, particularly when a sizeable proportion of the population began to refuse the services of the Church of England. The presence of a substantial nonconformist element in any local community will seriously distort the results obtained from the registers relating to that place, and although sometimes amendments can be made from surviving dissenting registers,[29] this is not always possible. Even when, however, no such distortion exists, the registers themselves are sometimes still faulty. There may for instance be a substantial under-recording of demographic events, especially infant mortality, while migration is totally unrecorded.

Nevertheless, where there is a good set of registers covering most or all of the community, they are very valuable indeed for local population studies. It is not

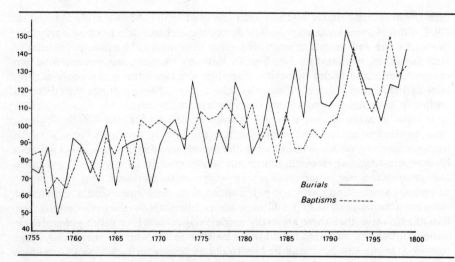

Fig. 4   Population in a Chester parish 1755—1800

(a) Crude totals of baptisms and burials, St John's parish, Chester. Such graphs can be revealing, not only of peaks and troughs but of other things. Thus the general upward trend in this parish is clear; Holy Trinity parish has a similar pattern. In both St Michael's and St Mary's parishes, the earlier period is marked by narrow fluctuations of roughly equal baptisms and burials, but after 1780 the two pull apart and the fluctuations are more extreme. In St Oswald's parish, baptisms plunge disastrously from 1790, although burials remain in the same range of fluctuations — perhaps an indication of increasing nonconformity rather than demographic trends. For these parishes, see map on p. 22.

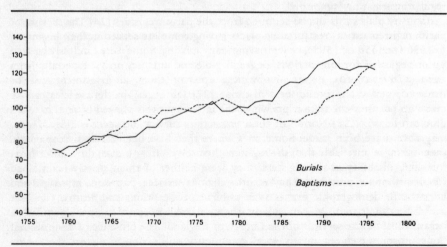

(b) Totals of baptisms and burials, St John's parish, smoothed out into seven year running averages to reveal the trends more clearly. This parish has a large extramural area.

really possible to move from the fluctuating figures contained in them to a total size of the community, although some attempts have been made in this field. It has been suggested, for instance, that a multiplier of 120 to the average annual totals of marriages may give a figure approximately in line with the community size.[30] This may work in a few cases: for Bourne (Lincs), the totals arrived at in this way are (1660–70) 840; (1717–21) 1,440; and (1781–5) 1,420 – totals which in two of the three samples are adequately close to those above.[31] But such figures may be easily vitiated by local factors, such as the popularity of some parishes for marriages[32] or by changes in fashions affecting the marriage age, and in general the multiplication in this way is too unreliable to be of value to the local historians. Other historians have tried to use a multiplier of 30 or 31 to the average annual totals of baptisms[33] to get population totals but without success; this method may have even less validity than the marriage approach. Such a measurement would give for Bourne some 1,550 in the 1660s, just under 1,000 for the years 1717–21, and just over 1,200 for 1781–5, considerably at variance with the pattern created from known total sizes. A combination of both methods to provide a range for the total population would seem best, if it is to be done at all.

On the whole, however, the use of the registers to estimate the size of the community is too unreliable to be worth attempting. Their chief value is for indicating whether a local community was growing in size or not. For this purpose, a comparison of the annual totals of baptisms and burials whether done in crude figures, five-year averages or five (or seven or nine) year rolling averages, may be made. It will reflect periods of high and low birth rate and of high mortality (see Fig. 4) which clearly call for explanation and which may, in their turn, throw light on subsequent population developments. But for many rural parishes the total numbers dealt with may be so small that the annual fluctuations will be artificially inflated.

Such crude totals, however, have limited value for discerning whether the population was or was not growing in size. What is needed is some comparison between births and deaths – or, in parish register terms, baptisms and burials, which is the nearest approach we can get to this data before 1801. The simplest of the processes of comparisons is that by which annual totals of burials are subtracted from the totals for baptisms, resulting in a plus or minus figure for 'natural increase' within the parish. These totals, if aggregated from a year taken as a base year, will reflect periods of increasing or declining population. Clearly an excess in the numbers of baptisms over burials would indicate either a growing community or one from which there was consistent and substantial migration; similarly, an excess of burials over baptisms may well point to a falling population. An 'aggregative analysis' of the totals from a good series of parish registers can reveal a great deal about the history of any community.[34] The following graphs (Fig. 5) for a number of parishes in the town of Chester (Fig. 6) from 1755 to 1800 indicate something of the fruit of this sort of analysis.[35] Some parishes show a substantial decline – St Oswald (with a large rural catchment area) in particular; while St Peter's shows a continual increase. Most (like St Michael's) however reveal a decline for the first part of the period and then a considerable increase from the 1770s or so. St John's parish follows the same pattern, but it falls off again seriously from the 1780s, though in this case the figures more probably reflect the under-recording of baptisms rather than true population decline.

Such studies have to be made on the basis of the parish rather than of the local community. In some cases, there may be gain in this; the growth or decline of different areas of those towns which had more than one parish may be traced. But in other cases, especially in rural parishes,[36] it may not always be possible to trace the pattern within any particular village, unless the parish and the village coincide. Further it must be remembered that although the trends may emerge in outline, the interpretation of this pattern and the judgements on which it is based are very complex indeed.[37] There are other sources which may help to corroborate or challenge the pattern. Topographical records like deeds and early maps may show increasing density of housing (or the reverse);[38] surviving houses and old photographs or prints may bear witness to considerable building activity at certain periods.[39] Poll books, rentals and surveys, taxation records, poor law accounts, all the other sources of local history, may throw some indirect light on whether the community was growing or declining at any particular stage of its early history. But it is from the process of aggregative analysis of parish register totals that the clearest evidence may be gained.

4

Nineteenth century sources
From 1801, the task of the local historian, at least with regard to this topic, is eased. For there survive the census records, the statistical summaries up to 1841

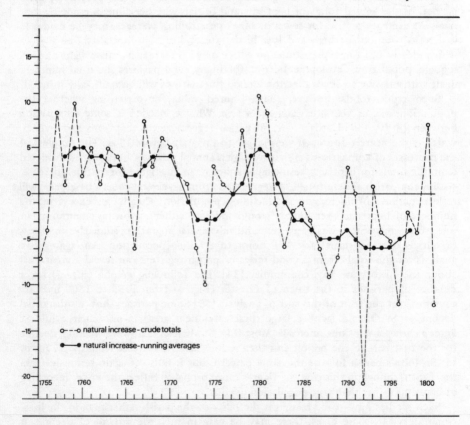

Fig. 5   Natural increase graphs for Chester parishes 1755—1800

(a)   St Martin's parish, with crude natural increase and natural increase smoothed out in seven-year averages. For very small parishes, the fluctuations of natural increase can hide the trends which can be shown by running averages. St Bridget also fluctuates within very narrow limits, ending with a net gain of O; it needs similar treatment. The cathedral parish has been omitted from this study, for its peculiar social position means that the burials and baptisms recorded there are often not strictly parochial.

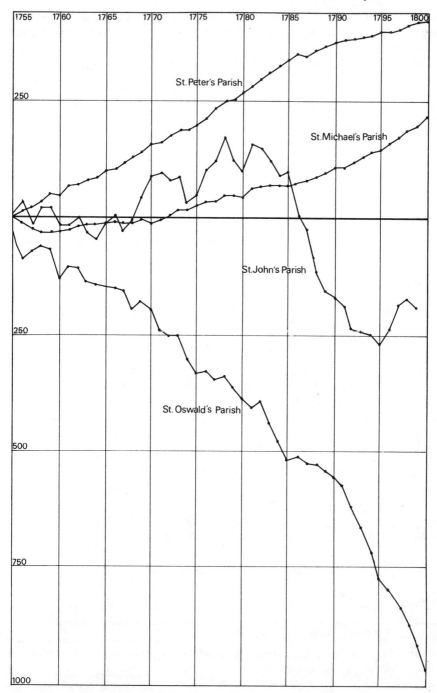

(b)   Graph showing different trends of population in some of the ten city parishes. St Michael and St Peter are both small central parishes, St John and St Oswald larger parishes with rural areas. Three other city parishes, Holy Trinity, St Mary and St Olave have patterns very similar indeed to that of St Michael.

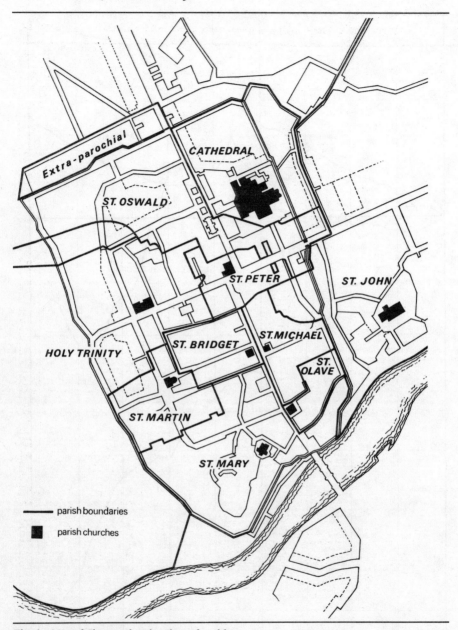

Fig. 6   Map of Chester, showing sizes of parishes.

and the schedules on which they are based from 1841 onwards.[40] For the purposes of judging the size of the community and the trends of growth or decline, the printed statistical summaries are enough (Plate 1);[41] indeed the totals are

Plate 1   Specimen page from the Census *Abstracts* for 1851, showing Richmond, Yorkshire. It ▶ gives population (1801—51) and houses. Other tables give further details. The small letters refer to notes which have been omitted from this extract.

No. of District	No. of Subdist.	SUBDISTRICT.	No. of Parish	Parish, Township, or Place	Area in Statute Acres	HOUSES 1841 In-habited	HOUSES 1841 Unin-habited	HOUSES 1841 Build-ing	HOUSES 1851 In-habited	HOUSES 1851 Unin-habited	HOUSES 1851 Build-ing	POPULATION PERSONS 1801	1811	1821	1831	1841	1851
537	1	ASKRIGG		**537 ASKRIGG.**[a]													
				Aysgarth, part of Parish—[*]													
			1	Aysgarth - - [b] Township	1174	61	3	–	62	3	–	268	293	293	332	269	253
			2	Carperby-cum-Thoresby Twnp.	4950	72	3	–	72	7	–	280	262	283	320	354	342
			3	Burton-cum-Walden, or West Burton, Townp.	6790	125	7	–	116	12	–	446	453	478	545	523	483
			4	Newbiggen - - Township	2000	27	1	–	24	2	–	121	130	128	122	132	130
			5	Thoralby - - Township	2840	63	3	–	63	6	–	313	310	342	272	299	288
			6	Bishopdale - - Township	4805	15	1	–	16	–	–	64	79	95	108	107	77
			7	Thornton Rust - Township	1923	36	2	–	36	1	–	130	120	135	158	178	158
			8	Bainbridge (w) - [bb] Township	14963	163	26	–	168	15	–	765	813	872	881	786	814
			9	Askrigg - - [c] Township	4751	174	27	1	159	21	–	761	745	765	737	726	633
	2	HAWES		*Aysgarth*, part of Parish—[*] [b]													
			1	Low Abbotside - [d] Township	5080	41	1	1	38	4	–	235	195	181	173	166	161
			2	High Abbotside - [e] Township	11150	117	6	–	120	1	–	559	585	641	589	574	588
			3	Hawes - - [f] Township	16872	342	24	–	374	12	3	1223	1185	1408	1559	1611	1708
538	1	MUKER		**538 REETH.**													
				Grinton, part of Parish—[†] [g]													
			1	Muker - - [gg] Chapelry	30262	276	15	2	280	8	–	1119	1339	1425	1247	1241	1321
			2	Melbecks - - [h] Township	10106	330	23	5	333	11	–	1274	1586	1726	1455	1633	1661
	2	REETH															
			1	Arkengarth Dale - [i] Parish	14256	254	31	3	266	7	–	1186	1529	1512	1446	1243	1283
				Grinton, part of Parish—[†] [g]													
			2	Grinton - - [k] Township	2934	114	10	–	117	7	–	518	649	689	696	594	598
			3	Reeth (w) - - [l] Township	5659	294	40	1	280	12	–	1128	1394	1460	1456	1343	1344
			4	Marrick - - [m] Parish	5560	113	13	3	113	7	–	474	499	621	659	648	555
			5	Ellerton Abbey - [n] Township (part of *Downholme* Parish)[*]	1490	11	–	–	10	1	–	(?)40	(?)44	47	61	56	58
539	1	RICHMOND		**539 RICHMOND.**													
				Downholme, part of Parish—[‡] [o]													
			1	Downholme - - Township	1394	24	2	–	28	4	–	114	225	113	104	121	129
			2	Stainton - - [p] Township	1851	8	–	–	7	1	–	(?) 39	(?) 47	54	44	47	40
			3	Walburn - - Township	1280	4	–	–	5	–	–	40	53	37	26	24	33
			4	Marske - - [pp] Parish	6557	49	3	–	47	2	–	239	247	290	290	274	244
			5	RICHMOND (w) - [q] Parish	2341	817	34	2	843	17	6	2861	3056	3546	3900	3992	4106
				Catterick, part of Parish—[†] [q]													
			6	Hudswell - - [r] Township	2831	56	16	–	59	11	–	127	253	305	291	258	245
			7	Hipswell - - [s] Township	2765	62	1	–	58	3	–	256	266	296	293	313	293
			8	St. Martins — [t] Ex. Par.	–			–	10	1	–	–	–	–	–	–	57
				Easby, part of Parish—‖ [u]													
			9	Easby - - - Township	940	15	–	–	20	–	–	85	113	105	79	105	114
			10	Skeeby - - Township	770	40	–	–	43	4	–	134	147	163	183	175	203
			11	Aske - - Township	1670	17	2	–	17	–	–	73	83	109	105	92	121
			12	Gilling - - Township (part of *Gilling* Parish)¶ [*]	4440	199	5	–	201	14	–	809	795	921	899	981	987
			13	Middleton Tyas with Kneeton Tp. (pt. of *Middleton Tyas* Par.)[**] [x]	3154	129	5	–	115	10	–	526	506	569	621	586	501
	2	CATTERICK															
			1	Moulton - - [y] Township (part of *Middleton Tyas* Parish)[*]	2954	52	–	–	54	4	–	174	179	236	190	209	227
			2	Brompton-upon-Swale [z] Township (part of *Easby* Parish)	1710	100	16	–	109	11	1	401	379	388	455	399	425
				Catterick, part of Parish—[†] [aa]													
			3	Catterick - - Township	1561	127	11	–	128	19	2	641	541	561	683	600	640
			4	Colbourn or Colburn Township	1318	28	2	–	25	3	–	138	139	133	163	142	122
			5	Scotton - - [bb] Township	1500	28	1	–	25	1	–	70	98	128	138	139	134
			6	East and West Appleton Townp.	1585	18	2	–	22	–	–	95	89	87	83	91	114
			7	Brough - - Township	1082	14	1	–	14	–	–	86	97	90	78	88	120
			8	Tunstall - - Township	1262	67	6	–	70	9	–	214	213	253	312	314	328
			9	Ellerton-upon-Swale Township	1609	25	3	–	28	4	–	116	111	140	147	152	144
			10	Scorton - - [cc] Township	2645	91	7	2	99	1	–	439	449	496	492	477	488
			11	Uckerby - - Township	756	7	–	–	11	–	–	75	50	52	50	40	61
			12	Bolton-upon-Swale Township	878	22	3	–	21	3	–	93	76	100	85	96	82
			13	North Cowton - - Township (part of *Gilling* Parish)¶ [*]	1321	76	7	–	78	9	–	282	322	270	264	273	312
				Entire Parishes of													
				[*] Aysgarth - - - - - -	77308	1238	106	2	1248	84	3	5205	5170	5621	5796	5725	5635
				[†] Grinton - - - - - -	48961	1014	88	8	1010	38	–	4039	4968	5300	4854	4811	4924
				[‡] Downholme - - - - -	5915	47	2	–	50	6	–	233	369	251	235	248	260
				[§] Catterick - - - - -	22599	592	56	2	609	57	2	2678	2600	2888	3066	2965	3014
				‖ Easby - - - - -	5090	172	18	–	189	15	1	693	722	765	822	771	863
				¶ Gilling - - - - -	10095	347	13	–	348	24	–	1396	1408	1516	1498	1618	1659
				[**] Middleton Tyas - - - -	6108	181	5	–	169	14	–	700	685	805	811	795	728

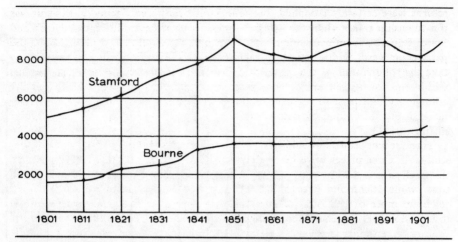

Fig. 7(a)   Population changes in Bourne and Stamford in the nineteenth century. These are represented as curves, although in fact they are based on ten-yearly totals and ought to be recorded in terms of block graphs; the common consensus is to show trends in this way.

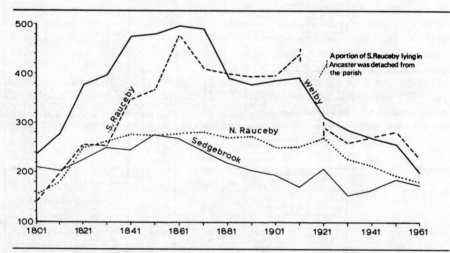

(b)   Population changes in four Lincolnshire villages in the nineteenth century showing the basic rural pattern with significant local variations.

available for many counties in the volumes of the Victoria County History of England.[42] These decennial totals, when compared, give a clear picture of whether any local community was growing or not. Thus for Stamford we can see the pattern of growth up to 1881 (with some fluctuations) and then a fall to the end of the century; Bourne's growth was somewhat different (Fig. 7). Similarly, the Lincolnshire villages of Welby, Sedgebrook and Rauceby can be seen to follow a pattern that is typical of many rural areas in the century in that the peak census was 1851 or 1861, although the difference between the two Raucebys immediately calls for some explanation.

Some of the problems which faced the historian when dealing with the sources before 1800 no longer apply. The census material is on the whole reliable;[43] the returns were certainly compiled for demographic purposes. Secondly, the unit was the township rather than the parish. It is thus possible to distinguish North and South Rauceby from each other, the minor hamlets within larger parishes, and the parishes or wards within the towns themselves. In the larger towns, it is desirable to take the subdivisions of the registration districts, for the large scale redistributions within the town itself are of very great significance to the general history of the community, not least to its demographic history. Changes in boundaries are clearly marked, but the frequency with which they occurred does make strict comparison difficult.[44]

Three recent studies of similar communities show something of the value of this study. All three places were not widely separated in size. Tickhill in Yorkshire was the smallest at 1,150 in 1801; Long Buckby (Northants) was 1,600 strong at that time, while Richmond (Yorks) was 2,861. They were all semi-industrial market towns in more or less rural settings, and very typical of early nineteenth-century towns. Moreover in general terms their demographic histories during the nineteenth century were similar (see Fig. 8). Nevertheless, it is the differences which are significant — why the fall in population should begin earlier in Tickhill; why Long Buckby did not seem to experience the slowing down of the growth rate in the 1830s that the others experienced, and so on.[45]

The different types of local community which emerge from a study of the census material may be classified roughly as below (Fig. 9). Not all villages were dying in the later nineteenth century; some were growing rapidly for a variety of reasons. Again, while towns grew, the decline of the city centres, at least in terms of population, can be clearly seen. What is much harder to see are those new communities, the new town suburbs which filled the spaces between villages, and especially the completely new settlements which sprang up in open spaces. These were situated within already defined registration areas (often the parishes) and are not always easy to see. The establishment of the little industrial villages of Westwood and Jacksdale in Nottinghamshire are not, for instance, recorded

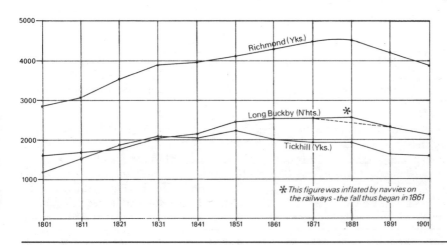

Fig. 8 Small town changes in nineteenth century population. Long Buckby, Northants, Richmond and Tickhill, Yorks. The trends in these three towns will be discussed below. These are totals, not rates of growth or decline.

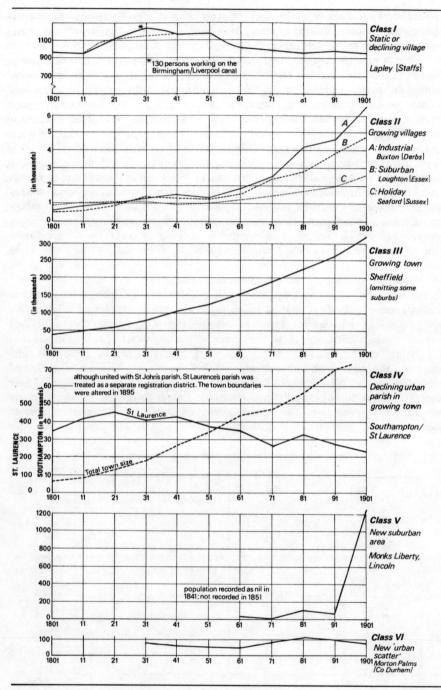

Fig. 9 The major demographic categories of local communities in the nineteenth century. Basically, town population rose and village population fell from the middle of the century. But some parts of towns witnessed population decline and some villages a rise, while a number of completely new settlements emerged.

separately from Selston, their mother parish. And this is unfortunate for they are among the most interesting of late nineteenth-century developments. Nevertheless on many occasions something can be learned even of these places.

While it may be suggested that the local historian of the later nineteenth century will in general find himself dealing with one or other of these classes, either with a village in decline or growing, or with a rapidly expanding town or a dying town centre, or with an entirely new settlement, either suburban infill or 'urban scatter', it must be stressed that the demographic pattern of any community is a story unique to itself. It is a story which can be easily traced, at least for the nineteenth century. The telling of this history in outline is not however sufficient. For there were many underlying causes for population change, and these throw a great deal of light on the economic and social development of the local community. And at the same time, the increase or decrease in population has had profound results upon the place, its economy and life. It is one of the tasks of the local historian to trace both these causes and the results of the changes in population in his chosen field of study.

Chapter 3

The structure of the community

1

The explanation of those general trends in population change which can be seen from the evidence so far discussed is clearly something which must occupy the mind of any local historian. He cannot be content with the mere statement that his chosen community was growing or declining in size, but must search out both the causes and the results of this rise or fall. This is a complicated field of study in which a good deal of recent work has been done and great advances made. It may be useful to summarise (in the most general terms) the reasons behind the increase or decrease of population in any community.

Any increase in population would seem to be related to one or more of three factors. Thus:

— more babies were born;
— more persons survived the hazards of disease and other premature causes of death;
— or more persons entered the community from outside.

Several of these factors, of course, worked together. Immigration was often most common among the younger and therefore potential child-bearing section of the community; while the decline of infant mortality itself would ensure that more adults of child-bearing age would be present in the community than in the earlier years.

Such factors however raise a further series of questions. Why did the birthrate increase at any particular period, if indeed that is one of the reasons for the growth in population? Is it because there were more parents or because each family was larger? Again the decline of mortality rates may be dependent upon factors like improved medicine, available diet, the cost of foodstuffs, or health legislation and amenity provision; while the reasons behind the increasing or continuing immigration may lie in social or economic factors, such as new industry or the town's amenities.

The increase of population thus provokes a series of questions which in their turn suggest further fields of enquiry. The same factors operate in reverse with a declining population. Fewer babies were born, more persons died, and/or significant numbers of persons left the community. The reasons for these developments would lie in such factors as the changing age structure in the group, disease and war, and the social and economic environment which led to migration.

In many of these questions, the local historian will pass from the purely local to more general aspects of his subject. Some of the factors involved, such as disease, diet and the cost of food, the social and psychological phenomena relating to the marriageable age and the age relationship of husband and wife, educational provision, the age at which people started work and retired, the time of year at which marriage and again conception took place, contraception and the spacing of the family and so on, are frequently determined by national or regional trends. On the other hand, specifically local factors may at times have predominated. The general pull of towns, at least in the nineteenth century, may be offset in any locality by the lack of available housing. The general improvement of health standards may not apply in particular urban developments. The task of the local historian is to try to assess what particular local factors are at play distorting or reinforcing the more general trends in progress.

In thus seeking to trace the reasons behind the increase or decrease of population in any community, the local historian is forced towards a complete social analysis of his subject. And in this analysis, a number of projects emerge clearly as of great significance.

First of these is an **age- and sex-structure analysis** of the community.[1] This will throw incidental light upon many other aspects of local history, such as the number of children for whom educational provision must be made and the number of elderly to be maintained. But its main purpose in demographic terms will be to assess the proportion of marriageable women in the group and their potential husbands. This should be linked with a study of the marriage rates within the community. How many married and unmarried adults are there? At what age did marriage normally take place? How long did a marriage last and how frequently did widowed (or divorced) partners enter a new union?

The second project is related to **the family and birthrate**. What was the average size of the family in the community? If this can be related to occupational or social groupings, to income levels, housing and the existence or otherwise of domestic help, significant patterns may well emerge. Did the wealthy brewer, living in a large house away from his place of employment and supported by a household of servants, have a larger or smaller family than an impoverished but well-educated cleric in a large parsonage, or the independent joiner whose house was also his workshop? How soon after marriage was the first child born? Simple birthrates are not in this context adequate; there are too many other factors involved. For instance, how frequently were children born? Clearly a couple who had five children in the space of some seven to eight years would help on the population growth rate a good deal faster than one which had the same number of children spread out over twenty years. A number of signs of early contraception have been detected recently. Perhaps most useful is an assessment of fertility — not just by crude rates of births related to the number of women aged 15–45, but more significantly by the number of daughters who live to become potential mothers (the net reproduction rate). Thus a rate of 1.0 would result in a static population, a rate of 1.5 would show a population capable of rapid growth, while a rate of 0.8 would indicate a falling population. Other methods of calculating fertility have also been suggested, such as 'the effective family' — i.e. the number of children who themselves marry.[2]

The third project relates to **mortality**. An assessment of the average expectation of life may be distinguished from a separate but clearly related study of the survival rate among births. Indeed, if it can be done, the most useful study would be one based on mortality rates for different age groups. One of the major troubles here is that there are extreme though often short-term fluctuations, both in time and in place. In a large town, some areas had a higher mortality rate than others. Further, some years were bad years for the whole of the group; other years were good years. Such fluctuations need to be explained once again against a background of climate, diet, costs of food, health legislation and provision and other factors. But the general trends, if discernible, are more important for the local historian than the fluctuations.

The fourth project relates to **immigration or emigration**. Is it possible to establish how many families or individuals joined or left the group? If so, what was it that drew them in or forced them to leave? How old were they when they moved? How far did they move? And was their migration a single event or was it a continuing process? How long did they stay? Once again, this needs to be related to age structure, to occupation, income level, social groupings and the provision of housing.

These are of course the major questions to pose concerning the community. Not all of them can be answered for every group at every period; some of them may never be answered at all. But they do become necessary to try to explain why, in any specific local group, the size of it was declining or increasing. And there are of course others which could be asked — family relationships and kinship groups within the community, and racial groupings (like the Irish or the Welsh) who formed identifiable subgroups[3]. The subject is a very wide one indeed.

With such a demographic survey, there are two main dangers. One is that the results may appear too static. It is necessary to take a cross-section through the community at a particular time in order to arrive at satisfactory answers. But all societies changed constantly, some faster than others, and the limitations of a static analysis approach must be kept clearly in mind. The other is of applying averages throughout the community, thus concealing extreme variations between different areas or groups within the whole. Once again an awareness of this possibility is necessary.

2

Population growth in England

The background to these population trends has already been discussed above, but something further may be added concerning the reasons behind the overall growth of population in the country. These reasons are not easy to assess — indeed, it is easier to find reasons for stagnation than it is for growth. Immigration into England was not significant in a demographic sense until the middle of the nineteenth century. Factors of environment, changes in diet, medical progress and the poor relief system (which, harsh though it could be, was still the most advanced in the world)[4] may all have helped to increase the birth rate and to reduce the mortality rate. That there was a substantial rise of population in western Europe in the eighteenth century would suggest that the increase was not directly related to the Industrial Revolution. There may also have been changing demographic trends inherent within the population.

Very little can be said about the reasons behind the population changes of medieval England, especially the early period of growth. A good deal is known about the Black Death, and some general views of the average expectation of life have been arrived at. There has been discussion on the average size of the family and household and on the marriage customs of the peasantry.[5] But few of these can be analysed in detail for any local community. It is for the period after 1600 that the useful material relating to demographic history is available.

Even here however there are problems. The real trouble is that the history of population in England before 1800 relies not so much on national statistics but on a number (indeed, so far a small number) of local studies. And these are of course subject to extreme variation. The picture thus is uncertain and large parts of it are still as yet undrawn. And what has been discussed has not resulted in any agreement among historians.[6] The samples are so far much too small to create an overall pattern. In this context the demographic history of any local community has a wider significance. After 1800, more is known, and thus most of the figures quoted relate to the nineteenth and early twentieth centuries.

It would seem impossible to make any clear statements concerning changes in age structure throughout the country as a whole for the seventeenth and eighteenth centuries; local variations are too significant. Until the birth rate began to fall at the end of the nineteenth century, it is likely that each age group successively exceeded the one older than itself, although the proportion of various groups clearly fluctuated as the expectation of life varied. The sixteenth century saw perhaps a smaller proportion of those under fifteen than did the seventeenth and eighteenth centuries. In the nineteenth century (for which firm figures are alone available) there was once more a lengthening of the age pyramid, with a decline of the ratio of those under fifteen years of age to those above fifteen. It is a mistake to assume that this figure remained constant (40% has been quoted without any firm basis) even in the nineteenth century (see Fig. 10), and this must have been equally true of earlier periods.

	1821	1851	1881
Under 15	38%	35¼%	36½%
15–45	44%	46¼%	44½%
Over 45	18%	18½%	19%

Fig. 10 Comparative percentages of the population of England and Wales by age-groups. The trends are slight but discernible.

It would seem that for most of the period 1600 to 1900, boys exceeded girls in the age range 0–12. Thereafter females predominated, surviving significantly longer. But in the age range 15–35, the imbalance may not always have been as large as it was, for example, in 1821. In the census for that year, males aged 0–15 exceeded females by 76,500, i.e. 1½% of that age range. From 15–40, the balance was dramatically reversed, with 309,700 more females than males, and this preponderance of females was maintained in the upper levels of the age structure.[7] It is probable that in most periods an even balance of males and females was achieved at about the age of fifteen years, but the fluctuation of this age even by a few years, which certainly occurred, must have produced significant demographic changes. This pattern, which we know certainly existed from 1801, varied slightly throughout the nineteenth century; in 1851, out of just over 15½ million adults above ten years of age, 8 million were female, 7½ million were male. From the 1880s, the imbalance of women to men increased considerably, a trend which has continued until the most recent censuses have shown some signs of recovery.

The way in which this imbalance affected marriage rates and the age at marriage is only now being examined. It has been suggested[8] that in the 1870s, some

26—28% of marriageable women in fact never married. Certainly the marriage rate fell, from 859 per thousand in 1850 to 818 per thousand in 1910, rising thereafter to 860 in 1921. Probably the marriage rate was less favourable before the nineteenth century.

Recent assessments of the general trends in the size of families and marriageable ages suggest that the average family (which is of course somewhat smaller than the average household) remained at a more or less static size of 4½ persons from the sixteenth to the early nineteenth centuries, although there was perhaps some slight increase at the end of the eighteenth century; by the 1870s, it had risen to rather more than 5, but thereafter it fell seriously until in the 1930s the national average was only 2. But this national average conceals the true size of families. Households with children (which seem to have been about 70% of all households at any one time) seem to have increased in size from approximately 6—6½ persons (i.e. 4½ children) in the late sixteenth century to about 7—7½ persons in the late eighteenth century. Most commentators agree that this increase was faster after 1740 than before this date — indeed, there may well have been a fall from the sixteenth century position for much of the seventeenth century, before a sudden spurt during the middle and later eighteenth century. But such general figures do not apply everywhere; there were large local and social variations and it is these variations which are significant, not the overall picture.[9]

Fluctuations in the rates of births and deaths are more easily seen. The birthrate probably fell throughout the period 1600 to 1900. In 1600, it was apparently about 40 per thousand; by 1700, this figure fell to 30 and it remained at or below this figure for much of the century. During the nineteenth century, it rose gradually to something between 35 and 40 per thousand. The rise was not however constant, and indeed it came to an abrupt end in 1871. Thus the figure of 34.1 (1851) which had become 35.5 in 1871 gave way to much lower birthrates, 28.7 in 1901, and 14.9 in 1939.[10] This drastic fall, perhaps connected with changing attitudes to contraception revealed in the famous trial of Charles Bradlaugh and Mrs Besant (1876) or in such books as Dr Dysdale's *The Element of Social Science, or Physical, Sexual and Natural Religion*,[11] reached its lowest level in 1933, at 14.4.

One trouble with these figures is that they vary with so many different factors — with social classes or occupations, with the age structure of the community or the balance between the sexes. How far the fluctuations reflected changes in fertility or changes in marriageable customs is not clear. For much of England, the age of marriage during the eighteenth century seems to have been late, some 27—28 years for men, 24 years for women (though there are some extreme local variations in this). Some of these differences of course occur in relation to different occupational groupings; it has even been suggested that the population of England rose after 1740 because the enclosure movement created more labourers who tended to marry earlier. It would seem however that the average age of marriage was fairly static for much of the sixteenth, seventeenth and eighteenth centuries,[12] but it may well have been higher during the nineteenth century and indeed reached its peak in 1911, when the average age at which women married for the first time was just under 26 years, falling back gradually until 1961 when it was 23.2. The average age relationship of husband and wife implied in these figures (a gap of only three years) was probably not constant throughout the period. Clearly a high rate of remarriage (when a widow with her established position might prove more acceptable to a young man struggling to set himself up, despite the age gap) would affect the fertility rate of the union, and indeed may prevent some younger females from ever being married at all. Indeed, it has been suggested that at any one moment, only 50% of fertile women (between the ages of 15 and 45) in western Europe were exposed to child-bearing, unlike many other parts of the world where it rose as high as 80%. In this connection of course, the illegitimacy rate becomes significant.

The average annual mortality rate, on the other hand, fell substantially from 1600 to 1900; throughout the Middle Ages it clearly stood at a very high figure. From 1600 well into the eighteenth century, it ran at about 30 per thousand, but it began to decline sharply from about 1780. By 1800, it had fallen below 25 per thousand and by 1820 was as low as 20 per thousand. It rose temporarily between 1850 (21.5) and 1870 (22.3), but thereafter it fell even below 20 per thousand, reaching 17.2 in 1900 and 11.6 in 1938,[13] after which it began to rise slightly. It must be remembered that these figures again hide large local variations — up to 1885, Liverpool apparently never recorded a figure below 26. Further, such figures hide differential age-mortality rates — for instance, infant mortality rates, after a fall in the middle of the eighteenth century, did not start to fall again significantly until about 1900, largely because of diseases like diphtheria. The general fall in the death rate became reflected in a rise in the expectation of life from a figure of about 32[14] for both sexes at the end of the seventeenth century, to 43.7 (men) and 47.2 (women) in 1881 and again to 61.8 (men) and 65.8 (women) in 1938.

Clearly such fluctuations are directly related to changes of diet, sanitation, housing and medicine which became more widespread in the nineteenth century. Significantly, of course, they are related to the pattern of plagues and diseases which swept the country at times. But, although it is possible to mark some periods as years of great crisis for much of the country, like the Black Death of 1349 and its successive waves of 1361, 1368 and 1375 or the later outbreaks in 1558, 1603 and 1625, or the Great Plague of 1665, or the disease-ridden years of 1728—9, local reactions to such periods, as Professor Chambers's study of the Vale of Trent clearly shows, were not always what one would expect. Similarly the coming of cholera in the nineteenth century, with its peak years in 1831, 1846—9, 1853—4 and 1865—6, may not be reflected in local population changes, even though it may be reflected in far-reaching changes of attitude towards public health shown in such things as the appointment of public health officers in Liverpool (1847) and London (1848) and in the Public Health Act of 1848. Plague of course has much wider significance for the local historian than just the deaths it caused; indeed, its impact on those who survived may in the long run have been more important. But in the pattern of demographic history, it is a factor to be reckoned with.[15]

Migration
The redistribution of population throughout the country, consequent upon migration between local communities, has already been discussed. The general patterns and trends of migration are clear. But such patterns may not be of much significance in tracing local movements of population. The causes of this movement are many and localised in effect. That significant numbers of labourers from a group of fenland villages in central Lincolnshire moved in the early nineteenth century to the Cleveland area of Yorkshire cannot be explained by the general trends of migration; the interpretation of this fact must be sought for in terms of the general development of both of these places.[16]

A final word must be added about the relationship between natural increase of population and migration. The term 'natural increase' can be used in two senses. On the one hand, it refers to an increase seen in the parish registers by the process of aggregative analysis. Thus the registers of the Chester parishes reveal a 'natural increase' or 'decrease' in their respective population. On the other hand, the term is also used of that process of increasing birth rate independent of the process of immigration. The population of Chester was rising in the eighteenth century. How much of this was due to 'natural increase' and how much to immigration? In other words, if there were no immigration, how fast would the population have risen naturally? Whether this is a possible calculation may be doubted, though some attempts have been made to assess the relative influence exerted by these two factors. Thus for London, it has been suggested that there was a 'natural decrease' from 1701 to 1781, followed by a slight 'natural increase' in 1781 to 1801 and a considerable 'natural increase' from 1801 to 1831. But at each stage immigration outweighed the early losses and reinforced the later gains.[17] Similar estimates have been made for other regions. The rural areas in both north and south showed a more or less constant pattern from 1701 to 1831 of natural increase offset by emigration. The urban north-west, however, had a pattern of natural increase offset by migration from 1701 to 1781, but from 1781 to 1831, the natural increase was reinforced by immigration.

These figures can only be accepted provisionally, for there is little firm basis for them. But it is important to realise that the 'natural increase' revealed by the parish register aggregative analysis is not the same as the 'natural increase' estimated in this way. All that the parish registers reveal is a rising or falling population. They do not and cannot say how much of this rise or fall is due to 'natural increase' or to migration. Both contributed to the figures to be found from the registers, but in what proportions they do not show.

3

Early sources

Before the detailed census records of the mid-nineteenth century, it is almost safe to say that such a detailed survey of local community population trends is only possible where very good parish registers survive. Very rarely do other sources throw light on the age structure of the group, size of families, birth and mortality rates or migration. There are some favoured groups for which a static analysis is possible[18] — an occasional census conducted for his own purposes by the local incumbent or some resident antiquarian, a house by house survey by one of the rating authorities or the like. But these are chance compilations and even more chancy survivals. Where they occur, the local historian must of course use them to the full, but in any case they will be unable to provide clues to any trends in the demographic history of the place under study. Only perhaps in the case of the censuses compiled in connection with the tax on baptisms, marriages and burials from 1695 to 1705, of which a number of local copies survive[19], is there hope of any comparison between communities, while a succession of such detailed records for one place is very rare indeed. On the other hand, some indication of migration may be obtained by a comparison of such lists of heads of households that survive, for instance in the Protestation Returns and the Hearth Tax Returns, with each other or with the parish registers.[20] But even this cannot always be done, and the results are not certain, for there may be more than one reason for the absence of a particular name from one or other of these sources. A survey of those marriage registers which record the original parishes of the partners can be done for a few favourable parishes.

This is not of course to say that the position is hopeless, that nothing can be known of population trends in any locality before 1851. Where good parish registers survive — that is, where they are complete (recording all three events of baptism, marriage and burial), legible, comprehensive in the sense that they are not vitiated by large dissenting groups, well maintained with full entries[21] and appear to be reliable, a good deal may be done, at least for the parish if not for the local community. Thus years of high mortality can be seen from the totals culled from the parish registers, and in some cases the factors relating to these peak periods, like plague as in the Trent Valley or high food prices as at Exeter, become apparent. Closer analysis of the crude annual totals may, in some cases, provide further information. Thus a comparison of monthly totals of baptisms may reveal peak periods for conceptions, such as Dr Mills's studies at Melbourn (Cambs) showed. These indicate a remarkable persistence of July baptisms for a whole century, 1741–1840, at least among the Anglican population of the parish. Where this can be compared with dates of birth (which the registers give from 1795 to 1830), it is clear that not all of this high baptismal rate can be accounted for by delays in baptism — there clearly was also a high autumn conception rate.[22] Similar study of burials may throw light on the death rate among the young and old during specific periods of the year.

There are limits however to the usefulness of these methods. A detailed analysis of the monthly figures of baptisms and burials for all the ten parishes of Chester for the second half of the eighteenth century failed to produce any coherent pattern at all (Fig. 11). A study of the ratio of baptisms to marriages which had taken place in the previous five years in each parish, in an attempt to get some indication of changes in the size of the family, similarly produced widely ranging figures without leading to conclusions.[23] The examination of the crude figures alone will not always be productive.

Such simple analysis of the registers can however be supplemented by the process known as **family reconstitution**. By this method of analysis, which is both laborious and exacting, entries in the different registers concerning the same person are brought together and related to those of persons of the same family. In this way, something of a biographical history of each individual in the community can be compiled. Experience seems to suggest that it is necessary to do this over at least three generations, or a period of about a hundred years, although the labour and the tedium involved may be very daunting indeed. This study can often be filled out with material drawn from other contemporary documents (such as estate records, like rentals or surveys, local government records like poor law accounts, or private records like wills) or non-documentary sources (like tombstones and monumental inscriptions or date stones on houses) to add significant details. Where it is possible to do a full static analysis of the community, clearly the final product of a comparison of the two analyses will be particularly valuable, for it enables the trends to be seen.[24]

From all of this data, one may be able to arrive at conclusions concerning the expectation of life, marriageable age, the age-relationship of husband and wife, size of family and infant mortality at different periods of the history of the local community. The mother's fertility, at least in terms of her age at the conception of her first and last child, the spacing of the children and the length of time between marriage and starting a family, the length of the marriage and the incidence of

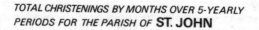

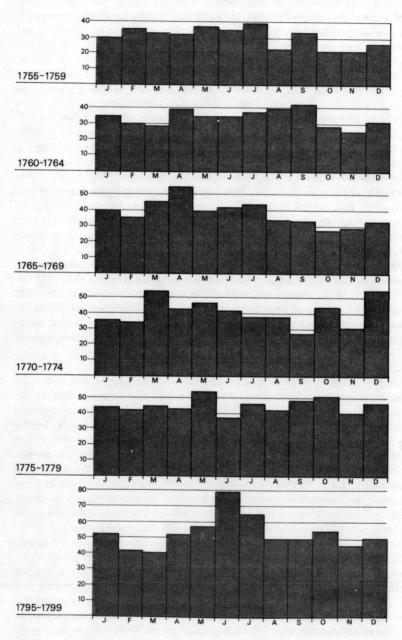

Fig. 11   Seasonality diagrams revealing trends in months of baptism, St John's, Chester, 1755–99. Similar figures for five-yearly periods may be drawn for marriages and burials.

remarriage, and such questions as whether the children waited until their parents were dead before getting married and how far the men went in search of their brides — on all of these topics, family reconstitution can throw light.

On the whole, however, little reliable information can be discovered concerning migration, although the number of persons in any period who appear in one register and not in one of the other two may help to indicate something of this.[25] Again, the compilation from this data of a complete age structure of the community at any one period is feasible, although it is not clear how reliable in practice it would be. But apart from these limitations, the process of family reconstitution is by far the most valuable way of assessing demographic trends in the local community.

4

Nineteenth century sources

The parish registers come to an end of their useful lives for demographic purposes in 1836 (in some cases a good deal earlier). It is true that they may be used to provide some ancillary information on known individuals, but their comprehensiveness declines steadily throughout the century and they can no longer reveal demographic trends except perhaps for marriages.

Fortunately, however, by then other more comprehensive sources have become available. From 1841 to 1871, the census enumerators' books[26] contain a good deal of information. It is true that they need to be supplemented by other records such as rate books, land tax returns, rentals, directories and newspapers, poor law records and school registers; but for the purpose of a demographic survey, many aspects of the study may be done from the enumerators' schedules for these years alone.[27]

A word needs to be added at this stage about these records. Clearly they have many advantages. They are the first purely demographic records to be drawn up, although the questions they were designed to ask are not always those which later students wish to answer. They were organised centrally and therefore are uniform in format and universal in coverage. They were official enquiries and therefore backed by great sanctions — often indeed with support from other official or voluntary bodies (in 1881, for instance, the bishop of Lincoln issued a special collect to be said in churches on the Sunday before the census was taken). Nevertheless, despite all of this, there are certain limitations to the schedules as definitive surveys. On the one hand, the incentives for evasion were still high — a fear of various forms of taxation or of conscription. Returns by householders were also rendered inaccurate by ignorance or uncertainty as well as by deliberate falsification. The 1881 census report itself commented that 'there is reason to believe that a considerable number of servant girls who are not yet fifteen years old represent themselves as having reached that age . . .'. These deficiencies in returns were most serious in the recording of young children: 'Even as late as 1911 the deficiency of the census records of children under two years of age would appear to have been over 6% of those of that age actually alive.'[28] On the other side, the enumerators themselves were not without handicaps. Some were not as literate as the registrars intended; many found it difficult to understand the rules drawn up for them, and impossible to ensure that their often unco-operative subjects understood them. Finally, the records were copied up and clearly some errors crept in at this stage, such as wrong totals at the bottom of pages or wrong sex indication.[29] (See Plate 8(b).)

Nevertheless, in general the records may be accepted with only minor amendments of the more obvious errors. And from these returns it is possible to make a survey of the local community in most of the aspects listed above. For this purpose the 1841 returns are not the most valuable, for they list only the names, approximate ages, marital status and occupation of the persons in them and whether they were born in the same county or not (Plate 2). The later census schedules were fuller, and the fact that there are successive returns for 1851, 1861 and now 1871, both provides opportunity for static analysis and enables population trends to be observed.

There is however a different problem facing the local historian here, and that is the very bulk of the material to be handled. It is easy enough to cope with a village with some 300—500 entries. With a group, it is equally possible to examine a larger community of up to 3,000, but above that there are great difficulties. Two methods have been suggested — random (or carefully selected) sampling methods,[30] or the use of computer techniques, as suggested by Professor Dyos.[31] This latter is not without its own hazards, for a computer can only answer the questions put to it and cannot suggest significant points. However, it is unlikely to be available to the average local historian, and he must be content, it would seem, to confine his attention to overall structures and sampling. Certainly the detailed analysis in terms of the projects discussed above is only possible to the local historian of the small or middle range of nineteenth-century community.

Age structure by sex

An analysis of the community in terms of the distribution by ages and sex is not easy before the 1851 census. The returns for 1801 and 1811 did not ask for the names of individuals and thus they do not contain ages, while those for 1821 included them as an optional item (in totals of 5-year groups). Nevertheless, there are age-sex analyses printed from the 1821 returns for many areas.[32] In 1831, only the number of males over 20 years of age was recorded. The first returns giving ages are those for the 1841 census, but the ages there given were often rounded down to the nearest 5 (except for children under fifteen). But for 1851 and the succeeding censuses, more exact figures are given. Of course, not all of these were accurate, especially among the old (through forgetfulness), the young women (for pecuniary or social reasons) and among infants. Further, some ages were missing — in 1841, as many as 52,565;[33] while a number of infants were omitted from the census altogether. Nevertheless, the censuses for the rest of the century achieved greater and greater accuracy and comprehensiveness. Thus assuming for the purposes of the study that the schedules list almost the whole of the community present on that occasion and excluding those (if any) whose ages are not given and cannot be deduced, it is possible to construct an age pyramid of the community. This can then be used to draw deductions concerning the nature of the community. Thus at Rauceby (Lincs), 47% of the population was below 20 years of age.[34] At Long Buckby (Northants) in 1851 (see Fig. 12), 37% of the population was under 14 years of age; two-thirds were under 30 years. Other features emerge from this local study, such as a shortage of men in the age range of 45—49, perhaps indicative of some local event in earlier years. Girls exceeded boys (but only marginally) from the age of 6—14 but were significantly fewer from 15—19. Thereafter they were greater in numbers from 20—29, but fewer from 30—45 and again from 50—59. In

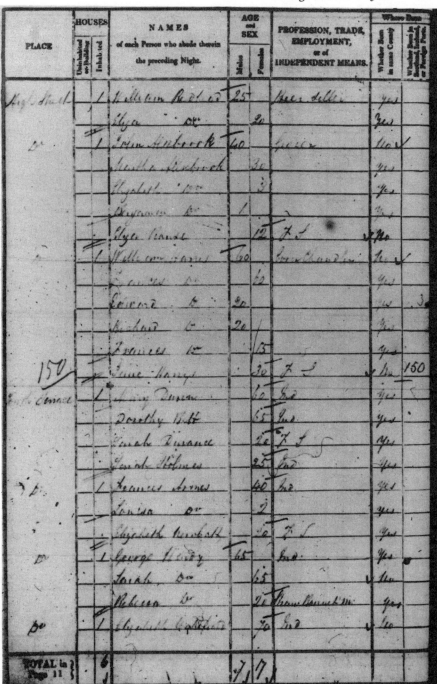

Plate 2 Page of Census Enumerator's book 1841, for South Rauceby, Lincolnshire. The limited range of the information provided here is clear. Although ages in 1841 were supposed to be rounded to multiples of 5, the enumerator here has recorded ages as they were given to him. J.C. stands for 'journeyman carpenter', F.S. for 'female servant', Y in the last column stands for 'yes'. For pages from the later books, see Plates 6 and 8(b).

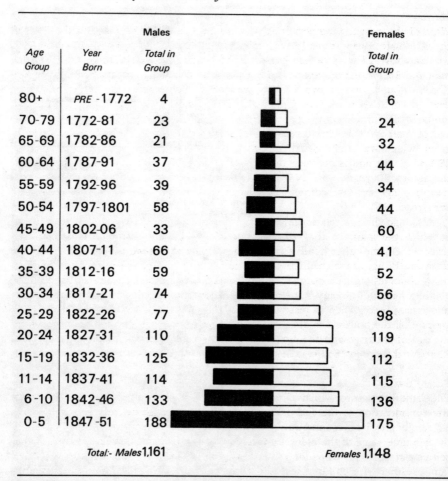

Age Group	Year Born	Males Total in Group		Females Total in Group
80+	PRE -1772	4		6
70-79	1772-81	23		24
65-69	1782-86	21		32
60-64	1787-91	37		44
55-59	1792-96	39		34
50-54	1797-1801	58		44
45-49	1802-06	33		60
40-44	1807-11	66		41
35-39	1812-16	59		52
30-34	1817-21	74		56
25-29	1822-26	77		98
20-24	1827-31	110		119
15-19	1832-36	125		112
11-14	1837-41	114		115
6-10	1842-46	133		136
0-5	1847-51	188		175

Total:- Males 1,161   Females 1,148

Fig. 12 The age structure of Long Buckby 1851. Note the fluctuations of the males and females in each group between the ages of 40 and 64.

no age grouping did the number of females greatly exceed those of the males in this specific instance; indeed above the age of 14, they were (most exceptionally) in total fewer in number.

A similar study for Tickhill in 1851 gives figures with some differences — 35.8% under 15, 17.8% being girls, 18.0% being boys. Males exceeded females up to the age of 35 and again 40—45 and 55—64. But this community was less unusual in that the overall proportions were 49.7% males and 50.3% females. At Richmond (Yorks), 53.5% of the population was female; 'the females outnumbered the males in every age-group except 5—14'. Tickhill was also unusual in its relative elderliness — 'only 70% were under 40' years of age; at Richmond this figure was 72.6%, at Long Buckby 75.5%, closer to the national average in 1851 of 76%.

Such an analysis covering all the available census returns can show changes in the structure of the community. At North Leverton (Notts) the 47.35% of under-20s in 1841 fell to 45.3% (1851) and to 44.3% in 1861, while the 9.78% of over-60s rose gradually to 9.85% and then to 12.75% in 1861.[35]

Marriage

What of the marriage rate within the community? In 1851, at Long Buckby, 344 of the 726 male adults above 14 were or had been married, some 61%; 485 of the 722 women above 14 were or had been married, some 67%. At Richmond, 36% of the men and 35.7% of the women had been or were married, a remarkably low proportion, making a total of two-thirds of the community unmarried. At Tickhill, however, it would seem that the figures were similar to those at Richmond, for married 'housewives' formed only 19% of the population. It is not possible to compute the age of marriage from the census books, but an analysis of the proportion of each group which was unmarried helps towards this assessment. Thus at Long Buckby 48% of all the adults between the ages of 20 and 29 years were unmarried; above the age of 30 years, only 11% were unmarried. It would seem from this that the marrying age in this community was late, although in the end few remained unmarried.[36]

Although the age relationship of husband and wife is clearly obtainable, the age at which the marriage took place is not known, except from the local marriage registers. On the other hand, some approximation of this age may be drawn from a study of the age at which the first child was conceived. For this purpose, a selection of the families must be made, for one cannot be certain that in some cases the elder children have not already left home. Families where the oldest child is aged six or under may be regarded as reasonably safe, but even this is not absolutely sure.[37] Despite all the limitations, however, some general conclusions may be drawn as to the age of marriage and the age of the parents when their first child was born. In Rauceby this age in 1851 was 26.[38]

Size of family

The same limitations which affect the age-at-marriage analysis are even clearer in any consideration of the size of families in the nineteenth century census returns. No family may be presumed complete until one of the parents has become infertile; by this time some of the older children may have left home. Thus at any one of the census dates, 1851, 1861 or 1871, a picture is given in most cases of a partial family, either with children still unborn or children having left home, permanently or temporarily. Nor is it possible to be certain which families were incomplete and which were complete.

On the other hand, the census schedules are the only systematic sources for such study, and some assessment of the size of household (as distinct from the family unit) can be made.[39] Thus at any one time, the mean size of the household can be determined: in Richmond it was 4.5 in 1851, while at both Tickhill and Long Buckby it was very slightly lower, 4.4. As further censuses are analysed, so trends can also be observed. The average household size of 5.23 at Burton Joyce (Notts) in 1841 became 4.7 in 1851, although at Bleasby nearby, the size remained much the same, at about 4.9.[40] A clearer view of the extended family, those with relatives of the head of the household living with them, also becomes apparent. At Long Buckby again, of the families recorded in 1851, 85% consisted solely of parents and their children, 9% of a 'three-generation family' while the rest consisted of relatives of the head of the household but without his children.[41] Lodgers were not common in that small market town but in other areas may be seen in profusion. If such a survey can then be related to the occupations of the households concerned, significant patterns can emerge.

Some useful information can thus be compiled on the household of the mid-Victorian period. Some were nuclear families, consisting of husband, wife and children only. It may well be significant to compare the spacing of these children, but so many unknown factors abound here (still-births and miscarriages, the number of children already dead, absences of the husband from home for work or war, etc.) that the conclusions can never be more than tentative. Other families were larger than the nuclear ones. Some of the children were married and may have had children of their own. Indeed, one of the problems is to decide in the three-generation family who exactly was the head of the household. Was the family one where the grandparents lived in as part of the family or was it one where grand-children and their parents were housed as well? Where there were grandparents or other relatives (brothers or sisters of the head, or more remote relatives like uncles or aunts), how many of them were dependants? What did happen to widows and widowers in this sort of society? Did they form any of the single member house-holds which existed? Who else lived alone? — in this, the occupation is clearly relevant. The frequency with which 'lodger' is used makes one suspect that the term hides other sorts of relationships which cannot now always be sorted out.

A good deal can thus be learnt about the structure of the local household. Never-theless, in the matter of family size, the process of census analysis is not so fruitful as the family reconstitution methods employed on the parish registers. Something in the way of reconstitution may be done from the successive census schedules, but in some respects the vital information is still missing.[42] Nor is there any other source which can provide this information at all easily. For some parishes, the Anglican registers are still of use after 1836, but this is on the whole very rare, while the registration certificates at Somerset House or locally are not always readily available for the study of a whole community.[43]

Mortality

The census does not inform the local historian of the age at which people died, although it is possible to use the age structure analysis to give some indication of this. There are, however, on occasion some other sources for mortality rates. The reports of the registrar-general, issued twice each year, contain national and regional figures which may provide some guide. Other government reports, especially those on Public Health and Urban Conditions,[44] may give some partial indication of the expectation of life in particular localities. Similar fruitful sources come from some urban authorities who commissioned local reports which often contain detailed figures. Thus the sanitary inspector of Arnold, just north of Nottingham, produced a report in 1853 which gave figures of mortality for this overgrown village. The average mortality rate per thousand for the previous seven years was 23.37 and the average expectation of life was 27½ years. Just under 20% died of infectious diseases throughout that period.[45] One-third of all the deaths recorded for those years were of infants under twelve months, and half of the total were aged under 15 years. It is thus not surprising that if an inhabitant of Arnold survived above the age of 20 years, he could expect to live to the ripe age of 56. Indeed 22% achieved or passed the age of 60.

Local reports of this kind may sometimes be supplemented by the information contained in the *Report of the Royal Commissions for inquiring into the State of Large Towns and Populous Districts* for 1844—5 (Plate 3).[46] Nottingham, for

Plate 3   Specimen page from the first *Report of the Royal Commission on the State of Large* ▶
Towns and Populous Districts, 1844, showing mortality rates in parts of Nottingham.

Town of Nottingham.

Report, in reply to Questions, by T. Hawksley, Esq.

46. The police have just begun to act as firemen, with what efficiency I have not had the opportunity of remarking. There are four or five very good engines under the control of the Municipal Watch Committee.

47. The general condition of the town with respect to health is singularly bad. The annual mortality is 2·84 per cent. The average duration of life amongst males is only 20·5 years, and amongst females 23·9 years; and yet the site of the town is decidedly salubrious, and the occupations of the people not necessarily unhealthy.

To arrive at a satisfactory conclusion respecting the actual sanatory state of the town, I have, with great care, analyzed the mortuary registers for the years ending June 1840, 1841, 1842, and 1843, comprehending the two years preceding, and the two years subsequent to, the census of 1841; and from these and other sources have been enabled to ascertain the rate of mortality, the age at death, the degree of density, and other of the more important particulars requisite in an investigation of the causes of human mortality.

The abstracts compiled from these documents, and the calculations based upon them, extending as they do to each of the 65 enumeration districts into which the town was divided by the Census Commissioners, are, I am aware, far too numerous and voluminous to be included within the necessary limits of this report. I have, therefore, condensed the more important facts into the following

TABLES showing the different RATES of MORTALITY prevalent in the differently conditioned Districts of the Town of Nottingham.

TABLE No. 1.—The Mortality of Wards.

a.	b.			c.		d.	e.	f.	g.			h.	k.	l.	m.
Wards enumerated in the order of their respective Rates of Mortality.	Population, excluding Public Institutions.			Space for each Person in Yards. Sub-districts.		Altitude above the Summer level of the River Trent in feet.	Number of Deaths in four years, excluding Public Institutions.	Proportion of Deaths per Annum to 100 of the Population.	Mean Age at Death.			Range of the Mean Age at Death in the Sub-districts.	Years of Life lost by each Person.	Approximate Proportion of Life lost by each Person.	Proportion of Deaths to Births.
	Males.	Females.	Persons.	Min.	Max.				Males.	Females.	Average.				
1. Park . .	2,186	3,047	5,233	24	..	40 to 180	408	1·95	29·4	29·3	29·3	18·5 to 39·3	0	0	1 to 1·31
2. Sherwood .	2,417	2,813	5,230	18½	..	60 to 200	421	2·01	20·0	28·2	24·3	20·2 to 40·0	6½	1/6 +	1 to 1·41
3. Castle . .	3,230	3,887	7,117	11½	81	12 to 70	662	2·32	19·3	26·5	23·0	24·3 to 33·4	8½	1/5 −	1 to 1·42
4. Exchange .	2,725	3,132	5,857	10½	66½	12 to 90	593	2·53	20·6	24·1	22·4	17·6 to 27·0	9	2/9	1 to 1·26
5. St. Mary .	3,172	3,984	7,156	9½	51	12 to 90	761	2·65	18·2	24·0	21·3	18·3 to 33·3	11	1/4 −	1 to 1·5
6. St. Ann .	5,051	5,469	10,520	8½	51½	50 to 150	1175	2·79	16·3	21·8	19·2	11·1 to 23·4	13½	1/3 −	1 to 1·2
7. Byron . .	5,117	5,912	11,029	8½	31	30 to 90	1368	3·09	17·3	18·7	18·1	14·3 to 27·8	14	1/3 +	1 to 1·2
The whole Town .	24,537	28,554	53,091	8½	..	12 to 200 Mean abt. 50	6032	2·84	20·5	23·9	22·3	11·1 to 40·0	9	2/9	1 to 1·21

TABLE No. 2.—Showing the Density of the Population, and the Mean Age at Death in differently conditioned Minor Districts of the Town of Nottingham.

Yards of Surface to each Inhabitant.	No. of Inhabitants per Acre.	Mean Age at Death.	Yards of Surface to each Inhabitant.	No. of Inhabitants per Acre.	Mean Age at Death.
Country	District.	40·0	13	376	21·7
40½	120	39·3	..	..	21·7
..	..	36 7	8½	568	21·3
..	..	36·6	25½	190	20·9
28½	170	33·4	9½	512	20·7
34	143	33·3	38½	127	20·3
48½	100	32·4	10½	460	20·3
30	161	31·8	..	..	20·2
36	135	30·8	11½	426	20·2
38½	126	30·6	17½	277	20·1
31	155	27·8	14½	330	19·7
33	147	27·0	20½	238	19·4
45	108	26·9	23½	206	19·2
31½	151	26·6	16½	292	18·7
38½	126	26·4	24	203	18·5
35½	136	26·3	51½	96	18·4
81	60	26·3	51	97	18·3
28½	170	26·1	27	180	17·8
24	204	25·9	10½	453	17·6
21½	230	25·4	16	307	17·1
22	222	25·2	..	..	17·1
50	97	24·5	13½	365	16·5
12½	389	24·4	16½	295	16·3
30½	158	23·6	..	..	15·5
22½	216	23·6	..	..	15·4
11½	418	23·4	16½	293	14·9
14½	336	23·2	13½	365	14·9
28½	171	23·1	11½	417	14·3
42½	114	22·4	..	..	14·3
66½	73	22·4	15½	313	13·2
18½	259	22·4	18½	265	13·1
20	243	22·2	11	438	11·1
10	492	22·2			

instance, is described in great detail in this important source. Thus various areas of the town were clearly shown to have had different life-expectancies. Those who lived in Byron ward only achieved an average of 18 years each, 44% of all infants in that area dying before they reached the age of 4 years. At the opposite end of the scale was the Park, where the expectation of life was 29 years, and only some 29% of infants died before their fourth birthday. What is also significant is the birthrate — 25½ per thousand in the Park, 37½ in Byron ward, and in St Mary's ward (where one could live to 21 years old) as high as 40 per thousand. A high birthrate did not necessarily mean a high infant mortality rate, for in St Mary's ward only 35% of live births died before the age of 4. Other types of surveys recorded mortality rates in relation to occupations and social classes. A private survey of 1839—41 showed that a Sheffield gentleman might live to 47, but the steel artisans of that town might only live to 19 years of age, lower indeed than the paupers in the workhouse (25½) or than other artisans (21½).[47] The variable factors are many and need explanation.

In the absence of such evidence, it would seem almost impossible to arrive at firm figures for mortality, any more than for age at marriage, for any particular local community in the nineteenth century, despite all the information available in the census.

Migration

An overall picture of local migration can be drawn from the statistical summaries of the census issued soon after the taking of each census, but this provides only the most general of accounts.[48] More detailed information can be gleaned from the census enumerators' books, although once again it will not be a precise picture. In 1841, the returns merely indicated, by a Yes or No, whether the person listed were born in the same county or not. From 1851, the census records the place of birth of each individual, sometimes quite specifically; in London, reference is made to areas as local as 'Old Kent Road'. It is thus easy to draw from this the percentage of the population which was not born within the locality. Thus 29% of the inhabitants of Long Buckby in 1851 were not born in the parish, a very low figure indeed. Most of these came from within a narrow radius of the town, 21% from within 20 miles. At Richmond, approximately 50% were non-natives; of that figure 16% came from places within a radius of 5 miles from Richmond. Most of the rest came from within 25 miles, and the overwhelming majority from rural areas in the north of England. Clearly a comparison with the same community 10 and 20 years later would establish the trends in migration, at least in these general terms. In Rauceby, almost 50% of the total population in both 1851 and 1861 were not natives of that village.[49] In two Nottinghamshire villages the percentage of inhabitants who were born outside of the county rose from 5½% in 1841 to 11½% in 1851.[50] There are some difficulties in presenting the range of migration intelligibly (see Fig. 13), and clearly this factor needs to be related to the occupations for the migrants. Nevertheless, despite the problems, the proportion of non-natives at various different times will become clear.

However, such an analysis leaves a number of unanswered questions. Apart from such problems as whether the migrants came from far and whether their last place of residence was urban or rural in character, there are other, more local problems. At what age had the migrants moved into the parish? How long on average did they stay? In other words, was there a significant pattern of emigration as well as immigration? Once again, it is not possible to be certain of the answers to these

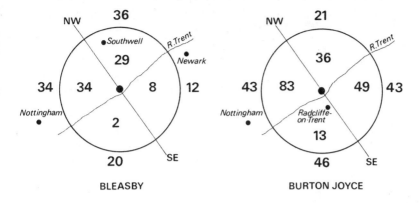

Fig. 13   Migration in two Nottinghamshire villages 1851; the circle represents a radius of 5 miles from the village. This is one method of representing places of birth; a series of concentric circles can also be used to reveal the pattern.

questions, but a study of the birthplaces of the children of the village helps to establish the frequency of moves on the part of their parents, and indeed their itinerary. For example, William Storer was an agricultural labourer who lived in Welby (Lincs) in 1851; he had been born there. But he clearly had not lived there all his life, for his eldest son (aged 8) had been born at Wilsford, his second son (aged 7) at Little Ponton, and his two daughters (5 and 3 years old respectively) at Welby.[51] Clearly Storer was a migrant, one of the 37% of immigrants rather than one of the apparent 62% of Welby natives, although all those places lay within 10 miles of his home village.

Finally of course, the census rarely reveals the reasons for migration. A study of the occupations of the migrants may throw some light on this; and occasionally the census enumerator adds a personal comment relating to some temporary increase of population (such as 'work on the railways') or a general trend ('emigration abroad' or 'movement to the manufacturing towns'). Most of these 'notes' were collected and added to the printed statistical summary. These clues are valuable ones which lead in turn to further subjects of study.

Census analysis in this way can go a long way towards helping to build up a picture of the local community. It must be remembered, however, that such a picture is not an end in itself. It is a search for the answer to a question, why was the community increasing or declining at any particular period? It is the community as a whole which is being sought, not just an analysis of its structure. And there is a great deal more to the community than its demography. For the growth or decline of the community may be affected by factors other than demographic. There may be economic changes which influenced migration; or social factors which limited mobility; or patterns of land ownership which prevented or encouraged development. In other words, it would seem to be rare for any community to be free to grow purely naturally. The resources and political structure of the community have always exerted a great influence on changes in population. And it must be to these topics that we now turn.

Chapter 4

Housing and the community

1

The growth or decline in population in any local community is clearly reflected in its domestic buildings. Men and their families must live somewhere. It is of course true that the relationship was not always a straightforward one. Houses did not always increase in direct proportion with population increase, for on occasion artificial limitations on building or money could result in a greater crowding of people into what housing existed. Even less does a fall in population reflect itself in an increase in the number of houses unoccupied. Many dwellings were of course destroyed or became dilapidated, while others became occupied by fewer people, especially as the average age of the members of the local community rose. Nevertheless, that there was a relationship between population and housing at all times is clear.

The local historian is thus faced with the problem of variations in the number of houses in relation to the variations in the size of his group of people. And in order to understand this relationship, he needs to examine the subject in a number of different ways. Three main groups of questions stand out in this connection.

Density per head of population
The first concerns itself with the houses themselves. How many houses were there and how did this number fluctuate over a period of time? To explain these fluctuations, the historian needs to examine the ratio of people to occupied houses, if it can be identified. There is thus the second question, how many of them were occupied? – the 'effective' house, if one may coin a phrase. The ratio then of occupied house to population will establish something of the average density of occupation – indeed, it gives the average size of the local household at any one time, with all its lodgers and servants and other families. This, contrasted with other communities and with later figures, can reveal some interesting trends and differences.

Such an average is however not really meaningful, for it conceals large internal differences. At South Rauceby, for instance, the average for the whole village in 1851 was 4.6 persons. But 25 people lived in one place, the Hall; exclude them and the figure drops to 4.3 persons, a significant difference in that context. Within a larger community there are similar variations, from the great mansion with a large household down to the small cottage or cellar dwelling occupied by two or even more families. The local historian thus has to look at the size of the houses, if possible, and how they were occupied. A truer indication of the real relationship between people and houses is not one of total population to number of houses, but rather the number of persons per room, but this is rarely a possibility for the local historian. Even an estimate of the numbers of persons in relation to the overall size of houses may be thrown out by such factors as whether they were purely domestic in character or partly business premises.

Groupings of houses: density per acre
This is one desirable range of questions concerning dwellings in the local community. But they in turn lead to a second group, the relationship of these houses to each other, especially the different types of houses. The topography of population may be significantly different from the topography of occupations or local government or religion, but it has its own value. It is affected of course by very many things — the physical relief of the site, patterns of land ownership, the economic structure of the community which may determine how far away people can live from their places of work, the land needed and (something quite different, as we know today) the land available for development, changes in local transport, social demands and many other similar factors.[1] Not all communities had the same need for building land; nor did the presence of a need, nor even the existence of an adequate economic reward, always result in the land being made available. Personal feelings as well as private interests played a large part in this, as in so much of our past.

The local historian's task, then, in this aspect of his study is twofold. He has first to determine the original nucleus (or in the case of large towns, the nuclei) of the early settlers, with all its geographical and political implications. And secondly, he must trace the process of growth or movement or decline, as the size of his community changed. Within larger places, especially in the later periods, there will be the study of any concentrations of particular types of houses — the so-called artisan or working-class house, or the middle-class and gentry houses — which may appear. And there will be the question of the relationship of the number of houses to the space available, the density of houses per acre.

The social structure of building
There is a third group of questions concerning housing, especially when the later pressure of population created in all communities, from small village to large city, a need for more dwellings. This relates to who provided them. Houses were needed and were in fact provided. Who built them? I do not mean by this the 'builder', for the study of the building trades really belongs to a discussion of occupations in the local community. Rather I mean the 'developer'. Who instigated the building and who paid for it? Sometimes of course the 'developer', the 'builder' and the 'occupier' were all one and the same person. But more frequently they were not. And this leads to another question, how were these houses occupied? — as tenants or as owners? How widespread was the availability of mortgages, enabling tenants to become (at least in one sense) owners? And is this pattern reflected in the length of time each family occupied their homes?

This discussion of what might be called the 'social structure' of housing has particular relevance to the later stages of urban growth, with the spread of large speculative estates or council estates, model villages, factory villages and the like. But its interest is not confined solely to that period, nor to the towns. In rural areas, there were whole villages which were owned by one landlord, where all or almost all the members of the community were tenants. These well-known 'closed' villages fall into two types, those with and those without a resident landlord. Here the provision of housing was always a matter of estate policy — the rebuilding or extension of existing houses and the siting and erection of new ones being matters for the landlord or his agent. Other villages, the 'open' villages (and there were of course shades in between), were essentially freehold communities, often with a good deal of land available for the putting up of new houses.[2] The distinction was not of course a static one. While North Rauceby remained a 'closed' village (indeed, still remains one), its 'open' neighbour, South Rauceby, went through an interesting phase during the nineteenth century when one of the principal landowners tried unsuccessfully to convert it into a 'closed' village by buying up other estates and building a large hall there. The distinction is also present in many towns, for the 'leasehold' town like Stamford or Cardiff presents many sharp differences from the 'freehold' town.

This pattern of housing proprietorship had far-reaching effects on other aspects of the community's life, on its occupations, local government, religious structure and the like. It has been suggested, for instance, that the size of the farms in 'open' villages differs markedly from those in 'closed' villages; certainly nonconformity in general spread earlier and with greater effect in 'open' villages (though there are of course many exceptions to this). In this respect, this pattern of ownership has a much wider significance than just its effect on housing.

The local historian thus may examine his local community through the houses, for the lives of the people depended to a large extent upon their dwellings. He can examine the number and type of houses in relation to the population in them; he can look for their relationship to each other, their topography; and he may seek to discuss the 'social structure' of houses, the hierarchy of landlord, owner-occupier and tenant, which in some communities so profoundly affected their character.

2

It is clearly impossible to deal adequately with the background of each of these three aspects of the history of housing in England. But wherever the historian may intend to go, he must start from the position that communities have always been changing and developing. This is as true topographically as it is of population. English communities have never been static. Once the original site had been chosen, whether this was during the prehistoric, Roman or (as in most cases) Anglo-Saxon settlements (or of course later), and chosen usually for reasons which subsequently became irrelevant (such as agricultural or other natural resources, water supply, ease of communications or defences), then began a process of change — a process which can be seen today more easily because of the more rapid nature and the larger scale of the developments. English history, if seen through the eyes of a time-lapse camera, would reveal a cloud of population spread over the island, constantly swirling about, never still for one moment, and growing more dense as time went on.

The shape of settlements
Early communities consisted in general of two elements, the place where the people lived and the place where they worked. Since most early settlements were agricultural, these two were often separate, the village site and the parish or 'town' lands. For the present study, the lands of the community are not as significant as the village or town site itself. Certainly, the discussion of the ratio of population per acre which is sometimes engaged in is relatively meaningless, for the significant factors here are the proportion of the land which was cultivated, the fertility of the soils, the use to which the lands were put, or the presence of industrial activity and

the like. Such factors differed from place to place, making it often impossible to say just when any particular community passed the point of reliance upon its own lands for its economic support.

Once this point has been passed, however, as it was in several towns by the later Middle Ages, the town fields became of significance mainly as potential building land, to be used as and when it was needed. For in the medieval town, apart from the continuing agricultural element, the place of dwelling and the place of work became more closely merged than they ever became in the purely agricultural settlement except perhaps in the discreet farmsteads of many parts of England. This process lasted on the whole until a twofold development once more began to separate place of work from place of residence. On the one hand, the development of large offices, factories and other buildings often involved the movement of substantial numbers of people to other parts of the town; thus whole areas of urban development became more or less devoid of residential buildings, exclusively devoted to commerce or manufacture or some similar activity. At the same time, changes in transport methods and in the 'psychology of housing' led to the development of suburbs. In some places the economic structure delayed this process, as at Nottingham where the lace merchants combined residence and working areas, or at Birmingham with its backyard workshops, but even in those places the process of differentiation set in during the later nineteenth century. Fairly rapidly, although of course at a different time and at a varying rate in each town of England, the domestic areas became once more separated from the factory or office areas; so far, modern attempts to repopulate central business districts have been unsuccessful.

The local historian, then, in dealing with the topography of population, is concerned with the area of settlement, that built-up part of the whole lands of the township. The early density of this area varied according to marked social, geographical and political considerations. In some places, dispersed settlements were preferred, perhaps because the land lent itself to exploitation more easily that way (as in high land or forest and fen areas) or because the social pattern of the settlers dictated individual family farmsteads. Elsewhere, settlements were more nucleated, on occasion it would seem for purposes of defence as much as gregariousness or economic necessity.[3]

What were the factors and the chronology of the pattern of change in this built-up area? Clearly it varied with every local community, but some common trends may be seen. The pattern whereby the site itself was changed, either by complete desertion or removal or by shrinkage or partial movement, is now well known.[4] What is less well traced is the process of change within the existing framework.

Three main factors have influenced changes in settlement patterns, what one might call 'natural' factors, 'political' factors and economic factors. Amongst the first, one might include climatic variations (which have been only just sufficiently marked during the 'historic period' to make discernible changes); or geographical changes, either slow-moving like changing sea coasts, soil erosion, the silting up or changing courses of rivers or alterations in water levels (perhaps the most important general consideration), or swift-moving like floods or forest fires; or the 'natural' disasters of plagues on people or stock. Warfare clearly was one of the 'political' factors affecting the local settlement, but there were others — the domination of the community by a landlord who could determine its size by his residence or non-residence (the presence of a religious house in any community can be regarded in this light, as well as that of the lay lord in his castle or mansion). Some owners developed newer planned settlements alongside or within existing ones,[5] while others restricted development. Changes in the lord's style of living, the creation of great houses and parks, of hunts and chases from at least the eleventh to the nineteenth centuries, all resulted in disturbances in the pattern of the settlement. Nor were such 'political' interferences confined to rural communities; there is little difference between the creation of an estate village in the nineteenth century and the philanthropic urban rehousing schemes of the same period.

Most important of course were the changes caused by economic factors. The development or exhaustion of natural resources, most obviously in mineral mining, quarrying and fisheries (causing the decay of several small ports) as well as forest and land; or changes in technical methods of farming (like the concentration on stock in the later Middle Ages or the seventeenth and eighteenth centuries' enclosure movement which resulted in some dispersal of settlements) or of industrial processes; changes in fashion which promoted one industry and depressed another; changes in transport which could both harm and help — the diversion of roads or the blocking up of rivers with weirs or bridges being examples of the former, drainage, canals and railways creating a wider hinterland all calling for increased market areas within the town at the centre being examples of the latter.

This list does not of course exhaust the influences on the settlement pattern of any local community. There are personal factors like the desire to live in towns, or social factors like an influx of gentry into towns or the presence of large numbers of resident single servants in farmsteads, all of which will affect the density with which people will live together. But at least such a list gives some indication of the wide range of factors which have controlled the pattern of settlement.

What of the chronology? Here again there is too much divergence to make any generalisation valuable. One cannot even generalise for villages. Some saw continuous and gradual dispersal of settlement, farmsteads moving out into the fields as colonisation progressed; other places started with a fairly diffuse settlement and continued a process of infilling. Nor was the process entirely related to population growth, for the general rule has been (until very recently) that the newer the house, the less dense its occupation. Thus a few new farmhouses outside a village left the older houses to be divided into tenements for the agricultural labourers. An increasing population could thus be housed in fewer buildings. Hardly any real chronology of topographical change has yet emerged for rural settlements.[6] Nevertheless there was a pattern for each local community and the local historian can trace this for his village area.

For the towns, something of a clearer general picture does emerge, although here again the local variations are enormous. Early medieval towns seem to have been very diffuse; the increasing population quickly spilled out into suburban areas rather than becoming concentrated in dense agglomerations. The early intrusion of populations in places like Mancroft at Norwich and the later planned 'new towns' usually took the form of a new settlement alongside the old rather than an increase in density of occupation. How long this process went on undisturbed is not clear, but the construction of town walls in many places during the thirteenth century and especially the coming of the friaries broke into several of these suburbs, as at Stamford and Canterbury. Shrinkage of the area occupied in most cases clearly preceded the Black Death. The later Middle Ages perhaps witnessed a process of de-urbanisation or at least very slow urban recovery. Many towns of 1600 seem to have been somewhat smaller in population than they had been in the late thirteenth century; they were certainly smaller in area.

Thereafter the process of physical expansion was determined by the growth of population and the land available. But one other factor emerged, the concentration within towns of different types of housing. No such distinctions can in general be seen within medieval towns, and it is not until the late sixteenth or early seventeenth centuries that areas of homogenous housing appear in many places; studies of the hearth taxes and other evidence suggest that by the late seventeenth century the houses of the wealthier were in the town centres, the slums and shanty towns were outside. But on the whole there was still relatively little distinction. The period from which one can speak of 'working-class' areas will vary with each place, but it would seem often to date from the late seventeenth and early eighteenth centuries. At Sheffield, for instance, to judge by the position of the new St Paul's church with its large number of rented pews, it becomes distinguishable from about 1740;[7] in Leeds, middle-class streets and squares emerged in the 1770s. At Nottingham the neighbouring gentry moved into Castlegate from the 1670s, following the Duke of Newcastle in the castle from 1674.[8] Later, as the gentry and wealthy merchants moved out, the larger properties became divided up and the gardens and innyards became crammed with small houses; in Stamford, this happened in the middle years of the eighteenth century. From the late eighteenth century onwards, such trends have become more marked, and in some ways make the task of the local historian easier.[9]

The urban revolution of the nineteenth century is part of the story of the fluctuations in topography, the use of land for dwellings and industrial buildings. And the process has continued to the present day and is continuing. Two factors which were not so present earlier influence modern developments − first, the relative ease of communications and the shorter working day, both enabling persons to live further away from their place of work, and secondly the presence of greater planning controls. On the whole, earlier towns just 'growed' like Topsy, although in some places some dominant individual or landed estate or borough authority could (at least for a time) exercise some control to create an improved situation. Elsewhere the market was open to the more normal forces of local interests. Physical features might present obstacles, as also man-made features like medieval or Civil War defences, and of course the shapes of fields. Patterns of proprietorial rights might prevent development, and indeed need a private Act of Parliament before the land could be freed. On the other hand they could encourage it. Sometimes, for instance, the allotments or commons made at enclosure were too small for any use save gardens or building, and thus new suburbs emerged, effectively planned by the enclosure commissioners.[10]

Dwellings

It is obviously impossible to write an outline history of housing in the space available here. For one thing, there is no complete survey as yet available. For another, local variations are once again most important. The local historian must learn to 'read' his buildings in their local context just as he must 'read' his landscape or town plan. Thus the average size of houses depend upon the land and building materials available as well as on the wealth and social pretensions of the builder; and what will be seen as common types of houses in one part of the country will be rarities elsewhere.

Nevertheless, some generalisations which may be of value to the local historian are emerging. Few medieval houses have survived into the present housing stock, and such survivals as there are are hardly typical, being representative of the more substantial, indeed wealthy, inhabitants — a fact which local historians must bear in mind constantly, in their desire to build as much as possible on the small evidence which survives. More is known of rural housing, which saw a massive reconstruction programme in the late sixteenth and early seventeenth centuries, a programme which meant much complete rebuilding, but also a not insignificant element of adaptation and extension of earlier buildings (especially the chambering-over of an open hall). Less is known of the development of urban housing. Both however saw the gradual extension of 'architectural' concern, especially with the house façade, from the relatively few great houses in the sixteenth century to the much more modest 'yeoman' and merchant houses by the late seventeenth century and the eventual emergence of planned terraces of increasingly small houses from the middle of the eighteenth century. But at any one period, the bulk of all housing in any town or village was 'vernacular' (or traditional) in style — planned and often executed by the owner and/or local jobbing builder, using local traditional plans, materials and methods. [11]

A few generalisations which emerge may be helpful to the local historian when he considers his housing. Plans on the whole developed two ways — down the social scale from the medieval open hall with its cross-wing extension(s), and up the social scale by elaboration of the single-unit peasant dwelling. On the whole, the size and standard of houses of the poorer classes have improved, while the size of upper-class housing has declined; the cottage and castle of today are not so far from each other as they were when William I ruled. Or houses provided *for* people were often better than those provided by themselves — the charity or town poor houses or the estate villages often compare favourably with the cottages erected by the labourers themselves. Again, house sizes have not necessarily increased but the numbers of rooms within them have. On the whole, too, the density of persons per house has declined. The medieval town house seems to have been densely occupied, only offset by the use of part of the premises for business purposes. Later, as functions became separated, town houses became smaller and more crowded, often subdivided. The process has not been a straightforward nor continuous one, as the history of one property in Stamford shows. It was built about 1702, alongside two earlier cottages which were joined together to form a second house. By the 1760s, both had been subdivided, the cottages into four, the newer house into two, but a few years later the latter was reunited. The whole complex was occupied by a group of carpenters and associated craftsmen, and from the 1770s the main house became a public inn under the title of Carpenter's Arms. The whole block remained as one house and four cottages until the middle of the nineteenth century when it was subdivided once more. [12]

The provision of houses

Less is known of the history of the social structure of housing. In general it seems the medieval inhabitant provided his own house, by purchase or building; his lord might help only by some slight and temporary relief from rent or by the grant of a site and/or building materials. Self-help, with neighbourly assistance, was the order of the day. The process of self-building however declined considerably during the seventeenth century, although it never died out completely. [13] In some ways, it was kept alive by the development of co-operative terminating building societies, starting in the Birmingham area in the 1770s and spreading rapidly into the north-west, [14] but even so, the total element of 'self-help' in this respect has declined.

Proprietorial building has not yet really been examined, and here the local studies are most important. One pioneer study is suggestive in its conclusions. C. Chalklin, studying several of the larger and more rapidly growing provincial towns ranging from Portsmouth and Bath through Birmingham to Nottingham, Liverpool and Manchester for the period *c*. 1750–1820, found that four main groups of persons were engaged in the activity of supplying dwellings for the increasing population in these towns. These were craftsmen-builders (who might be erecting houses either on contract for others or as their own speculation), developers who employed builders to erect new houses, sometimes for their own residence, investors who bought already-built houses, and a fourth group who provided funds in the form of mortgages. In all of these six places most of those who had houses erected came from middle ranks of traders in the town concerned; the absence of leading industrialists and merchants and of the larger landowners was significant. They built in small units, ranging from one or two to perhaps ten or twelve dwellings per undertaking. Most building projects involved the outlay of no more than a few hundred pounds, since before the 1790s a block of eight or ten small working-class tenements of two, three or perhaps four rooms might be erected for under £500. It seems clear, too, from the fact that in the majority of the towns most of the houses built were kept for some time in the hands of the developer, that the purpose of building was investment. Local factors predominated to determine when the great building periods took place. In most of the towns there were two main bursts of building, from the later 1780s until about 1792 and from just after 1800 for a number of years, although this varied from place to place; thus Portsmouth had a 'wartime building boom' in the early 1780s while construction was muted in Bath, Manchester and Nottingham. In most of the towns, additions to the housing stock were on a bigger scale in the 1780s and 1790s than in the 1760s and 1770s, and again in the two decades after 1800 than in those before that date. Yet most projects continued to be on a small scale both in terms of the number of houses built and financial outlay; it is only exceptionally that the growing demand is reflected in the erection of blocks of 40 or 50 or more working-class tenements as a single undertaking. [15]

The nineteenth century

What then can we say of the local community in the nineteenth century?[16] Generalisations concerning the average size of house are not really meaningful. That there was a national housing density of 5.3 in 1871 may merely reveal that there were places both above and below that figure.[17] At Long Buckby, the density was 4.2, at Richmond it was 4.9. On the other hand, within the local communities, areas of types of housing are clearly emerging. Trains, trams and buses were encouraging the growth of suburbs, with their semi-detached houses standing in their own gardens. Other areas were very densely occupied indeed, with houses ranging from the small cottage to the large mansion greatly subdivided. Dense 'rookeries', greatly overcrowded, had grown up in some areas of what had once been larger houses, although no place in England seems to have equalled Dublin where in 1861 almost half the population lived in single-roomed dwellings. But elsewhere the density was high. In Leeds, 88% of all houses were back-to-backs; it was the pockets of middle-class housing which were exceptional. Of course, there were mixed areas; Professor Beresford has traced how the artisan-type house invaded the polite West End of Leeds. But elsewhere in the towns, large areas were wholly devoted to small artisan dwellings. The type of housing in these urban areas has by now been well explored.[18] Much less is known however about the areas of middle-class housing. Flats had been developed from about the 1850s, but were still rare until the end of the century, while the terrace was becoming unpopular — indeed they virtually ceased to be built from 1890 until after the First World War.

Rural areas were similar. A good deal of rebuilding had greatly improved the average size of the labouring cottage, while the density of persons per house was lower now than it was in many working-class areas in the town. But the working of the Poor Laws still kept down the numbers of houses in many villages, while others, the so-called 'open' villages, grew rapidly. Much less of the detail is however known for rural areas. Were new houses built during the first half of the century, only to become vacant in the later years of declining population? If so, where were they built? — as infilling or out-spreading? More studies are needed before conclusions can be reached. The Union Chargeability Act of 1865 relieved the pressure of the poor rates, thus potentially allowing more building of houses in 'closed' villages, but in fact this resulted in very little change in the number of houses — it came too late to affect these communities, which were already declining in population.

Development in almost all towns was proceeding apace. The larger houses were spreading along the main road frontages first and only later to the areas behind. It was a piecemeal process, unlike the building of working-class areas. By now, most of the gardens and yards in the old nucleus had been filled. The pressure thus came onto fields and, when they became available, they were commonly developed *en bloc*[19] — although it is surprising how long it often took to complete a street or a block development.[20]

The way in which land was sterilised or became available for development is also being explored. The grip of the common owners at places like Great Yarmouth and Grimsby had by now been broken, but there were still estate holders, large or small, who were unwilling (or unable) to sell; among the factors which helped to de-sterilise much-needed land in or near our largest towns, the pressures of bankruptcy and death in overcoming personal prejudices seem to have been among the most effective. At the same time, some attempts were being made to clear the worst of the 'rookeries' under the adoptive Workmen's and Artisans' Dwellings Act of 1875 and this resulted in a greater demand for building land. At the same time there were other clearances in many towns. The city centres were in many cases becoming exclusively devoted to commercial or administrative functions; the population was being forced to move out. This was not true in Leeds, where the central in-town population continued to rise until after 1901, but in Southampton,[21] the central parish of St Laurence is a good example of this trend.

Professor Beresford's study of housing in Leeds[22] provides a number of examples of some of these trends. The changes which took place in a plot of land called White Cross Close, turning it eventually into Brown's Yard and Square, are typical of that process of development which exactly conformed to the boundaries of the fields into which houses were now being placed for the first time. It was a long narrow field of some six acres on the east side of the Leeds to Harrogate Road, which was turnpiked in the late eighteenth century (Fig. 14(a)); it became bounded

Fig. 14   From White Cross Close to Brown's Square, Leeds   ▶
(a) White Cross Close and other closes, 1691—1780.
(b) Plan 1803 showing Sayer's house and garden A1 and B, Brown's house A2, and terrace 3—16.
(c) The Close, 1815, from Giles and Netlam's map of Leeds.
(d) 1815, one of a pair of larger detached houses east of Brown's Yard, with garden and warehouses at the rear.

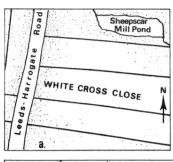

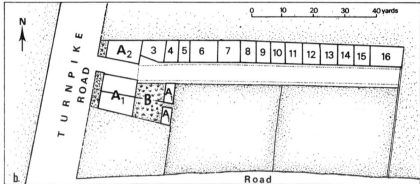

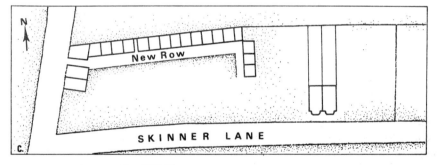

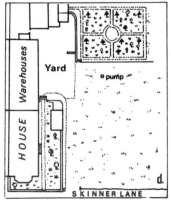

on the south by a new road (Skinner Lane). By 1792, William Sayer, victualler, had built a house and garden in the middle of the road frontage. In that year, the owners of the plot (a merchant family called Denison) sold it to a property speculator called Paley, who in turn sold the northern part of the field to James Brown, master bricklayer. By 1798, Brown had built a second roadside house and a terrace of four one-up one-down blind-back houses (Land Tax returns); by 1803, this 'New Row' had been extended to fourteen houses, reached from the main road by a long yard (Fig. 14(b); Plate 4(a)). Between 1803 and 1814, the yard was closed by a further three blind-back houses on the east end (Plate 4(b)). A little further east, within the same field, a detached pair of larger houses with bay-windows were built about the same time; behind them lay some warehouses (Fig. 14(c); 14(d); Plate 5(b)). After some years, the space between these two houses and Brown's Yard (as it was now called) was filled in 1834–8 with back-to-backs, part of which became known as Brown's Square, a small area made up of one-room houses at three levels, cellar, ground floor and upstairs (Fig. 15(a); Plate 5(a)). The warehouses were next converted to dwellings by Charles Smith, a butcher, in 1843 (Plate 5(b)). By 1849, additional houses had been built fronting on Skinner Lane, completely filling the Close (Fig. 15(b)). The various censuses reveal this process and the types of occupants (Plate 6). Except for the cellar dwellings which were closed about 1870, most of the houses of the former field were inhabited when slum clearance began in 1951 (Fig. 15(c)).[23] The process of development was a long-drawn-out one.

What of the social structure? At Leeds, the pattern was one largely of develop-ment when a customer appeared, and this seems to have been true elsewhere. The analysis by Professor Dyos of the development of the London suburb of Camber-well from 1840–1900 is one of the fullest studies of development so far made.[24] Most of the finance came from the speculative builders themselves or from Building Societies. A number of societies, one or two of them large national bodies, others smaller and more localised, were involved in lending money. None of them seems to have developed any estate itself in Camberwell, although they did so elsewhere, but they promoted the builders — the smaller supporting the owner-occupiers, the larger ones the speculative builder.

Most of the work thus was done by these builders, although their activities were beginning to decline by the 1870s. Some of the early development work was done by the National Freehold Land Society (later the British Land Company) but in general its activities were restricted to helping the smaller speculative builder. There was at least one insurance company in the field also, but its intention was to deal only with the early stages of development (in the end, however, it was forced into larger-scale work on the site). But it was the smaller builder who provided most of the homes in Camberwell. By the 1870s, a few larger firms had emerged, building sixty houses or more and in the end being responsible for about one-third of all the houses in the area. But the rest were erected by the smaller firms, with a total development of thirty houses or less, often much less.

Most of these houses were built 'on spec'; there was no prospective purchaser in view when they were begun. The speculator was usually the builder himself — nine-tenths of Camberwell's builders were aiming to sell the houses they built at a hand-some profit for themselves. They were local men, buying up land as it was made available and building what they thought the future residents of Camberwell would wish to live in.

Such development was piecemeal — 'the building of Camberwell's streets was the

Plate 4　Brown's Square, Leeds

(a)　One-up one-down blind-back houses, built 1798—1803; 17—25 Brown's Yard.

(b)　Three blind-back houses built 1803—15, closing the east end of Brown's Yard.

Plate 5 Brown's Square, Leeds (*continued*)

(a) One-room blind-back houses on three levels: upstairs *centre*, ground floor *right and left* and cellar dwellings *right and left*. Photograph *c.* 1949.

(b) Former warehouses at rear of semi-detached larger house, built 1793, and converted to dwellings in 1843.

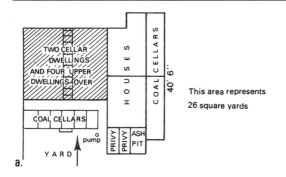

This area represents 26 square yards

a.

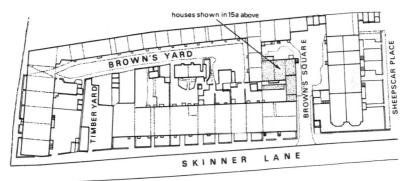

houses shown in 15a above

b.

SCHEDULE.

Reference numbers and colouring on map. 1.	Description and situation of the lands. 2.	Owners or reputed owners. 3.	Lessees or reputed lessees. 4.
Pink			
1	Dilapidated dwelling-house, 19, Skinner Lane, and area		
2	Dilapidated dwelling-house, 21, Skinner Lane, and area		
3	Dwelling-house (partly over Ref. No. 7), 2, Brown's Square		
4	Dwelling-house (partly over Ref. No. 5), 3, Brown's Square		
5	Dis-used passage leading to the rear of No. 19, Skinner Lane		
6	Dwelling-house (partly over Ref. No. 5), 4, Brown's Square	Trustees of the late Henry Bingley :— John William Pickles Charles Reginald Brooke	
7	Bow-way and conveniences adjoining No. 2, Brown's Square and No. 12, Brown's Square		
8	Court adjoining Nos. 3, 4, 5, and 8, Brown's Square, steps and ash-places		
9	Dwelling-house, 5, Brown's Square, area and steps ..		
10	Dwelling-house (over Ref. No. 9), 6, Brown's Square, passage and steps		c.
11	Dwelling-house (over Ref. No. 12), 7, Brown's Square,		

Fig. 15   From White Cross Close to Brown's Square, Leeds (*continued*)

(a) Brown's Square, 1842. The arrow indicates the direction of the photograph in Plate 5(a).
(b) 1849, the Close completely filled: from O.S. 5-foot plan.
(c) Part of schedule from Leeds, Skinner Lane No. 1, Housing Confirmation Order 1951 listing the houses in Brown's Square.

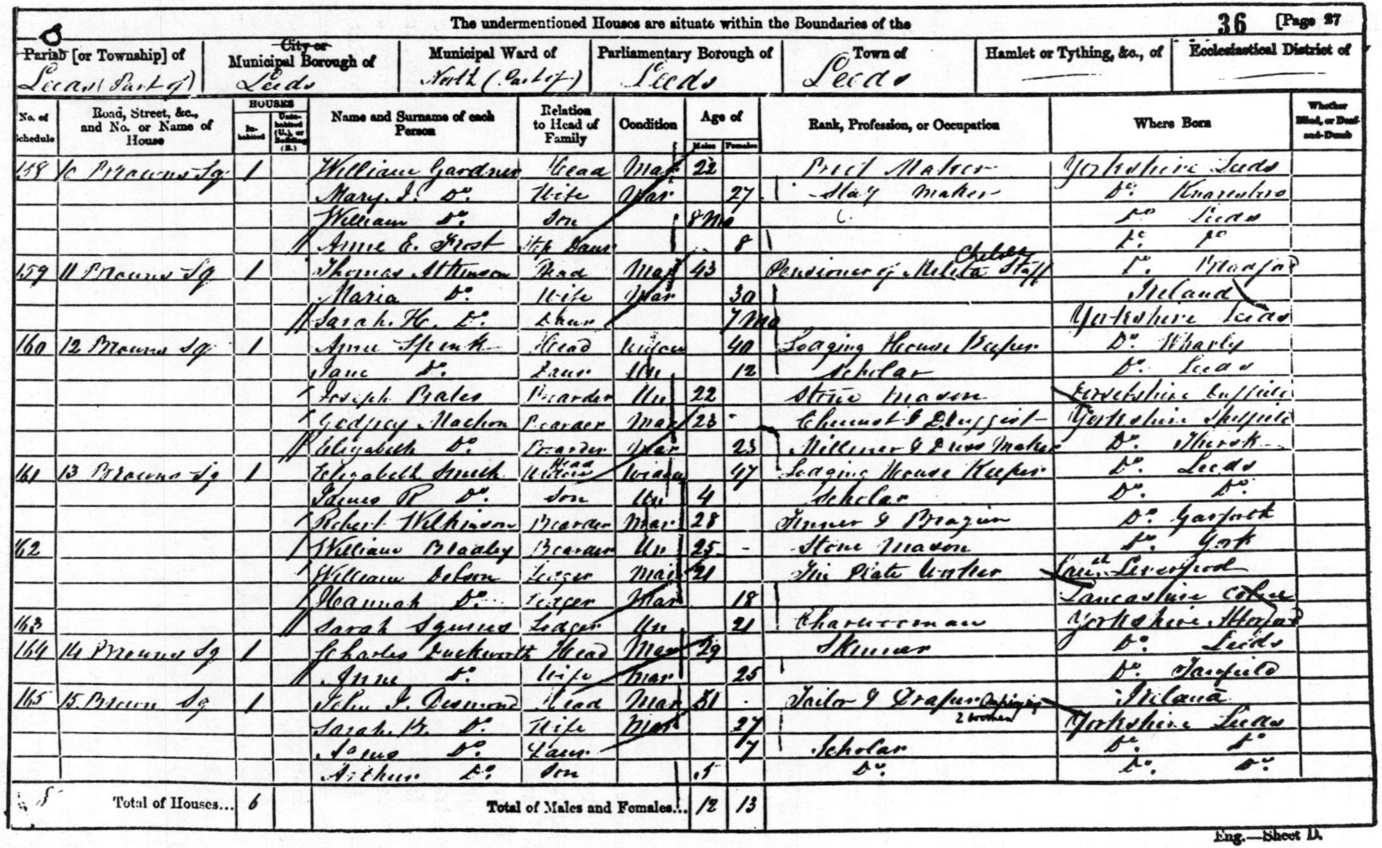

The undermentioned Houses are situate within the Boundaries of the — 36 [Page 27

Parish [or Township] of	~~City or~~ Municipal Borough of	Municipal Ward of	Parliamentary Borough of	Town of	Hamlet or Tything, &c., of	Ecclesiastical District of
Leeds (Part of)	Leeds	North (Part of)	Leeds	Leeds	—	—

No. of Schedule	Road, Street, &c., and No. or Name of House	Houses: Inhabited	Houses: Uninhabited (U.), or Building (B.)	Name and Surname of each Person	Relation to Head of Family	Condition	Age of Males	Age of Females	Rank, Profession, or Occupation	Where Born	Whether Blind, or Deaf-and-Dumb
158	10 Browns Sq	1		William Gardner	Head	Mar	22		Brick Maker	Yorkshire Leeds	
				Mary J. Do.	Wife	Mar		27	Slay Maker	Do. Knaresboro	
				William Do.	Son		8 Mo			Do. Leeds	
				Anne E. Frost	Step Daur			8		Do. Do.	
159	11 Browns Sq	1		Thomas Atkinson	Head	Mar	43		Pensioner of Militia Staff (Chelsea)	Do. [illegible]	
				Maria Do.	Wife	Mar		30		Ireland	
				Sarah H. Do.	Daur			7 Mo		Yorkshire Leeds	
160	12 Browns Sq	1		Anne Spink	Head	Widow		40	Lodging House Keeper	Do. Wharfe	
				Jane Do.	Daur	Un		12	Scholar	Do. Leeds	
				Joseph Bates	Boarder	Un	22		Stone Mason	Derbyshire [illegible]	
				Godfrey Machon	Boarder	Mar	28		Chemist & Druggist	Yorkshire Sheffield	
				Elizabeth Do.	Boarder	Mar		23	Milliner & Dress Maker	Do. Thirsk	
161	13 Browns Sq	1		Elizabeth Smith	Head	Widow		47	Lodging House Keeper	Do. Leeds	
				James R. Do.	Son	Un	4		Scholar	Do. Do.	
				Robert Wilkinson	Boarder	Mar	28		Tinner & Brazier	Do. Garforth	
162				William Bradley	Boarder	Un	25		Stone Mason	Do. York	
				William Dobson	Lodger	Mar	21		Tin Plate Worker	Lanc. Liverpool	
				Hannah Do.	Lodger	Mar		18		Lancashire Colne	
163				Sarah Squires	Lodger	Un		21	Charwoman	Yorkshire Otley	
164	14 Browns Sq	1		Charles Duckworth	Head	Mar	29		Skinner	Do. Leeds	
				Anne Do.	Wife	Mar		25		Do. Fairfield	
165	15 Brown Sq	1		John J. Desmond	Head	Mar	31		Tailor & Draper employing 2 workmen	Ireland	
				Sarah B. Do.	Wife	Mar		27		Yorkshire Leeds	
				Jane Do.	Daur			7	Scholar	Do. Do.	
				Arthur Do.	Son		5		Do.	Do. Do.	
	Total of Houses...	6			Total of Males and Females...		12	13			

Eng.—Sheet D.

Plate 6 Census book, 1861, for Brown's Square, Leeds. Note the details of employment given under occupation.

unconcerted effort of many builders'. The process of co-ordinating efforts, of sharing neighbouring sewers, for instance, was one fraught with long delays. Thus developments took a long time to be completed. It was rare for whole streets, let alone whole districts, to be built by one firm, so that the general character of the area was eventually determined by the end product of many builders. But there was a cohesion in design which helped towards this general character.[25]

How far this picture is typical cannot be determined until other studies have been completed, but on the whole it accords well with the Leeds picture. There were of course some variations. The work of Building Societies (some of them by now Permanent) and Housing Trusts was not negligible, especially in the north.[26] Nor was the small investor insignificant. Professor Beresford has pointed out in Leeds the prevalence of the unit of four back-to-back houses, built with a mortgage by the occupant of one unit, and with the rent from the other three units paying off the mortgage. In such rented property, the tenants changed quickly; so indeed did many of the owners, as Professor Beresford's studies have shown for Leeds. In other areas, however, ownership and occupancy were more stable.[27] The pattern of owner-occupied, tenanted and mortgaged property in each town was an individual one, but one which did not change very significantly throughout the century. Virtually nothing is known of rural development at this period, but it is likely that it was mainly estate development handled by the agent, with a small amount done by the owner-occupier under direct contract to a builder. The development of the tied cottage in the nineteenth century probably increased the amount of tenanted property in the country. Once again, more studies are needed here.

3

Sources before 1800: numbers of houses

How then may the local historian find out about the three main aspects of the houses within his local community — their size and use; their relationship to each other; and the pattern of landlordship? What are his sources?

There is virtually no way of finding out comprehensively about housing in the community before the nineteenth century census. The earliest indication of numbers of houses (apart from a few rare surveys or rentals in closed villages) comes from the hearth tax returns. Not all of these are comprehensive however, and the local historian must be convinced that the local commissioners included *all* houses (including those exempt from the tax) before he can rely upon them. But a careful use of hearth tax returns (which indicate a *minimum* number of rooms) with contemporary probate inventories, censuses and/or family reconstitution would yield some fruit.[28]

Local censuses of houses for some of the larger towns become more common in the later eighteenth century and early nineteenth century, and clearly relate the number of dwellings to growing population. Thus a local survey of Nottingham in 1779 records some 3,191 dwellings for a population of 17,584, a density of 5½ persons per dwelling.[29] Most of these surveys appear in contemporary descriptions and they were often produced to be used in some local political controversy. Others, for smaller communities, were produced by local incumbents, like that for Letheringsett (Norfolk) in 1822.[30] Such surveys do not usually include empty houses and are frequently guesses rather than careful counts. Rather better, where they exist, are those estate or other plans of villages and towns on which all the dwellings may be recorded. When these have the tenements numbered and the occupants enumerated, as in some surveys or enclosure and tithe plans, they are particularly useful. They may still have limitations; it may not be easy to distinguish houses from out-buildings, nor empty ones from occupied ones. But they will certainly help.[31]

House sizes and use
The records for individual houses and their occupants are more numerous.[32] Series of deeds, leases and estate records, together with parish rate books, probate inventories and (for parsonages and adjacent properties) glebe terriers, enable one to construct a view of the development of some houses, but not all are so fortunately recorded[33] and in any case the records must be treated with care[34]. Occasional sources give a glimpse — fire insurance records, sale notices, newspaper advertisements and memoirs being amongst the most useful — as well, of course, as field surveys. Looking at old buildings intelligently can almost always result in a good deal of information about them (as well as in many additional problems, of course — not all buildings carry date stones and those which do are sometimes of a quite different date!).[35]

Topography
Topographical growth is probably better recorded. Once again, there is no substitute for field work — a long hard look at the streets and the layout of the place. There is other, non-documentary material such as street names and parish boundaries.[36] Most important of course are early maps,[37] some local and unprinted, others made for wider circulation. Such maps exist in some numbers, produced to accompany awards or deeds or estate surveys or printed accounts of the place or for many another reason. And then there is a profusion of documentary source material, from contemporary comment (from Leland onwards) to deeds. The process of infilling can often be clearly traced from deeds and may be related to early maps and to existing buildings. Especially valuable are the Enrolled Deeds (of Bargain and Sale) in the quarter sessions' records, consequent upon the statute of 1536.[38] An examination of the hearth tax by areas (parishes or wards of a town), classifying the houses into groups of exempt, one hearth, two hearth, three to five hearth and more-than-five hearth houses, can begin to reveal areas of at least somewhat larger houses (as in Exeter).[39] This is too large a subject to develop here, but a great deal can be traced about the growth of almost any local community before the nineteenth century. A study of some of the successful accounts already produced, as for instance in the *Atlas of Historic Towns*,[40] may show how it is done, but one must always beware of presenting too static a picture. Dr Urry has shown how, in even a short space of time, the face of Canterbury was changing.[41]

Social structure of housing
The evidence for the social structure of housing is scanty. Open and closed villages may of course be revealed from statistics of landownership such as the land tax returns among the quarter sessions papers, mostly of the period 1780 to 1832, listing owners and occupiers. Similar information may be obtained from enclosure awards or estate and manorial records. But urban areas are more difficult. It is not difficult to discover whether any town were mainly leasehold or freehold, but to analyse the way in which new housing provision was made is a larger task.

Chalklin's analysis of the builders was based on an exhaustive survey of local occupations from sources such as directories, wills (which reveal house ownership) and probate inventories, on newspaper accounts of development and advertisements of houses for sale or to be rented, and above all on extensive collections of deeds, as well as a body of miscellaneous source material drawn from contemporary writings such as diaries (like the *Life of William Hutton*, a bookseller of Birmingham, written by himself and published by his daughter in 1816) or political and polemical writings such as Sir F. M. Eden's *State of the Poor* (1797). There are of course other town sources, especially the borough records (leases, deeds, rentals and rate books) where the corporation was a substantial landholder. But the task is no easy one, even where there is plenty of material.

4

Nineteenth-century sources: housing densities

From the nineteenth century, there is more evidence and each of our three main themes may be treated more easily.

The density of population per house can be seen from the census returns. From 1801, the printed abstracts record for each place the number of inhabited houses, those empty and (from 1811) the number of those in process of building, as well of course as the total population. One can thus tell how far the number of houses was related to the population of the place concerned. At Leeds, where there was no central depopulation until after 1901, the ratio of houses to population throughout the nineteenth century can be seen as follows:

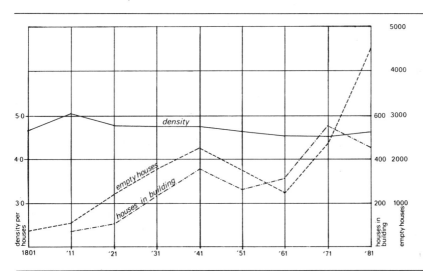

Fig. 16 The density of population per house in Leeds, 1801—81. The graph also shows fluctuations in the numbers of empty houses and houses in building recorded in the censuses. [42] Boundary changes were made after 1881.

This relationship can be expressed in terms of different communities or different parts of the same community, and also in terms of trends within the community during the course of the century. Not all communities were of course alike, even similar sized ones. At Rauceby, there was a constant difference between the two villages, North Rauceby (a closed village) being much more crowded than South Rauceby; at the same time, it is clear that in 1851, nearly the peak year of population in each village, there was in fact less density of occupation than both before and after that year.[43] For the larger towns (but not for smaller settlements) the census abstracts frequently give the figures for different areas or parishes and thus internal comparisons can be made.

Housing areas

For many towns, the census can be supplemented from other official source material. Throughout the century, a vast (and still only partially explored) library of reports was compiled, and several of these deal with housing. Some were national, like Chadwick's *Report on the Sanitary Condition of the Labouring Population* (1841–2) or the invaluable and extensive *Report of the Royal Commission on the State of Large Towns and Populous Districts* (1844–5)[44] (Plate 7) or (for country districts) the *House Accommodation of Rural Labourers* (1864), all containing detailed local information in their Appendices. A later one is the important report of the Royal Commission on the *Housing of the Working Classes* (1885). Others were local. Thus for instance in Leeds, Robert Baker, the medical officer of the Poor Law Guardians and later factory inspector, wrote a *Report of the Leeds Board of Health* (1833), a second report upon the condition of the town based on a door-to-door statistical enquiry taken in 1839 which he published in the

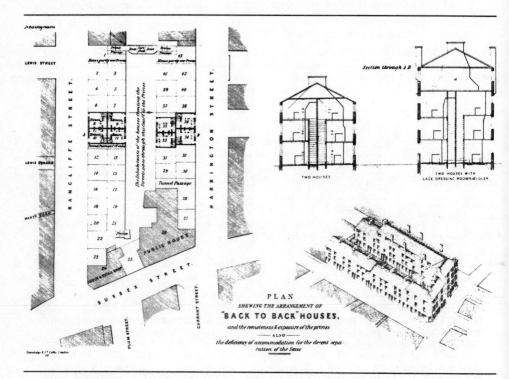

Plate 7 Page from first *Report of the Royal Commission on the State of Large Towns and Populous Districts*, 1844, showing housing in Nottingham. The detail here is not unusual.

Journal of the Royal Statistical Society in 1840, and a further report on the state and condition of Leeds in 1842; and his work was supplemented by others like Vetch, the sewerage officer. Many of these describe housing areas and conditions in great and lurid detail.

Since the census records provide further evidence of the types of house occupation, such as multiple families or the presence of lodgers, visitors and servants, a good deal may be drawn from them. In most towns, the addresses will be given, at least in the form of street name (see Plate 8(b)), and it is thus possible to compare areas in more detail. North Quay, Weymouth, for instance, in 1861 would seem to fall into two distinct parts. At one end lived the coal and corn porters, three of them sharing their houses with lodging families; at the other end lived a master builder, a master butcher, a 'Fundholder' (aged 80) with his resident nurse, and a master baker, all with large households. There seems to have been some overlap in the middle of the street (the small household of a corn porter which included his 21-year-old prostitute daughter may have been occupying part of one of the larger houses), so that it is unfortunate that the houses themselves have now disappeared to indicate the precise way in which the road was divided up. Such a study for small

LANDOWNERS.	OCCUPIERS.	Numbers referring to the Plan.	NAME AND DESCRIPTION of LANDS AND PREMISES.	STATE of CULTIVATION.
Parker Mary	In Hand	184	House, Garden &c.	
Pidcock Mary and Harriet	In Hand	186	House and Garden	
Pidcock Sarah	In Hand	190	House, Shop, and Yard	
Pearson John	John Wigley	229	House and Shop	
Porter James	In Hand and another	233	Two Houses and Shop	
Robinson Ellen	In Hand and another	18	House and Garden	
Reuben Sarah	In Hand	104	House and Garden	
Riddlesden Thomas — John (Executors of —)	In Hand	185	House, Garden &c.	
Salt Thomas	In Hand and others	13	Four Houses, Gardens &c.	
Spencer Samuel	In Hand	71	House, Shop &c.	

Plate 8(a) A page from Ashbourne, Derbyshire, tithe award, 1849. Note the house and shop (71) of Samuel Spencer. In rural areas, the last column usually contains an indication of 'arable, meadow or pasture', etc. Such awards, listing owners, occupiers, acreages and names of fields with land use, together with a plan, were drawn up after the Tithe Commutation Act of 1836 for most places where tithe had not been extinguished during earlier enclosures. The coverage is thus variable; the south and west of England have a large number of such awards, while in the east there are few — less than a third of all villages in Leicestershire and less than a quarter in Northants having such awards, while in Kent, Shropshire and Devon, there is almost complete coverage.

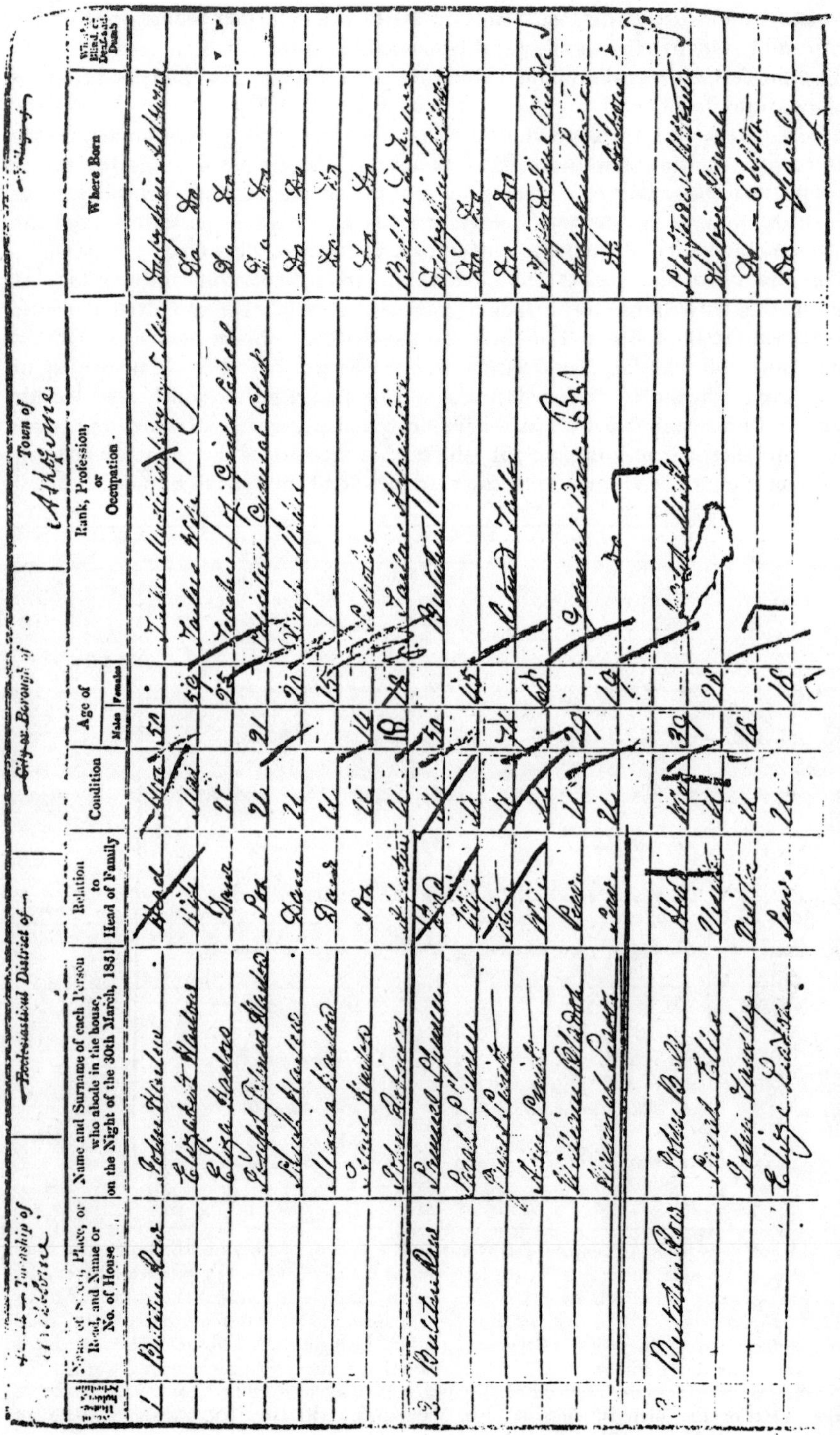

1

Town of Ashburne

No. of Schedule	Name of Street, Place, or Road, and Name or No. of House	Name and Surname of each Person who abode in the house, on the Night of the 30th March, 1851	Relation to Head of Family	Condition	Age of		Rank, Profession, or Occupation	Where Born	Whether Blind, or Deaf-and-Dumb
					Male	Female			

Plate 8(b) Census book 1851, Ashbourne, Derbyshire. The household of Samuel Spencer, with two servants, is shown in Butcher Row. Note the error in the age column which has been corrected at some later calculation.

areas can be most rewarding, but for larger areas, sampling by streets may be the only possible way of arriving at general conclusions.

This process of 'house repopulation' from the census books alone however has its limitations. For one thing, one cannot be certain that the entries on the schedules do in fact go from door to door consecutively down the street; the numbers in the census are not street numbers, as any comparison with a town directory will show. Indeed it is clear that on occasions the order was changed, by accident or design. In any case, for villages the streets are not recorded, and the order probably merely reflects the shuffling of the original returns.

For the process to be taken further one must turn to other sources. At Ashbourne (Derbyshire), for instance, Adrian Henstock has been examining the 1851 census returns (Plate 8(b)) in relation to a tithe award and plan of 1849 (Plates 8(a) and 9).[45] The fruits of this study (see Fig. 17) are beginning to appear. Thus one end of Church Street was clearly dominated by the larger houses of people of independent means; the other end was more mixed. The backyards behind the main streets were densely occupied, while the large eighteenth-century houses on the street frontages were less crowded. The distribution and type of houses which had resident servants and the location of social groups can be clearly seen from this study.

For larger places, the absence of a tithe apportionment map can be made good from a number of sources such as rate books or gas or water company account

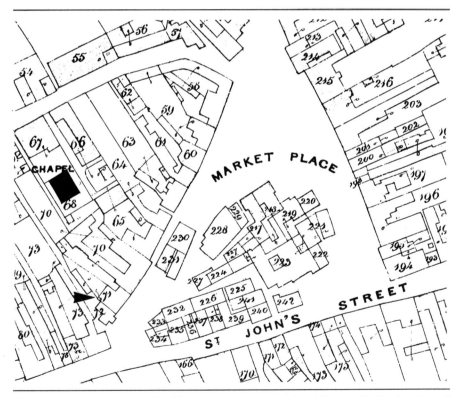

Plate 9 Part of the plan of Ashbourne accompanying the tithe award. The location of Spencer's shop can be seen (71).

Fig. 17   Map of Ashbourne showing (a) houses with servants and (b) houses in western part of town where the heads were described as having independent means.

books. Among the most useful are those town directories which give addresses. Nineteenth-century directories are of immense importance to the local historian.. They begin in fact in the last years of the previous century, mainly on a national scale, such as the *Universal British Directory* which had sections on many major towns. But local ones also appeared very early, the earliest being apparently Sheffield's in 1763.[46] There were two main parts to any directory — the introductory sketch which outlined the history and other useful items of more contemporary life of the community, and the list of principal inhabitants (see Plate 10). Some had maps, but these are often the least useful part of the books. County directories soon appeared covering the villages. It was not long however before the introductory sketch began to be separated from the lists of residents and separate 'guidebooks' appeared. But the directory proper still kept the two sections and appeared at regular intervals. In this lies its immense value for the local historian.[47]

There are however shortcomings in these books. They are frequently out-of-date, even those which are not (as some undoubtedly were) pirating the material of previous issues. Some directories merely copied the earlier works without any attempt at revision: there were some interesting law suits over this. But the fact that there are such runs of directories and that many were conscientiously revised, enables several uses to be made of this source.

For the present purpose, their main value lies in the addresses which began to appear during the century. The earliest lists of residents were alphabetical, often without addresses; then came the addition of street names. It was however the guidebooks which converted these lists of residents into street lists, often in the 1870s. And from this point on, house repopulation becomes relatively easy. There are still problems. The census and the directory do not always tally. The re-numbering of streets, especially in central areas, often causes difficulties. But the task can be attempted.

The relation of the census books and field surveys is another aspect of the same theme being developed in Birmingham.[48] And from these and similar studies, it is possible to arrive at conclusions about the groupings of housing within given areas, those (for instance) with servants and those without, those occupied by large or small families, by the young or the old, by Irish immigrants or some other distinctive social or occupational grouping. It is the Leeds Housing Project conducted by Professor Beresford and Professor David Ward which has probably taken this study furthest.

New development

The location of new building in the nineteenth century can also be seen. There is a vast range of sources here. The census returns, compared with each other, will give total figures area by area. Local deeds and rentals are still very important, but they can be supplemented by the accounts of the local water and gas companies. These will indicate occupiers and the date when these services began — in fact, of course, the date of connection to these services rather than the date of erection, but with the larger type of house these two dates will be much the same. Borough rate books (Plate 11) similarly describe occupants and can be used (where they still exist) to show how frequently the occupants moved. Other local official records like the records of Improvement Commissioners, or records in the custody of the local authority like deposited plans of new housing (especially after the nineteenth century health legislation which many boroughs gradually adopted), or minutes of the various local committees such as the Public Health Committee — all these may

350   WIRKSWORTH HUNDRED.

BOOT AND SHOE MAKERS

+ Atkin John, Sturston ln
* Beardsall John, Compton
Brandrith Luke, Butchery
Brandrith Thos. King st
Cope Joseph, Market place
Harrison Thos. Derby New rd
Hollis Robt. Dig st
Howell John, & toy warehouse
    Market place
Johnson Samuel, warehouse,
    St John's st
* Land Wm.
Potter Charles, Church st
* Smith James
Street Joseph, Church st
* Stubbs John, Clifton ln
Tarr Wm. Dig st
Tatlock Thos. Market place
Wigley John, Market place
Willis Thos. Butchery

BRASS FOUNDERS

Davenport Wm. Market pl
Harlow B. Wyatt, St John's st
Haywood James, Market pl

BRAZIERS AND TINNERS

Allen Joseph, Market place
Barnes Thos. Butcher's row
Howard Geo. Back lane
Howard Gervase, Dig st

BRICKLAYERS

+ Brown Elisha (maker)
    Compton
+ Brown Thomas, Compton
+ Brown Wm. Compton

BRICKMAKERS

(*See Bricklayers*,)

BUTCHERS

Etches Mary Ann, Butchery
Froggatt George, Butchery
Frost Richd. (pork) Church st
Marples John and George,
    Butcher's row
Miers Wm. Butchery
Needham Wm. Butchery
► Spencer Saml. Butcher's row
Tomlinson Wm. St John's st

CABINET MAKERS

(*See Joiners.*)

CHEMISTS & DRUGGISTS

Baker Harriet, St John's st
Genniss John, Market place
Greaves George Brailsford,
    St John's st
Whitham John, St John's st

COACH BUILDERS

+ Hall Thos. & Son, Compton

CONFECTIONERS

Bass John, St John's st
Porter James, Butchery

COOPERS

Eyre George, Church st
Needham Robert, Market pl
Williams George, Market pl

CORN FACTORS

Bass John, St John's st
* Eaton Joseph, Compton
Oakedon Edward, Church st

CORN MILLER

* Eaton Joseph

CURRIERS AND LEATHER CUTTERS

Boam Jonathan, King st
Hobson John, Market place
Spencer John, Market place

EMERY AND COLOUR MANUFR.

* Handley Thomas, Compton

FIRE & LIFE OFFICE AGENTS

Farmers and Graziers, John
    Hardstaff, St John's st
Manchester, Robert Hobson,
    Market place
Norwich Union, Thos. Barnes,
    St John's st
+ Phœnix Fire and Pelican
    Life, Ph. Dawson, Compton
Sun, Harriet Swindell, Mar-
    ket place
Yorkshire, John Hardstaff, St
    John's st

GLASS, CHINA, AND EARTHEN-WARE DEALERS

Eadin Elizabeth, Market pla
Smith Fanny, St John's st

GROCERS & TEA DEALERS

Marked • Tallow Chandlers

* Barnes Thos. Butcher's row
Bradley Septimus & Nephew,
    Market place
Clark John, Dig st
Coxon Thos. St John's st
Foster Thos. Market place
Genniss John, Market place
Hall Ralph Hudson, Mkt. pla
Hardstaff John, St John's st
Mellor Thos. St John's st
* Mountfort Thos. John, Mar-
    ket place
Tomlinson Jno. (late Heaton)
    Market place
Tomlinson John, Market pla
Walker Samuel, St John's st

HAIR DRSSRS. & PERFUMERS

Poole Edward, Dig st
Redfern Luke, Dig st
Shipley Wm. & fishing tackle
    manufacturer, St John's st
Wilson Wm. St John's st

HATTERS

(*See also Drapers*)

Barton Rt. (mfr.) Smith's yd
Hooworth Wm. St John's st

HOP AND SEED MERCHANTS

Edensor Wm. Back lane
Foster Thos. Market place
Hall Ralph Hudson, Mkt pla
Morris James, St John's st
Tomlinson John, (late Hea-
    ton) Market place

HOSIER

Tunnicliff John, St John's st

IRONFOUNDER

* Bassett James, Compton

IRONMONGERS

Allen Joseph, Market place
Barnes Thos. Butchers' row
Haywood James, Market place
Howard Gervase, Market pl

JOINERS & CABINET MAKERS

Marked • are Builders.

* Birch Charles, Spital hill

Plate 10   Page from Bagshaw's *Directory of Derbyshire 1846*, for Ashbourne. Spencer's name can be clearly seen under Butchers.

survive to throw light on individual developments. The house plans are indeed a most important and so far largely neglected source (Plate 12). In Birmingham, as in other places, they survive from 1876, after the 1875 Sanitary Acts came into force, giving the council power to demand such plans from prospective developers. In

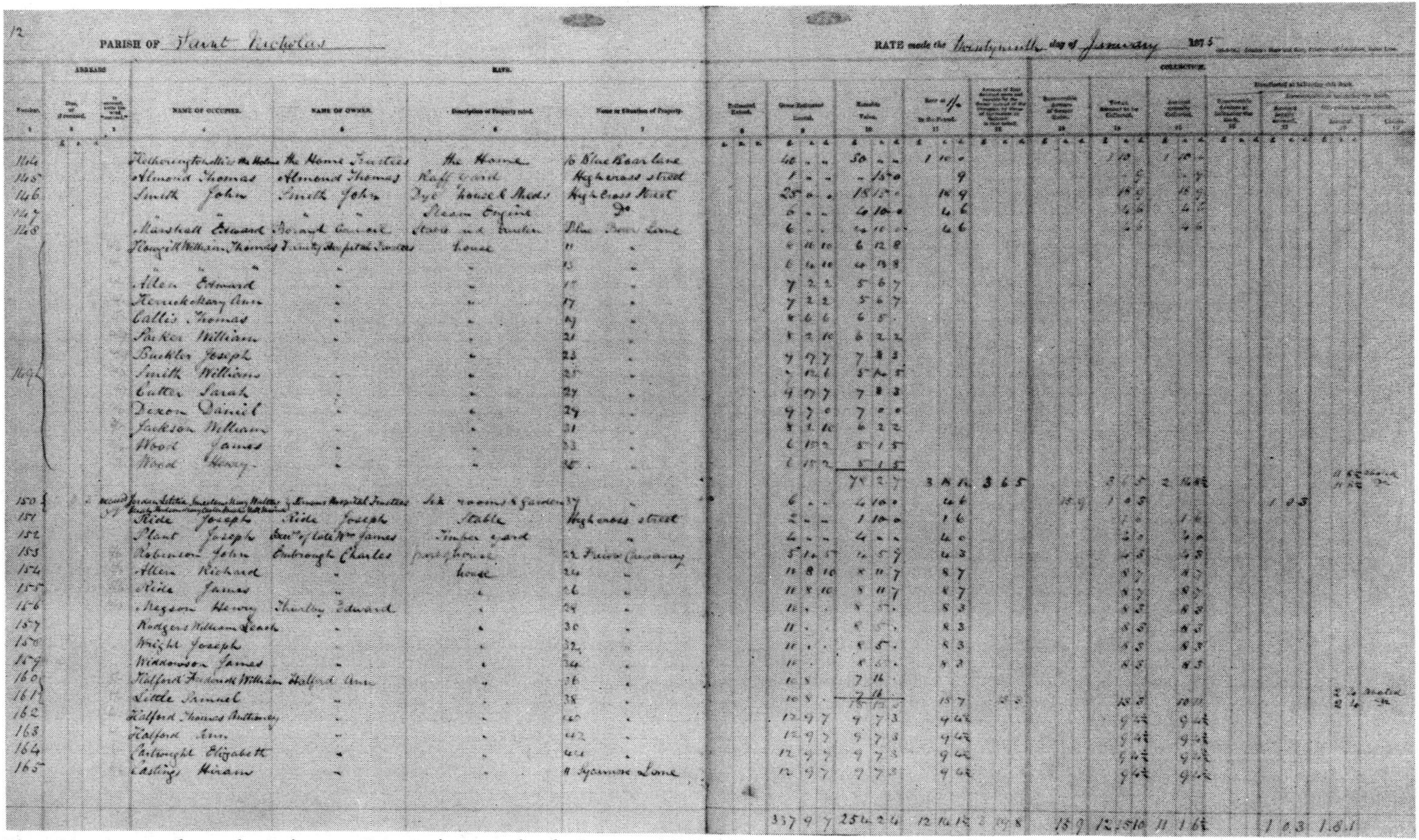

Plate 11 A page from the Leicester Corporation rate book, January 1875. This refers to part of the centre of Leicester, not to the newer development around the town. The properties may be seen to be subdivided. The Home mentioned in the first line is a Home for Penitent Females. Trinity Hospital trustees owned a block of houses as part of their endowment. Item 150 refers to a small almshouse with six women. Note the 'steam-engine', rated separately. From this source, the extent of owner-occupied and rented properties may be traced.

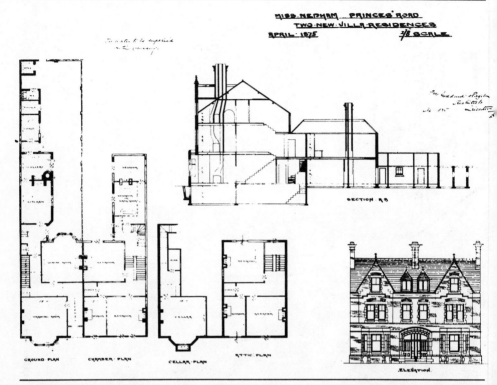

Plate 12   An example of the local authority deposited plans authorised under the Public Health legislation and local bye-laws. This refers to a new and relatively high-class development of semi-detached houses on the outskirts of Leicester, 1875. The elevation is not always provided; local authorities did not require it until much later. Note the separate flues, insisted on by Leicester from the late 1860s. These houses still stand, part of the University precinct.

other towns they exist from an earlier date, for the health legislation of 1848 made it possible for some towns to require them if they so wished.[49] The use of these plans, together with field surveys, will reveal a good deal about changing standards of house building in the local community. Professor Dyos was able to use a most valuable series of monthly returns by the District Surveyor in his study of Camberwell, but it is not yet clear how far such records survive for other communities.[50] Another important source is the series of reports of the local police commissioner, where they are available. Local newspapers, especially the advertisements of houses and land for sale, and national journals like *The Builder*, estate records and sale notices (Plate 13) among the records of estate agents and solicitors, are basic sources, while living memories, biographies and diaries will help to add flesh to the bare bones of figures, as will literary sources.

And then there are maps of varying descriptions. The main source here must be the large-scale O.S. maps (see Plate 14(b)). These are of varying dates but by the 1870s almost the whole of England had been covered. The earliest maps were published in the 1850s, but several of the Midland counties had to wait until the late 1880s before their surveys were completed.[51] The uses of these maps and the detail they contain are both very great indeed, especially when coupled with the

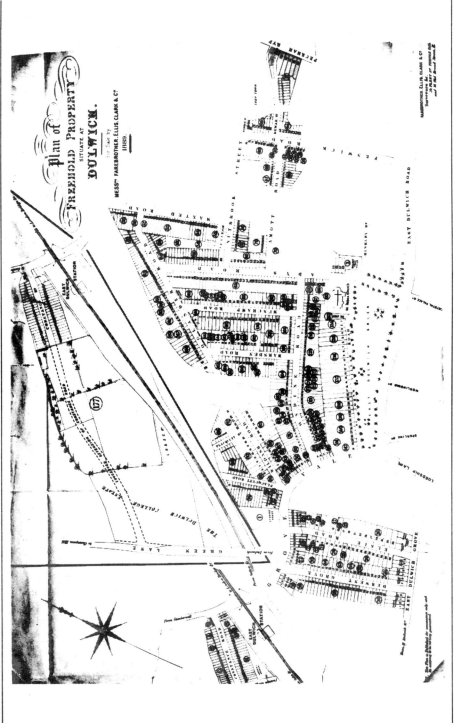

Plate 13 Plan taken from particulars of sale of freehold ground rents in Camberwell, Surrey. The particulars themselves show owners and occupiers and the amount of the ground rents.

Ordnance Survey area books which describe land use up to 1878. From them, with the other records, the local historian can trace the process of growth (or in villages, decline[52]) in the built-up area of the settlement, the existence of estates and the reasons for their location. The most useful way in which this can be presented is in a series of maps, showing the process of development from start to finish.

Tenure

What of the social structure of housing? Until the records of the various Building Societies become more generally available, there are limits to what can be done in this field, but the annual reports together with the records of local housing charities like the Leicester Domestic Mission[53] can show something of this movement. Most building firms were small businesses and their records rarely survive. Rate books and tithe awards help, as they usually record both owner and occupier, so that the number of tenants may be seen; so also for rural areas the land tax. Indeed, the rural areas are relatively well served. In 1873, there was a parliamentary enquiry into landownership, the details of which were published in 1875.[54] A large number of local lease books survive for private or public estates. But a good deal more needs to be done before this aspect can be said to have been even briefly examined at all, and the local historian's surest guides are those studies, like Professor Dyos's, which have already charted the course.

Chapter 5

Earning a living

1

How did members of our local community earn their living?

This is an easy enough question to ask. But it is not such an easy question to answer. The sources are often scarce and the interpretation of the scattered material is difficult. And before it can be answered there are a number of subsidiary questions which need to be posed.

The size of the working population
For instance, there is a group of questions concerning the number of those who worked, the breadwinners within the community. Not everyone of course earned their living. Infants in arms, the old and the sick did not work; nor did the leisured classes or the unemployed. So the first set of questions must be related to the size of the working population. Here the age structure of the group becomes important in indicating how many children there were below the minimum working age. Clearly this age varied with social classes, with the level of wealth, with the particular occupation engaged in, or with the nature of educational provision and other factors, and none of these was static in any community. It is the task of the local historian where possible to determine at any one time what was the minimum age at which persons began to work and how many young people within his community were so engaged.

Of the adults, three main groups will fall outside this study. First, there were of course the women left in charge of families and households (excluding of course paid housekeepers); but even here there were some hidden workers — wet nurses, paid foster mothers and the like. Secondly there were sick adults. It would seem almost impossible to arrive at firm figures for this element but it must always be borne in mind. Thirdly there were the able-bodied who were unemployed either because of indolence or because of lack of opportunity. There were of course peak periods of unemployment, but one wonders whether at any time there was ever complete full employment in any local community. It is thus a mistake to assume that the working population comprised all adults, or even all adult males, in the community. Local conditions varied enormously and must be examined separately.

Finally there is the problem of the old. How long was the working life? Did it vary with particular occupations? Were there periods when men worked longer than at other times? Problems concerning retirement provision as well as education and poor relief are relevant factors in any examination of the working population in a community; the various aspects of our study are closely interrelated.

What the historian is thus left with is the working population. And this needs to be broken down into men and women. A number of women at all times worked and it is sometimes possible to trace how many. Once again, as with child labour, the relation of this to wealth and the type of occupation done can be revealing.

Occupational analysis
Having established the size of the working element in the community and the fluctuations in this group at different times, the next question is the analysis of the occupations themselves. It may be possible for the local historian to pick out one or two key jobs done in his community, like the ribbon weavers of Coventry or the smith of Birmingham, although establishing the justification for such a selection can be difficult. How is importance in this sense to be assessed? Is it a matter of wealth, or of how many persons are engaged in any particular occupation? Too often the choice may become an arbitrary one.

But more important is an overall statement of the economic activity of the whole of the working force of the community. Here we run into a problem, springing from the fact that no generally accepted classification of occupations exists.[1] This makes detailed comparison between communities or between the same community at different periods difficult, for each historian has adopted his own classification to suit his particular community. Modern categories are not helpful because of the great changes in types and structures of employment in the last hundred years. There is now for instance a different emphasis on manual and white-collar workers. The various groupings of trade unions show how difficult it is even today to achieve satisfactory categories. To apply these to the past is unwarranted. For one thing, there is a modern conception of the relationship between social class and occupation which did not exist in the past.[2]

The local historian thus has to invent his own classification. And this will vary with the period, the type of community being studied, the area of the country, the range of occupations within the community and indeed the type of source material available for the study. Professor Everitt, in two studies of Northampton at about the same time, one from a poll book of 1768, the other from apprenticeship records, has used different classifications in each case.[3] Other historians use other categories.

There are a number of reasons why none of these classifications is satisfactory for general use. For one thing, there is the problem of dual and often unrelated occupations. Dual occupations are common in most early communities. Few innkeepers for instance were able to get a living on their victualling alone, especially in rural areas. Some, like the landlord of the Greyhound at Folkingham[4] or of the Horseshoe at Long Buckby, kept farms, while others ran small businesses such as joinery or brickmaking. Urban pubs were frequently in the tenancy of those engaged at times in other occupations. Pubs are no doubt a special case, but many other examples of dual occupations can be found in any community. Many early industries originated in the secondary occupations of rural workers.

A second problem is that people were rarely consistent in how they described their occupations, with a resultant blurring of distinctions. James Hopkinson for instance called himself a cabinet maker; he was apprenticed as a joiner and furniture maker. His category would seem to be clear. And yet his memoirs make it clear that for most of his working life he ran a furniture shop in Liverpool, and the directories record him as a furniture broker[5]. Is he thus to be classified as a craftsman or a shopkeeper? Further, in many early lists of occupations, social categories like esquire or gentleman get mixed up with occupational descriptions. Professor Everitt found 47 gentry in the Northampton poll book of 1768. Were they all part of the non-working group in the community, or did they conceal some who ought to be among the professions or the trades? After all, both James Hopkinson and his father who ran a grocer's shop called themselves gentlemen. But even when the description is consistent, there may be uncertainty in the titles themselves, speaking from the past. What does 'ostler' mean in its seventeenth- and eighteenth-century context? What precisely is a 'knocknobbler'?

But the real difficulty over the classification of occupations does not come so much from these problems but from the changing nature and status of early employments. The domestic character of industrial economy up to the late eighteenth century (and often later) meant that many workers were both manufacturers and retailers. A tanner was also a leatherseller, a shoemaker sold as well as made shoes. Many printers up to the mid-nineteenth century were also publishers. It is thus almost impossible to distinguish clearly between members of the manufacturing, retailing and service occupations in any past community.

In these circumstances, an historian might well despair. Even if he were able to devise categories which satisfied himself and applied to his particular subject (and this is possible), it would seem that he cannot hope to please his fellow historians or to produce work which can successfully be used for comparison. The temptation is to avoid anything detailed; it may be felt safer to stick to general categories, such as professionals, land workers, crafts and trades. It is however precisely the last two which cause most of the difficulties. In the end however the historian must not lose sight of his real objective in the mass of detail; all that is needed is a general statement of the preponderance of economic activity and major changes in the whole community, not an argument over a few persons in specific categories.

Nevertheless, it must not be forgotten that we are dealing with individuals, not just a group. And in this context one or two occupations can be significant. Especially is this true of the relationship of occupations to the family structure. Did occupations follow in families? At Bourne (Lincs), for instance, a local tannery (originally run jointly with a large farm consisting mainly of grazing) descended not from father to son but from father to nephew to son-in-law, the farm itself being the main family inheritance. How far did members of families follow the same occupation as the head of the household?

Such a study of occupations in the local community needs to be set in a wider context. Clearly they were related to the needs of and natural resources available to the community, and any discussion of this subject ought to include an account of such natural resources. Nevertheless, the economy of any place and the changes in that economy were not always directly tied to these resources but may be the result of other factors, such as traditional activities or one man's ambition and endeavours, especially in the later development of large-scale industry. The mills of West Ham were ancient before the middle of the nineteenth century, and the later chemical works were foreshadowed in their use for gunpowder and fertiliser-making. On the other hand, Boots, Raleigh and Players all grew in Nottingham because of individual enterprise,[6] and the same is true of particular industries in other places.

Structure of employment

Apart from the size of the working group in the community and the nature of the work done, there is one other set of questions. This relates to the 'social structure' of the economy, that is, how the work was structured. In agriculture, the pattern of landlord and tenant farmer set against the owner-occupier may be related to the size of farms, the type of agricultural practice, the employment of labourers, the machinery used and a host of other similar topics. Industrial society lends itself particularly to such a study of the bonds between those engaged in different parts of the processes essential to the industry concerned. Was the relationship one of employer (supplying equipment or materials or both) and employee, and if so, how many men (or women of course, and indeed children at times) were involved? Were the units large or small? Was the system a factory one or a domestic one or some other form, like the 'cottage factories' of Coventry? Were the profits cumulative at each stage of the process of manufacture or was the system based on speculative processing with substantial profits accruing in the end to the one 'master' who controlled all the processes? The range of variations was enormous and needs to be explored.[7]

And this leads to another question. What was the nature of industrial relations at any one time and how did they develop within the local community? Did groups of employed or employers band together to achieve mutual benefits? One danger here is the reading of the past in terms of the present. The journeymen gilds of the Middle Ages were not embryo trade unions, any more than the gilds merchant were Chambers of Commerce or the liveried companies early Industrial Confederations. A true understanding of such associations must be sought in terms of their own days, but in so far as they arose out of the economic structure of the local community, out of the occupations of the members of that group, they also need to be discussed.

There are thus three main groups of questions which the local historian may ask concerning the economic activity of his chosen community — what was the size of the working population? what was the nature of their occupations? and thirdly, how were such activities organised? Once again, the danger inherent in such an approach of presenting too static a picture is obvious — and one part of the local historian's task must be to trace the changes which took place in each of these aspects of his study throughout the period which he has undertaken to examine. For changes there were, not always determined by local factors but nevertheless greatly affecting the lives and fortunes of the people within the local community.

2

Any account of the background to this theme would constitute a history of the major developments in English economic history throughout the last fifteen hundred years. It would indeed be rash to attempt it in the space available. Nevertheless, some general points may be made.

Agriculture

For rural communities of course, agriculture must be the predominant theme of the local historian.[8] Other economic activities must not however be underestimated. In almost every community, often very small villages, groups of non-agricultural workers existed. There were almost always those we should nowadays classify as professional — men like the parson, schoolmaster or doctor who serviced others on the basis of some advanced educational requirements. Men and women were engaged in crafts of various sorts — supplying such domestic needs as pottery or cloth or houses themselves; or servicing the agricultural workers, like the wheel-wright; or processing the food by milling or brewing. Most of these activities were engaged in at home, often combined with other employments. Other persons (or sometimes indeed the same) engaged in trade in shops or markets. This was probably true of all but the very smallest settlements; indeed, the only clearly dis-tinguishing feature of an early town is that in that community, this latter group of occupations predominated. Others were engaged in the exploitation of the natural resources other than the soil, by fishing, hunting, forestry, iron smelting and mining. As time went on, all these occupations became subject to increasing special-isation and diversification and in many communities they grew in importance. Nevertheless, despite all of this other activity, agriculture predominated. It even played a large part in urban economy until the middle of the eighteenth century; several large towns, like Norwich and Bristol, had their town fields until quite late and farmers lived within the urban areas, being an important constituent of the community.

One of the main interests in agriculture for the local historian throughout the ages lies in its changing significance to the local community. What were the changes in the proportion of the population involved in agriculture? On the whole, the proportion declined, although even in 1851 there were still more people engaged in agriculture in England and Wales than in any single industry. Methods of farming improved, creating higher yields for less labour, and thus the proportion of agricul-tural labour in most communities declined as time went on. But the progression was not a simple nor a direct one — the size of the agricultural labour force fluctuated from time to time, often quite violently.

A similar tendency can be seen in relation to the area of land under cultivation. During the first great increase of population in the early Middle Ages, the total expansion of cultivated land by assarts and colonisation was enormous. Later, better farming techniques enabled higher yields to be derived from smaller acreages. Thus marginal lands could be used to better advantage generally by being grazed (a feature of the fifteenth and sixteenth centuries). On the other hand, the improved practices enabled some marginal lands to be farmed for the first time by the enclosure of heathland and the drainage of fenlands, characteristic of the seven-teenth and eighteenth centuries.

A further major theme of agricultural history is land use — the balance between the different types of farming, arable, pastoral and mixed. The development from hunting and pastoral to arable is well known. Later changes were of course more complex and more localised in character. In general, purely arable farming pre-dominated until the middle of the thirteenth century. Then came a long period of emphasis on stock, sheep from the thirteenth to the sixteenth centuries and cattle in the seventeenth and eighteenth centuries; associated with this was a process of enclosure, often labelled (but just as often without any justification at all) as 'enclosure by agreement'. The so-called 'agricultural revolution' has been a matter of debate,[9] but there is no doubt that the eighteenth century saw far-reaching changes in almost all parts of the country, frequently associated with a process of enclosure which Parliament facilitated by the passing of Acts, the appointment of commissioners and the recording of the 'awards' drawn up. Somewhat later came a return to arable farming but with a difference — large areas were subordinated to crops grown to support livestock rather than for direct human consumption. At the same time, new crops and machinery, changes in the relationships between land-owners, farmers and agricultural labourers, new forms of farm structures associated with the enclosure movement, and other major developments ushered in a new era during which agriculture became 'industrialised'.

Finally, the local historian should become aware of the changes in the internal organisation of agriculture within his community. The so-called 'death of the peasant' in England has become a common theme of recent writing — but the date at which the decline of peasant farming commenced has so far proved elusive. The family unit of subsistence farming, characteristic of so many other countries and persisting in some parts of England until the early nineteenth century at least, gradually gave way to a differentiated society of large farmers (freehold or tenant) employing landless wage labourers. The date of this change has varied from the fifteenth century to the eighteenth century and certainly differed widely from region to region. And the factors controlling these changes are also being debated — whether shortage of food or of labour. Margaret Spufford, in her important study of three Cambridgeshire villages, traces a relationship between the decline of peasant farming and years of famine, but it is likely that the story has a longer and more complicated history than her study indicates. In the West Midlands, for instance, the process can be seen at work much earlier; and it seems likely that in other parts of England a substantial waged labouring force has been a significant element from as early as the tenth century. On the whole, however, the trend has been towards larger and larger farms with a growing differentiation in society created by fewer farmers within the community, although on occasion the process could be reversed. Clearly, changes in the size of farms and in the numbers of men employed on them are of major significance in the story of any local community.[10]

The trouble with such a generalised picture is that it often does not apply to the individual rural community. Many places seem to show very little change until the eighteenth or nineteenth centuries; in other places there has been a constant process of agricultural re-ordering. Local factors are clearly most important here. It is true that the new ideas spread, that improved communications at times eased the process of specialised production for markets far away, that the development of banking helped capitalisation and improvements, although here again the reactions of individuals could promote or hinder the newer developments. But there were limits to these processes; the pattern of farming in any locality was of course to a very large extent determined by the soils, physical features and climate in the area concerned, and these were relatively stable over long periods. Changes in the overall economy of many rural communities were small and infrequent.

Trade

If some rural areas show few signs of change over long periods, the towns present a very different picture. Here agriculture ceased to be the predominant occupation at an early stage. In some places of course it was still significant, especially in towns of late enclosure like Nottingham, but this continuation of the agricultural interest was largely for political rather than for economic reasons and is of interest to the local historian for political and topographical purposes rather than economic. In urban communities, agriculture is rarely of great economic importance although it persisted into the nineteenth century.

However any individual town may have started, whether in military, administrative, religious or economic activities, there is no doubt that the market soon became its most important feature. Further, however much we may stress other aspects of the town's trade, however significant long-distance commerce may appear because of the wealth of individual merchants, the really important economic activity of any town (save perhaps London, almost always an exception) was its regular shopping, its short-distance weekly markets and annual fairs. In this sense, every town was intimately tied to its region. The marketing history of English towns is still very obscure.[11] In the medieval period, it would seem that some markets were active over considerable distances but in a small range of goods; there was a very large number of smaller markets, but many of the most important domestic necessities were produced within the household itself. As such crafts became increasingly specialised, as more well-made domestic necessities like cloth, furniture and shoes became available from specialist manufacturers, and as at the same time the great medieval markets declined, so it seems the smaller market towns profited, catering for the needs of a limited area and often overlapping with other nearby market towns. The sixteenth and early seventeenth centuries saw some hundreds of these towns scattered throughout the countryside. And competition continued to increase. As communications improved, so the town's market region grew. Thus many of them died. Some indeed had been still-born, like a number of the artificial creations of the twelfth and thirteenth centuries — a species of estate development which continued in some form or other until the nineteenth century, with spa towns and later private attempts to establish industrial development.[12]

But the interest in the local history of towns is not confined to those which did not succeed. Towns were immensely versatile, especially the successful ones. In the late seventeenth and eighteenth centuries, some of them can be seen to have developed as social centres for the neighbouring gentry. And this resulted in the significant growth in the late seventeenth and eighteenth centuries of the service industry for the gentry — hotels and victuallers, suppliers of all sorts of necessary and luxury goods, in the increase of professional activity, especially bankers and lawyers, and above all in the growth of domestic service. It is from the mid-eighteenth century that the domestic servant really becomes an identifiable element in the economic structure of any local community in England.[13]

Industry

The development of industry is really too large a theme to be expounded in full here. One or two points may however be noted. Early industrial development was not always associated with towns. The clothing industry of the fifteenth and six-teenth centuries was largely non-urban, as were of course the later coal-mining and lead-smelting and some other forms of industrial activity. But the towns saw far-reaching changes in this as in other respects, both in the types of economic activity engaged in and in the structure of the various types of industry. The local historian must be aware of the continual adjustments in the types and forms of industrial activity engaged in within his community.

How far the pattern may be generalised is still not clear, nor is it probably of great significance for the local historian. For to say that industries began locally in small units and became increasingly mechanised, specialised, centralised and large-scale in their operations is not to say much, for the chronology of these changes varied so enormously.[14] The different types of pottery industry had, so it seems, gone through this process by the end of the Middle Ages; brick and tile making, originally local and ephemeral in the sense that the industrial activity was engaged in when and where the bricks and tiles were needed, had begun its process of mass-production by the fifteenth century. On the other hand, it can be argued that the textile industry did not achieve this goal until well into the nineteenth century and is indeed still undergoing the process of centralisation. In any case, these tendencies were counteracted by an opposite development, the proliferation of more specialised activities, both in industry and trade. The different industrial processes came to be done separately, while an increasing variety of goods were put on the market. The range of occupations in almost all towns thus increased as time went on. Patterns of wealth similarly changed, largely it seems away from trading sections of the community to the manufacturing, but this is probably not true in all cases.

It is thus the individual stories of industrial and commercial development rather than the general picture which must interest the local historian most. And here the importance of the entrepreneur and especially the landowner and his agent as the promoter of change has been emphasised in recent studies. Agriculture and industry were not far removed in the early stages of the Industrial Revolution; both were seen as different aspects of the exploitation and processing of the natural resources available to the estate holder.[15] Not all industries, of course, emerged at the instigation of the landed interest. Many were small concerns of an independent nature, while others were wholly divorced from the rural and agricultural parts of the community. But in each case, the organisational structure of the industry owed most to the nature of its origins. Nor is the story confined simply to organisation; fluctuations in fashion, in methods of production and in materials all combined to produce new industries and trades. The Essex 'bays and says' gave way to silk and lace making and strawplaiting, just as Birmingham nails gave way to cars. And such changes involved radical restructurings of the way particular industries were carried out.

Industrial relations

The picture thus is a changing one and highly localised. And this is similarly true of the size of the working population; local factors predominated at any one time. Child and women labour varied with the type of industry engaged in, its structure and with the availability of labour — and perhaps with the determination of some local employer to exploit the resources at hand. The length of the working life again depended upon local factors, such as the poor relief facilities available or whether the industry was organised into a domestic or factory system. And industrial relations similarly varied from place to place, from industry to industry. The more general urban riots of the late eighteenth century, whether associated with low wages (as in East Anglia in the 1820s and 1830s) or high food prices (as at Nottingham in the 1790s) or political reform (as at Bristol in 1831), the attacks on machinery in both rural and urban areas in the early nineteenth century, the early combination movement of the first part of the same century and the political revolts of the second and third quarters of the nineteenth century, may all appear to be of general character, but they were in fact localised and need local studies to explain them. It is not until the late nineteenth century that truly national movements emerge, fostered by newer and faster means of communication in the railways, postal services and telecommunications.

The later nineteenth century

The situation in the later nineteenth century is thus too complex (and indeed too well-known) to warrant more than a few words here. Generally speaking, the working element of the population was substantial. There was a very high rate of child employment, which did not decline until the last quarter of the century; even most liberals thought that nine or ten years of age was a reasonable age at which to start work, while four or five was common in some domestic type industries. But legislation (effective from the 1860s), educational provision and the spread of factory employment began to reduce child employment significantly, although the employment of women remained more or less static.[16] The size of the working population was further reduced by growing unemployment, although this is still difficult to assess. Leisure too was spreading; hours became shorter and bank holidays became more generally acknowledged by legislation in the 1870s. All these trends may be found reflected in the local community.

That the balance of occupations throughout the century changed hardly needs comment. Agriculture employed more than one-quarter of the working population in the early part of the century; by the end of the century, this figure was down to about one-tenth. How far this reflected the changing fortunes of the industry, the high yields of the Napoleonic war period and the depressions of 1815—50 and from 1870 until into the twentieth century, is not clear. There were some increases in building, in transport and in trades, larger ones in professional and domestic services; while on the other hand, the numbers engaged in manufactures actually fell. But such figures, while they show the trends, may be of little significance in any particular place studied by the local historian. The growth of domestic service is however of particular interest, for its spread was not even throughout the country — 'thus in London the proportion [of servants to the total population] . . . was one in 15, in Brighton one to 11, and in Bath one to 9'.[17] At Rauceby, the figure in 1851 was one in 10, at Richmond, rather less; at Tickhill, one in 12 and at Long Buckby, only one in every 23.[18]

Such trends have some significance for the local historian. But to attempt to describe the very complicated developments in the organisation of industry during the nineteenth century here would be irrelevant. For each industry and each locality had its own story. What may be said of most large towns is that the period saw the emergence of some (perhaps not very many) large factories, often in areas once occupied by large houses. It is not clear whether the legislation which sought to control conditions within many of these factories in fact resulted in some inhibition in their development, but at least such Acts and the measures prepared to enforce them created many of the records by which we can see the process more clearly. Nor were the changes solely in industry. Commerce too saw the erection of huge memorials to the permanence of the shopkeeper — corn and coal exchanges, large shopping complexes (Exchange Buildings *par excellence*), great business houses and hotels. Some of these functions were of course still combined; the Lace Market at Nottingham comprised workshops and warehouses as well as salerooms. But much industry still remained on a small scale, and its destruction (as at Coventry)[19] was a painful process.

It was a process which resulted in urban and rural unrest and in the development of trades associations, a development by now well charted.[20] The earliest trades societies of the late eighteenth century, banned under the Combination Acts of 1799—1824, are not well recorded, nor can they be easily traced in the localities. The Grand National Consolidated Trades Union of 1834 was certainly both 'grand' and 'national', but it never became 'consolidated'. From the 1840s however came a different movement, finally (but hesitatingly) approved of in 1871 by the Trade Union Act and subsequent legislation. At much the same time, other forms of co-operation emerged, beginning with the Rochdale 'Equitable Pioneers' — a measure of self-help parallel to the trades associations.[21] It is against this background that local developments in industrial relations are to be placed. And these

are peculiarly local — at York, for instance, the development of workers' associations in the early part of the century was almost completely inhibited by the
opposition of one man, George Hudson.[22]

3

Sources: the labour force

There are few comprehensive sources for the study of local economic growth before
the nineteenth century, and some of our themes can only be examined in outline, if
at all. It is for instance very difficult to secure evidence of the proportion of the
community which was engaged in gainful employment. Domesday Book itself
records such population for the late eleventh century in each village, but it does not
give the other figure needed, the total size of the group. For many years thereafter
there is no clear picture. From the seventeenth century, poor relief and local
charity records may help to indicate the numbers of the old, the sick and (sometimes) the unemployed. A careful study of the recipients of poor relief, especially
in relation to family reconstitution work, still needs to be undertaken. There is no
indication however as to how many children were employed, and at what age,
before the great government enquiries of the nineteenth century.

Nor, at the other end of the scale, is there any real evidence of industrial relations before the early nineteenth century. There were local riots, well discussed by
contemporaries, especially antiquarians, and their reports are not without
value.[23] There are a few early combinations like the Nottingham framework-
knitters' associations of the early nineteenth century whose records survive, at least
in part.[24] But for the rest, the local historian has to rely on chance records,
business accounts (in which class of course fall the many and extensive collections
of estate records) or biographies of the more prominent local magnates. Such is not
the material for a systematic analysis, although it is of course most valuable.

Analysis of occupations

In the study of the economy of the community however, the local historian is
better off. There are sources which can indicate the major fields of activity of many
of its working members.

Agriculture is in some respects well served, better indeed than for any other
occupation. Large collections of estate records, rentals, surveys, manorial accounts
and court rolls,[25] survive to help indicate the extent to which the members of the
community were engaged in filling the mouths of their own families directly. Such
surveys are not confined to private records. The medieval enquiries made on the
death of any major royal tenant often resulted in a detailed account of the
estates.[26] Much later, the enclosure award may give a tenurial structure of the
community, although it rarely indicates how the tenants' farms were organised
under the landlord. This information can sometimes be gleaned for the eighteenth
century from a study of the land tax returns, if it is not available from estate
rentals.[27] Probate inventories may also help to indicate the type of farming in the
list of crops and stock remaining on the death of some of the more prominent
inhabitants. A valuable indication of the major types of farming engaged in within
the parish may be obtained from tithe schedules where they exist, or from glebe (or
more properly parish) terriers which sometimes list tithing customs.[28] The
terriers may also help to reveal the structure of the farming practice in the community, should the glebe land be described as scattered throughout the open fields

or gathered together in closes; early enclosure can sometimes be detected in this way, as also from court rolls and other estate records.

The enclosure movement was of course a major factor in the development of English agriculture, and the local historian concerned with places which were affected by enclosure must try to examine both the process and the results of enclosure within his own community.[29] Such a change was indeed far-reaching, not just in the effects it had on agricultural practice and on tenurial arrangements but also on the life of the community — on the position of the parson, for instance, on the freedom of movement of the local inhabitants, and of course (and probably most profoundly) on the psychology of village co-operation. Nevertheless such an event as enclosure must be kept in proportion. In some villages, it never occurred at all or indeed affected such a small fraction of the total parish lands as not to be really noticed. In others, it was merely part of a long and continuous process of land-change, a process similar to and often parallel with the constant changes we have already seen affecting the built-up area of the settlement. In some places it is clear the 'townlands' were for ever being readjusted, redivided, reallotted. Thus a picture of pre-enclosure (when such an event can be closely dated) field systems which can on occasion be obtained from early surveys and plans among estate records or reconstructed indirectly from field names listed in enclosure awards or (rather later) tithe awards, does not tell us anything about a *permanent* system before enclosure. It merely shows what the pattern of farming was at any one time. For some villages it may be possible to do more, to show something of the continuous process of change. There is more to the subject of course than this. Indeed such is the size of the topic, with such a wealth of source material,[30] both documentary and non-documentary, that it would be impossible to list here all the types of sources dealing with the local history of English agriculture. Nor would it in fact be very meaningful; for as the agricultural practice and estate management of Derbyshire differed from that in (say) Norfolk or Kent, so the types of records and 'field survivals' (as one may term the many forms of non-documentary agricultural source material, from field boundaries and names to marl pits and village pounds) will also differ.[31] There are, especially towards the end of the eighteenth century, several general surveys organised by the Board of Agriculture, which covered most of England county by county;[32] and more detailed accounts appeared in many local newspapers. But the coverage is not systematic, and the local historian is always faced with the problem of finding exactly what evidence there is for his own chosen locality. Probably the best introduction to the range of source material available for such a study is to examine the contents of some successful study such as Dr Thirsk's work on the seventeenth century or Dr Grigg's on the eighteenth century.[33]

Urban occupations

The general surveys of agriculture may be paralleled for towns (at least in part) by the accounts which visitors or diarists recorded in a long series from Leland (or indeed from William Worcestre in the fifteenth century before him) through the eighteenth century of Arthur Young (*Six Weeks' Tour*) into the nineteenth century of Cobbett.[34] Leland's description of Birmingham is well known:

'there be many smithes in the towne that use to make knives and all maner of cuttynge tooles, and many lorimars that make byts, and a great many naylors. So that a great parte of the towne is mayntayned by smithes',[35]

but it is only one of many. And there are other more purely local descriptions:
county and borough histories, like Morant's *Essex* (1748) and Drake's *Eboracum*
(1736), often contain brief accounts of local industries.

The testing of these books' subjective impressions by hard facts is rarely possible
for the early urban communities. Before the 1841 census there is no regular source
which will give a full account of the occupations of all the working members of the
local community. There are some rare individual surveys, like the list of Coventry
occupations in 1522 and the Northampton taxation of 1524 which records the
occupations of the taxpayers;[36] but these are exceptions.

Most of the information about occupations in towns before 1841 comes from
three main series of records, the poll books, registers of freemen and apprenticeship
papers. *Poll books*, which record the votes in parliamentary (and in a few rare cases
some local) elections, only survive for those corporate towns which were involved
in such elections. They range in date from about the 1760s to the 1860s and list the
voting members of the community together with the votes they cast for the various
candidates; many of them also give a note of the property by virtue of which the
voter was entitled to his franchise. Such a list might not even cover all the major or
wealthy persons in the town, and certainly it omits the humbler inhabitants, thus
under-recording those domestic industries on which so many places at this time
relied. Nevertheless, a reasonable cross-section of the community would seem to be
recorded in most poll books (see Plate 30(b), p. 168),[37] from which some
evidence as to the major economic activities within the place may be drawn. Thus a
study of the 1812 poll book for Chester suggests a preponderance of leather and
wood workers, with the river trade occupying a more or less insignificant element,
perhaps a hint at the decline of the river Dee.[38] Many of the cordwainers were
still concentrated together, in Hanbridge and in Foregate Street, an indication of
the way such poll books (and the slightly later directories) can help to reveal the
topography of industrial and commercial activity within a town.

Registers of freemen similarly only exist for corporate towns. They usually
record the name and occupation of the person admitted as freeman. A good deal of
their value lies in the fact that there are often long runs of them. Thus it may be
possible to trace something of the changes in balance in the economy of the town
from the fifteenth century (or even earlier) to the eighteenth century by examining
the proportion of occupations so listed.[39] Sometimes this has been linked with a
study of office holders in the borough on the grounds that these would reflect the
economic structure or at least the most prominent occupations in the town, but
this is doubtful. For a few boroughs, rate books will serve much the same purpose
as freemen's rolls.

Perhaps the least useful of these three sources are the records concerning
apprenticeship — registers kept by the corporation in some towns, quarter sessions
registrations of apprentices for the unincorporated town or rural areas, newspaper
advertisements for apprentices, and some surviving books from about 1720 now in
the Public Record Office which relate to the tax on apprenticeships of the late
seventeenth and early eighteenth centuries. There is a good deal of information
about the boy who was being apprenticed, his parents and their place of residence
and the master and his trade in these papers. Once again, a long run of these may
show some economic changes within the community as the period progresses, but it
must be stressed that they are not in any way systematic.

These papers, like the poll books and the rolls of freemen, presuppose questions
about the economic organisation of trade and industry and thus (for instance) may

omit factory and many domestic type industries. How far such omissions can be made good by a study of large numbers of *wills* and *probate inventories* [40] for the community is still not clear, but it is unlikely that even these will give a balanced account of the general structure of the economy, especially in the smaller town. In any case, the survival rate of probate inventories varies considerably from place to place, while their compilation seems to have become more occasional from the 1720s or 1730s. But their great value lies in their inventories of stock or equipment which cannot be gained from other sources. Local deeds and lease books may also reveal occupations. Perhaps more reliable, because they cover a genuine random sample of the population, are those parish registers which record occupations. Another source, as yet hardly used by local historians, are the militia papers of the late eighteenth century, now kept among the records of the quarter sessions, [41] a source of value for some rural areas.

The end of the eighteenth century saw the beginning of local directories, and for the first time some general surveys of particular localities is possible. The *Universal British Directory* for instance records that in Birmingham, the 'hardware' town, there were ten times as many metal workers as there were builders, ten times as many general tradesmen and craftsmen as professional men. [42] These are of great value for overall surveys.

Evidence of individual occupations and industries can be drawn from a wide range of source material. Among the most useful documentary sources are the eighteenth-century fire insurance records. [43] These give the insurance valuations on buildings associated with particular industries and trades. Business records before the eighteenth century are rare, certainly compared with the richness of estate records, but they do on occasion survive. There are of course many miscellaneous references to local economic activities; the recent publication of fifteenth-century coroners' reports for Nottinghamshire throws some light on the early coal industry among other things in that area. [44] But one of the most valuable sources in this connection is the whole field of industrial archaeology — surveys of surviving or pre-existent industrial housing or plant [45] — kilns, furnaces, mining equipment, saltpans, factories and small workshops. It is important to reiterate that surveys of this sort are not an end in themselves; their purpose is to tell us about the people of the past and how they went about the business of earning their livings; but equally it is important to realise that no full account of the economic activity in any locality can ignore the physical remains that that activity produced.

4

The picture for the nineteenth century is once again different. It is not just that we can study the subject in greater depth or more systematically; rather, we can for the first time ask some of the questions with some expectation of finding out the answers.

The working population
The size of the working group in any local community can, to some extent, be determined from the census records. The growth of the interest of the census officials in occupations was slow. In 1801, general counts were made of the numbers engaged in agricultural work, or in trade, manufacture or crafts, or thirdly in some other occupation. These three categories were kept in 1811 and 1821, but

the numbers of families rather than persons were recorded. In 1831, a wider system of classification (seven categories in all) was used but it only dealt with men over the age of twenty years. On the other hand, useful material relating to the distribution of trades and crafts in each town and county is contained in the *Abstracts*.

It was not however until 1841 that personal information relating to age and occupation was provided, and this survives in the enumerators' books. These give the occupations as described by the person himself (Plate 2). In the general instructions, the enumerators were given some guidance as to terms and classifications to be used but it would seem that in general they accepted what they were told. This of course creates some problems, but on the whole the occupations listed there may be accepted.

On the other hand, as we have seen, some of those recorded (like girls in domestic service) may have falsified their ages because of their occupations.[46] Certainly there is some unreliability in the ages of particular groupings, especially domestic service. There were also errors, like the boy of two months recorded as 'scholar'. Nevertheless, common sense will sort out the most obvious mistakes; and an analysis of the ages at which children were listed as being employed (part-time or full-time? – this is not of course recorded), if related to social and occupational groupings, will give some indication of the average age at which children in particular industries started work. Such findings can be tested against the often very detailed material included in the numerous government reports into either the employment of women and children or particular industries.

The average number of women at work as well as the types of occupation in which they were engaged can similarly be determined from the same two sources, the census books and government reports. The unemployed, the sick and the retired constitute a more intractable problem. The census does on occasion record 'retired' and 'pauper', although these persons are clearly under-recorded in the schedules for a variety of social reasons. Again, from 1851 the census records those who were deaf, mute and blind, but not those with other forms of disability. Unemployment is not recorded; the census does not tell us whether the 'coal porter' was employed or not at the time of the return. Something may be recovered from Poor Law statistics and from the returns made by charities.[47] A full study relating the census to local poor law records would yield great fruit, but this is not always possible.

Range of occupations
The census is perhaps most useful in the general analysis it affords of the economic structure of any community. Once again, there are the problems of obscure, uncertain or inaccurate descriptions and deliberate falsifications, but these are unlikely to unbalance the picture very much, except perhaps in the domestic service category, where the deficiencies may be serious.[48] There are certain checks on this, the occupation recorded in the marriage registers after 1813 and those listed in directories often providing useful counter-information. It may be added at this point that an analysis of the changes in the nature of the economy of any particular locality is not really feasible from nineteenth-century directories, despite their fullness and regularity of appearance. They are too selective to provide a sure guide and they too often copy one from another. This is not to say they have nothing to tell us about the economy of any particular place during the nineteenth century. They have much light to throw on specific occupations, on the topography of industry and on the growth or other changes in particular industrial concerns;[49]

they are especially valuable towards the end of the century for which the census books are not yet available.

Nevertheless for a balanced account it is to the census that one must turn. Here we can get some idea of the total distribution of workers among the various occupations. The problem of classification is still a serious one, and the census office itself realised it. After each census from 1831, the meanings of the categories used were discussed in a special report devoted to occupations.[50] These contain figures which have some value. But it is important to remember that, except where girls and boys are expressly mentioned, they refer only to those over the age of twenty. The 1851 census report on occupations is perhaps the fullest, with a large map of England entitled *Distribution of the Occupations of the People*, but once again, its value for local studies is limited. The census reports from 1841 to 1881 were summarised by Charles Booth[51] and this provides much useful material on the general trends.

It is the census books which are the most valuable in this connection, and many studies have been done on them. In Rauceby, for example, a Lincolnshire farming parish where a third of one village (South Rauceby) and a half of the other village were at work in 1851–61, half of the working population in 1851 was engaged directly in agriculture as farmers, agricultural labourers or agricultural servants (it is in practice virtually impossible to see the significance in the distinctive terms). A further quarter were employed as domestic servants – interestingly enough, rather more in North Rauceby (the closed village) than in its more open neighbour, South Rauceby.[52] Long Buckby (Northants), a larger rural settlement, was different. Just over 1,000 out of the total 2,300 were in fact employed, most of them (about one-third of all the working population) in shoemaking. Only one-tenth were household servants, while agriculture and the food and clothing industries employed twice as many persons as domestic service. Many of the shoemakers were young – indeed a full half of all those in the community aged between fifteen and nineteen were engaged in this industry, while there were a further 59 youngsters below fifteen years of age similarly employed. It was apparently a home-based craft but little of its organisation can be seen; more can in fact be seen of the farms than of the workshops in this small town.

At Tickhill (Yorks) a community of about the same size, just under half (43%) of the total population in 1851 were at work, including 77 children (one-tenth of the total child population of the community) and 57 housewives (rather more than one-eighth of that section). Agriculture was the main occupation here (44%) but domestic service was also prominent (one-fifth of the working population). Trades and crafts, as in all communities of this size, formed a major part of the whole economy, well over one-quarter. Of the farms, there were several large ones, but the average labour force was on the whole small. Richmond (Yorks) was twice the size of these two latter communities. Here the working population was 42% of all inhabitants in 1851. One-third of these comprised women, while one-twentieth (81) were children under fifteen years of age. Agriculture accounted for only one-tenth, domestic service for one-quarter. One of the most important industries was papermaking, but most of the working inhabitants were engaged in the service crafts or in trade, for Richmond catered for a large surrounding region. More than a third of all workers were skilled craftsmen and 13% were tradesmen and shopkeepers – high figures compared with the 20% and 7% respectively at Tickhill.[53]

The use of the census schedules thus in a total analysis of occupations can reveal significant patterns. It is relatively easy to do this for communities of this size but larger places require more sophisticated techniques.[54] Thus Professor Dyos for Camberwell computerised a 3% sample (household heads only) for the 1871 census. His classifications are of course very sophisticated, and it is not surprising that domestic service was one of the smallest categories in his group.[55] Elsewhere, sample techniques may be adopted like those used by Armstrong for York (every tenth household, with some variations) or those of Lawton for Liverpool in 1851.[56] Lawton selected seventeen areas within the borough and outside, with samples ranging in size from 153 to 1,138 persons, and portrayed his results by means of proportional circles (Fig. 18). The variation in occupations within the sample areas, such as the distribution of professional, industrial and commercial workers, is striking. It is clear that when dealing with a population of this size (more than 375,000), a sampling method is the only practical solution, although even this will result in very large numbers being dealt with (14,000 in Liverpool).

Such a study does not exhaust the interest in the economic structure of the local community. There is the topographical development of local industry and commerce, for which the use of maps and field surveys is an essential ingredient (see below, pp. 111–13). It is always possible to under-estimate the commercial activity in any local community, probably because much of it was carried on in a minor way and was largely unrecorded. But it formed the core of the economic activity of most towns, especially the smaller market towns, and it was never negligible even in the larger industrial centres like Liverpool or Manchester.

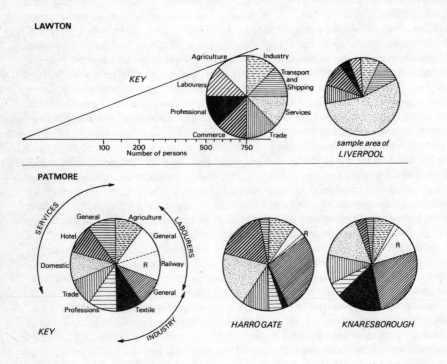

Fig. 18 Diagrams to show the distribution of occupations in the towns of Liverpool, Harrogate and Knaresborough. There are other ways of representing the facts.

Individual occupations

Records relating to individual occupations are of course much fuller in the nineteenth century, although it is strange how little can be found out about agriculture at this time. From 1851 it is true, the census recorded the size of the farm and the number of farm servants employed, but the figures are often ambiguous and rarely tie in with other evidence. Nevertheless they have some value. On the other hand, it is frequently impossible to determine what type of farming is engaged in even when estate records survive, for tenants seem to have been left very largely to their own devices. There is some evidence from government reports — the series of *General Views* were continued by the Board of Agriculture well into the nineteenth century and were supported by other records, like the 1801 acreage returns (in the Public Record Office).[57] Local records, like the land tax, are particularly useful for the early part of the century; from the middle of the century there are numerous tithe papers, often associated with the various Tithe Acts of 1832—46 and the local awards drawn up subsequently. From 1866, the Board (later the Ministry) of Agriculture collected returns on land use, while the Ordnance Survey had land use surveys covering much of England up to the late 1870s. Two large government reports on *Agricultural Employment* (1867—9) leading to the regulation of the gang system[58] can provide some local material but they are not among the most valuable of the nineteenth-century blue books; the Royal Commission on Agriculture produced more useful reports in 1882 and 1894.

These parliamentary papers really come into their own when examining specific industries.[59] Whether one is dealing with coal-mining or textile manufacture or market trading, there are detailed reports, prepared by government departments, royal commissions, select parliamentary committees or local government agencies. Behind the formal reports lie the summaries of evidence and in many cases unpublished minutes.[60] The range of subjects covered is immense. From the point of view of our present study, the most useful reports are those devoted to specific industries (like the *Report of the Select Committee on the Silk Trade*, 1832) or groups of workers (like the *Report of the Assistant Commissioners on the Employment of Women and Children in Agriculture*, 1843) or places (like R. Shapter's *Report on Exeter*, 1845). But many of the more general reports, especially those emanating from the Children's Employment Commission of 1842—3 and later from 1862 to 1867 (six reports in all), contain a wealth of local information about particular industries. 'In addition to the larger distinct workplaces which may be more properly called "factories" and many of which are named "Works"', wrote the Children's Employment Commissioners in 1864, 'there are in the yards in which Birmingham abounds . . . a vast number of small workshops, forming either separate floors or parts of floors in the same block of buildings, and in some of these cases renting the steam power needed for the work . . . or standing alone or attached to houses' (what elsewhere were called 'shops').[61] It is well known that much of the evidence was 'loaded', just as the famous report of the commission into borough management which preceded the Municipal Corporations Act was hardly impartial. But this does not invalidate the more sober (and sobering) material relating to ages, hours of work, conditions of employment and frequency of injury and death in relation to particular occupations or particular localities. The official reports may be supplemented by more private commentaries, frequently written for much the same political and social motives as the government blue books. Gravenor Henson's *History of the Framework-Knitters* (1831) is only one of many. Some were published separately; others appeared in journals, like Leifchild's survey of

Plate 14   West Ham: the growth of an industrial centre.
(a) Map of the parish in 1855, from the local government ('Dickens') report.

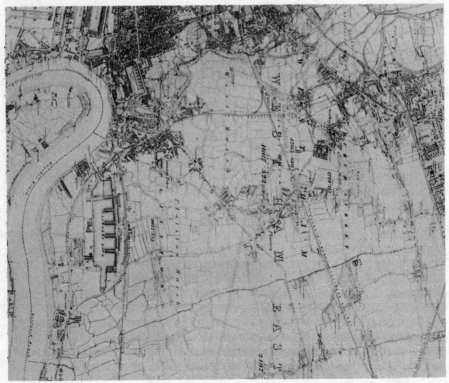

(b) Map of the parish in 1875, taken from the first edition O.S. 6 inch map, *c.* 1860–70, with some later detail. (The orientation has been changed to match the above map.)

Property rated, but unbenefited by Commissioners' Scheme.   19

the streets were impassable ; yet with all this the inhabitants WEST HAM are now subject to an eighteenpenny rate under the Commissioners' Act. The cholera has raged very much in this district. Small pox and typhus are now prevalent there."

Mr. *Ashdown* handed in the following list of twenty ratepayers, rated in the aggregate at 28,305*l.*, who in his opinion could by no possibility receive any benefit from the Commissioners' scheme, but who, in common with the whole of the parish, would be subject to the eighteenpenny rate.

Twenty of the principal Ratepayers.	Railways Manufactories and Buidings.			Principally Land.		
	£	s.	d.	£	s.	d.
Eastern Counties Railway -	11,155	5	0			
Mure & Co. - -	2,050	5	0			
Mare & Co. - - -	2,004	15	0			
J. Tucker - - -	1,970	10	0			
W. Adams - - -	-	-	-	1,885	0	0
T. Curtis - - -	1,360	0	0			
*Victoria Dock - - -	-	-	-	1,169	15	0
Northumberland Coal Co. -	892	0	0			
Peto & Co. - - -	860	0	0			
East London Water Co. -	727	0	0			
Silver & Co. - - -	550	0	0			
Ireland & Sons - - -	-	-	-	549	15	0
Howard & Co. - - -	544	0	0			
R & T. Wagstaff - - -	-	-	-	614	0	0
S. Gurney, Esq. - - -	-	-	-	517	10	0
Ireland, Joseph - - -	-	-	-	448	5	0
West Ham Gas Co. - -	400	0	0			
Messrs. Tothill & Co. - -	314	0	0			
Widdicomb - - -	-	-	-	293	0	0
	22,827	15	0	5,477	5	0

* This amount will of necessity be very largely increased as the profits of the docks are developed.

Mr. *Alfred Robinson* condemned the plan of the Commissioners, and advocated the application of the Public Health Act as likely to be the most economical and effectual means of getting a good system of drainage for the district.

Mr. *W. H. Dean* spoke to the want of drainage throughout the town. He not only corroborated the previous evidence, but extended it to the whole parish. The usual drain is a cesspool ; in some instances a still more objection-

---

Plate 15   Page from the 'Dickens' report 1855 on the state of West Ham.

Plate 16 (overleaf)   Page from one of the Special Properties Rate Books, West Ham. Note the entry 533, relating to Gould's Mill.

Life and Labour in the Coalfields (largely Tyneside) in *The Cornhill Magazine* (1862), or the account of the Black Country in *The Edinburgh Review* (1863), and others in places like *The Fortnightly*.[62] From these sources, official or commercial (like *Bradshaw's Handbook to Manufacturing Districts* of 1854) or private, it is possible to discover a good deal about local industries.

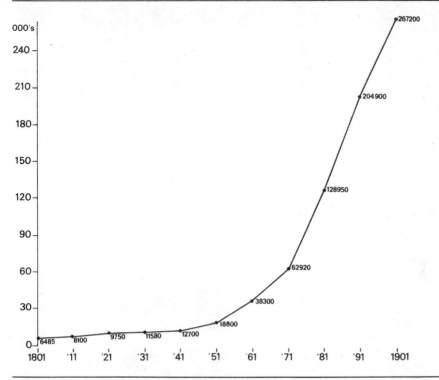

Fig. 19 Population growth in West Ham, Plaistow and Stratford. It is not possible to distinguish between the three settlements in the parish before 1851.

West Ham

A recent study of West Ham (Essex), prepared for the *Victoria County History* of Essex,[63] shows something of the value of these sources. The overall pattern of the growth of Metropolitan Essex since 1850 was first described by Professor Ashworth, using mainly census material, directories, blue books and other official publications.[64] His study emphasised the importance of economic influences on growth, and showed the different occupational patterns in neighbouring towns like West Ham, Ilford and Walthamstow. One feature to emerge from his study (a complication for the local historian) was the separation of homes and workplaces in the area. In 1921, for example, over 54% of the occupied population of the nine Metropolitan Essex towns were working outside their own towns, mainly in London. How far should the occupations of such commuters be regarded as part of the local history of the places where they live?

Professor Ashworth's work showed the influence upon West Ham of the royal group of docks and of industry along the Lea and the Thames. His study has been followed by a separate industrial history of each town in Metropolitan Essex. In the case of West Ham a detailed survey was made of the manufacturing industries, how many firms were there and what they produced. In 1800 West Ham was a large parish with three settlements, Plaistow and Stratford as well as West Ham village (Plate 14). It was still mainly rural but contained an ancient industrial fringe along

VIEW of the RIVER LEA BRIDGE and STRATFORD VIADUCT as now constructing for the EASTERN COUNTIES RAILWAY COMPANY.

Plate 17   West Ham: the development of a local industry.   (a) The Eastern Counties Railway, *c.* 1838, showing an old mill at Stratford Marsh. Such mills, recorded in the Middle Ages, began to diversify their output by the sixteenth century (gunpowder, etc.)

Plate 17(b)   Gould's Flour Mill, High Street, Stratford, 1969.

the Lea at Stratford Marsh. By 1900 it was one of the greatest manufacturing centres in southern England (Fig. 19).

The basis of the study was a survey carried out for the *V.C.H.* by West Ham Borough Libraries by means of a questionnaire addressed to all the principal firms, including some (like Howards of Ilford) who moved away. Some firms had published their own histories. Local directories (especially Kelly's county and town series) and official guides proved very valuable, and local newspapers like the *Stratford Express* were also used. A *Report to the General Board of Health on the Sanitary condition of West Ham* (1855) provided some information on recent industrial growth (Plate 15). It was compiled by Charles Dickens's brother, and was followed up by an article in *Household Words*. Even more important was *West Ham, a study of social and industrial problems* (1909), written by E. G. Howarth (head of the Trinity College, Oxford, Settlement at Stratford) and Mona Wilson, on behalf of the Outer London Inquiry Committee. The minutes and rate books (Plate 16) of the local authority and the records of the commissioners of sewers (the drainage authority) were also useful.[65] West Ham's central reference library also provided a great collection of photographs, prints, pamphlets, cuttings, sale catalogues and other records.

The above sources were used to prepare an introductory section followed by short histories of some 180 firms, past and present, grouped according to the Standard Industrial Classification.[66] West Ham's main groups were chemicals, engineering and food-processing. The growth of Stratford Marsh illustrates the continuity of much nineteenth century industrial development (Plate 17). The ancient City Mills, for example, had been used in succession for corn-grinding, fulling and papermaking before going over to chemicals. The railways were crucial to the

Plate 18   Cotton factories built in Oxford Street, Manchester, in the later nineteenth century. Manchester was one of the earliest city centres to become largely deserted.

growth of the town. The Eastern Counties Railway built their main workshops at Hudson Town (renamed Stratford New Town after George Hudson's disgrace). A branch line to the Thames led in the 1850s to the building of the Victoria Docks and the development of Silvertown, named after the rubber firm of S. W. Silver & Co. One of the largest employers of labour was the Thames Ironworks at Bow Creek, one of several shipyards on the Thames which were eventually forced out of business by northern competition.

Structure of industry

A good deal more could be learned about industrial relations, the growth of the Co-operative Societies (the Stratford Company later became the London Co-op) and the use of foreign labour and management (for instance in the sugar refineries and chemical works). An examination of these aspects of the 'social structure' of the local economy relies very heavily upon government and local reports. The casual labour system in the docks at West Ham and its social results on the local community are for example fully explored in the 1909 report. Something of the size of firms (like the farms) earlier in the nineteenth century can be seen from the census books: 'John Desmond, Tailor and Draper employing 2 women' (Plate 6); but there are signs that fear of taxation or some other reason led to some evasion in this entry; certainly the figures for farm employees are frequently suspect. Other evidence comes from business records which now feature more importantly. Many and extensive are the files of correspondence, account books, order and delivery books, company minutes, wages sheets, stock books and production papers and a host of other such records emanating from particular concerns. Most of these collections are still in the hands of the businesses themselves (or their successors) and are often not accessible to the local historian, but a number have been deposited in local record offices, although the total survival is indeed very small compared with the vast total originally created.[67] Local directories similarly sometimes indicate the size of industrial concerns; Blackwell's *Directory of Sheffield* of 1828 gives a clear picture of the small scale of most of the businesses engaged in the cutlery industry at that time. Diaries and memoirs, like the Hopkinson one already cited, can vividly portray the relations between men and employers, the renting out of tools in workshops, the provision of sewing machines for women at home.[68] The records of the embryo trade unions themselves, and especially ephemeral printed matter like songs and hymns which the workers' associations produced, become useful from the second half of the nineteenth century. Most important are the local newspapers for the whole period – the local historian can never get far away from the newspapers at any time during the nineteenth century. Indeed, for the rural movements, the newspapers are often the only sources available, although some printed accounts of particular events do survive,[69] while the movements of the earlier part of the century are illuminated by the quarter sessions papers dealing with wage disputes and machine breaking, as well as by locally produced pamphlets and some miscellaneous references.[70] Industrial archaeology too may have something to say on the way factories grew (Plate 18). But it is to the blue books that once again one must turn. The eleven reports produced in two years (1867–9) by the Royal Commission dealing with Trade Unions are masterful compilations with much local supporting material.

Note on occupation classifications

There are many, probably insuperable, difficulties in the way of devising a universally applicable code of classifications, especially one which might apply to both industrial and non-industrial communities. The value of such an agreed code is obvious but so far there are great divergences among historians.

Omitting those who classify themselves with non-occupational titles like esquire or gentleman (i.e. the leisured classes) or pauper (the unemployed), the simplest system is one based on very general categories:

1 non-productive occupations: professional – clergy, teachers, lawyers, medical men, etc. – and service.
2 those engaged in direct exploitation of natural resources – fishermen, sawyers, miners, iron smelters, etc. (agriculture would clearly demand a separate subsection)
3 processors of raw materials (crafts and industries)
4 distributors of finished products (trades).

Such widespread categories however need to be differentiated, for those engaged in agriculture may be farmers or employed labourers. Nor will this simple classification do for industrial societies; nor indeed, because of the confusion between crafts and trades, will it suffice for pre-industrial societies.

One of the problems in the way of devising a system which will be adequate for purposes of comparison is to determine whether the classification should be based on what was being done (e.g. industry or commerce) or on the materials used (such as leather, textile and metal workers or builders or food and drink and clothing retailers) or on whether the workers were employed or not (as labourers and servants). Some systems mix these categories up.

Professor Everitt, in his studies of market town poll books and probate inventories, has devised a system of classification, as follows:

1 Gentry
2 Professions (and armed forces)
3 Innkeeping and wayfaring (i.e. travelling merchants, factors, etc.)
4 Processing trades — brewing, wool, leather (tanning), etc.
5 Retail trades — food, clothing, miscellaneous.
6 Crafts — metal, leather, clothing, wood, building, fine crafts, miscellaneous.
7 Landwork (which could include farmers and labourers)
8 Servants

His analysis of apprenticeship records however, adopted somewhat different classes, highlighting the difficulty of using one set of categories for all records; but it makes comparison almost impossible.

J. E. Vincent, in his analysis of poll books, uses a different classification:

1 Gentlemen and farmers
2 Professional and commercial
3 Publicans
4 Labour
5 Business
6 Craftsmen and skilled workers
7 Retailers
8 Miscellaneous

He recognises[71] that it is impossible always to distinguish between employer and employed in the poll books.

The same problem defeated the census enumerators. Charles Booth, in his 1884 summary of occupations from 1841 to 1881,[72] took the compilers of the *Abstracts* to task for not doing this, but Dr Ogle from the registrar-general's office replied[73] that although 'special directions were given on the schedule that every worker should state whether he was master or man, . . . workmen would not do anything of the kind'. So the census officials themselves used 'safe' categories from the first introduction of occupations in 1831:

1 Agriculture (employers, occupiers not employers, labourers)
2 Manufacturers or makers of manufacturing machinery
3 Retail trade and handicraft (masters or workmen)
4 Capitalists, bankers, professional 'and other educated men'
5 Labourers employed in labour not agricultural
6 Other males 20 years and over (except servants)
7 Male servants 20 years and over
8 Male servants under 20 years
9 Female servants

Such categories are of limited use to the historian.

The classification most commonly used in the analyses cited above is that devised by P. Tillott in his work on Tickhill, although it has been somewhat revised by other workers:

Tillott	Fieldhouse	Greenall
1 Farmers	1 Farmers, farmers' sons, smallholders	1 Farmers
2 Agricultural workers	2a Skilled agricultural workers 2b Agricultural labourers	2 Agricultural workers
3 Tradesmen	3 Tradesmen and shopkeepers	3 Petty entrepreneurs, shopkeepers, traders
4 Craftsmen	4 Craftsmen and skilled workers	4 Skilled craftsmen
5 Industrialist/ manufacturer	5 Industrialists	(Not used)
6 Mining	6 Mining	(Not used)
7 Professions	7a Upper professional 7b Lower professional and military	5 Professions, teaching
8 Clerical	8 Clerical	6 Clerical
9 Servants	9a Upper servants 9b Lower servants 9c Servants for hire	7 Servants
10 Independent	10 Independent	8 Persons of Independent Means
11 Victuallers	11 Victuallers, Innkeepers, Lodging house keepers	9 Semi-skilled and service workers
12 Labourers	12 Unskilled labourers	10 Labourers and unskilled workers
—	—	11 Supervisory workers

Then there are a number of 'socio-descriptive' titles:

H. Housewives	H. Housewives	H. Housekeepers
P. Paupers	P. Paupers	P. Paupers
R. Retired	R. Retired	R. Retired

With two (or three) other categories:

C. Children (including scholars)	C. Children	
NO. No occupation given	NO. No occupation	NO. No occupation V. Visitors

There are of course other categories used in census analysis. Lawton for example used the following for Liverpool, closely followed by Patmore, studying Harrogate and Knaresborough [74] (Fig. 18):

UNIVERSITY COLLEGE LIBRARY SWANSEA

Lawton	Patmore
1 Industry	I Industry — 1 General 2 Textile
2 Agriculture	
3 Transport and Shipping	
4 Services	II Services — 1 Domestic 2 Hotel 3 General
5 Trade	III Trade
6 Commerce	
7 Professional	IV Professions
8 Labourers	V Labourers — 1 General 2 Railway

On the other hand, Alan Armstrong uses the six major 'classes' created in 1950 by the Registrar-General, thus:[75]

I   Capitalists, manufacturers and professional
II   Smaller shopkeepers, lower professional, farmers
III   Skilled labourers and self-employed shopkeepers
IV   Semi-skilled labourers
V   Unskilled labourers and domestic servants
VI   Housewives, spinsters and retired.

The trouble with this classification is that class III becomes enormous, even after adjustments have been made. Professor Dyos, in a discussion of this problem, has elaborated the scheme considerably, but it is unlikely that many local historians will need such sophistication except when dealing with large urban areas. In any case, it is not clear whether modern social conventions should intrude into categories of occupations.[76] The census authorities themselves use other categories than 'socio-economic' ones — employment status and economic position. Indeed, at least two different lists of some 27 categories each are in circulation.[77]

The basic problem facing the local historian is not a comparison between a past age and today but between two communities at the same or different periods. The categories must therefore be capable of application to both pre-industrial and at least early industrial communities. For this purpose, it would seem that the scheme devised by Mr Tillott is probably the most flexible that has so far been devised. But whatever one is used, it is important that local historians should use only comparable schemes for comparative studies, and above all, to think in terms of the past he is dealing with rather than in twentieth century terms.

Chapter 6

Transport and communications

1

The occupational structure of the local community, just like its demography, has a topographical aspect which the local historian may be able to trace in at least two ways. On the one hand, there is the region within which the community is placed and to which it is closely related. On the other hand, there is the relationship of those buildings or lands within the place itself which relate to the occupations of the people who lived there.

The region
The economic structure of any local community depended to a large extent upon a wider area than just the parish or township lands, especially in those places where there were sizeable industrial or commercial interests. A market naturally relied upon and catered for a region, both for the supply of goods and for prospective purchasers. Similarly, industries needed raw materials and labour as well as marketing outlets, and these could often only be obtained from a distance. Even purely agricultural communities were never entirely self-reliant. All of them had a need for some market to obtain goods or to dispose of their produce. At the same time, many farms were cultivated as part of a widespread complex of estates and perhaps specialised in some produce or other under central management, like the great medieval sheep farms of the fenland monasteries. Every community was part of a wider region, a natural one or a man-made one, and changes within the hinterland could cause changes in the local economic structure as new resources in labour and materials became available or old ones were removed.

The relationship between the local community and the region was one of transport and communications rather than just simply one of distance. If on occasion goods could not be brought easily to a nearby market but could be taken more readily to another some few extra miles away, then the local community was more closely attached to the further market centre than to the nearer. The area within which any place was set was thus determined by the ease of communications. There were, of course, many things which affected this — physical features like rivers or high land, man-made facilities like roads, bridges and tunnels, or indeed man-made restrictions like marketing privileges and immunities. And if this is true, then changes in the patterns of communications could create new regional boundaries. This has been demonstrated in modern times by the construction of motorways, by which places formerly remote have become easily available because they lie close to the new routes, while other places earlier regarded as lying within relatively easy travelling reach now seem more distant.

Regions thus depend to a large extent on communications. These have been constantly changing throughout man's recorded history. Thus regions themselves are never absolutely static, are frequently altering, if only marginally. Rivers have become silted up or canalised; roads deteriorated or were improved; the mechanics of transport changed. And each of these affected the area that the local community depended upon. Of course, such changes are not the only ones to influence the regions. Changing fashions and a greater prosperity could result in large towns going further for fresh food, thus creating a demand for improved communications. It was the call of the London markets for live stock rather than salted meat which helped to establish several of the so-called 'drove' roads in eastern England. The region and its roads (or other means of transport) are inextricably conjoined.

It must not be assumed that these changes were always forced upon the local communities by outside influences of the natural persuasion of irresistible geographical and economic forces. This was far from the truth. Some of them were, of course; opposition to the railway movement in the nineteenth century was frequently as futile as resistance to the modern motorway bulldozer. Other changes, however, were created from within the community, in the search for new outlets or new enterprises. But communications had two ends — and it must have been very rare for both ends, let alone the communities in the middle, to agree beforehand on the needs and mutual benefits which made the newer means of communication desirable. The question 'which end did it start from?' is not an unreasonable one to ask of any new project in communications.

The relationship between the local community and its region was a Janus-like one, with two faces. On the one side, changes which took place within the region were bound to affect the local community. The fluctuations in the Cornish tin mines, for instance, or the changes in agricultural produce in eastern England consequent upon the enclosure of the heaths and marshes caused the decline of old markets and industries or the creation of new ones. Thus population itself could be affected by the ease with which surplus labour could leave the community or extra labour could be drawn in, if necessary. On the other hand, new means of communications, often developed to meet this kind of situation, would bring a whole new hinterland to bear upon the community and thus would change its economic structure and indeed its social composition. It was to changes in patterns of communications (or rather the lack of them) that Norwich owed the loss of its textile industry to the West Riding of Yorkshire.[1]

Local topography
But changes in the pattern of communications not only affected the economic and social structure of the local community; they frequently affected the topography of the economy within the place. New roads were laid down in and around the town; new industrial or commercial interests were established. What is more, there is often a direct physical relationship between the pattern of communications and the manufacturing and distributive industries. The location of factories and warehouses at or near railway stations is well known; the development of hotels along the line of urban turnpike roads can similarly be charted. How many canals have a Wharf Road or something analogous? There are many other features to this study of the topography of communications. Even rural communities were affected, especially by the passage of a nearby railway.

Transport and communications are only one of many factors affecting the economy of the local community. But it is an important one. Indeed, in one sense the whole of this chapter can be seen as a preliminary enquiry before attempting to discuss the economy of the local community. In isolating it for special study, it is not intended to give undue prominence to it. Rather it will serve as a case study of the ways in which changes came about and how the local historian can trace them.

The questions the historian may thus ask in relation to this topic would seem to come down to three. First, what was the existing (or natural) pattern of communications and to what region did this pattern relate the local community? Secondly, what changes came about in this pattern? Why and how did they take place? Were they locally inspired (and financed) or the result of outside pressure? And thirdly, what results did these changes have upon the local community? — in terms of the region which surrounded the place, and its internal population, economy and topography. There are, of course, other aspects, but these would seem to be the major ones.

2

Rivers

The general outline of development of the main means of transport — roads, waterways and railways — in the historic period is by now well known and hardly needs repetition here as a background to local studies. Nevertheless a number of general points emerge. Only the railways are capable of a close chronology, certainly in their origin — the other two are equally ancient. The use of water transport did not start with the canal age of the Duke of Bridgewater. It is often forgotten how important water traffic was in the Middle Ages — not just in towns like London where the Thames was the main high road for both goods and passengers, nor just for the main river ports like Bristol on the Avon or Chester on the Dee. For all sorts of goods through much of English history, the rivers (aided and abetted by man) were as much arteries for traffic as were the roads. In 1301 Edward I held a parliament at Lincoln, and the goods needed to feed his extended court during the session arrived in that town from all over the east midlands and north country, as much in boats or on rafts as on wheels or on foot.[2]

Roads

This use of waterways was not entirely due to the bad roads of the Middle Ages; indeed these bad roads are probably another great misconception. There were roads, and good ones, in medieval England. The Gough map of the mid-fourteenth century[3] shows that several of the Roman roads had lost their earlier significance but very few of the important ones were completely lost. Many were carefully maintained and to these were added others, more local in character but still useful and used.

Nor was this road system static; the local historian must be aware of the changes within his region. Some of these were the result of natural development, others of human agencies. Especially important was the building of bridges, regarded for much of the Middle Ages as a special work of piety and frequently resulting in important deviations of routes. Many of them were completed long before the earliest maps were drawn and can only be traced in the course of detailed field studies on the ground itself. It would now seem, for instance, that there were several crossings of the river Welland at Stamford instead of just one 'ford', a fact deduced from fieldwork and completely lost in terms of the later records relating to that town.

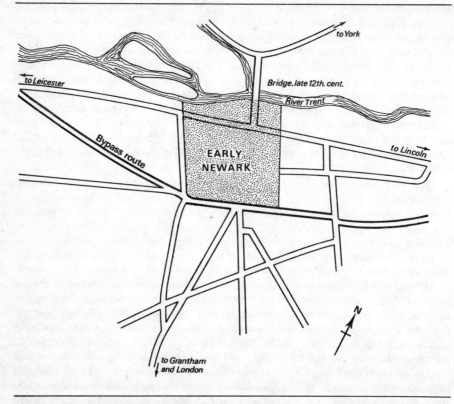

to York

Bridge, late 12th. cent.

to Leicester

River Trent

Bypass route

EARLY
NEWARK

to Lincoln

N

to Grantham
and London

Fig. 20   The medieval by-pass to the walled town of Newark.

Some of these changes had far-reaching results, others were purely of local significance. Newark (in Notts) provides a good example of both of these. Here a bridge
was built over the Trent about 1170, the first and only crossing of this great river
below Nottingham. The result was the creation of the Great North Road, running
through Huntingdon, Stamford, Grantham and Newark and on to York via
Doncaster, in place of the earlier road through Nottingham. One bridge brought
beneficial results to several communities many miles away, but harmful results to
others like Nottingham and Lincoln.[4] On the other hand there were many more
local changes. At Newark again a route by-passing the defended town eventually
became one of its main shopping thoroughfares, and such a process is not unknown
in other towns (see Fig. 20). Rural colonisation and land reclamation similarly
created new local roads, while others died out through lack of use or deliberate
obliteration. The process was as unceasing as migration and was, of course, very
closely related to such redistribution of population.

It is thus apparent that the chronology of road changes was much the same as
that of the major factors affecting population movements. Enclosures and the
formation of private estates had their own consequences in the pattern of routes;
indeed much of the process was a formalisation and restriction of passage rights
over areas where previously there had been much informal traffic. Heath roads
emerged, backlanes along the edges of built-up areas, set roads over common land,

lanes between urban property. It is unlikely that there was ever any let-up in the process. Especially important in all of this was the fossilisation of private property. The creation of parks saw local diversion of roads; some early enclosures cut off older roads. The increasing permanence of the common fields system which seems to characterise many local communities in the seventeenth century itself provoked larger measures of enclosure (mostly parliamentary), and in these cases complete new systems of internal roads became possible. Probably the only political incentive for the creation of major new roads came in the first half of the eighteenth century, when the Jacobite rebellions provoked the work of General Wade (1726–37) and later John Metcalf of Knaresborough (Blind Jack), but the small scale of these efforts is shown by the fact that from 1767 to 1792, the latter built only about 180 miles of new road.

How far the deterioration of roads in the seventeenth and eighteenth centuries was due to neglect or to increasing traffic or indeed to that process of restriction of common rights of passage so that more traffic had to pass over narrower routes is not clear, but deteriorate they did, as Arthur Young demonstrated in the 1770s. And this precisely at the time when, as recent work has shown, they came to be used on a systematic basis more heavily than ever. The importance of the road network to drovers and especially to carriers, the former defining the through-routes and the latter defining the local region at the centre of which stood some larger or smaller market town, caused increasing concern.[5] The result, at least for most of the more important routes between major centres of population, was the turnpike system; for urban areas, increasing measures for paving and improving the streets; and for rural areas, increasing enforcement of the parochial system of maintenance.

One of the most important of these for the local historian is the local turnpike movement, beginning in the very early eighteenth century and spreading rapidly throughout the country. It is sometimes forgotten that turnpike trusts rarely created *new* roads. Most of their work was devoted to improving older roads or (by a process of straightening) to turning minor roads into major ones. Some new roads were however established over heathland, generally in association with enclosure projects; others were closely linked with drainage systems or other land improvements. New bridges (at least made possible in some cases by canalisation of river channels) opened the way for newer, shorter routes. Nor was the work of the trusts restricted to the open spaces between settlements; within several towns, new roads were cut or others improved. The trusts were at the height of their activities by the 1760s and they continued in existence well into the nineteenth century – not indeed as providers but at least as maintainers of roads and collectors of tolls.[6]

Despite the development of waterways, the roads remained the major bearers of traffic throughout the whole of this period. Particularly important to the local community were the older, non-turnpiked roads, maintained by the parish under legislation of 1555. On these roads, local residents had to provide labour for four (later six) days each year or provide carriage, under the supervision of a surveyor, elected by the parish or, after 1691, nominated by the justices.[7] Rates were soon collected in lieu of service in many communities. But the parish was unequal to the task which was made more difficult by two main developments. On the one hand, there was the substitution of widespread wheeled traffic (corn waggons and stage coaches and the like) for pack and post horses. On the other hand, the development of canals and main turnpike roads created a demand for ancillary service roads, much as the motorways are doing today. This was especially true of the towns where new roads were laid out by paving commissioners to join turnpikes, like London Road in King's Lynn (Norfolk) in 1804—5 (Plate 23).

Canals

The growth of canals, of course, was not confined to the eighteenth century; nor did they start with the Duke of Bridgewater although it can be said that His Grace's project, with its immediate and spectacular results on the local price of coal, opened the Canal Age, the development of a national system of waterways.[8] There were very many earlier 'new cuts' and river improvements. Exeter in 1564—7 first developed the process of raising water by means of locks, and several local navigation Acts followed, like that for Stamford in 1570. In the early eighteenth century a number of connections were made between rivers.[9] Much of the seventeenth and early eighteenth centuries' drainage movement was as closely related to traffic as to land use, in two ways — the channelling of rivers through their flood plains often made them navigable and it certainly made them bridgeable. Nevertheless, it was the opening of the coal traffic from Worsley to Manchester in 1761 which caught the imagination and speculative instincts of contemporaries, and a flood of new projects followed — James Brindley's second link of Manchester to the Mersey in 1776, the Grand Trunk Canal (1777) joining the Mersey to the Trent (the first route across England from east to west and at Harecastle the first really long canal tunnel of nearly two miles) and the Thames—Severn canal joining with the Stroudwater navigation in 1789 coming soon after in quick succession. Nor were there just new canals dug; old rivers were rehabilitated for traffic. The peak period for canal and navigation Acts was from 1760 to 1795, but there continued a regular stream into the 1830s until a complete network had been created, representing a vast investment in terms of money and labour.

Although compared with some European examples English canals (and canal boats) were small, they had a profound effect on the English local community. Whole towns grew up because of them, from Brigg (in Lincs) to Stourport (Worcs). Within others, the canals brought new developments, like the establishment of Trafford Park in Manchester in the 1890s (a late example, it is true, but in some respects merely the culmination of much earlier development).[10] But it was not only the immediate towns which benefited; the impact of the canals was felt in many fairly remote parts of rural England, where even today Anchor Inns may be found on the edge of stagnant pools. They were particularly important for the carriage of goods, especially coal — indeed Birmingham grew up at the heart of the Midland complex of canals. But passenger traffic was not unimportant and it was on the rivers of England that steam packets were first developed, just as canals provoked the first establishment of reservoirs. It may be hard to trace exactly the influence of a canal on the communities it passed by, but it certainly affected the people considerably.

This raises the question of the origin of the canal urge in any local community. There are signs that there was a demand for more waterways than were ever finally established. The residents of Stamford, for instance, talked constantly and at length about several projects to connect their town with the Midlands, with Leicester or Melton Mowbray or Grantham (and thus with the Trent), but nothing ever came of the scheme. The men of Grantham proposed a connection to Newark but in the end it was the longer route to Nottingham that was built. Such discussions, whether abortive or not, form the stuff of local history, for they reveal the community in action, trying to promote its own interests; while the strains which making such a project work imposed on local resources (not least the local banks) show something of the strength and weaknesses of the local economy. The involvement of the community in the project is a sure sign of the major impact of these waterways on the community. The same is true also of coastal shipping for ports on or near the coast.

Nineteenth century

The situation in the early nineteenth century was thus one of rivalry between water and road, a friendly rivalry, not bitter. In King's Lynn, for instance, coaches to London began to replace water traffic from the mid-eighteenth century. The turn-pikes reached their hey-day in the great age of the stage coach (*c.* 1810—40), with some 23,000 miles of road maintained from tolls charged at some 7,800 toll gates. Improvements in route planning by Thomas Telford and others, and in road making, maintenance and administration by McAdam and others, were having their effect; but there was also growing hostility. The riot of Rebecca's sisters (1842—3) was only one of several local incidents revealing the strength of popular opposition to road tolls. From 1830 (when there were more than 1,000 trusts) amalgamations and discharge resulted in a rapid fall in numbers, especially after the parliamentary committee of 1864, to about 200 in 1880; in 1895, there was only one trust left.

The whole administration of roads was changed in the course of the nineteenth century. The 1835 General Highways Acts established some elective highway boards in place of the paving commissioners; from 1862, highway districts could be formed from unions of parishes reluctant to continue road maintenance on their own, but only a few were in fact so established. In 1878, the Highways and Locomotives Act, the first to establish that roads must be 'adopted' before being maintained, created the designation of 'main road' whose maintenance was subject to the supervision of first the quarter sessions and later (from the Acts of 1888 and 1894) of the County Councils. The various reforms in urban government during the century enabled further internal road development, especially associated with the railways, to be undertaken. Restrictions on traffic, like medieval town walls and gates, were removed, and roads were widened. Road surfaces improved immensely, the mud or cobbles and stone flags giving way gradually from about the 1860s to asphalt or granite or wood blocks.

If roads came into new hands, the canals died, sometimes a slow lingering death, at other times a sudden Damoclean disaster. Their costs and slowness told against them, and from the 1840s they felt the competition of railway traffic. But it was the railway companies who generally served the *coup de grâce*, on occasions apparently undeserved.

Railways

The sudden appearance of the railways on this scene is a story by now well rehearsed, from the early horse tramways and cast-iron 'plateways' in colliery areas. The development of private or indeed of the first public railways from the Act of 1801 setting up the Surrey Iron Railway Company affected very few places, while the tale of the early trials of the steam developers is not of great significance to the local historian. The general movement for railways in almost every corner of the island began in 1830, and like the 'canal rage' began at Manchester with the line to Liverpool. In 1837, during the first of the railway 'manias', Birmingham was joined to Lancashire and in 1838 to London. Huge sums were involved; the latter line cost some £5½ million. The start was slow but from 1845 to 1855 came a great spurt. There was very little planning save the over-riding political supervision of

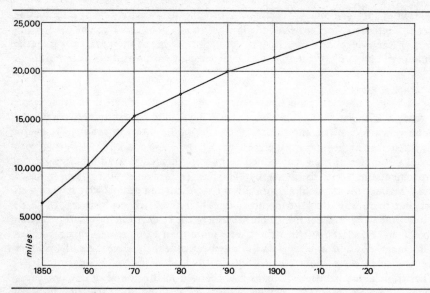

Fig. 21   Railway mileage increase in nineteenth century

Parliament. More than 600 main line Acts and some 500 extensions or alterations were authorised by Parliament by 1850, of which some 6,620 miles of line had been completed. It was the rivalry of companies which dictated routes and services.

After 1850 there was a slow process of amalgamation of companies until the government began to discourage it from the 1870s, but the building of the tracks (improved ones, made of steel, with better signalling and other technical advances) continued unabated (Fig. 21), from 6,600 miles in 1850 to 23,400 in 1910. Apart from the Great Central route into Marylebone (1893), the main line system was completed by the 1870s. Thereafter it was a process of infilling or the opening of new tunnels (like the Severn in 1886) and bridges making for shorter routes.

The importance of all this to the local historian is obvious. First there were the main lines. Why did they run here and not there? Not all such decisions were taken at a long distance from the local community. Colonel Sibthorp, the Lincoln M.P. who bitterly opposed the new means of transport, was matched by George Hudson ('I'll mak all t'railways come to York') or Colonel Tomline, 'the Lord of Orwell' at Felixstowe, whose private railway (jocularly called the 'Tomline') was built in 1875–7 in the hopes of promoting a dock town there (and at the same time to snub a neighbour, J. C. Cobbold).[11] Coventry was by-passed for the sake of Birmingham, to the grief of many of its citizens who saw their goods 'whirled by their own doors'.[12] Then came the process of building local lines and the heart-searching that this involved, the haggling over land values, the frequent replanning of local lines and so on.

And the results were enormous, although, of course, they depended to a certain extent on the frequency of the local services. It is really not clear whether the railways did kill viable local markets and fairs; there was a good deal of care taken to build strategic stations. But the ease with which goods, especially those now being mass-produced for the new customers, could be obtained from places far away affected communities many miles from the railheads. The standard of living in most parts of England was irrevocably altered. But just as important was the effect on mobility. The neighbouring town and all its amenities became that much closer; jobs and holidays could be pursued more easily; in 1851 a Nottingham joiner could get married in a St Pancras church simply because he and his bride were on a visit to the Great Exhibition.[13] A new dimension had come into the lives of the members of the local community.

Harrogate marks a number of these trends clearly. The first railway lines opened there in 1848–9; by 1862 when the central station was built, there were frequent and fast services to Leeds, York, London and the north, and these services improved as time went on. The result was there for all to see. Holiday visitors, often breaking their trips from Scotland back to London, increased greatly in the course of three years,[14] from about 12,000 to some 20,000 by 1850; by the 1860s, this had become about 30,000, by 1890, 50,000 and by 1910, 75,000. Secondly, more commuters from Leeds and Bradford settled in the new estates being built in the town, like Victoria Park. This can be seen, not only in the scale and kind of building work going on but in the increase in the numbers of daily trains to Leeds — 10 in 1862, 12 in 1874, 16 in 1887. Changes came over the economy too, with 'quality' shopkeepers, formerly seasonal only, now settling permanently in Harrogate, while building became a major industry, based on good local stone and wealthy customers. At Starbeck (once a separate village), railway workshops and other industries developed. The population of the borough more than trebled from 1861 to 1891.

The results of the railways were not only felt in the economy and way of life of the people; they were also profoundly felt in the very shape of the local settlement. At first, up to the late 1850s, most stations were built on the edges of towns; it was only later that 'the Centrals' were established. Then they were often put among the most crowded parts of the towns, clearing away acres of 'rookeries' but creating a worse housing shortage than before.[15] St Pancras station is one of the most remarkable of these stories. It was built on land 'occupied by a canal, a gas-works, an ancient church with a large and crowded graveyard, and some of the most atrocious slums in London; and through it all ran the Fleet River'.[16] There were two main housing areas, Somers Town (a decayed area) and Agar Town, a 'shanty town' of the worst sort which had grown up in the early nineteenth century. The railway company bought out the landlords in the 1860s, and the latter evicted the tenants without compensation so that demolition and railway development could begin (see Plate 22, p. 124).

The coming of the station was only the start of much reconstruction. Generally its immediate presence lowered the status of the neighbouring residential areas. More frequently industrial works came to be centred around the station. At Harrogate the location of the station determined the location of the main hotel development;[17] thus Low Harrogate captured the shopping and hotel interests to the exclusion of High Harrogate, cut off as it was from the new station. New or widened roads to link the commercial areas with the station were everywhere planned and often built.

Lincoln is a particularly good example of this development. Around the head of the waterway system (Brayford Pool, the junction of the Roman Fosse Dyke, reconstructed in 1741–5, and the Witham Navigation, 1760–6) and along the side of the Witham, there developed the large warehouses which are still a feature of the area (Fig. 22). There were breweries and maltings in both Brayford Head and Waterside. Bone and seed crushers, coal merchants, corn millers and millwrights congregated in this industrial belt; in 1842 Lincoln's two main ironfounders were in the

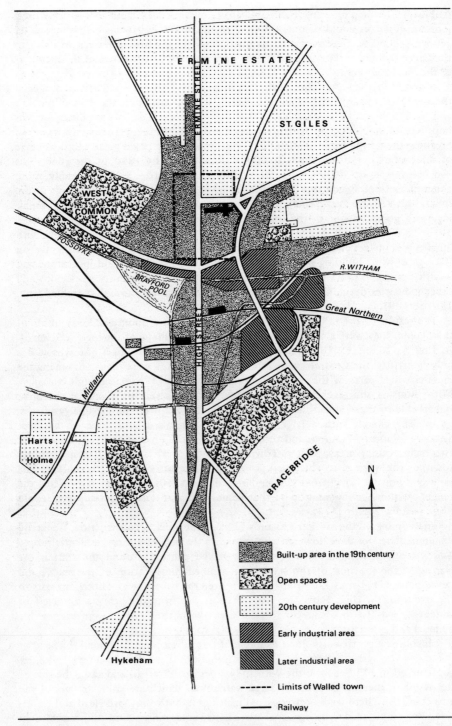

Fig. 22 Plan of Lincoln showing modern development.

Plate 19 Aerial view of
Lincoln from the east. In the
centre back is Brayford Pool,
the junction of the Fosse Dyke
and the River Witham (which
leaves the town *centre front*).
The first industrial area lay
around the pool and between
the river and the old city which
lies on the *right* of the photograph. The railway yards and
the newer industrial area *bottom
left hand corner* can be clearly
seen.

neighbourhood of Waterside. The first railway (the Midland Company line to Lincoln from Nottingham and Newark) opened in 1846 and two years later a loop line of the Great Northern from Boston was completed. The Midland station was situated to the west of High Street, nearer to the water of Brayford. But the Great Northern outdid its rival by buying out the Fosse Dyke and Witham Navigations. Their new station was set to the east of High Street with an imposing railway hotel. Already there had been some industrial development in this region but it was the railway which promoted the establishment by 1856 of Clayton, Shuttleworth and Co. and of Robey & Scott, both of them situated closer to the main route to London, Manchester and Sheffield. There is little reason to doubt that it was the presence of the station which encouraged the industrial development to the east of Sincil Dyke until the area became the centre of Lincoln's heavy engineering industry (Plate 19).

Such concentrations of industrial and business premises were continued in the 1860s and 1870s by the rapid development of internal transport systems. Buses, first appearing generally in the 1830s, were frequent and well used by the middle of the century and carried large numbers of persons. Steamboats were also used but declined in numbers. On the other hand, local railways quickly developed; horse (and later steam) trams became common from the 1870s; the London underground commenced in 1863. Whole systems of suburban railways and tramways prolifer-ated, enabling commuting to become the normal way of life for the middle-class worker and again creating great changes in urban topography. Similar developments were not unknown in rural areas, for trams on occasion ran through the countryside while the single track branch line served much the same function as the suburban railway round the larger cities. The effects of the railways were ubiquitous.

Some places of course were created by the railways — industrial centres like Crewe and Swindon and holiday resorts like Skegness (Lincs) and Seaford (Sussex). Skegness is particularly interesting. The small village on the coast was already becoming a watering place with three hotels and a number of lodging houses by the 1870s; there had been 'bathing machines' from at least 1784. But population had fallen from 1841 in common with other agricultural and fishing communities. The first plans to bring the railway to the east coast were based on a desire for docks rather than the possibility of holiday traffic, but these never materialised. In the early 1870s however, the earl of Scarborough took up the railway cause and in 1873 a branch line from Wainfleet was opened. Thereafter the earl laid out Skegness on his own land as a resort town. The Great Northern Railway Company took no part in this process (as they did elsewhere) but co-operated in making excursion facilities easily available. The development however was the work of the Scarborough estate and it affected the whole shape of the town[18] (Figs 23 and 24).

Seaford (Sussex)
Not all resorts were created out of nothing by the railways. Several were flourishing earlier in the century on a basis of steamboats and coaches — especially those (like Margate) near London or others (like Rhyl) near Lancashire and in south-west Scotland. But it was the railway which promoted these (and other newer centres) beyond recognition, as well as changing holiday patterns. At Seaford (Sussex), the coming of the railway did not mean, as it had for Doncaster and Peterborough, a very rapid change in the town's character. It did however arrest a long process of stagnation and make possible the development of 'the least gay of the chain of south coast seaside places',[19] extending its area and accelerating its population

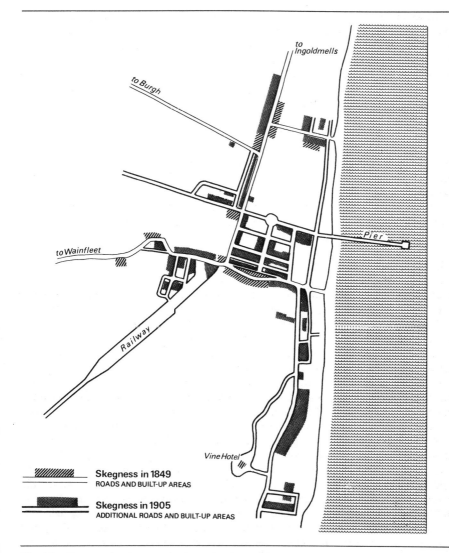

Roads and built-up areas legend:

Skegness in 1849
ROADS AND BUILT-UP AREAS

Skegness in 1905
ADDITIONAL ROADS AND BUILT-UP AREAS

Fig. 23   Skegness development in the early nineteenth century.

growth. The line was a single track, 2¼ mile extension of the London, Brighton and South Coast Railway's line from Lewes to Newhaven. Although it was authorised together with that line in 1845, it was not opened until June 1864;[20] why is not immediately apparent.

The town itself was a long decayed medieval port, cut off from its former trade by the accumulation of longshore drift and shifts in the Ouse estuary, so much so that only ten of its inhabitants in 1851 had any connection with the sea, as fishermen. It was a huddle of indifferent buildings, separated from the sea by a marshy common which flooded regularly. The corporation, a survival of minor Cinque Port status, owned this and a small baths adjoining the beach. A few gentry and London merchants owned houses in the town, probably to escape the fleshy delights of

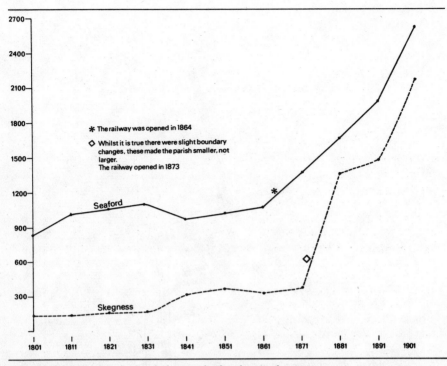

Fig. 24   Growth of Seaford and Skegness in the nineteenth century.

Brighton. Otherwise, its population was largely agricultural, with the small service element its size demanded. The population had fluctuated between 847 and 1,098 until 1861, when it began a steady rise from 1,054 to 2,615 in 1901 (Fig. 24).

The line itself came in at the west end of the town; it was unambitious but required considerable engineering. For much of its length, it crossed salt marshes and needed embankments; nearer the town, it had to cross some low hill outcrops through cuttings.[21] This provided a workable gradient and the track ran fairly straight, avoiding expensive curves, to a small terminus, enlarged when the line was doubled in 1905. Its construction provided shelter for a small string of later Victorian villas and rows of workers' cottages. In turn, the embanking of the promenade towards the end of the century sheltered the track at its most exposed point.

As the line was being constructed, a local landowner, Dr Tyler Smith, put forward a modest proposal for expanding the resort. He acquired a 299 year lease of the salt common from the corporation, and began a small development of hotels and boarding houses, with an Assembly Rooms on the site of the baths (Fig. 25).[22] This did not progress easily – a major flood swamped the site in 1875. Only when the railway company extended the Newhaven harbour defences in the 1890s did the bay become more sheltered. Even so, the small line of grey hotels was separated from the older town by open land until recently. The beach lacked sand and Seaford never became a day tripper's Mecca. It did acquire in 1864 a gas works, the indubitable sign of urban growth, and a small group of shops near the station gradually widened the services available to the population. The town grew slowly into a modest resort for the quieter middle classes who came increasingly to choose

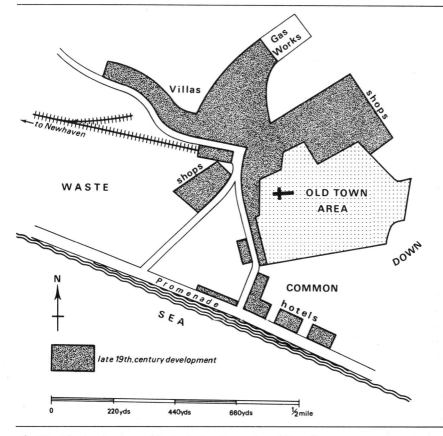

Fig. 25   The development of Seaford after the coming of the railway.

it as a place for retirement as well as holidays. It is very doubtful whether this would have happened without the 2¼ miles of single track.

Many other examples can be given of the way in which the coming of the railways affected the life of the local communities. Few changes in communications have had such far-reaching and sudden effects as did the steam monsters in the second half of the nineteenth century. Perhaps it may be matched by the decline of the many small ports around the coast, killed by the silting up of river estuaries and the increase in size of ships as well as by railway competition. Some kept alive on the increasing holiday traffic, aided this time by the railway and the development of hotels. But others, like Burnham Overy and Blakeney in Norfolk, fell into insignificance, only partially to revive in the twentieth century with the coming of the car. The story is of course still going on.

3

Sources: early roads
As with so many of these topics, there are no sources for a systematic study of transport and communications in the local community before the nineteenth

century. Rather it is a piecing together of scattered fragments and drawing deductions from casual references. It is Domesday Book, for instance, which hints that the main road to York ran through Nottingham. For local routes, the evidence becomes more tangible. Although there are virtually no direct records relating to marketing activity, a study of estate accounts and household accounts may show how far the effects of individual markets reached, where people went for their goods. In the sixteenth century, for instance, the Hatchers of Careby in south Lincolnshire went not only to the nearby markets at Stamford, Grantham and Stow Green but also as far as Newark, Nottingham, Spilsby, Melton Mowbray and indeed into Derbyshire — well over 30 or even 40 miles from their estate.[23] Passing references in the archives of neighbouring places may be important in this connection; it is from Leicester borough records that we learn that Leicester merchants had stalls in Stamford market. Clearly the local historian must be prepared to search for hints about his local transport system, especially in the records of the nearest large town. The same thing is true of early water traffic — estate and business papers, some government returns like taxation accounts and many other miscellaneous sources may be drawn upon to provide a few notices of the nature of river trade. The description by Defoe of King's Lynn in the 1720s:

'a well situated Town, at the Mouth of the River Ouse . . . which gives it a vast Advantage in Trade . . . the Merchants of Lynn supply about 6 Counties wholly, and 3 Counties in part, with their Goods, especially Wine and Coals . . . they bring in more Coals, than any Sea-port between London and Newcastle; and import Wines than any Port in England, except London and Bristol. Their Trade to Norway, and to the Baltic Sea is also great in Proportion, and of late Years they have extended their Trade farther to the Southward,'[24]

shows how valuable such contemporary comment can be on this, as on so many other aspects of the local historian's task.[25]

The most important source however is clearly the map, combined with field studies. Early maps were largely concentrated on routes between towns, like the medieval Gough map and Ogilby's *Atlas* of the late seventeenth century. This latter is particularly important not only for the places it describes but for those lying near to the routes. Such early route maps are not always available but there are others. Several counties now have lists of early printed maps and these are invaluable for the study of early road systems. As long ago as 1907, Sir Hubert Fordham traced no less than 60 printed maps or editions of maps for Hertfordshire and 46 for Cambridgeshire for the years before 1800, and other counties are similarly well placed. Even where these do not exist in such profusion or provide little information, a careful study of modern maps can yield a great deal of fruit. Early roads, sometimes now vanished or mere footpaths or green lanes, can often be traced across the ground. In areas of extensive agricultural reorganisation, the older system may have vanished; but generally some of the main roads still survive even in those towns where development was most dense in the nineteenth century. And even where new roads were laid out, as in the enclosure movement, they were laid out for a purpose, to fit the current patterns of movement.

Within the parish (urban or rural) the minutes of the vestry and especially the accounts of the highways' surveyor, where they survive, may reveal much of traffic and the state of the roads; and the records of quarter sessions will supplement these. Within the towns, these are paralleled from the late seventeenth century by the records of paving or improvement commissioners as at Exeter or by corporation injunctions concerning road maintenance. Again, poor law records may indicate where paupers came from and where they were sent to in cases where settlement was denied, thus throwing some light on the routes through the locality. In the same way, the accounts of noble households will on occasion give the roads followed by peripatetic lords. It is most unlikely that none of this material will exist for any particular locality. But this may be true of a few places and in this case the local historian must rely upon the modern map with a close study of the ground and the liberal use of common sense.

For turnpikes, where they apply, the local historian is on surer ground. The companies which were formed to run the trusts left behind them a considerable body of records. There are, it is true, relatively few comprehensive collections of company records — minute books, accounts of tolls, leases of toll bars, investment of capital in road improvements and the like[26] — though some of these do exist, often among the papers from solicitors' offices or in County Record Offices. But if a turnpike road existed through or near a local community, it can be traced fairly easily. There are many published guide maps showing the routes and the location of the bars, and there are often the toll houses themselves scattered over the countryside.

Details of the running of these turnpike roads can be discovered from two main sources. Turnpike trusts were both subject to regulation and at the same time dependent on the public, and in both respects the records reflect their position. On the one hand, there are the records of the supervisory bodies. Parliament was concerned, especially with the initial establishment of the trust (usually for a limited period) or the terms of subsequent alterations and extensions. In the process of passing turnpike Acts, large accumulations of records were created and those which survive (there was a disastrous fire in 1834) are now in the House of Lords Record Office. Apart from the Act itself, there are in many cases plans, minutes of committees, petitions, lists of subscribers and other financial papers. A search of the *Journals* of both houses may reveal the stages in the parliamentary procedure.[27] And such trusts, once established, were from 1792 made subject to the regulation of the local J.P.s. Thus among the records of the quarter sessions are a number of turnpike papers, plans, lists of tolls, returns of revenue collected and the like, in addition to copies of the most useful of the parliamentary papers.

Apart from the formal papers however, there are the records of the trusts' dealings with the public, most noticeably in the newspapers. Advertisements of the lease of toll bars and notices of tolls themselves emanate from the clerk of the trust. Local comment on the opening of new roads as well as travel incidents, the amount of traffic (and especially concern at the decay of commerce when it occurred) may be found in these pages. Public meetings to promote schemes and meetings of shareholders are often reported. It is rare for the local historian of transport to be able to ignore the local press with impunity.

Water routes

The same range of source material, company records, parliamentary papers and quarter sessions records, are needed for any account of water traffic and canals.[28] Rather more of the canal companies' records survive than turnpike trusts, for most of the canals and many of the docks were bought out by the railways and in some cases the records have passed into the possession of the British Transport Historical Record Office. Other bodies, especially the courts of sewers and the Navigation Companies, were taken over by the River Boards, and minute books, letter books, ledgers, inventories and the like may be found among the papers of these authorities. There may be miscellaneous records as well, like correspondence relating to the canals among private estate papers. But once again it is the newspapers which provide the less formal details and often the bulk of the information as in the case of river traffic. Especially valuable here are parliamentary papers relating to neighbouring canals, for new projects led to counter-petitions rehearsing the disastrous results which would flow if the scheme was allowed to go ahead. Similarly the records of other towns affected by the trade may yield information; it is among the records of the port of Hull that much light can be found for the flow of traffic on the Trent.[29] The papers relating to the abortive Stamford canal are among the borough records and others exist similarly, often with their own reports, plans, minutes of meetings and the like, while the urban corporation often had some say in the control of river traffic. Finally, at the end of the period, J. Phillips's *General History of Inland Navigation* (1795) provides an easy point of reference for most local schemes.

It is not easy to study the early topographical effects of changes in communications and such studies have not yet been done at all widely. But field surveys, the study of the location of industrial monuments, of street and field names and early maps all help to show something of the concentrations of early industries and may suggest some of the many reasons for them.

4

Nineteenth century sources

The nineteenth century is different only in that many more records survive. It is thus possible to trace this subject in greater detail for almost all communities. But the range of sources is much the same. There is a growing body of parliamentary papers, especially the official reports (blue books), on all aspects of the subject.[30] Parish roads became increasingly subject to the supervision of the clerk of the peace's office, and returns of local expenditure may often be found among the papers of the quarter sessions. Parliamentary returns were called for on several occasions but most of these contain county totals only, not the expenditure of the more local units. The most important of these are the returns for 1818 and the reports of the Royal Commission on Roads established in 1840.[31] The turnpike trusts and their fortunes are fully traced in the successive parliamentary reports which dealt with them. Accounts were submitted from 1824 and local evidence collected from 1836.[32] The abolition of the turnpikes produced a series of most valuable papers, among them the returns of the roads taken over by the local highway boards and the returns of turnpike roads 'dis-turnpiked', 1871–8.[33]

Roads without services are like empty houses. Details of the traffic, especially the main through-traffic like stage coaches, may be obtained from newspaper notices, a few surviving posters and from local directories. The latter come into their own in several respects, for some of the information they supply cannot be obtained from other sources. They reveal for instance local carriage and postal communications, especially for rural communities. New urban roads are also generally recorded here as well as in the newspapers and borough records. In addition fuller series of large-scale maps survive; at least nine printed maps are known to exist for nineteenth-century King's Lynn, for example.

There are fewer parliamentary reports covering all canals; indeed, the earliest

			1	2	3	4	5 6	7	8	9	10	11	12	13	14	15	16	17	1	2	3	4
	Harrogate	Dep	7 58	8 45	9 20		11 32		2 8	2 59	4 15		6 40		8 30		9 0		10 7			8 15
	STARBECK								2 13													
	PANNAL		8 7		(a)				2 21				6 48				(e)		10 17			8 23
	WEETON		8 16		(a)				2 28				6 56				(e)		10 25			8 30
	ARTHINGTON JUNCTION		8 24		9 42	11 17	11 48	1 32	2 35	3 19	4 32	6 22	7 3		8 47		9 17		10 32			8 38
	Ilkley	Arr	9 4		10 22		12 35				5 37		8 15									
	Ilkley	Dep	7 45		9 10	10 45		1 0				5 50										
	HORSFORTH		8 34	9 5	9 52	11 27	11 58	1 42	2 45	3 29		6 22	7 13		8 55		9 25		10 42			8 47
	HEADINGLEY		8 41		9 58	11 33	12 5	1 48	2 52	3 35		6 38	7 20		9 1		9 31		10 49			8 55
	HOLBECK JUNCTION		8 51	9 18	10 5	11 39	12 15	1 54	3 2	3 44	4 48	6 44	7 28		9 10		9 40		10 55			9 5
	Leeds (New Station)	Arr	9 0	9 25	10 15	11 45	12 30	2 0	3 10	3 50	4 55	6 50	7 35		9 20		9 50		11 5			9 15
	Bradford Mid.	Arr	9 35	9 45	10 58		12 55		3 35	4 50	5 50	8 5			9 55		10 35		1 40			9 55
	Bradford, G. N.		9 50	9 50	10 50		1 0	2 30	3 30	4 35	5 50		7 55		9 50		10 45		11 30			10 40
			a.m.	a.m.	a.m.		p.m.		p.m.	p.m.	p.m.				p.m.							p.m.
Midland Railway.	**Leeds**	Dep	10 30	10 30	10 30		12 45		5 10	5 10	5 10				10 5							10 5
	Sheffield	Arr	11 55	11 55	11 55		2 15		6 35	6 35	6 35				11 35							11 35
	Derby		12 50	12 50	12 50		3 10		7 35	7 25	7 35				12 22							12 22
	Birmingham		2 20	2 20	2 20		5 0		9 30	9 30	9 30				2 2							2 2
	Bristol		5 35	5 35	5 35		7 55								5 55							5 55
	London (Euston Sq.						8 15								6 0							6 0
	London (St. Pancras)		4 0	4 0	4 0		6 40		11 0	11 0	11 0				4 15							4 15
			a.m.	a.m.	a.m.		p.m.		p.m.	p.m.	p.m.		p.m.				p. m.		a.m.			
L. & Y. Ry.	**Holbeck**	Dep	9 20	9 20	11 3		12 45		3 55	3 55	5 3		8 4				10 3		11 8			
	Manchester, (Victoria)	Arr	11 35	11 35	1 46		3 15		6 15	6 15	7 30		11 10				1 10		2 0			
	Fleetwood		2 25	2 25	4 40		7 5												9 0			
	Liverpool, (Exchange)		1 0	1 0	2 55		4 28				9 5								4 5			
	Holbeck	Dep		10 15			12 50		4 8	4 8	5 18		7 55									
	Wakefield	Arr		10 35			1 13		4 32	4 32	5 45		8 20									
	Barnsley	"		11 20			2 0		5 20	5 20	6 50		9 10									
	Goole	"		11 48			2 15		5 45	5 45			9 55									
			a.m.	a.m.	a.m.		p.m.		p.m.	p.m.	p.m.		p. m.						p. m.			
L. & N. W. Ry.	**Leeds** (New Stat)	Dep	9 10	11 0	11 0		1 0		4 0	4 0	5 30		8 30						12 0			
	Huddersfield	Arr	9 51	12 0	12 0		1 44		4 50	4 50	6 13		9 25						1 0			
	Manchester, (Victoria)		11 0	1 35	1 35		2 55		6 25	6 25	7 15		10 45						2 35			
	Liverpool, (Lime street)		12 12	3 5	3 5		4 20		8 20	8 20	8 45		12 35						8 15			
			a.m.	a.m.	a.m.		p.m.		p.m.	p.m.	p.m.		p.m.		p m.				a.m.			p. m.
G. N. Railway.	**Holbeck**	Dep	10 28	10 28	10 28		1 4		3 28	3 45	5 28		9 58		9 58				11 9			10 8
	Doncaster	Arr	11 19	11 19	11 19		1 57		4 19	5 0	6 19		10 50		10 50				12 20			11 0
	Retford		11 47	11 47	11 47		2 27		4 47	5 57	6 47		11 25		11 25				1 13			11 30
	Peterboro'		1 20	1 20	1 20		4 8		6 20	7 35	8 20		1 16		1 16				4 30			1 16
	London, King's Cross		3 10	3 10	3 10		6 0		8 10	9 35	10 10		3 20		3 20				7 45			3 20

(a)—No. 3 stops at Topcliffe and Baldersby to set down Passengers from Stations north of Thirsk. On Thursdays it stops to pick up passengers for Ripon. It is Government from stations on the Knaresborough and Pateley Bridge Branches and north of Ripon only, and, when required, stops at Wormald Green, Pannal, and Weeton, to set down Passengers from such Stations

(b)—Government from Stations East of Northallerton to the Great Northern, Midland, London and North Western, and Lancashire and Yorkshire lines. It stops at Wormald Green for First Class Passengers. It conveys Government Passengers westward, arriving at Thirsk by the 7-15 a.m. train from Newcastle.

(c)—Stops at Welbury when required. It is Government from Stations north of Newcastle.

(d)—Stops at Topcliffe and Baldersby on Mondays

(e)—Stops at Topcliffe and Baldersby to set down Passengers booked from Stations north of Thirsk, and at Wormald Green, Nidd Bridge, Pannal, and Weeton to set down Passengers booked at Stations north o Ripon only. Government Passengers are conveyed by it from Harrogate and intermediate Stations to Leeds.

Passengers are booked to Leeds via York by the Mail trains leaving Berwick at 9-5 and 12-2 p.m., arriving in Leeds New Station at 10-49 p.m. and 3-10 a.m.

☞ For Trains between Ferryhill, Stockton, and West Hartlepool, see page 24

Plate 20 Harrogate–Leeds timetable for 1870. The pattern of commuter trains can be clearly seen. There were ten trains on weekdays, two on Sundays. The morning concentration (7.58–9.20 a.m.) can be matched by a group of return trains from Leeds in the early evening. Note the reference to 'Government' trains, those with a statutory fare structure aimed at providing cheap travel.

useful one is that for 1883 while the most comprehensive (and essential guide for any local study) is the *Report of the Royal Commission on Canals* (1906—11).[34] There are however numerous reports on individual undertakings which should be examined. This material can once again be backed up from the other sources, for great local concern was expressed about the decline of the waterways.

The fact that the railways came late, when parliamentary procedures were well developed, accounts for the vast bulk of record material relating to this topic. Each scheme had its own report and from 1837 there was a long series of general reports and enquiries. Returns of traffic as well as details of capital and equipment were made annually by each company, and there is much useful local material here; rates and fares may be obtained from 1881 (a paper which also covers canal charges).[35] The same is true for much of the internal traffic facilities in nineteenth-century towns; from the 1870s until well into the twentieth century, a series of parliamentary papers listed the returns from all tramways,[36] containing a good deal of local information.

Light on the more transient and permanent effects of the coming of the railways will be thrown by most of the other kinds of nineteenth-century records. The census books will reveal the short-term labouring force employed on construction and the longer term changes in the proportion of those engaged in the transport industries. At Corby (Lincs) for instance, one-fifth of the recorded population of 958 in 1851 were railway labourers and although many of these came from neighbouring villages, they were rarely Corby natives. Newspapers of course regularly recorded railway events and services, as did directories (especially those relating to communities particularly dependent upon such traffic like the railway towns and the holiday resorts). Nineteenth-century timetables do still exist and some are being reprinted (Plate 20). Local estate and business records will contain many significant details; in 1850, the Ancaster estate sold building materials to the G.N.R. during the building of the route from Peterborough to Grantham.[37] There are papers among the borough or county quarter sessions records relating to the railways, especially deposited plans. And there are other scattered references in many odd places, all grist for the industrious mill of the railway historian.[38]

But by far the most important sources for local railway history lie among two sets of records which are not easy to use. The House of Lords Record Office[39] contains many papers relating to individual railway projects, some effective, others still-born. The most rewarding of these papers are the minutes of the committees which heard evidence for and against each project. Here may be found a wealth of local and indeed not so local evidence (Plate 21). Opposition and support for the Boston railway for instance came from as far away as Leeds. And the evidence has a more human element than the printed reports. In 1882, a Skegness witness told the committee of the House of Commons that on the August Bank Holiday, some 20,000 trippers arrived in the resort but that, because there was only one track, they could not all get away — 'many hundreds spending the night in waiting rooms or in the streets'.[40] Some of the more formal papers, especially the plans, survive in local copies, but the most rewarding material lies buried among these largely unindexed committee papers.[41]

There are other government collections of papers relating to transport history, especially those of the Board of Trade which for much of the period had powers of supervision over the railways.[42] But beyond these official sources lie the records of the British Transport Authority. These are not deposited but maintained (like some other authorities such as the National Coal Board) in a separate record office

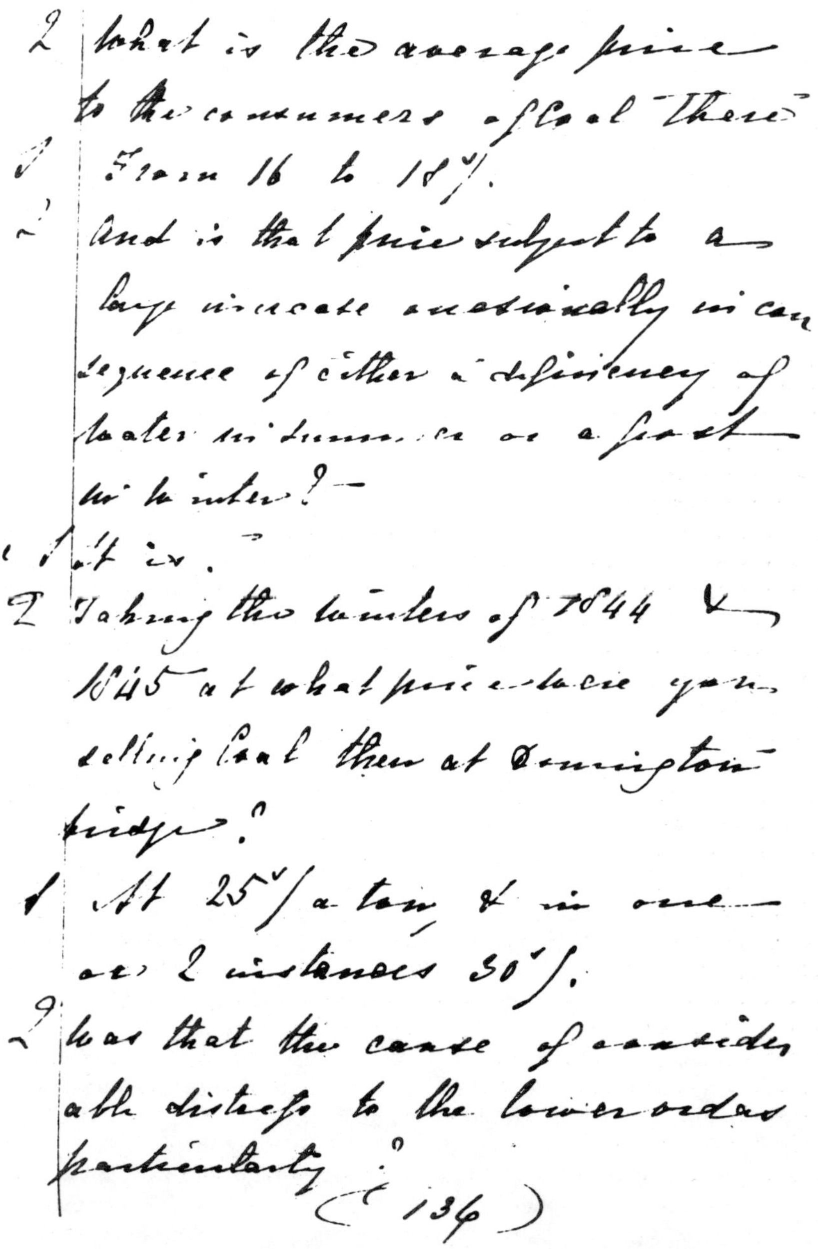

Q   What is the average price
to the consumers of Coal there?

A   From 16 to 18/.

Q   And is that price subject to a
large increase occasionally in con
sequence of either a deficiency of
water in summer or a frost
in winter? —

A   Not is.

Q   Taking the winters of 1844 &
1845 at what price were you
selling Coal there at Donington
bridge?

A   At 25/ a ton, & in one
or 2 instances 30/.

Q   Was that the cause of considerable
able distress to the lower orders
particularly?

(136)

Plate 21 A specimen page from one volume of minutes of the committee looking into the petition for the establishment of the Ambergate, Nottingham and Boston Railway. This contains part of the evidence of Joseph Dodds, a corn, coal and linseed cake merchant of Donington (Lincs); he is referring to the cost of carrying coal, an annual total of 6,000–7,000 tons from Derbyshire (by canal) and some 2,000–3,000 tons from Yorkshire by sea. He was a witness in favour of the railway.

Plate 22(a)   St Pancras Station, 1971.

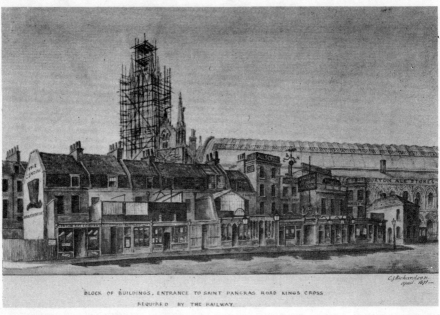

BLOCK OF BUILDINGS, ENTRANCE TO SAINT PANCRAS ROAD KINGS CROSS
REQUIRED BY THE RAILWAY.

(b) Drawing of the building of St Pancras Station, 1871; the shops in the foreground disappeared in the course of construction.

in London. There is a wealth of local detail here, relating not only to the railways nor just to canals as well but also to docks and roads as well as suburban transport systems. The sources here include both manuscript and printed records. There are company papers (minute books, financial accounts and records of work undertaken, etc.) as well as many miscellaneous items like letters, and many plans and surveys. Especially valuable, as with the parliamentary papers, are the Minutes of Evidence submitted along with particular projects, with arguments both for and against the particular local proposal.[43]

And when all the paperwork is done, there are still the monuments themselves, erected by an enthusiastic nation on navvy (often foreign) labour in an outburst of speculation which has rarely been rivalled. Now fast being dismantled, nevertheless much the best local source for the study of the railways are the tracks, the bridges, the stations and other equipment which may still be seen all over the countryside. Surely the best evidence for the building of St Pancras Station in 1863 is the station itself (Plate 22).

Chapter 7

The bond of religion

1

The community which the local historian has undertaken to study existed as a group of people resident in one place, engaged in mutually dependent occupations. This in itself might give such a group adequate identity of interests. Nevertheless, it is still possible to ask the question, what was it that bound them together? What made them into a community? Clearly it was not just a matter of residence, though this must have helped in days when settlements were more distinctly separate than today. There were other matters of common interest, and the agencies which each community created to promote these interests will be discussed later. Here we are rather more concerned with the abstract bonds of society, immaterial and informal — 'culture' as a whole. In this, such factors as language or common social structures and aspirations played a very large part; so did a considered identity as part of some larger recognisable whole. But in the end, the common adherence to sets of ideals and ideas must be the predominant characteristic of social bonds.

Out of this general discussion, I wish to isolate one major strand for more detailed discussion, religion (and in particular, Christianity). Partly this is because it is relatively easy to examine from the materials which survive. But in addition religion is a useful subject for analysis, for it not only united the community but it also on occasion divided it. In many ways, it was the politics of yesterday.

The main difficulty with the subject however is that, although we can study the formal framework with relative ease, there is little real evidence of the quality of spiritual life. This is not of course a feature confined to religious history. It is for example similarly true of housing conditions; we can study rows of nineteenth century working-class houses but not so easily the life within them. But it becomes particularly acute when analysing the consequences of spiritual ideals. There are of course many personal statements of faith but they often leave the impression of having been contrived rather than spontaneous. Even such individual expressions of piety as occur in wills or on monumental inscriptions will seem to most people to be formal, written with an eye to the reader. The heartpourings of a John Donne do not always strike one as being altogether devoid of histrionic effects. In all this the historian, like the contemporary, is forced into personal judgements of motives in an attempt to understand the religious life of the past. What does need to be asserted is the reality of religious experience. People could on occasion be self-less, be inspired to go off into the wilderness by an ideal, or simply in everyday life live in a way which reflected their spiritual understanding. James Hopkinson's un-affected and good humoured spirituality must have been paralleled by thousands more in his day.

Nevertheless, religion is never purely personal; in almost all cases, it has a strong social content as well. At all times the many various branches of the Christian religion have had enormous influence on the local communities of this country. I do not only mean by this those aspects of religion which concerned themselves with social affairs, like Shaftesbury's rescue of young destitutes in the nineteenth century. Religion formed social organisations, groups with expressed allegiances, and these can be assessed in terms of the local community in a way in which the quality of spiritual life cannot. If then this chapter seems too concerned with formal establishments of religion rather than with spiritual movements, this must be the justification.

Religion in the local community had thus two main results. First it created some form of social bond, although of course there would always be an element, however small or informal or even hidden, which would not accept such a bond. The first questions that arise then must be related to the strength and to the spread or decline of religious adherence throughout the community. How far was religion accepted within the group? How significant was the element left outside?

Religion however has always been divisive as well as cohesive. Smaller groups within the community arise, each claiming their adherents. Thus the next group of questions concerns the varying forms of provision for religious practice. What sort of groups existed? The development of sectarianism is of great significance, as are the relations between the various bodies.

But religion affected the community in another way, for it was the mainspring of much of the charitable activity which took place within the group. There was in many cases a concern for those outside the administrations of the religious organisations, a desire to proselytise, to convert. And with that ran a concern for the less fortunate members of the community. It is true that much of the local charitable enterprise was not specifically religious in nature; a great deal more was only formally religious and expressed local rivalries rather than sentiments. Nevertheless, that the expression of religion in terms of concern has been a feature of all ages of the past may be accepted by all but the most cynical, just as it clearly was the foundation of much of the self-help which inspired men like Thomas Cooper the Chartist to educate and elevate themselves to useful social functions.

This concern may be assessed in a number of ways. One of the most significant seems to be the physical location of the various institutions within the community. Religion, like the community's population growth and economic activity, has a topographical aspect. The siting of churches and chapels within the village or town may reflect to a very large extent both the origins of the religious groups and their willingness to adapt themselves to changing situations. But there are other ways of assessing 'mission'. The length of time ministers served their cures may reflect not just the value of the benefice or the comfort of the manse but something of the idealism of the incumbent and the satisfaction or otherwise his task gave him.

The major questions then that the local historian has to ask himself within this sphere of his study are threefold. First, how important was religion among the community? How widespread was its acceptance? What proportion of the population was among its active or its more formal adherents? Secondly, what religious organisations were there in the community? If more than one, what relative strengths did they each enjoy? When and how did they originate? And what were their relations, the one to the other? What sort of persons predominated within each organisation? And thirdly, what sort of activity did they engage in? Were they inward looking or 'full of good works'? What attempts did they make to deal with the problems of their contemporary society, to reach those outside? In this, all the evidence is needed, whether it comes from documents or memories or the buildings themselves or the location of the buildings. There are many ways in which the life of the churches may be assessed.

2

The background against which the local historian has to place the religious development of his local community is necessarily the growth of Christianity in this country. It is the archaeologist or the anthropologist rather than the local historian who have to concern themselves with significant relics of paganism, although very recent studies in folklore have indicated how persistent some of these relics have been; and it is not until the present century that there has been sufficient spread of rival creeds to merit serious attention in most local communities. Nor need the actual process of the conversion of England for long occupy the attention of the local historian, though this may affect his account of local parochial arrangements, some early monastic communities and even some later patterns of landownership. For the means of the conversion were twofold; individual missionaries (whose field of activity may sometimes be traced in church dedications) and mission stations, known generally as 'minster churches', many of which later became early monasteries or parish churches in episcopal or monastic hands.[1]

The medieval church
The main characteristics of the medieval Church (at least so far as the local community is concerned) are its diversity within a formal unity and its comprehensiveness. The comprehensiveness was expressed in two ways. Within the local community, we may presume an almost total adherence to the faith. There were virtually no agnostics, no atheists, and the number of non-practising Christians (except in some of the remoter areas of more dispersed settlements) was very limited indeed. Every member of the community, we may presume, was baptised. Those who died in normal circumstances were certainly buried, very few without Christian rites. Most marriages were performed in Christian ceremonies. Nor was this completely formal, for the comprehensiveness of medieval Christianity was expressed in the way that the religion affected the whole of life. God was involved in all human activities; He was always present and thus was often treated with that disrespect that characterises man's relations with his familiar companions.

Medieval religion thus was a unifying influence within the local community, both in the sense that it demanded a common allegiance from all the members of the group and that it coloured all that the group did, communally or individually. But this is too simple, for behind the formal unity expressed in a common adherence to the institution of the papacy there lay deep and real divisions. The Christian Church has never been one, however strong its apparent links may have been. The regular clergy (the monks living technically cloistered lives of prayer and meditation and the canons living together united in service for the community) were bitterly resented by the secular clergy, the priests and curates with parochial duties. Nor were the regulars themselves united, for what might be called the 'high Church' reformed order of the Cluniacs (which originated in the tenth century and arrived in England in the eleventh century) were themselves the cause of further discontent from the more puritan-minded reformers of the twelfth century, the

Cistercians and their followers. But on one point all the regulars were agreed — indeed, they were even united with the secular clergy in their hostility to their new-fangled rivals of the thirteenth century, the friars. While the movement of the thirteenth and fourteenth centuries to establish endowed chantries and rather later parish gilds with their own chaplains was not always welcomed in the parishes, let alone by the monastic and mendicant orders.[2]

There may thus, in any medieval local community, have been a variety of religious provision for the members of that group. Almost everyone fell within a parish and contributed to the support of the church and its staff of clergy by tithes and offerings as well as in most cases by the loss of a certain amount of common land which the parish priest held as a glebe farm. Parishes, established in the tenth and eleventh centuries, were not however static. New ones (especially in the towns) were created out of earlier ones up to the early thirteenth century (and in a few cases thereafter); boundary changes were common, and several died out (especially in the thirteenth century when friaries disrupted some town parochial arrangements, and in the fourteenth and fifteenth centuries when falling population consequent upon the Black Death denuded many suburbs). Nevertheless most parish boundaries (especially in rural areas) were static for very long periods.[3]

The parochial arrangements of any community however did not form the sole Christian provision there, especially in the towns. From the twelfth century particularly (although there were of course many earlier ones and one or two later — there was even a trickle as late as the fourteenth and fifteenth centuries) there were the monasteries. We tend perhaps to think too much of these institutions as landowners, estate holders, rather than Christian praying and serving bodies, but most of them did make some religious provision for the local community in which they found themselves. From the thirteenth or the early fourteenth centuries there might also be the friaries (almost only in towns), aimed at social work and missionary activity in the surrounding region. These were very popular, much resorted to by the gentry and upper classes, especially for burials. There were in addition hospitals and non-parochial chapels, attended for regular worship. Private chapels were endowed within parish churches and were served by their own chaplains. The socio-religious gilds sometimes had a separate chapel, or at other times found their home within a parish church. All of these formed part of the provision for the community, an expression of its faith as well as a means of pastoral concern.

The picture is thus one of multiple provision, often with an element of rivalry within the community. It is true that for many villages the pattern was a simple one, of parish church with (or even without) chapels of ease. But it is rare for there to be one church solely for one community, even in rural areas; in the west, there were frequently several townships within the cure of each local church, while in the east, where there were more village churches, chapels abounded, both separate ones or chantry and gild ones.[4] In the towns of course the picture was more complicated. Thus medieval Stamford had no less than fourteen parish churches, two major monastic institutions and probably some five or six minor ones, at least twelve gilds, three or more hospitals, four or more chapels and a host of other religious interests.[5]

But what of the quality of this life? Unfortunately, there is very little real evidence. Contemporaries wrote of the corruption of the Church and deserted the formal bodies to establish new ones. The mendicant friars particularly attracted charges of insincerity and abuse. Most of the sources are literary or legal; and little is said of the large amount of good work that was done, for that was unremarkable (although the letter of John of Monte Corvino, a friar archbishop in Peking, can equal any nineteenth- or twentieth-century missionary report[6]). Probably the best evidence of the decline of religious life in the medieval Church is to be found in the search for spiritual satisfaction and community life *outside* of the established organs of Christianity. Some of these movements were persecuted for heresy, like Wycliffe's Lollards in the fifteenth century. Others, like Margery Kempe or the numerous parochial anchorites or the brethren of the Common Life in the Low Countries, were not, although the Church always found it hard to tolerate such enthusiastic and often ill-disciplined activity. The search existed throughout almost the whole of western Christendom and it is a moot point as to whether the gild movement of the later medieval centuries was a part of it or not.

Reformation
The Reformation swept over England as a storm.[7] Such a title cannot of course refer just to the violent changes of formal adherence associated with the successive reigns of Henry VIII, Edward VI, Mary and Elizabeth, although these were real enough. In terms of the local community, what happened was in some sense a real conversion — either from indifference or strong adherence to the old religion to a brand of protestantism which was both different and on the whole tolerant. For there is little doubt that the 'papist' majority of the 1540s had become by the 1570s a protestant majority. How this transformation came about is not altogether clear. There were many missionary teachers, especially among the parochial clergy, active in this. Leading the opposition in many cases were the regular orders, like the Dominican friars who stood up and resisted the protestant vicar of St Martin's (Lord Burghley's church) in Stamford, and their dissolution helped to undermine the old religion.

Papists
But the old religion survived, despite the strong flow in the opposite direction. The movement was not without its element of witch-hunt but the story is a local one rather than a national one. The long series of parliamentary statutes (1581–1606, and again in the late 1650s) imposing restrictions on 'papists' were not always enforced in the various localities of the realm. And thus there were survivals, sometimes submerged for long periods (and therefore scarcely known to the local historian), later to re-emerge as significant 'recusant' groups. Generally these were associated with prominent estate owners, although adherence to Catholicism was not one entirely based on one's tenantry.[8] When Irnham (Lincs) for example passed to an Anglican owner in the early nineteenth century after a long period of papist ownership, the family Catholic chapel is reputed to have been removed to nearby Corby (Lincs) for the convenience of the worshippers who were not solely tenants. But without the support of the larger landowners, such pockets were unlikely to have survived, cited as so many of them were regularly into the courts of quarter sessions. The legislation of 1700 and 1715 concerning papist estates gave a lever for local attacks on some of the more prominent of these persistent Catholics, but it was rare for such persecution to last long. By 1791, when the Catholic Relief Act allowed the groups to reveal themselves openly, it seems that in many places they had been tolerated for a long period already; the later Catholic Emancipation Act (1829) and the re-establishment of the hierarchy in 1850, both made under the pressure of substantial Catholic immigrations and of conversions

among the noble and influential, merely set the seal on earlier decisions taken in a multiplicity of local communities.

Dissenters

Apart from the Catholics there were other nonconformist or dissenting groups. The basic theme of the post-Reformation Church has been fragmentation — or the re-iteration of medieval divisions in new guises.[9] Disputes over religion split the nation in the Civil Wars; they split the counties by the exercise of the Test Acts (debarring those who would not conform to the Church of England from office); they split towns and villages between Church and Chapel.

How far such disputes promoted the growth of irreligion is not certain, for some reform movements (especially the Methodists) claimed they originated to cope with such a growth. But there seems to have been a decline in adherence to religious bodies; in some communities even the formal rites were no longer sought. How widespread it was cannot be determined. It may well be that until the nineteenth century, there was no more irreligion than in medieval communities — it was equal indifference. But there are signs that much of the population was slipping through the net of organised religion even before the growth of large towns broke great holes in the net. What has become clear is the concentration of dissenting groups in villages of divided landownership, decayed market towns and rural areas of dispersed settlement; it is these social conditions which seem to have provided the climate in which nonconformity could flourish.

The decline of religious adherence took place despite the increase of religious provision for the local community. In this movement, the growth of nonconformist groups is most prominent. From the start of the reign of Elizabeth to the 1620s, most of the puritans sought to work within the Church of England. Thereafter they moved outside, at first abroad. From 1642, at the call of what later became the Long Parliament, they came back to England to establish new groups. Calvinist and puritan, they formed the numerous congregations of Independents (later either Presbyterians or Congregationalists) and Baptists (later the Particular Baptists) with some smaller extreme groups. The Quakers were formed in the late seventeenth century and spread most rapidly then, making little further advance after the middle of the eighteenth century. There was of course some persecution, both during the Interregnum when the Presbyterians predominated and especially after the Restoration, culminating (after an abortive effort at toleration in 1672–3) in the statutes of 1681 and the years following. But toleration (except for the Unitarians) came in 1689 and with it further religious groupings, marking off the 'Old Churches' from the 'new dissent'. Arminianism, the opposite theological pole to Calvinism, became active in the eighteenth century by the establishment of General Baptist churches and especially by the Methodist mission. At first a spiritual movement within the other churches (and indeed often using others' buildings) with little intention of forming its own establishment, the Methodist community was forced into this action by rejection.

The rest of the story, so far as it affects the local historian, is of further divisions, although there were also some amalgamations of independent congregations like the Baptist New Connexion in the 1770s and the General Baptist Union in 1813 (which in 1831 absorbed the Baptist New Connexion). Most of the Presbyterian chapels died out or joined the Congregational Union (1832) or the Unitarians. This latter was a trend in doctrine which affected the General Baptists particularly in the eighteenth century. The Methodists split on many occasions. In

1796—7, the Methodist New Connexion was established in rivalry with the Wesleyans. The Primitive Methodists of Staffordshire (1810) and the Bible Christians of Devon (by 1815; formally established in 1831) spread to other parts of the realm. These three were however for many years quite small compared with their rivals: in 1827, there were about 237,000 Wesleyans against 30,000 Primitive Methodists, 10,000 members of the New Connexion and 8,000 Bible Christians. The future lay with the first two only; by 1860, there were 130,000 members of Primitive congregations. Between 1849 and 1857, a further series of secessions and expulsions resulted in the Wesleyan Reformed Church and other associations, most of them eventually coming together into the United Methodist Free Churches. Rationalisation came in 1907 when the United Methodist Church joined together all the smaller bodies, leaving the Primitive Methodists and Wesleyans to join with this body in 1932. Similarly in 1891 came the Baptist Union. But these later amalgamations hardly affected local communities for by then the pattern of chapels had been established. There were other groups, offshoots of the evangelicalism of the eighteenth and nineteenth centuries — the Countess of Huntingdon's Connexion, the Plymouth Brethren (which soon split into two) and (much later) the Salvation Army from 1878.

Such movements were clearly divisive within the local community. Many of them arose from schisms within existing groups; others were certainly aroused to hostility by the actions and teachings of their neighbours, resulting in a war of sermons and pamphlets. The Baptists of Norwich decreed in 1753 'that it is unlawful for Any so to attend upon the meetings of the Methodists or to join in any worship'.[10] Some aimed quite deliberately at particular social groupings within the community, although how far the final pattern by which in many places the Wesleyans seem to have become largely middle class while the Primitive Methodists were largely labouring workers was the result of early policy decisions is in doubt. Nearly all were united in hostility to the Church of England. Nevertheless this divisiveness can be over-estimated. Many were the local parsons who encouraged the early Methodists and even built chapels for them; a number of members of the local aristocracy encouraged their servants and tenants in what they saw as a movement of spiritual activity — church in the morning, chapel in the afternoon. Nor did any religious group hold a monopoly of religious morality; it is quite clear that there were good and bad nonconformist ministers and Anglican parsons alike.

Anglicans

The Church of England itself was not static during all this period. Indeed much of the growth of irreligion must be laid at the doors of the Church of England. It is not that the Church was unwilling to change; rather it was that such changes as did occur were largely irrelevant to the needs of the people within the community. There was too much internal argument; the Anglicans were not immune from the same disputes as troubled their nonconforming rivals. Although the Church of England aimed to be as comprehensive as the medieval Church, the Reformation in England was by no means unanimous, the reformers not united. Not all left the Church of England when its pattern was established by Elizabeth. For nearly a century the extremists sought on a local basis to mould the Church into a different pattern, one of Presbyterian organisation as in Scotland or on the continent or one of independent congregations characteristic of the later Congregationalists. Thus for most of this period there were local controversies within the Church of England, Laudianism versus puritanism, as at Grantham where the hostility between the incumbent and the more extreme 'lecturers' led to the celebrated 'altar controversy' in the early seventeenth century and much bitter local feeling.[11] The struggle came to a head in the disruption of the Interregnum when the successive parochial ejections and intrusions (or indeed the just-as-significant continuations in incumbencies) reveal the stages of the rivalry.[12]

After the failure of these attempts, confirmed in 1660 by the Restoration of Charles II, came a period of more formal religion in the Church of England[13] coupled with persecution of all nonconformists. In many cases, parish livings became family property served by poor curates; at Coningsby (Lincs) two families alone held the benefice for 150 years. Elsewhere churches suffered from falling income. The establishment of Queen Anne's Bounty in 1704 tried to help but still the poverty resulting in non-residence and pluralism, the formal observances of the Age of Reason and the great fear of all forms of 'enthusiasm' led to real spiritual hunger. Much of the local interest of this period relates to disputes over clerical tithes, a great source of contention ever since their enforcement in the tenth century. Some had of course been commuted by now into regular money rents, and the enclosure movement saw some attempt to extinguish these by granting the parson some allotment of land in lieu of tithes. But much remained uncommuted until the great series of Tithe Acts in the early nineteenth century. On the other hand, if tithe was enforced, worship was often neglected; the story of the goose sitting on her egg in the pulpit is unhappily not entirely fiction, if rare. It is true that galleries were built and pews were rented (and thus presumably used) but church activities were on the whole formal and undemanding, and some at least of the pew rents were levied in order to pay the bills for maintenance, just as they were paid as a status symbol or a piece of estate development.

Nor does the situation change much until the nineteenth century, despite some increase in the value of benefices related to the work of the Governors of Queen Anne's Bounty and to the enclosure movement. An attempt to cope with non-residence by the establishment of parsonage houses was only partially successful. In the towns, much of the concern seems to have been to fight off unions of parishes or the establishment of new churches. The Evangelical Revival of the late eighteenth and early nineteenth centuries brought the first real signs of life. It was promoted mainly by two groups, academics and wealthy landholders and merchants, but it was not a remote movement. Its effects were felt in many parishes, especially in the relations with the nonconformists.

Nineteenth century: church building

The nineteenth century thus opened with a slowly reviving Anglican Church, a Catholic Church emerging from several generations of exclusiveness, a declining group of 'Old Dissenters', a new enthusiastic Methodist movement but very prone to schism, and a largely alienated population. It is this latter which creates the main theme of concern to the local historian.

One problem is that there were too few churches, and for all their building the denominations were quite unable to keep up with the rate at which the population grew. Thus, whereas in 1801 there were some 58 seats per 100 heads of population, by 1851 this had fallen to 45. It was of course worst in the towns; in 1801, less than 42% could get into any urban church or chapel and this fell to 37% by 1851. Some places were particularly bad; in Leeds in 1816, the Anglican churches could house only some 3,400 out of a total population of 64,000, but this town and nearby Manchester (one of the largest single parishes in the country) were notorious

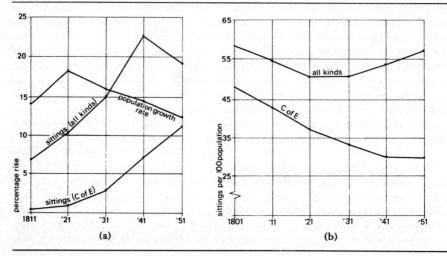

Fig. 26(a)   Comparative rates of growth of church sittings and population in the first half of the nineteenth century.

Fig. 26(b)   Sittings in relation to population 1 : 100 heads and the Anglican share of it.

for their problems. In rural areas, there was provision for some 69% of the population, but even here it fell to 61% in 1821—31 (Fig. 26).[14]

The churches tackled this problem. At first, it was the nonconformists who made most progress. In the rural areas, their efforts were maintained for the whole of the first part of the century, although from 1831 the Anglicans became close rivals, so that by 1851 the lost ground had been recovered, a total provision for 70% being recorded for rural areas in that year.

In the towns, the nonconformist effort, especially great from 1811 to 1831, was not maintained much beyond that date; then the Anglican provision began to close the gap. But it was still a long way behind in 1851; indeed its total provision throughout the whole country had fallen from 48% in 1801 to just under 30% in 1851. Less than one-fifth of the adult population of England could attend an Anglican church if they so wished. In the early years of the century came a half-hearted attempt to counteract the increasing alienation of the town dwellers by building new churches — the so-called Waterloo churches, built to two basic designs by government grant between 1818 and 1833. But it was from about 1840 that the real Anglican effort was made; for the first time the rate of increase in church provision exceeded the rate of population growth in both town and rural areas.

The total effort of all this building has not yet been fully assessed, but the average cost in Leeds of a new Anglican church was about £4 per sitting, while for the Methodists it was some £3 per sitting and elsewhere was lower.[15] There was a good deal of central help available, with bodies like the Church Building Society (founded in 1818 and incorporated in 1838) advising local communities and making often substantial grants, but even so most churches and chapels had to be built on mortgages.

Coupled with this was the movement to set pews free from rents and thus to get the artisan classes into church. The trouble was that so many of the new churches (especially the evangelical ones) needed the rents for their endowment, while the older ones needed them for maintenance. But as rents rose (and they existed in the nonconformist churches also, but generally at lower levels), so did the cry for free seats, and a good deal of progress was made locally here. The Tractarian and ritual movements of the middle of the century were especially opposed to such rents and brought increased vigour to local churches. But once again they sprang from the clergy, not from the laity, often emanating from ecclesiological societies. The church restorations of the nineteenth century were more often an expression of this new interest or of lay patronage rather than a genuine demand by the laity for more suitable places of worship, and they were in any case frequently divisive in the local community. The new movements do not seem to have brought the people in.

The churches in 1851

What then was the situation in the middle of the nineteenth century?[16] It would seem, from the census of religious activity taken in 1851, that in the country as a whole something like one-third of the adult population might be expected to go to church regularly; occasional attenders would increase this figure considerably, while of course nominal but non-attending adherents would raise the total of professing Christians to something nearer two-thirds, if not indeed higher still. But these overall figures conceal very great differences. In the rural areas and smaller market towns like Colchester, Exeter and Bath, the regular attenders were in excess (sometimes considerably) of the national average; in most of the large towns the figure was lower, often greatly so, though there were a few exceptions. It would seem that it was the urban working classes who most refused the administrations of the Christian bodies.

Non-Christian bodies hardly existed at all, save for small communities of Jews in some places. The 'fringe' Christian bodies such as the Mormons were only just beginning to make headway and the eastern religions are not formally recorded. The local community thus in the middle of the nineteenth century would be divided between practising Christians and some Jews on the one hand and a mixed body of non-practising and non-believing residents on the other, the exact proportions of which can never be known.

In terms of provision, most local communities had more than one religious group. A small village like Rauceby (total population in 1851, 644) had a church with two Sunday Schools, a Primitive Methodist Chapel and probably a small Wesleyan group in North Rauceby as well as other options available in Sleaford nearby. A town the size of King's Lynn (1851, 19,355) had in that year two medieval Anglican churches and one chapel as well as one new (1846) parish church; there was an old-established Roman Catholic church with a dependent chapel (1828); three 'Old Dissenting' congregations, Particular Baptists, Quakers and Independents (formerly Presbyterians and then Calvinistic Methodists); a Unitarian offshoot from the Baptists (1811); four Methodist chapels of differing persuasions, as well as a Jewish synagogue — fifteen places of worship in all, with seating available for some 65% of the population.[17]

The larger towns had still more assorted provision. The fullest study made so far in this respect is for the steel town of Sheffield.[18] Whether the pattern that emerged there is typical cannot be known until further work has been done.

Sheffield

Two religious surveys, the one of 1851 and a second in 1881, enable some estimate to be made as to the total effect of religion on the community. In 1851, out of a

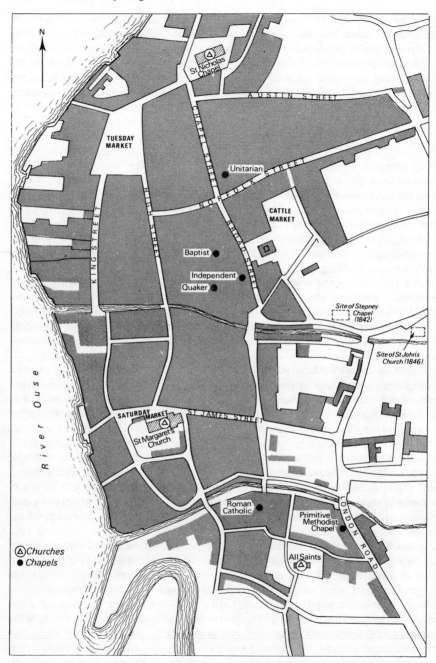

Plate 23　Map of King's Lynn 1830: based on Wood's Survey, 1830. The town defences lie to the west of this map, but there was virtually no building in this area until later in the century. The site of St John's Church (1846) and Stepney Chapel (1842) are marked. The new London Road can be seen with its first chapel, Primitive Methodist. Other nonconformist churches soon moved to this main thoroughfare from the back lanes and yards.

population of over 135,000, some 43,500 attendances at church were recorded. It is difficult to assess how many heads these attendances registered, but it is likely that the number of persons attending twice would reduce the figure to nearer one-quarter than one-third of Sheffield's total population. In 1881, when the basis of the count was much the same (although the number of Sunday School scholars would by this time be very substantially reduced), the comparable figures were as follows:

Population	*Attendances*
284,400	87,750

making it probable that just under a quarter of all the inhabitants of Sheffield were in church or chapel at least once on that Sunday. Some slight leeway had been lost during the thirty years but it was not significant.

What is significant is the change in provision over the same period. In 1851, there were 70 places of worship recorded — 23 Anglican (6 of them mission churches), some 26 Methodist of all varieties, 10 Independent and a number of other congregations (Plate 24). By 1881, this number had nearly trebled to 196 churches and chapels, at a time when the population of Sheffield had only slightly more than doubled. The expansion of the provision was not equally shared between the major denominations. The Anglicans probably just equalled the rate of Sheffield's population growth by doubling their provision to 50 churches. The Independents had a similar rate of growth, 10 to 22 chapels. Some minor congregations were lost and at least 4 Salvation Army citadels and 2 Presbyterian churches had appeared. But it was the Methodists who shot ahead, at least in terms of chapels, from 26 to 96. Many of these new churches or chapels were however small; the Anglican accommodation rose from 19,500 to 32,750 seats, the Methodist from some 14,200 to 41,000. In other words, the *average* Anglican church in Sheffield fell in size from 850 to 650; the average Methodist chapel fell too, from 550 to 340, a slightly smaller rate of decline.

This story of increasing provision must be put into its context of earlier growth. Thus the Anglicans in 1800 had had only 6 places of worship in a town of some 45,750, while the Methodists of all shades had only 3 chapels; the 'Old Dissenters' had 7 places in all, a figure increased in 1851 to only 16. Great efforts were made by the Anglicans and Methodists to expand their work centres. Indeed, in the twelve years before 1851, the Anglicans alone erected a total of 14 new churches, an achievement unparalleled until the 1930s.

So much for provision, but what about support? Here it would seem that the Anglicans made the greater strides. Its average total congregation[19] was actually higher in 1881 than it had been in 1851, some 676 against the earlier 647. The average Methodist total congregation fell disastrously from 600 to 300 and this probably included a larger number of double attenders than in the Anglican congregations. In this respect the 1881 figures are unfortunate, for the Methodists (especially the Wesleyans) were only just beginning to recover from a very bad patch and major advances were made between 1867 and 1900 when the Wesleyans alone built or rebuilt 28 chapels in the city. But the Anglican church in this town had outstripped its nearest rival.

There is a good deal that can be said about the life of the churches and chapels in the community, the freeing of rented pews in church and chapel alike, the scale of the building operations, the schools, the many activities helping to fill the leisure time of the church members, the internal divisions and secessions. Something is

Plate 24   Section from map of Sheffield, 1833, printed in Pinnock's *Penny Cyclopedia*. This shows the location of the six Anglican churches and 20 chapels, as well as other public buildings in the town. Key: 1 St Peter's Church, 2 St James's Church, 7 Friend's Meeting House, 11 Methodist Chapel, 12 Independent Chapel, 13 Independent Chapel, 14 Baptist Chapel, 15 Independent Chapel, 16 Methodist Chapel, 17 Independent Chapel, 22 Primitive Methodist Chapel.

known of the work of some prominent members of the religious organisations in the public causes within the city. How far the location of the churches and chapels reflected an onslaught on the working-class areas of the town or an over-provision of the newer middle-class suburbs is not immediately apparent. We can see something of the missionary activity in open air and theatre sermons, in the Town Mission, in the Workmen's Mission and the Pleasant Sunday Afternoon movement, an effort which was apparently largely ineffective. Perhaps the divisions and consequent rivalries between the Christian bodies seemed important at the time; perhaps they still appear too important to the local historian. What was clearly significant was the total contribution that religion made as a social bond in the life of the people of Sheffield in the nineteenth century.

The later century

Sheffield reveals the trends for the rest of the nineteenth century.[20] Denominational and internal competition continued after 1851. The 1851 census showed that the two main religious groups were almost equal in total numbers. On the whole the Anglican Church was more strongly supported among the rural communities than in the towns, though there were towns which provided exceptions. In Exeter, 30% of the town's population attended the Anglican churches, 19% the nonconformist places of worship; in King's Lynn, the comparable figures were 23% and 29%. The Roman Catholics were confined to small pockets except in the north, especially Lancashire. The nonconformists on the whole were better supported in towns but their adherents in many rural areas were not negligible. Numerical support of course did not determine the influence of the separate bodies in the community. The smaller bodies of Congregationalists and Unitarians were especially prominent in local government and the Quakers and the Baptists in industrial and commercial activity, while the Primitive Methodists, although numerically strong in large industrial towns, were rarely as influential.

Much of the energies of the churches went on the re-ordering of services (especially among the Anglicans) and the re-building of churches (among all bodies). In King's Lynn, for instance, the three medieval churches were extensively restored (one twice) between 1860 and 1887; five of the six nonconformist chapels existing in 1812 were rebuilt, while two founded before 1845 were also rebuilt (one at least twice) between 1850 and 1883 (Plate 25). Nor was this pattern unusual; throughout both the towns and the countryside, builders and architects grew rich on 'restorations' and rebuildings. Some of this was caused by the need for larger buildings and by urban redevelopment, but much was for liturgical purposes, genuine maintenance or prestige. In rural areas and in some towns, most of the Anglican work was inspired by patrons, landowners or great industrial or civic magnates; but the chapels were largely rebuilt by congregational efforts and large mortgages.[21] It is probably in the financing of the work that the main significance of the rebuilding of the nineteenth-century churches for the local historian lies.

There were other reasons for this building. Internally, there were still secessions. At King's Lynn the Wesleyan Reformers set up a Tabernacle in 1853, joining the New Connexion; in 1858, the General Baptists established themselves in South Lynn, while in the following year the Union Baptists seceded from the Particular Baptists, receiving support from some of the Independents. Nor were the Anglicans exempt from divisions — the Additional Curates' Society and the Church Pastoral Aid Society led the two wings of the Church of England in intense rivalry.

Plate 25   Contrasting church building, King's Lynn:

(a) Stepney Baptist Chapel, built on the street frontage in 1842 by voluntary subscriptions at a cost of £2,600. This was a middle-class church, with only 250 free seatings out of a total of 1,000.

But there was also a sense of outreach. The Church of England was slower in establishing new churches, perhaps hampered by its legal position; but in a long series of statutes devoted to church buildings and new parishes (1818 to 1888), Parliament gradually eased the way for the rationalisation of church structures by replacing the process of Act of Parliament with an Order in Council. Large parishes were carved up; thus at West Ham, the single parish of 4,000 acres was split into no less than seventeen parishes. In King's Lynn, apart from the new parish church established in 1846, there was a 'School-Church' built in South Lynn in 1863, 'the seats [of which] are open benches', and an iron room was established as a mission in Railway Road in 1881. On the whole this process was still misdirected to the town centres; it was not until the 1870s that the churches followed the chapels into the suburbs.

The nonconformists had gone there from at least the 1850s or even earlier, often giving up rented accommodation to build their own halls. The Roman church at Lynn set up a chapel in Coronation Square as early as 1828, and removed its church to the London Road in 1843 (Plate 23). The major Wesleyan congregation transferred from North Clough Lane into the main road of Tower Street and established two other chapels in London Road (1862) and North End (1883). And with this process went the freeing of pews from rents; the chapels had got rid of this feature quite early. In 1880 the Salvation Army replaced the interdenominational Town Mission of 1843. Indeed, apart from the Friends for which no figures survive, the churches and chapels of Lynn by the 1890s were able to seat rather more than 12,750 of Lynn's total population of 19,053.[22] Throughout the country, missions were run in down-town areas such as docks and slums, or to temporary groups of workers like the railway navvies.[23] 'We have twelve brethren', reported St Clements' Baptist Church in Norwich as early as 1836, 'who are employed every Sabbath in visiting the courts and yards in the neighbourhood of our chapel'. The revivals of the nineteenth century climaxing in the great Moody and Sankey tour of 1873, and the more limited blossoming of church and chapel activities (like the large Sunday schools and Bible classes or the Pleasant Sunday Afternoon movement of the 1880s) show something of the concern of church and chapel alike for those not so far reached by their local provision. But by the end of the nineteenth century, the general trend may be discerned by which the nonconformist groups began to lose their wealthier, more educated and more influential supporters, to leave them weakened but not totally ineffective to face the mission of the twentieth century.

The relationship between religion and class implied in these trends has recently become the subject of debate of which the local historian should take notice. It is possible that this will reflect itself in the local community. More important to the local historian is the identity now being established in some areas between non-conformist affiliation and early trade unionism — a relationship which was however unable to weather the stresses of the Great Depression and its sequels during the first forty years of this century. Here is new ground still being explored, to the knowledge of which the local historian may add a great deal.[24]

◀ **Plate 25(b)** St John's Church, built in 1845—6 almost entirely by private subscription at a total cost of £6,160; the only new Anglican church in the town, and set in discreet gardens, it had 800 free pews out of its total of 1,000.

3

The sources for the study of the religious development of the local community are exceptionally prolific, largely because the churches and chapels both created and preserved records in the nature of their activities. Further, the close relations in this country between the established church and the state meant that the state was continually interested in and active on behalf of the church, and thus extensive documentation can be found among the public records.

Medieval sources

Evidence of the size of the local religious community during the Middle Ages just does not exist. Central taxation records like clerical subsidies may indicate the surprising number of clergy who staffed the churches,[25] but the size of their congregations is not known. Nor is there any evidence for the size of the non-religious element in the population.

On the other hand, record material relating to the provision made by the Church for the local community abounds. Some of it comes from national sources like Domesday (only incidentally, for this was not intended to be comprehensive; a study of church fabric suggests that a large number of pre-Conquest churches are not mentioned in the Domesday Book) and various other surveys.[26] Bishops' registers survive to indicate which churches were parochial; sources for chapels however consist of incidental mentions and many must remain unrecorded. Monastic institutions, friaries and hospitals are more fully documented and may most easily be checked up in the local *Victoria County History*.[27] Chantries and gilds (often in practice indistinguishable) are in many cases recorded in the 1389 gild returns and the 1548 chantry certificates as well as in the long series of inquisitions which were associated with their establishment.[28] It is rare to find however any evidence for relative adherence, save wills for friary burials.

It is thus not difficult to outline the provision available in the local community. But it is the quality of the spiritual life and the activity of these bodies which escape detection. Medieval church building does not reflect attempts to cope with increasing population. It may not even reflect individual or group piety, for much of the building was done by a few individuals and seems more to reflect the pattern of patronage than community loyalties. Donations and legacies, traceable in the wills of prominent local inhabitants, may give one clue but must be assessed with caution. The records of the church courts may throw some light upon those 'extramural' movements like the Lollards, but these sources are notoriously difficult to use and the chance of finding something relating to one specific locality extremely remote.

If we can say little of the parishioners, we might hope to say more of the clergy themselves and their churches. The siting of some of the institutions, especially the friaries which were noted for building on marshy sites, may just as well reflect the stage at which they entered the town as their concern for the deprived urban parishioner. Something may be learned from the length of incumbency of the parish parson, but this really depended upon the nature,[29] location and wealth of the benefice; nor can we be certain in many cases whether the parson were resident or not. Even when we know of a long-living resident parson, there are no tests as to whether he were active or indeed a conscientious pastor of his flock. Chaucer's '*povre parson*' is an ideal type, unlike his fellow pilgrims completely lacking in personal characteristics. Perhaps Chaucer felt his picture was unreal.

Post-Reformation sources
The records for the Church and the churches after the cataclysm of the Reformation are fuller and easier to use. Thus an attempt at a more complete religious survey may be made.

What evidence is there in the local community of the decline in at least the formal adherence of part of the population? Virtually nothing, except for the lamentations of contemporaries over the failure of the church(es) to come to grips with the masses — and these are rare before the nineteenth century. There are the records of the church courts once more and also the quarter sessions, but does the presentation of some individual for persistent neglect of the parish church indicate the presence of irreligion or perhaps nonconformity? The decline of services recorded in visitation returns is evidence of lack of provision rather than of desire.

The development of ecclesiastical provision of all sorts and their activities can be traced more easily. This can most easily be done in two main series of Anglican records.[30] The first are the visitation records, especially the occasional surveys in which the local incumbent was asked to indicate what rival groups existed and sometimes how many adherents each had. Some, like the Compton return of 1676, were of national coverage; most are however diocesan. They are full of local detail: the vicar of Bourne (Lincs) noted two conventicles in 1705—22, one Anabaptist, the other Quaker, while in 1788—92, there were some 15 protestant dissenters and 10 papists resident in the parish out of 300 families. The second main records are those certificates to be found from 1689 among the diocesan or quarter sessions papers — a licence for the 'Protestant Dissenters called Anabaptists [who] have erected A house for the Publick Worship of Allmighty god At Kirton in Lindsey' (May 1762, signed by eight members of the congregation).[31]

Each of the dissenting groups may be traced further in other records. The survival of papists can often be seen in quarter session presentments (though sometimes these fail to distinguish between papists and protestant dissenters) and especially in the series of records associated with the various outbursts of persecution, such as the requirement that papists were to register themselves (1657) and their estates (from 1717) in quarter sessions. Even after 1791, Catholic chapels had to be registered with the quarter sessions. Hardly any of the records of papist congregations survive but something may be learned of local activities from other sources.[32]

Many of the other bodies possess both central and local records. Chapel minutes and account books dating from the late seventeenth century may still exist in private hands; the Quakers were particularly insistent upon the creation and preservation of records, and their minute books and accounts of their congregations at various levels (from the particular meetings to the monthly and quarterly meetings) and especially their record of 'Sufferings' are most valuable accounts of local congregations. Lists of members of particular sects and the many surviving nonconformist registers, mostly now in the Public Record Office, may help to determine the size of the dissenting group and (if related to hearth tax returns or occupations) its wealth and social connections and especially how far afield its influence was felt, for (save in the towns) most nonconformist congregations drew from several settlements rather than just from one. Local newspapers and the many tracts and pamphlets produced by local congregations, where they exist for the eighteenth century, will reveal a good deal of the activities of these rival Christian churches. There are several lists of protestant congregations of the eighteenth century.[33]

What of the Church of England itself? Surprisingly, the field is not rich. We can continue to learn of the value of the benefice from a number of sources. There are a few central records such as John Ecton's *Liber Valorum et Decimarum* (1711) recording changes in parishes since 1535; it was revised in 1786 by John Bacon under the title *Liber Regis*. There are records of Queen Anne's Bounty in the Public Record Office. There are more numerous local and diocesan benefice papers, which for instance may include, apart from the church terriers, much relating to tithes. Surveys and valuations were taken on occasions by diocesan authorities and occasionally (as in 1603—4 and 1649) on a national scale; many such surveys were taken during the Interregnum.[34] A study of the enclosure award (where it exists) can be most revealing: it is not at all rare for a previously unattractive living to become a good deal more desirable after the enclosure had commuted the trouble-some tithe into a substantial agricultural estate. Again the fortunes of the parsonage house may be traced, once more an influence upon the status and person of the incumbent.[35] But there is less evidence for his activities. Many bishops or archdeacons tried to record where an incumbent was non-resident or where he employed a stipendiary curate, but such attempts were never exhaustive nor persistent. Lists of services were similarly made on occasion, but probably the returns represent an ideal rather than actual practice. Again alterations to the fabric such as pews, galleries and organs, as recorded in faculties, may reflect changes in human standards as much as alterations for divine service, while pew rents or church rates, culled from churchwardens' accounts, may show some measure of local involvement.[36] More valuable are the occasional notes in the parish records, especially the registers; and indeed the regularity and detail with which these records were kept and returns made to the diocesan office can reveal surprisingly much about the character of the incumbent or his curate.[37]

Is there much to be learned of the religious activities and allegiances of the parishioners? The welcome given to the Reformation by the protestant parishioners of St Andrew's in Norwich is unusual both in its survival and in the 'versifier' who expressed it.[38] The destruction of church furniture recorded during the sixteenth century[39] is certainly some evidence of the spread of protestantism but it might of course have been inspired by relatively few influential persons. The ejections[40] of the middle of the seventeenth century may once again reveal at least the pressures on the teaching members of the religious groupings. But for most places there is little to be learned about religious concerns for much of the eighteenth century, except what appears about services in visitation returns.

4

The religious census

The starting point for the study of the local community's religious history in the nineteenth century must clearly be the 1851 religious census (Plate 26).[41] For the first and last time, the census authorities managed to persuade both the Church of England and the dissenters to accept a count of heads — not a count of verbal adherence but attendance at a place of worship on one particular Sunday. The

---

Plate 26   The religious census 1851

(a) Return for St John's Church, King's Lynn, showing when it was built, how it was paid for, ▶ the number of pew rents as well as the congregation.

Census of Great Britain, 1851. *246 - 2 -1 -1*
(13 and 14 Victoriæ, Cap. 53.)
A RETURN

he several Particulars to be inquired into respecting the undermentioned CHURCH or CHAPEL in England, belonging to the United Church of England and Ireland.

similar Return (*mutatis mutandis,*) will be obtained with respect to Churches belonging to the Established Church in Scotland, and the Episcopal Church there, and also from Roman Catholic Priests, and from the Ministers of every other Religious Denomination throughout Great Britain, with respect to their Places of Worship.]

NAME and DESCRIPTION of CHURCH or CHAPEL.
Saint John the Evangelist, King's Lynn, a New Parish Church (6 & 7 Victoria chap 37)

WHERE SITUATED.	Parish, Ecclesiastical Division or District, Township or Place	Superintendent Registrar's District	County and Diocese
	New Parish of St John King's Lynn Situated in Blackfriars Road	King's Lynn	County of Norfolk Diocese of Norwich

WHEN CONSECRATED OR LICENSED	Under what Circumstances CONSECRATED or LICENSED
September 24. 1846	As an additional church

In the case of a CHURCH or CHAPEL CONSECRATED or LICENSED since the 1st January, 1800; state

HOW OR BY WHOM ERECTED	COST, how Defrayed	
By Parliamentary Grant Grant from Church Build'g Soc's Grant from Diocesan Soc's Private Subscriptions	By Grant fr. Ch. Build Soc's By Parliamentary Grant Diocesan Ch. Build Soc Parochial Rate Private Benefaction, or Subscription, or from other Sources	£400 500 100 5160
	Total Cost......£	6160

V.		VI.		
HOW ENDOWED		SPACE AVAILABLE FOR PUBLIC WORSHIP		
	£			
l	Pew Rents........ *abt* 60	Free Sittings	804	
e	Fees .... *abt* 5	Other Sittings	200	
e	Dues		*1004*	
or Permanent En- } wment .... }	Easter Offerings ...... Other Sources	Total Sittings...		
	150			

Estimated Number of Persons attending Divine Service on Sunday, March 30, 1851.				AVERAGE NUMBER OF ATTENDANTS during Months next preceding March 30, 1851. (See Instruction VII.)			
	Morning	Afternoon	Evening		Morning	Afternoon	Evening
General Congregation }	390	60	432	General Congregation }			
Sunday Scholars	175	258	—	Sunday Scholars			
Total..	565	318	432	Total...			

	REMARKS	The Pew-rents are employed to defray the expenses of the Church. The afternoon service is only on the last Sunday of every month & is attended by the scholars besides those of the Parish.

I certify the foregoing to be a true and correct Return to the best of my belief.

Witness my hand this   31st   day of   March   1851.

IX.   (Signature)   C.F.E. Hankinson

(Official Character)   Perpetual Curate   of the above named St John King's Lynn

(Address by Post)   King's Lynn

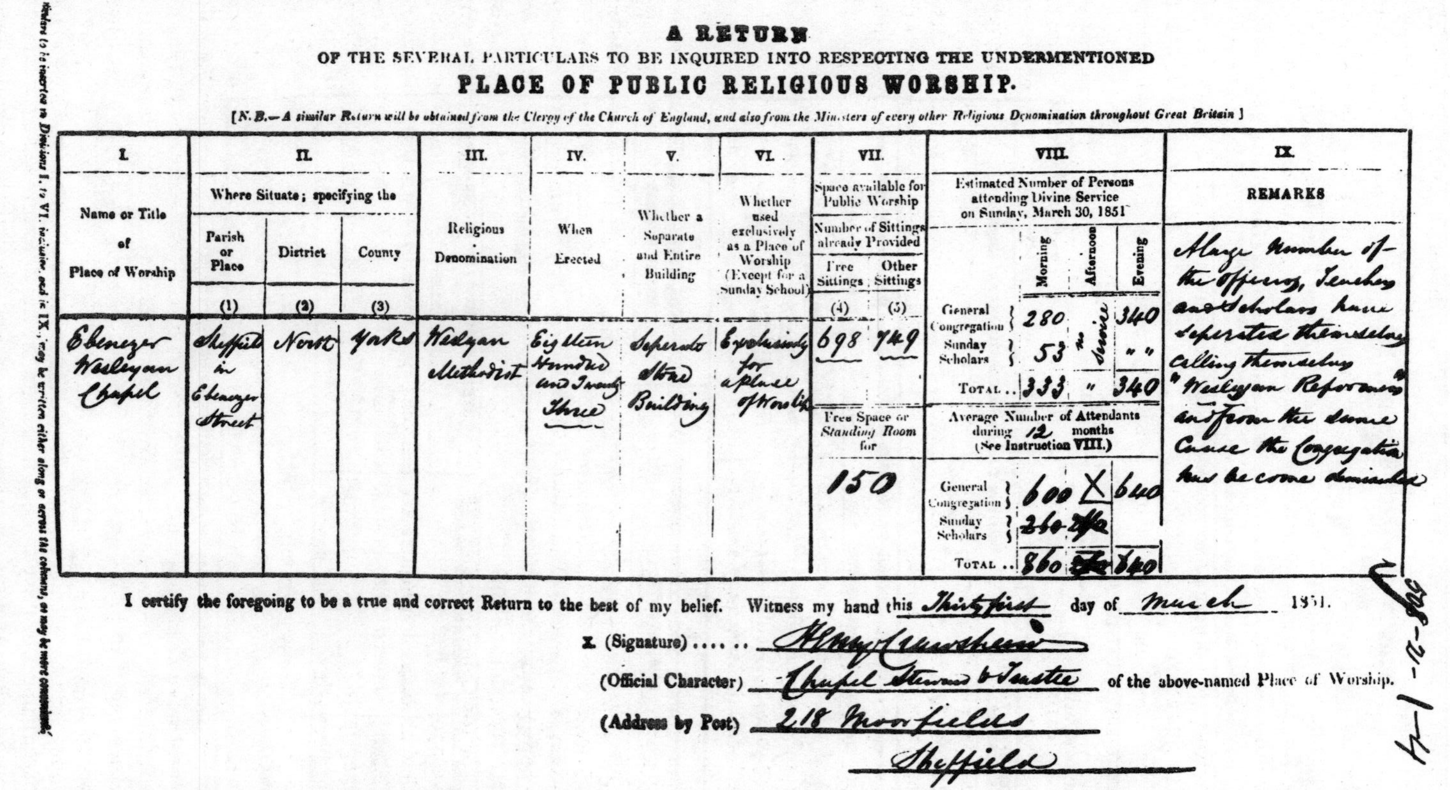

A RETURN

OF THE SEVERAL PARTICULARS TO BE INQUIRED INTO RESPECTING THE UNDERMENTIONED

PLACE OF PUBLIC RELIGIOUS WORSHIP.

[*N.B.—A similar Return will be obtained from the Clergy of the Church of England, and also from the Ministers of every other Religious Denomination throughout Great Britain.*]

I. Name or Title of Place of Worship	II. Where Situate; specifying the Parish or Place (1)	District (2)	County (3)	III. Religious Denomination	IV. When Erected	V. Whether a Separate and Entire Building	VI. Whether used exclusively as a Place of Worship (Except for a Sunday School)	VII. Space available for Public Worship: Number of Sittings already Provided: Free Sittings (4)	Other Sittings (5)	VIII. Estimated Number of Persons attending Divine Service on Sunday, March 30, 1851	Morning	Afternoon	Evening	IX. REMARKS
Ebenezer Wesleyan Chapel	Sheffield in Ebenezer Street	North	Yorks	Wesleyan Methodist	Eighteen Hundred and Twenty Three	Seperate Stone Building	Exclusively for a place of Worship	698	749	General Congregation	280	" Service	340	A large number of the Officers, Teachers and Scholars have seperated themselves calling themselves "Wesleyan Reformers" and from the same Cause the Congregation has become diminished
										Sunday Scholars	53	"	" "	
										TOTAL	333	"	340	
								Free Space or Standing Room for		Average Number of Attendants during 12 months (See Instruction VIII.)				
								150		General Congregation	600	X	640	
										Sunday Scholars	260			
										TOTAL	860		640	

I certify the foregoing to be a true and correct Return to the best of my belief. Witness my hand this Thirty first day of March 1851.

x (Signature) ..... [illegible]

(Official Character) Chapel Steward & Trustee of the above-named Place of Worship.

(Address by Post) 218 Moorfields Sheffield

Particulars to be inserted in Divisions I. to VI. inclusive, and in IX., may be written either along or across the columns, as may be more convenient.

Plate 26(b) Return for Ebenezer Wesleyan Chapel, Ebenezer Street, Sheffield, a new suburban chapel built in 1823 with seats for nearly 1,500, half of them free; the minister complains that the Wesleyan Reformed movement has split his church and reduced his congregation.

record itself is full of holes, especially for the local historian. Indeed it may well be of more value to the general historian for, apart from some overcounting among the nonconformists, the relative national proportions may well be accurate.[42] It is the detailed local studies which may reveal the defects of the survey. Sharp practice was not unknown; figures were often only rough guesses, giving adequate opportunity for them to be inflated by several only-just-honest means, while some enumerators refused to make any returns at all, like 'The Vickar [of Long Buckby, who] disapproves of the census therefore declined to fill up the form'.[43] The returns thus are not complete, nor indeed was compulsion used against those who failed to fill them in. What did happen was that local enumerators made attempts to fill in the census on behalf of the defaulting clergy. But at least 2,500 churches were seriously under-recorded.

Nevertheless this record can give us the first clear guide to several of our questions. It records the population said to be in church or chapel on that Sunday, at the same time as the census gives the total population figures for the community. Thus at King's Lynn, apart from the Quakers, some 10,045 (or 51% of the population) attendances at 15 churches or chapels on 30 March 1851 were recorded, but how many individuals this represented and how many of them were adults or children are not clear. It tells us how many churches and chapels there were at that time, when they were built (it must be noted that the date here refers to the building, not to the establishment of the congregation), what was their size and what was their relative support in the community. It throws light on the way the church or chapel thought of itself by the number of rented pews it still had. And it may well have incidental information in the comments attached to the return.

The local historian may thus start from this point to explore his main religious projects for the nineteenth century. There is little evidence for the *growth of irreligion* among the community. The census was followed in many cases by editorials in local newspapers; at Sheffield, there was a whole series of articles by a journalist called *Criticus*. Unfortunately there is no later comprehensive evidence for the growth in any particular community of the irreligious element in the population, for Church (which had suffered badly in the comparison) and chapel could not agree on the basis on which a second census should be taken. There were however several local ones like the Sheffield survey of 1881 or that for Bristol (1881) or for Gainsborough (1887–8) conducted by the newspapers, or the series in Liverpool (1881, 1891 and 1902);[44] they survive in manuscript form or published in local newspapers or occasional publications, for this was a matter of great public concern. The nearest one to a national survey was a private census published in 1872 by Edward Miall[45] but it cannot command anything like the same respect as the official census.

Other nineteenth-century sources

The *growth of provision* can be seen for both rural and urban churches in a variety of sources. Early in the century, dissenters' certificates were still required and were apparently more effectively enforced immediately after the Places of Worship Act of 1812; but they soon (1852) ceased to be required altogether. Thereafter local directories and date books, parish and diocesan papers, together with local newspapers and church magazines as well as the buildings themselves and old prints of them, may help to tell the story in detail. Central government records such as local Acts of Parliament or Privy Council notices in the *London Gazette* help to show the creation of new Anglican parishes, while a parliamentary paper[46] surveyed

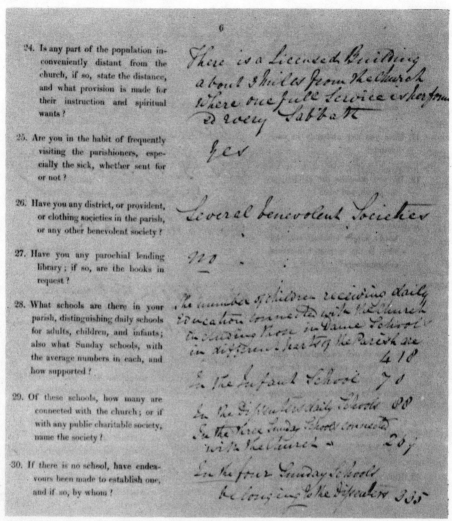

6

24. Is any part of the population in-
conveniently distant from the
church, if so, state the distance,
and what provision is made for
their instruction and spiritual
wants?

25. Are you in the habit of frequently
visiting the parishioners, especially the sick, whether sent for
or not?

26. Have you any district, or provident,
or clothing societies in the parish,
or any other benevolent society?

27. Have you any parochial lending
library; if so, are the books in
request?

28. What schools are there in your
parish, distinguishing daily schools
for adults, children, and infants;
also what Sunday schools, with
the average numbers in each, and
how supported?

29. Of these schools, how many are
connected with the church; or if
with any public charitable society,
name the society?

30. If there is no school, have endeavours been made to establish one,
and if so, by whom?

Plate 27(a)   One page from the visitation return 1845, for Wymondham, Norfolk. Other
questions relate to schools, charities, chapels and other subjects.

parochial livings as a consequence of the increasing sums available to the Governors
of Queen Anne's Bounty. There were other reports, one in 1818 on Anglican
churches in relation to growing population, several on non-residence and plurality
(1835, 1849, 1850), one in 1851 on Church Rates and another in 1857—8 by a
Select Committee of the House of Lords into the *Deficiency of the Means of
Spiritual Instruction and Places of Divine Worship in . . . Populous Districts*. The
records of the Ecclesiastical Commissioners reveal details of the finances of
Anglican churches,[47] while similar central material may be found for nonconformist chapels in the record offices of most of the major denominations, such
as the Baptist Union, the Methodist Church and the Society of Friends, and in their
Year Books.

   This concern with finances reflects the large amount of *church building* which

Wymondham Society
List of Members Dec 1896

No.	Name	Address		No.	Name	Address
1	George Lane	Middleton St		22	William Bullend	People St
2	John R Smith	Town Green		23	James Kent	do
3	Charles Higgins	do		24	Ann Buttush	do
4	William Minns	Norwich Road		25	Benjamin Mills	Back Lane ...
5	Mary Woodbine	Kidds Moor		26	Clarissa Drake	Dampate ...
6	Charlotte Lane	Middleton St		27	Maria Howchin	Chapel House
7	George Howes	People St		28	Emily Kent	People St
8	Mahala Howes	do		29	Clara Higgins	Chapel House
9	Elizabeth Thurston	Kidds Moor		30	Annie Childs	Cock St
10	Ann Smith	The Lizard		31	John Howes	Battle Row
11	Elizth Hipperson	Fairland St		32	Elizth Howes	do
12	Martha Minns	Fairland ...		33	Esther Norton	Dampate ...
13	James Knivett			34	Alice J Smith	Town Green
14	Ellen Knivett			35	Ellen Gooch	Fairland St
15	Amelia Elsey	Railway Road		36	Miss Cowling	Bridewell St
16	Jabez Boom	Middleton St		37	Mary ... Mitchell	Folly Lane
17	Robert Swatman	Norwich Rd		38	Ernest Higgin	
18	Walter F Pitts	Bun & Brown		39	Harriett Wells	
19	Jessy Blazey	People St		40	Rebecca Swatman	
20	William Jacobs	Fairland				
21	Harriett White	do				

Plate 27(b) Part of the Wymondham, Norfolk, Methodist Society list of members for 1896; it shows addresses and, in the margin, whether they left the society *L* or died *D*.

was done during the century. Apart from these, the most important sources here are twofold. The diocesan papers include detailed faculties for work, mortgage documents (starting in 1778 under Gilbert's Act) and a considerable amount of correspondence which is often intimately revealing. Bills, estimates and plans often survive. And secondly there are the newspaper accounts of the reopening of buildings after restoration, often giving full details of the work done and the methods adopted to pay for it. Ecclesiastical societies of various forms, many with diocesan branches like the Church Building Society, and local antiquarian societies show in their annual reports and other records something of the work done, while several journals like *The Builder* and the *Ecclesiologist* contain details of local church building.

Fourthly, there is the question of *support*. Lists of members may survive: in this, chapel records (Plate 27(b)) are usually more informative than parochial papers. The Methodist Conference published annual membership totals from 1766; for Anglicans, there are returns of Easter communicants from 1891. The unofficial censuses reveal the strength of the denominations; in Nottingham an assessment of 1833 gave some 5,800 Anglicans against a total of 12,000 nonconformists.

Similarly, on the whole the *activities* are better recorded for the chapels than for the churches. For the Anglicans, there are the parish records, registers of services among them. Especially valuable are the visitation returns which are now fuller (Plate 27(a)) rather than the formal and uninformative records they were in the

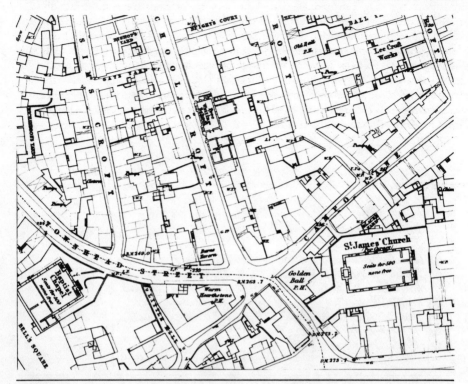

Plate 28   Section from O.S. large-scale 10 feet to the mile town plan for Sheffield, 1853. Note the church of St James (590 seats, none free) and the Baptist Chapel (500 seats, none free). This area is included in the 1833 map, see Plate 24. *Crown copyright reserved.*

eighteenth century.[48] There is a lot of evidence on the parsonage house, and the value of the benefice will be most clearly seen in the tithe awards, subsequent on the Act of 1836.[49]

The chapels lack much of this kind of material. But they still possess many records, minutes, accounts, correspondence and lists of activities — and a range of pamphlets, printed sermons and all the rest of the essential accompaniments to religious controversy.

And from these sources one may be able to assess something of the spirit in which all this was done, the *sense of social conscience and mission*. Here the subject of pew rents becomes important. The local struggle is recorded in the newspapers, where many advertisements for pews also appear; while the first large-scale O.S. town maps (10 feet to the mile scale) record the numbers of sittings in churches and chapels (Plate 28). These maps are also important for the study of the distribution of the churches and chapels, a further sign of the sense of mission to the community.

But apart from these simple tests, the local historian is dependent upon personal comment, in obituary notices in the newspapers or in memoirs, literary accounts of the local community or oral tradition. 'The Dissenters are strong in Newark, but not activated by the spirit of Dissent', wrote Gladstone during the course of his 1832 parliamentary campaign in that town.[50] In Corby (Lincs), living memory records that the Anglican and Roman Catholic congregations were more friendly disposed to each other at the turn of the century than either of them was to the dissenters. Such reminiscences are invaluable for many aspects of our subject and (in their printed form) are much more common than might be supposed. The Kilvert diaries are perhaps some of the most famous, but Ellen Buxton's notebook tells in some detail of the 'temporary church in Colne House gardens' during the restoration of Cromer church in 1862.[51] Local chapel and church histories contain many such reminiscences. But for much of the period the intangible nature of local religion will remain obscure.

Chapter 8

The concerns of the community

1

A question as to how the affairs of the local community were managed presupposes always that there were some clearly definable matters which concerned the group as a whole. Such an assumption has already been made by asserting that the proper subject of local history is a community, i.e. a group of people bound together by certain common interests. This does not mean of course that these common interests were necessarily common to all communities; the major concerns of a nineteenth-century seaside resort like Brighton are not those of the residents of a Staffordshire industrial village at the same date or of a scattered Shropshire sheep-farming society in the sixteenth century. Each community had its own range of public matters which indeed were not static but changed as the centuries passed. Other aspects of our study are of general interest: some economic changes will affect a Norfolk farming community as much as a Cornish mining village and a West Riding textile town; patterns of landownership, agricultural structure, religious organisation and social aspirations are among the factors which have made for changes in all places. But when we try to examine what were the matters of common interest within a particular local community, we find a multiplicity and a diversity which throws light on the distinctive character of each town and village. It is in the promotion of these common affairs that the real significance of its local government lies.

It is important to realise this, for it is much too easy to assume that the government of any local community was simply an administrative matter, a study of the machinery by which some of the common concerns were regulated. And this is not strictly true. Local government perhaps more than regional or national government was an expression of the society which formed the community. Each group of people created structures suited to its own needs. And for this reason local government worked. Indeed, it can be argued that local community affairs ceased to be managed naturally when, in the nineteenth century, the central authorities imposed more or less uniform structures of government on all the towns and villages of England, willy nilly.

This is not to say that true local government (by which we mean that the administrative decisions which involve the governed intimately should be taken by those most affected) always existed in earlier times, only to be destroyed by the nineteenth-century legislators. For the extent of popular involvement has varied considerably from place to place and from time to time. There were village groups governed by paternalist landlords (like Squire Donnithorne in *Adam Bede*) or indeed by despotic squires and their agents, like Roger Wendover's servant

Henslowe.[1] On the other hand, there were groups which from very early times wielded a good deal of influence over their own fortunes. The question cannot thus be framed, how did the local community manage its own affairs? — for some of its affairs were never in its own hands. For most of England for most of the time the majority of decisions concerning the future welfare of the local communities were taken by a few privileged persons. Rather the question must be put in the form, how were the affairs of the local community managed? How were their common interests forwarded, their common concerns safeguarded? Such an approach clearly dictates the way in which the local historian will tackle his study.

The first task is to select the subject to be discussed, for the machinery devised for its handling will vary from theme to theme. The identification of such subjects is indeed a formidable task. There is always a danger that the local historian will search in the past for matters which concern government today rather than let the past speak for itself. Nevertheless, there are some matters which would seem to concern all communities at all times, for they arise from the nature of communities themselves. Such is the treatment accorded to the needy members of the group — the young and the old, the sick and the poor. Again, most communities tried to ensure that individuals in the pursuit of gain or of pleasure did not exploit or inconvenience other members of the common group. Some communities took steps to protect minorities from persecution by the majority, and most attempted to protect the majority from aggressive and lawless tendencies on the part of a few individuals. Or there was the management of common property in the common interest. Matters thus of education, poor relief and welfare, public amenities, toleration and crime prevention may appear sufficiently widespread to be looked for in all local communities and to be commented upon where absent.

The second task is to identify those agencies which the social structure of the community created to deal with these spheres of common interest. And in this there was a balance maintained. In general, there seem to have been three main sorts of provision to meet the varying needs of the community. There were the formal agencies, with a legal (sometimes a statutory) basis for their authority. Secondly there were voluntary bodies, charitable institutions or informal groups wielding patronage with philanthropic concern. And finally, there was always a measure of self-help. Each community constructed its own pattern to meet particular problems; each story will be a different one, although composed of these three elements. There were of course other factors; during much of the nineteenth century, for instance, commercial interests provided a fourth element which does not seem to have been always as prominent in earlier periods. But for much of the period of our study, these three in varying proportions were involved in dealing with local community concerns.

Local government cannot thus be conceived of solely in terms of administrative machinery and certainly not only in terms of statutory or chartered bodies. Individuals exercised enormous influence and patronage within these fields; groups of persons combined to provide voluntarily what was not regarded as the legitimate object of the formal bodies of government. Indeed, the main characteristic of pre-nineteenth century local government in the formal sense was how limited was its field of activity. It was not a matter of charitable bodies or co-operative self-help filling the gaps left by the administrative machinery; rather the formal agencies were set up reluctantly where self-help and charity were inefficient, open to abuse or no longer regarded as the appropriate agency to handle a particular problem.

Having discovered the particular balance which his local community worked out in relation to the theme under consideration, the local historian must then assess the functions of each of the agencies involved. How were they structured? How were their decisions carried out? Each agency had some executive officers, although often not full-time, nor expert, nor salaried. Clearly the type of body concerned, the number, title and duties of the officers and the length of time they held office, the income and expenditure and work done must be explored, as well as the relations between the various agencies.

Having identified the fields of common interest and the body or bodies which tried to cope with them, and having seen them at work, a number of further problems arise. One is the question of the basis of authority in the community. Why should any individual or group act in relation to the community in a certain manner? Why for instance should a medieval lord of the manor control public amenities, or an eighteenth-century landlord control all the housing of a village? Why should a group of liveried gildsmen rule over the affairs of a whole town? Does their authority derive from inherited position, wealth, education and professional status, landlordship or some such factor; or does it spring from some common acceptance based upon some measure of control over those who wielded power?

This immediately raises the question of the involvement of the whole community. This may be seen in at least three ways. First there is the *election* of officers and members of the various bodies as well as representatives to those higher bodies (notably Parliament) which increasingly came to interfere with the community's purely local existence. In this, the matters of concern to the historian of both town and village will be the numbers of those entitled or not entitled to take part, the numbers of those who actually did so, and the grouping of the electors into parties based on local or national issues. Secondly the community had to support these agencies financially, and an examination of the *level of rates* or voluntary income can be very revealing of the measure of local support. But further, the *membership* of these bodies needs to be examined to see how widespread was the basis of power and how active were the members of the local community in their own government. Who served on its various boards and committees and trusts? Who were the members of (for instance) municipal corporations and what factors governed the various changes in personnel of these and other local bodies? What sort of persons acted as local officials, and what were their particular interests in the problem they were attempting to deal with? Who for instance were the nineteenth-century highways officers or sanitary officers, and how far were they involved with the community they served? The fact that in Corby (Lincs) the vicar was the most active promoter of one of the 'godless School Boards', became its chairman and regularly visited the Board School when it was established, throws a good deal of light on that local community where there were already voluntary Roman Catholic and Methodist schools. The same thing may be said of earlier periods; we still await a detailed study of the local government of an eighteenth-century village, and an analysis of its parish officers in terms of the community in which they lived and acted.[2] It is not without significance in the history of Rauceby that the incumbent, John Pugh, was one of the surveyors of the highways for most of the time of his residence in that village at the end of the eighteenth century. The nature of those who governed and their relations with the governed are of great importance in understanding the local community. Considerable variations will be seen according to the type of community, whether it is a parish or manor or borough and so on.

The final problem is how effective these bodies were. This cannot always be seen as a rivalry between voluntary and official bodies, the one appearing because the other was or became ineffective, although it often seemed like this to contemporaries. For, as the problem arose from out of the community itself, so in the same way certain answers arose from the community. The real question is how far the problem was solved. Did the medieval tithing system really help to keep down crime? Did the voluntary and statutory bodies, private charity and poor law officers, between them keep the problem of the underprivileged within manageable proportions in our given local community? It is perhaps in this final question, the most difficult of all to answer, that the true view of the local government of English communities as a joint enterprise of voluntary and 'official' bodies and self-help can really be seen.

2

There are, we have seen, three main elements in the development of local government in England, the statutory bodies or other agencies based on authority, the voluntary agencies and the practice of 'self-help'. The history of local government cannot be described simply in terms of a growth of activity, of increasing interference in the lives of members of the community. Nor can it be represented simply as a transition from one of these agencies to another. All three have been active in differing proportions at all stages in the development of the local community, although of course the forms that these have taken have been so varying that it may at times be somewhat difficult to classify them easily.

The middle ages

The medieval community was largely regulated by authoritative bodies and self-help. The system of administration of the medieval manor is still not completely clear, nor the relations between the manorial authorities and those non-manorial members of the community. Indeed it now seems likely that practice varied so greatly between local settlements, even those which were adjacent, that little in the way of generalisation can be made safely. A 'free tenant' on neighbouring manors could mean widely differing things in practice, whatever the lawyers might say. Relations between the manor court and the township assembly varied in different places according to ancient custom. But that there was in each community an element of both self-help and authority in the regulation of its affairs seems to be quite clear.

The basis of the authoritative agencies would seem to have been landlordship. It was this which gave, for instance, the Abbot of St Albans his right to insist that the inhabitants of the village might not use any corn-grinding equipment save the lord's mill, or the lord of the duchy of Cornwall his control over the tin-mining of the Cornish residents. But such an authority came to be challenged from two main directions. On the one hand, there was the royal authority gradually interfering with private custom, insisting on a 'common law' for all the king's subjects or at least for all his 'free' subjects. Thus the local lord had to justify his claims to take toll and to hang thieves or else lose such rights. Growing interference by the king's local agents, the sheriffs and then the escheators and (from the middle of the fourteenth century) the justices of the peace, came to whittle away local seignorial authority.[3]

On the other hand, there came constant pressure from the lord's tenants for an increasing amount of 'self-help'. This only became effective where the pressure came from organised groups. Thus it was largely in the towns that authority became transferred from landlords to tenants. The burgesses of Exeter for instance were able in the fifteenth century to overcome hindrances to their coastal trade which the Countess of Devon had imposed in the thirteenth century, by building a canal to by-pass her toll-stage on the river. It was not a transfer to the whole body of the community but to certain sections of the inhabitants organised in a gild or a closed council. It did not in the end justify the plea of 'self-help'; it merely changed the basis of authority from one of landlordship to one of chartered privilege, and in the course of it gave rise to many bitter feuds between rival in- and out-groups, as in London and many other towns. Nevertheless, as a recent study of the membership of the borough council of Stamford in the fifteenth century has shown, the transfer was effective. It was the burgess council, elected by the more privileged members of the whole community, which administered the affairs of the town, in so far as they were administered at all.[4] The evidence is that these councillors took their duties seriously. Incorporation was not opting out of government; it was in fact the means of opting in, of becoming more responsible rather than less responsible.

But the activities of these formal agencies of regulation were very limited. Much of their work was an attempt to enforce a measure of self-help. The residents were to pave their streets, light them and cleanse them and dispose of their own rubbish. The council of Great Yarmouth in 1552 appointed one of themselves 'daily to see that the gutters, drains and Rows may be kept clean and amended'; the council did not offer to do it for the inhabitants. And self-help was limited too. It was left to the voluntary (mainly religious) bodies to try to deal with some of the more severe problems of the local community. It was the friars who attempted to cope with the problems of urban overcrowding and plague; it was they and the monks who offered alms to the poor and the unemployed. Medieval hospitals cared for the aged and the sick, while all parts of the fragmented medieval church provided educational facilities. Much self-help came to be expressed in socio-religious gilds which, like the famous gilds of Coventry, provided poor relief and burial clubs for the middle rank of medieval urban society. From the late fourteenth century onwards, a few purely secular trusts for charitable purposes were established but generally they were of ephemeral nature.

It was for this reason that the Reformation created great changes in this sphere, as indeed in so many others. A large number of the voluntary agencies vanished or came under authoritative control; thus for instance religious schools came under the supervision of the local burgess council, while so many medieval hospitals passed into private ownership, either for their property and functions to be absorbed and lost or for the charity to be re-endowed with a new name. The benefactions of the medieval clergy were similarly lost with the creation of the married priest, to be replaced with a much greater element of private charity from individual members of the community, as wealth became more widely diffused.

Such a change in the field of voluntary activity reflects changes in the basis of authority. For the landlord element declined on the whole. The formal attacks on seignorial privilege had weakened it, but the eventual death of the manorial authority did not come about on the battlefield; it withered and died from an excess of profit-making. This of course is not true everywhere, but it is significant that the new 'manors' which emerged in the fifteenth and sixteenth centuries lacked administrative functions; the titles were purely for prestige. It is on the other hand clear that in some circumstances, especially where there was considerable building within the township, manorial authority became stronger, for it was in the lord's interest to assert his ownership of the waste. But such action could only take place (as in Manchester where the court leet lasted until the Improvement Commissioners took over from it in the nineteenth century) in places where there was no corporation and where the parochial interests expressed in the vestry were weak. On the whole seignorial (or proprietorial) authority was declining; the enclosure movement did not help it in any way.

The manor court thus became more or less a land registering and rent collecting body, although it could still appoint manorial officers. The court recorded transfers of manorial land, collected the entry fines, took rents (sometimes disguised as amercements) for houses built on the manorial waste, and in general left the regulation of the affairs of the community to that community. Even when we find the manor court legislating for the control of agricultural practice, there is a suspicion that the local community is using the court merely to record (and if possible, to enforce) decisions which the village community itself had already agreed, although of course some lords were still actively using their courts to regulate their estates.

The parish and the county

What then replaced it? From the late fifteenth century, it was the parish or township which became to a large extent the unit of civil government, and it remained so for nearly three hundred years with significantly little change. This is not to say that in many rural areas the landlord did not wield very great power over both his tenants and their neighbours. Closed villages still existed, often with minimal parochial administrative machinery. But alongside the estate there grew up with statutory encouragement a coherent body (the vestry with its churchwardens) with considerable powers and a number of officers charged (like the constable) with preserving law and order, or (like the surveyor of the highways) with providing common amenities, or (like the overseers of the poor) with dealing with social problems. The involvement of the community in this process varied from time to time and from place to place. In some townships, officers were elected and held office for one year only; in others, their period of duty could extend for several years, while in others again, service was by rota among a specified number of tenement holders. The body (where it existed) which lay behind these officers, the vestry, might be self-perpetuating or elective, open or select.

The whole system has been described so frequently that no further repetition is needed here. One might just add two words. The variation between different localities might still be very great, despite the legislative background to the authority of the civil parish. And secondly, the local work was largely routine; very little real freedom was left to the parish officers.[5] On occasion there are glimpses of initiative: at Holt in Norfolk, the parish register for 1599 (two years before the first Poor Law of 1601) recorded, 'In this yeare was the house for the poore builded by the Towne'. But this is on the whole rare.

For this initiative, one has to turn to the justices of the peace.[6] Just as the local community existed within a wider economic region, so it existed within a wider administrative region, the county. This unit cannot be too strongly stressed in the seventeenth and eighteenth centuries: 'In some respects the England of 1640 resembled a union of partially independent county-states, rather as Canada today is a union of self-governing provinces.'[7] There was, at least among a certain class, a real sense of community in the county, just as there was in the village and town, and it persisted despite much mobility from shire to shire. Lambard's much-quoted introduction to his *Perambulation of Kent* echoes the sentiments of that class of county gentleman which was united by intermarriage, social pretensions, speech and even (paradoxical though it may seem) by its very divisions. In some counties, like Gloucestershire, the major families were strongly polarised, while other counties were much less deeply divided. The class was not a closed one – coal miners like the Willoughbys and industrialists like the Strutts could enter the Nottinghamshire scene in the seventeenth and eighteenth centuries.

And the powers of these justices were real. Collectively for instance, they maintained some bridges and supervised weights and measures; individually, they could appoint some parish officers, supervise the local poor law officers, check the parish accounts and maintain order. Their duties and powers were regularly being increased; their presence was felt everywhere. They lost some of their work in places to turnpike trusts or Improvement Commissioners; they came themselves to rely upon specialist officials and paid servants. But they still controlled the local administration in most of its aspects.

The corporate towns had their own justices, chosen from among themselves. Much of the interest in borough administration from the seventeenth century onwards lies in the relations between the borough justices, the corporate authorities and the parish officers – although the growth of authority in the civil parish did not affect these communities quite as much as their rural counterparts. Religious controversies particularly played their part in this triangular relationship. Leeds is a celebrated example of a religious struggle over the control of the parochial offices, but similar things happened elsewhere. The relations at Nottingham between the (Anglican?) parochial officers and the (largely nonconformist) corporation which drew most of its members from one of the major Independent chapels in the town, the robing room of which became known as 'the mayor's parlour', explain much in the eighteenth-century history of that town.[8]

On the whole, the towns reveal an increasing tendency towards oligarchy. The fifteenth century saw some early and unsuccessful attempts to limit this, but as time went on the corporation in most places grew away from the community. The struggles over the charters which so many towns experienced in the late seventeenth century seem to have contributed to this. But whether these corporations became more, or less, active in the field of local administration, whether they became more effective or not, seems to have depended upon some local leader, some effort of initiative by an individual or small group.

There is indeed some difficulty in distinguishing clearly between the voluntary and the formal aspects of government. The Great Yarmouth corporation in the seventeenth century for instance ran an orphans' fund. 'Town lands' were held by a number of boroughs for charitable purposes. Indeed, for some of the non-corporate towns, a new kind of local authority sprang up, administering the 'chamber lands' and with this assuming wider responsibilities.[9] Where charity provided the poor houses, the town did not need to. And charity was very active indeed. Each community varied in the numbers, range and activities of its charities but very few had none at all. Such charities created links between communities; the inscriptions to Thomas and Mary Deacon in Peterborough Cathedral record their bequests to the poor of Peterborough, Spalding and Fleet,[10] binding together three communities in their charities. But the charitable movement was above all else a parish-based movement. It was membership of the parochial community which entitled one to benefit, and in a very large number of cases it was the parochial officers who administered the trust.

Decline of the parish

The decline of the parish came about in the late eighteenth and early nineteenth centuries. It became recognised that for some purposes of social provision the small township was not necessarily the most effective body. At first unions of parishes for such things as poor relief and the provision of workhouses (from the Workhouse Test Act of 1722 and Gilbert's Act, 1782) were created. Later, from the 1830s, new authorities were established, quite independent of the older civil parish officers — boards for Poor Law (1834) or Health (1848) or Highways (1862) or Education (1870), each with its own elected body, its own officers, its own rates.[11] Early in the nineteenth century the parish lost its own elected constable when the county quarter sessions and the boroughs were authorised to set up police forces. The parish became, as the Webbs saw it, 'squeezed to death'.

It was, of course, the towns which felt this proliferation of authorities most. From the late seventeenth or early eighteenth century they had seen the arrival by local Act of Parliament of separate commissioners for police or for improvements such as cleaning and patrolling the streets or lighting and paving them or for slum clearance or for the provision of amenities such as new roads or an adequate water supply or (rather later) gas distribution and the like. These functions were rarely performed by one body in any town. Sometimes they were undertaken by the borough council, often by one or more independent bodies;[12] on the other hand, private enterprise in estate development or in the provision of water and gas supplies was at times the main moving force. In west Norfolk, for instance, gas for Dereham and King's Lynn was the monopoly of the Malam family; at Stamford, the whole town was supplied with water by the Exeter estate. The reform of about two hundred of the corporate boroughs by the Municipal Reform Act of 1835 increased the number of different authorities, although in general it gave a nucleus for the growth of further local government. Local Acts of Parliament continued; Liverpool promoted no less than nine between 1858 and 1883. But by that time most of them added to the powers of existing authorities rather than set up new bodies. By the middle years of the nineteenth century, the collage of local administration had reached its most complex form. The establishment of the county councils in 1889 marks the beginning of that continuing process of creating comprehensive local government structures which has accompanied the devolution of authority from local hands to larger and more remote bodies, a process that the present reorganisation is still pursuing.

Nineteenth century: local variations

What then was the picture of local government in the middle of the nineteenth century? It is one in which there is more active concern in the problems of society than there had been at any time before, but the approach was still a piecemeal and even at times a reluctant one. A fever in Manchester helped to create the demand for a Board of Health in the town as early as 1796, but it was not until a second wave of cholera broke out over the country in 1845—6 that neighbouring communities like Liverpool did much about their provision or that national concern was aroused. A problem was thus identified and separate machinery was devised to deal with it. The result was an incredible variety in form and activity in the field of local administration. There was no common pattern. The old parish officials in some places became ineffective; in others they retained their powers. Manor courts still appointed officials: as late as 1855 the town of Wimborne (Dorset) was 'governed by a constable and bailiff with tithingmen for the several tithings within the parish, who were appointed at the manorial court held annually at Michaelmas'. Thus rural parishes might range from those with no real form of local government at all (save that provided by the nearest Board of Guardians) to those with very active vestries. Towns were even more diverse. The old chartered corporations had fallen apart — some were reformed into active municipal authorities, while others were by-passed and dwindled into insignificance, the real power passing to other bodies like Improvement Commissioners. The unchartered towns all developed along individual lines, with manorial officers, vestry, Boards of Guardians, charity trustees, Improvement Commissioners and many other bodies jostling each other, challenging and quarrelling and getting in each other's way. Even in London it was the vestries or district boards (unions of parishes) which were the real authorities, with the Metropolitan Board of Works attempting to bring order out of local chaos.[13]

Confusion thus reigned. There were separate, often overlapping, boards, councils and committees for each aspect of local concern which the official bodies came to be interested in. Professor Best quotes the reply of one official when asked who was responsible for the public health of his local community (1869): 'The local Board of Health, two Burial Boards, the Board of Guardians, the Superintendent and district Registrars, and the Inspector of Factories and his subordinates.'[14]

The town of Exeter provides a clear example of this.[15] Here the corporation (called 'the chamber') became the city council after 1835. It managed the town's property, ran the police and the town's market and built the canal (running into difficulties in the process). But most of the town's amenities were provided by the sixty or so Improvement Commissioners, established since 1688. They paved, lit and patrolled the streets and provided sewerage. Only six of their members came from the corporation. An Act of 1832 revised their constitution but as a body they survived until 1867 when their functions were taken over by the Streets Committee of a reformed corporation (called, for confusion, the Local Board). Then there were the members of the Corporation for the Poor, set up by local Act in 1696 (amended in 1788), who collected the local poor rate. Their activities were supplemented by the Exeter Relief Society, a voluntary body. A Board of Health was established by the Council, originally to replace the Improvement Commissioners, but for a time the two bodies rivalled each other. A School Board, set up in 1871, completed the formal provision. Three commercial undertakings provided other amenities: the Water Company, which the Council bought out in 1878, the Exeter Commercial Gas Company, which the Council failed to buy out, and the Exeter Sewerage Manure Irrigation Company, which the Council did not need to buy out, for it failed. Housing was provided by two main interests, the Exeter Improved Industrial Dwellings Company and the Exeter Freehold Land Building Society (from 1857).

As official bodies proliferated, the voluntary urge does not seem to have declined in the second half of the nineteenth century. It was still expressed in most areas — in the country by the provision of schools or village halls or other social amenities; in industrial areas by housing schemes or hospitals or cultural and leisure provision. Self-help too became more active, more insistently heard. From the 1850s local amenity societies emerged, often leading to the provision of parks and other facilities. But the later nineteenth century marked a period in which the statutory bodies became more and more active in the field of social welfare.

In this they were spurred on, but not controlled, by central persuasion which similarly witnessed a proliferation of bodies (the Central Board of Health, the Charity Commissioners, the Local Government Board, the Committee of the

Council for Education and very many other bodies). At first, Acts like the 1848 Public Health Act were adoptive; it was only later that they became compulsory. From the 1870s came a movement for greater interference; the era of isolation was over. The new Municipal Corporations Commission of 1876 dealt with many of the smaller boroughs, and some new local government areas were set up in 1877 and drastically revised in 1894, when the Boards of Health became Urban District Councils. But the smaller bodies were not squeezed out; the 1894 Parish Councils Act established elected councils in all villages with more than 300 population (and indeed in smaller ones, if they so wished).

As local authorities became more centralised and more comprehensive, so they became more self-conscious. The great rebuilding of town centres of the second half of the century reveals that local government, like other aspects of the history of the community, has a topographical dimension. Some of the rebuilding was part of a programme of slum clearance or other improvements; but others were simply an assertion of title within the community. Led by Birmingham (1832–61) (Plate 29), Manchester (Athenaeum, 1836–8) and Liverpool (St George's Hall, 1839–56), most towns revealed their civic dignity and increasing administrative responsibilities in edifices worthy of the community in which they stood.

This may lead us to underestimate the voluntary and self-help aspects of local community concern in the later nineteenth century. But this would be a mistake. All elements were active. The problems were bigger; a larger effort was needed on the part of all agencies to overcome them. The involvement of the community was greater than just the process of local elections and politics.

Involvement

But the process of local elections and politics was important. In this connection, the interest of the local historian will centre on the question of rates. 'Since the commencement of the present century', wrote a commentator in King's Lynn, 'nothing more remarkable is known to have occurred here than what has been

Plate 29(a)   Birmingham Town Hall, started in 1832 but basically an expression of the reformed corporation — a symbol of civic self-consciousness in its style and situation.

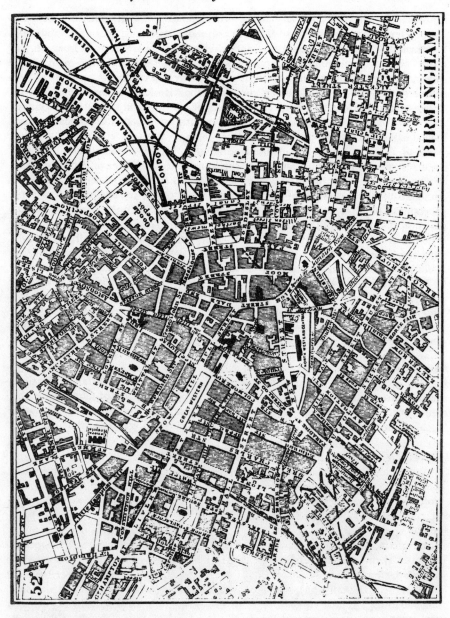

Plate 29(b)   Map of Birmingham, from *Bradshaw's Handbook to the Manufacturing Districts of Great Britain,* 1854. Note the early concentration of public buildings.

produced by the operation of new taxes and new laws — especially our poor and paving laws. These certainly have borne and are still bearing hard upon a large portion of the industrious inhabitants.'[16] This tale was repeated elsewhere, and often. Rates rose alarmingly and created reactions within the community. Elections were fought bitterly and retrenchments were made soon afterwards. In Birmingham, a town poll of 1855 in which the Council was defeated led to the resignation *en bloc* of the Finance and Public Works Committees. In consequence a party of Economists organised by the Ratepayers' Protection Society secured control of the committees, dismissed the borough engineer, replacing him by his assistant at half his salary, halted the programme of improvements and quarrelled regularly with the Town Clerk. After ten years of 'inefficiency', Thomas Avery began to bring some order into the city's affairs and five years later, in 1870, Joseph Chamberlain began the programme of 'High Rates and a Healthy City', though in fact the main cost of improvements came not from higher rates but from more of them and from other sources.[17] Rates were not of course the only local issue. In York, a small Tory group outmanoeuvred the Liberals over the establishment of a police force but when they came to power they promptly did what they had objected to in opposition.

Clearly such disputes highlight the question of the basis of authority. Where did real power lie in the community and why? In rural areas, landlordship had been undermined although it was never insignificant. How could it be when, for instance, one-third of the soil of Nottinghamshire as late as 1876 was owned by three lords only? But even in villages there was increasing involvement of the people in their affairs. This was more particularly true of the towns — the various reform Acts of the nineteenth century had seen to that. Thus at Exeter there were changes in the parliamentary electorate after the Reform Acts of 1832 and 1867, with an increasing working-class element clearly apparent,[18] challenging the predominance of the Conservative professional and merchant classes and 'the second tier' of Liberal small businessmen.[19] And towns varied. York (unusually) elected their Improvement Commissioners but the corporation was closed; the early struggles thus centred on the Commission elections.

Involvement in elections and involvement in terms of paying rates — these were increasingly widespread. Involvement in service was also increasing as the proliferation of bodies called for the energies and time of the local residents in membership of the various Councils, Boards and Committees. Not all of the community of course was able to serve; it was largely confined to the tradesmen of the town. In Birmingham, over half of the Council in the 1840s were owners of small businesses, most of them manufacturing. The bigger businessmen, however, increased their representation especially after 1851 when the Streets Commission (the local Improvement Commission) was taken over by the Town Council; but in 1855 when the Economists gained control, they became less significant; it was the smaller men who once more predominated, especially the licensed victuallers. With Chamberlain's reforms, there were again changes — big business and professional men becoming the important elements; the smaller interests fell to only 15%.[20] The involvement of at least a number of members of the community is clear. But there were some contradictory trends. Officials were becoming more permanent, expert and thus less directly responsible urban servants. And the units of local government themselves were becoming larger — the 1870s saw many considerable borough extensions. It is a matter of gains and losses, and each local story has its own tale to tell.

3

The major sources for such a widespread study are equally extensive, for many of the agencies which concerned themselves with these matters created and preserved records for themselves. Although most of the bodies set up to deal with specific problems have now ceased to exist, in most cases their concerns and with them their records have passed to other bodies. Even where there was no obvious heir, there seems to have been an inbuilt tendency for such records to survive. After all, they were for many purposes legal documents and were consulted frequently. Only in one main aspect is there any serious deficiency. The self-help aspect of local government is seriously under-recorded. In the nature of things, it was less organised, its efforts were more ephemeral and its personnel on the whole less articulate, less literate. Such activities required less in the way of precedents or previous records to enable them to be pursued. Most of the voluntary work was recorded in some way or another but generally hardly as fully as those 'official' bodies with permanent or semi-permanent officials.

It may once again be best to divide the period before 1800 into two for this purpose — pre-Reformation and post-Reformation — for as we have seen the sixteenth century saw major changes in the distribution of functions and concerns between the three main groups of agencies. The problems, however, remain the same: what were the concerns of the community, what agencies existed to meet these concerns and on what authority, how far did they involve the members of the community, and how effective were they?

Medieval sources

The main sources for this study consist of manorial records. Not every village, of course, had a manorial structure, nor do the records of every manor which did exist survive. But this must be the starting point. In this respect, the *Victoria County Histories* are quite correct to stress the descent of manorial title (even though their studies rarely go on to inquire into community concerns). Tracing the descent of a manor is a tedious task, and the local historian may be thankful to the *Victoria County Histories* where it has already been done.[21]

The most useful of these records are manor court rolls and custumals which may show the range of the concerns of the court. Those which survive are mainly for religious houses. Where these records do not survive, there are two main supplementary sources — the Hundred Rolls, a great survey of local government of the 1270s, often listing all those who claimed any rights of lordship in the community;[22] and the Inquisitions *post mortem*, especially those which include extents (or surveys).[23] There are other inquests, one of the most valuable of which is the series known as *Ad Quod Dampnum*.[24]

For medieval boroughs, the sources provide a different series of problems. The manor court may still survive; so may the hundred and even the sheriff's court; at Nottingham, the Mickletorn Jury, apparently a descendant of the court leet jurisdiction, continued until the nineteenth century. Indeed, some of these agencies may even have become more active at different stages of the town's development; in Stamford, the royal steward came increasingly to interfere with the corporation in the early sixteenth century. The question of the relationship between these institutions thus arises. But more often the history of town government is one of the growth of different privileged groups, the early gilds and the later corporation. Here the study of local charters becomes essential. For most places, the charters have been printed, but details of all of them can easily be obtained.[25] Especially valuable are the borough records themselves — minute books, list of officers, records of officials or committees, such as chamberlain's accounts, etc.[26]

Voluntary efforts may be traced in such records as the return of gilds (1389) and the chantry certificates of 1548.[27] But the subject is fraught with difficulty, for there is no overall survey for the local community. There are many miscellaneous references to charitable uses in bishops' registers and other sources, and such material becomes particularly profuse at the time of the dissolution of the monasteries. The task is a difficult one for the medieval local historian, for he needs to hunt for his material and can never be sure he has in fact covered everything.

Post-medieval sources

For the period after the Reformation, the most prolific sources are those relating to the official bodies. To trace these in any local community, the obvious starting-point must be the records that they themselves created. The manor may continue to exist; it may even be revived in the seventeenth and early eighteenth centuries. In these cases, where the manor court rolls survive, they should be examined carefully, especially to discern the links between the parish (or borough) officers and the manorial officers.[28] But on the whole the manor declined, and as a sign of this, in many places the manorial constable became a parochial officer, chosen in the vestry. The parish itself created numerous records, described in detail by W. E. Tate in his book, *The Parish Chest*. Vestry minutes, churchwardens' accounts, records of the overseers of the poor or the surveyors of the highways, constables' accounts and the like may be found in an average parish chest. But there are many parishes for which they do not survive and in these cases the local historian must rely upon what scattered information he can collect. Thus the names of the churchwardens may be recorded at times in the church itself or in the registers or on church terriers or on the bishops' transcripts. The quarter sessions papers will contain much relating to the local poor law, but these are not always available and are usually quite inadequately indexed. Certainly, however, they must be used for any full analysis of the subject. They regularly in the eighteenth century contain returns of local rates, and can on occasion be supplemented by parliamentary returns, especially in the early nineteenth century. So that even for those places where there are no surviving records of parochial administration, a good deal can be learned from other sources.

Most towns are better placed in this respect, especially those which were chartered boroughs. Their papers are frequently plentiful and are sometimes printed.[29] They may contain charters, a larger number of deeds and lease registers for town property, minute books, the legal records of the borough courts (including the quarter sessions) and the like. The corporation as a whole and each of its officers or committees produced many evidences of their work. Again the quasi-municipal bodies created many records and these generally passed into the possession of their successors; thus the papers of the Exeter Improvement Commissioners are now among the archives of the Corporation, while the papers of the town trustees of Ely and of the charities at Peterborough survive.[30]

The records relating to voluntary work are more patchy. The charitable interests fall into two categories, the endowed and the unendowed. The latter often left no survival but their work may be recorded in the local newspapers. Thus we may find advertisements for a Hospital Sunday or some other special effort to raise and distribute funds. Again wills provide much information on charities, both unendowed and endowed. But the endowed charities are better provided with memorials and their papers often survive in the parish chest, corporation archives or local solicitor's office. They throw a lot of light on such topics as the origin of the trust, its duties, the nature of its trustees and officials (if any), the management of the endowment and the persons who benefited. Lists of charities are sometimes found on church terriers or painted up in the church itself. But charities were ephemeral in their nature[31] and many were lost by the time of the great Charity Commissioners' Report of 1819—40. Nevertheless this very detailed report, listing all known local charities with full particulars, is still the best starting-point for the enquiry. In addition, there are, of course, the buildings themselves, the poor houses, charity hospitals, almshouses and the like, still surviving.

Nevertheless the answers to many of our questions will still be elusive. What concerns of the community were not catered for? How much self-help was there? How far was the community as a whole involved? How effective were these agencies? Some of these subjects are better known for the towns than for the villages. Poll books (Plate 30(b)) or lists for parliamentary elections may survive as early as the fifteenth century,[32] but matters relating to internal elections are rarely recorded save in borough minute books and then only for the most important issues.

One difficult question relates to the basis of authority within the town or village. Here the local historian has to make an assessment of the social structure of his local community. This has many problems which will be discussed more fully below. Nevertheless an analysis of both the chosen members of the corporation and the officers in terms of landownership, wealth, occupations and the like may reveal something of the basis of power. In this connection, the records of the enclosure and estate papers (especially deeds) and taxation records (especially the land tax) are most important. But in the end authority in the local community, although clearly related to one or more of these subjects, depended upon the exercise of personal initiative, upon an individual's activity, his social enterprise. It was the efforts of many concerned individuals, often at some sacrifice to their personal interests, that decided what in fact was or was not done in any local community. Thus, much of the best material relating to local government is to be found haphazardly amongst the private papers of the community's leaders.

4

The problems for the nineteenth-century historian of local government are very great indeed, for a number of reasons — the great multiplicity of agencies, the growing pressure of the problems and the ever increasing bulk of the record material. But it is ungrateful to complain that there is too much when the earlier studies have suffered because there was too little.

It is relatively easy to trace what *agencies* existed in any one locality. An inspection of the local directories is almost certainly the quickest method to secure this information for rural areas, although they sometimes omit one or two of the more general authorities. For the towns, the directories also have their uses, but most important are the borough records themselves. These continued to proliferate as the councils took to themselves more responsibilities.

Parish records exist for most of the century but they gradually decrease in bulk and usefulness. The parish poor law papers more or less cease from 1834, although the vestry minutes carry on. For this and other aspects of his study the local

ROTTON PARK WARD ELECTION.

THE BALLAD OF A BARROW.

Air - - - - - - "*The Whistle*," - - - - *By Robert Burns.*

I sing of a Barrow, from Bull Street, wheeled forth,
By Baker and Chamberlain, up to the North,
To the Liberal Committee, whose help was implored,
To send it to Council for Rotton Park Ward.

If this Barrow was empty, well, what did they care?
The more they could fill it, if once it got there;
It was trim and well painted, its handles were wide,
And upon it the mighty Screwmaker could ride.

So the old women whispered, and rumour did swell,
That the Barrow would go in, with lantern and bell,
To the Council, and then to the Sewage back stair,
To wheel in the Chamberlain, soon to be Mayor.

But then, a commotion arose in the Ward,
"Shall Screwmakers rule us? Is Baker our lord?
"Awake ye good Burgesses! trusty and true!
"Let them quake that would wheel such a Barrow on you!"

Then Sadler rushed out, and he harnessed his steed,
And leaders around him came up with all speed;
They Bearded the Baker, and dared to maintain,
He should not have a Barrow to play with again!

They sought a good man, with an eye for a flaw,
In a bill of expenses, or vote against law ;
And one who would dare in the Council to fight,
For this Ward so neglected, and argue its right—

To be sewered and drained and made wholesome and clean
That the poor might be healthy, the wealthy serene;
One who lived in the Ward, one who saw what was wrong,
And would strive to remove it with time and with tongue.

SAMUEL TONKS was the man who was chosen at last,
Though a veteran in years, not too slow nor too fast,
In Council experienced, well knowing his way,
And a daring opponent of waste and delay.

Vince and Collings they thundered, Sam Timmins he roared,
Herbert Chamberlain threw his "old clothes" at the Ward;
Poor Baker the Quaker, they made such a clatter,
He vowed he should soon be "as mad as a Hatter."

Did they push the Barrow, or sugar the Tea?
Did they give out currants and raisins all free?
If not, with sweet vows and with tongues smooth as oil,
They begged their opponent their game not to spoil.

But spite of their promises, speeches, uproar,
The Barrow they could not get in at the door!
While TONKS the Ward Champion, nobly be bore him,
And drove the "*Alliance*" and "*League*" all before him.

The Burgesses said "Take your Barrow outside!"
" To Bull Street or Edgbaston wheel it" they cried,
" For, spite of *the screw*, and your canvass and din,
"**The People's own Candidate, TONKS shall get in.**"

Plate 30(a)   Local government poster, Birmingham

This poster refers to a local authority election in November 1873. Joseph Chamberlain was first elected mayor in 1873, which explains the line: 'To wheel in the Chamberlain, soon to be mayor.' In fact, despite the tone of the poster, Richard Cadbury Barrow was elected; Samuel Tonks who had represented another ward for 17 years, never represented Rotton Park Ward.

historian needs to look further afield, to the records of the local Boards or Unions supplemented by quarter sessions papers and parliamentary returns.

Political issues are, of course, recorded in the newspapers and in the pamphlets and posters (Plate 30(a)) which were produced, many of which have survived.

9

	C.	P.	K.	M.
Borne, John, gentleman, Albany-place, Cowick-street ...		1		
Borne, Henry, gardener, Sanford-street ...			1	1
Boston, F., butcher, Kenton & New Bridge-st, St. Edmunds	1		1	
Boulter, James, cellarman, Brook Green			1	1
Boundy, Samuel, accountant, Magdalen-street	1	1		
Boundy, John, joiner, Waterloo-place	1	1		
Boundy, George L, clerk, Friars	1	1		
Boutcher, William, painter, Paris-street			1	1
Bovey, Robert, gentleman, Friars Walk			1	1
Bowcher, Edward, gentleman, 26, Dix's Fields ...			1	1
Bowcher, William, tailor, Parr-street	1	1		
Bowden, George, Cottage-court	1	1		
Bowden, George, Dymond's-court			1	1
Bowden, Thomas, sawyer, Limekiln-lane	1	1		
Bowden, John, Polsloe Villa, Heavitree		—		
Bowden, John, bricklayer, Alma-cottage ...			1	1
Bowden, William, bricklayer, Summerland-row ...	1	1		
Bowden, John P., plumber, Parr-street	1	1		
Bowden, John, sawyer, Commercial-road		1		
Bowden, Charles, carpenter, 3, Chapple-buildings ...			1	1
Bowden, W., painter, 8, Spring-tr., York-road, Lambeth	1	1		
Bowden, William, stone mason, 52, Bartholomew-street...	1	1		
Bowden, Edward, tailor, Longbrook-terrace			1	1
Bowden, Edwin, independent minister, Heavitree ...	1	1		
Bowden, William, milkman, St. David's-hill			1	1
Bowden, Robt. H. R., yeoman, Woodbury Salterton (fr.)			1	1
Bowden, Wm. sawyer, Brunswick-place	1	1		
Bowden, John, labourer, Lion's Holt			1	1
Bowden, Wm., sawyer, Summerland street	1	1		
Bowden, Thomas, junr., sawyer, Townsend-court ...	1	1		
Bowden, Thomas, sawyer, Townsend-court	1	1		
Bowden, Henry, accountant, Melbourne-place			1	1
Bowden, John, ironmonger, Magdalen-street			1	1
Bowden, William John, 23, Okehampton-street... ...		—		
Bowden, David, Elm Grove-road		—		
Bowden, James, Woodbine-place		—		
Bowden, John, Waterbeer-street	1	1		
Bowden, Henry, North-street...			1	1
Bowdidge, George, West-street			1	1
Bowers, Henry, carman, Paul-street	1	1		
Bowers, George, Edmund-square	1	1		
Bowring, Henry, tailor, Parr street	1	1		
Bowring, Sir John, Knight, 3, Claremont Grove ...	1	1		
Bowring, John Charles, Larkbeare, St. Leonards ...	1	1		
Box, Rev. H. A., Parker's Well House		—		
Boyce, John, gentleman, Union-terrace	1	1		
Boyce, James, labourer, Black-boy-road			1	1
Boyce, Josheph, carpenter, Par-street...			1	1
Boyd, the Rev. Archibald, clergyman, the Deanery ...			1	1
Brackenberry, James, Silver-terrace, Heavitree... ...			1	1
Bradbeer, Henry, brushmaker, Friars-walk ...	1	1		
Bradbeer, Thomas, North-place		1		1
Bradbeer, George, carpenter, Olave's-square ...	1	1		
Bradbeer, William Robert, brushmaker, Exe Bridge ...	1	1		
Bradbeer, Robert, brushmaker, Paragon-place ...	1	1		
Bradbeer, Joseph, brushmaker, St. Sidwell-street ...	1	1		
Braddon, John, Currier, Magdalen-street ...	1	1		
Braddon, Benjamin, boot closer, King William-terrace ...	1	1		
Bradford, Thomas, reporter, Parr-street			1	1
Bradford, Robt., gardener, Albert-street	1	1		
Bradford, James, shopkeeper, Paris-street ...			1	1
Bradford, George, joiner, East Wonford			1	
Bradford, James, joiner, Summerland-street ...			1	1
Bradford, William, shoe maker, Pancras lane			1	1
Bradford, George, Prospect-place, Rack-street ...	1	1		
Bradley, William Henry, reporter, Salem-place ...	1	1		
Bradley, John, painter, 154, Fore-street	1	1		
Bradley, William, decorator, 159, Fore-street ...	1	1		
Bradley, William Henry, draper, North-street	1	1		
Bradley, Matthew, gent, 1, Richmond-terrace, St. Leonard			1	1
Bragg, George, builder, Portland-place			1	
Brailey, Charles, chemist, Heavitree	1	1		

Especially significant are the poll books (Plate 30(b)) which continue to record parliamentary electors up to 1872. A study of these for any community, when related to census and other material, can be most revealing. Local rate books throw a great deal of light on the electorate, for with varying rates, a £10 householder in York or Birmingham was not the same as in London, even in the early nineteenth century.

The local newspapers not merely inform us of local political controversies, especially those surrounding the great elections in town and county, but they themselves reflect such controversies. It must be stressed that despite what the newspapers called themselves they did not always follow party lines. They did, as occasion demanded, change party allegiances. A good example of such changes (and thus of the necessity for the local historian, in order to assess a political situation in a mid-Victorian town of some size possessing three weekly newspapers of different political complexions, to read all three carefully and to collate and compare them) may be seen in the elections in Southampton in 1859—60.[33] Here the Liberal party had controlled the parliamentary representation for the previous dozen years, helped by the powerful backing of the port's leading steamship company, the famous P. & O., whose managing director had been one of the sitting members throughout that period. A by-election in 1859 caused by the elevation of the other member to the peerage gave an opportunity for the growing discontent of the party's more radical section with what they called 'P. & O. domination' to find expression by their putting up W. D. Seymour, who some years earlier had sat for Sunderland, against the new candidate brought forward by the moderate, well-to-do (and P. & O.) elements who had hitherto led it. The local Tories had no strong nominee available and no prospect of winning the ensuing contest, and many of their more progressive or Tory-Radical members seized the chance of splitting their rivals by voting for Seymour, who was successful. He also received some support from London protectionist shipping firms anxious to check the rise of Southampton and the P. & O.

These factors, however, led some of the Radicals whose cause Seymour had championed to begin to look askance at him. Thus the Tory *Hampshire Advertiser* in supporting Seymour declared that its rival the Hampshire *Independent*, long the local Liberal organ but moderate or even Whiggish in tone, had 'ignored the young tradesmen and merchants, the working-class votes and the labourers . . . and attempted to goad the public into subservience to its infallibility'; while the *Independent* retorted that Seymour 'comes here . . . to play the same game as he played at Sunderland in 1852 when he was elected by the cross-votes of Tories and Radicals to the displacement of (another) Liberal'. Meanwhile the Radical *Southampton Times*, newly founded by the breakaway elements that had brought Seymour in, tempered its praise by warning him that 'unless he played his cards better he would lose his newly-won seat at the next election', since 'on one or two occasions, at public meetings, he had been supported by his Tory opponents instead of his friends. Let him [it adjured him] identify himself more closely and thoroughly with the Bright and Cobden men.' For a full and balanced appreciation of this situation, in the main a typical one at that time but possessing special complications in an important and rising port, an adequate and critical study of all three papers and the attitudes they adopted on each particular occasion is essential.

The newspapers are, of course, a key source also in a survey of the voluntary efforts in the field of community concerns. But in this, the main starting-point must once again be the report of the Brougham Charity Commission from 1819.

The forty-four volumes of this report provide a wealth of local information about endowed charities with many plans and figures. There were later reports issued by the Commissioners for Charitable Uses (from 1853, the Charity Commissioners), and other records relating to charities (especially apprenticeship papers) are to be found among the files of the Department of Education now in the Public Record Office. Parliament carried out a number of county surveys of charities at the end of the century. The records of local trusts in the nineteenth century exist, often in bulk, for there were large numbers of law suits relating to charities, but they are not always available. Most important, however, are once again the newspapers, for charities needed publicity and (like Hiram's Hospital in Barchester) were often a matter of considerable local interest, if not controversy. There were thus many public notices in these papers. It is from this source too that *self-help* may be traced, as well as in pamphlets and other local publications.

The less formal charitable work as well as the major charities themselves may be recorded in the diocesan or local church and chapel records and in private papers. Correspondence and memoirs are particularly valuable; Ellen Buxton noted at Christmas 1861: 'This afternoon we went to the Alms houses near here [Leyton-stone, Essex] and gave to each of the people half a pound of tea and a pound of sugar, which they liked very much.' Such personal glimpses can throw light on a number of different aspects of the study, such as the officials: 'Six years ago [My dear Father] was elected Chairman [of the Hospital], and there ought to be a new Chairman every year, but they found he made such a good one, that they have had him now for six years.'

For a study of *effectiveness*, the most important sources are the official reports of Parliament and local officials. The blue books on Public Health, on Housing, on Factories or on particular industries are full of information about local government.[34] The annual reports of the various committees or officers contain a wealth of basic material and will often show how effective these agencies have been in coping with their problems. A list of the sort of records used for the study of Exeter may be seen in Dr Newton's book on *Victorian Exeter*. Boundary commission reports, returns relating to elections, poor law reports, education reports, police reports, housing reports, industrial reports all throw light on how Exeter managed its affairs. The borough itself printed annual reports concerning its finances and public health, and there exist the minutes of its council and the committees. Exeter is not unusual in the wealth of its material. Many other places had reports of museums and libraries, of sanitation, of the borough surveyors as well as the more normal run of borough records. Where these do not survive, they will usually be fully discussed in the local newspaper.

Not much of this local material survives for rural areas. But Parliament was still interested in these parts of the country. The Report on the working of the laws of settlement in 1850 throws a lot of light on the way in which many villages managed their common concerns; the survey of landlordship in the 1870s,[35] if compared with the tithe or enclosure award, can reveal something of the changing basis of authority for these groups. But on the whole it is rare to be able to see in any rural community how involved the people were in running their own affairs.

Chapter 9

Social welfare

1

We have seen that the provision of facilities for social and other problems in the local community has in the past been done by a combination of agencies. Of these, the three most important were the formal local government bodies, charitable institutions or philanthropic individuals and a measure of self-help. The balance between these elements has been almost indefinitely variable and constantly changing.

What follows are three examples of this. There are others which could have been discussed. For instance, it is becoming widely recognised that the question of law and order in earlier communities was a crucial one. Attention is now being given to the history of social controls, the law and the members of its profession, and to the problem of violence and disorder. So far as the local community is concerned, attention is focused on the history of the police, on the crimes and the criminals and on the measures taken to combat them.[1] Or we could have taken the provision of public amenities to make life more tolerable — cleansing and paving of the streets, lighting, water, sewerage and other sanitation measures. But the three which have been chosen are now on the whole well-worn roads and cover all main sections of the community. Thus social welfare concerns the provision made by the group for the poor and needy; education deals with the problem of the young and the illiterate adult; while finally all able-bodied persons within the local community had needs for leisure and recreation, and these needs were met largely within the community itself. And in examining these three examples, we shall see clearly the integration of the different agencies in satisfying the common needs.

The basic pattern in dealing with each of these topics is much the same. The size and nature of the problem will first need to be assessed. The various agencies involved in its solution, the reasons for their presence in this field and their activities and relationships, will next concern the historian. Thirdly, the extent of the involvement of the members of the community in the work of these agencies by their active interest, financial support and personal service, may be followed by a final assessment of the effectiveness of the community's reaction to the problem which it had identified.

The needy
Social welfare concerns itself with the needy members of the local community. But 'need' has first to be recognised, to be defined. Each age has of course determined these needs differently. Nevertheless there are certain common features. There will always be the sick, the deformed and the mentally ill. It is unlikely that the

historian will ever be able to quantify these elements in the population of his past community; they are probably completely indeterminable. But they were always present and at times (for instance during the many outbreaks of epidemics which our country has seen for at least the last six hundred years) they could amount to proportions of political significance. In addition, there were the aged, often indistinguishable from the sick but never of course politically important. There were also those deprived of their families, the orphans and widows. The treatment of the old and isolated can often be the touchstone of the community, but on the whole the local historian has only a few glimpses of this.

And then there were the poor. How poor is poor? There are many variable standards. Today a family is technically 'poor' if it has no telephone. Past communities seem to have had few clear guidelines on this subject. For some, there was need if a family could not provide for old age or at least if it could not bury the dead decently. For others, it was a matter of bad or overcrowded housing. For still others, a man and his family were not poor until they were starving. But although poverty was relative, it was always present and to some extent recognisable, whatever the standard employed.

There were two kinds of poor, the employed and the unemployed. And these two categories were subdivided by contemporaries once more into two, the deserving and the undeserving. For poverty was brought about by a whole range of causes and these created very different attitudes towards the poor. For the employed, poverty might be caused by dissoluteness (especially drunkenness) rather than by exploitation, by low incomes. For the unemployed, the problem was more complex. Some were sick, others unemployable because of their characters, while still others were unwilling to work. But for large numbers the problem might rather be that there was no work for them to do. The historian must not only assess the size of the problem of poverty within his local community but also its causes, both real and apparent, for it was the latter that determined the ways in which the community members sought to relieve the problem.

How then did the local community cope with the problem of its needy members? They certainly existed. Did it merely leave them to the attention wherever possible of its smaller constituent units, the families? Were formal agencies established with sanctions and powers of compulsion? If so, how were they organised and what did they do? Or was the problem left to voluntary resources and to such measures of self-help as the needy organised for themselves? In almost every community in fact, a balance was struck between these agencies. There were many changes in the balance, many fluctuations in the fortunes of the various bodies engaged in the work; but it was rare for there not to be these three elements at any one time.

Whether this increased the involvement of the community or not is a matter of conjecture. But such involvement expressed itself in several ways. The sick and the aged had to be tended and in some cases hospitals built. The poor had to be fed, clothed, housed and if possible employed. Time, money and thought had to be given by some at least of the other members of the community. How many did in fact so give and so serve?

And finally the local historian should attempt an assessment of whether all this work had any effect at all. Here of course are completely unquantifiable judgements, the 'ifs' of local history. What would the situation have been if these agencies had not so worked? Some factual basis for the assessment may be drawn from such questions as how efficient and expert were the officials engaged in the work, how long did they serve, on what basis did they dispense poor relief and the like. It may even be possible to assess whether the united efforts of the community kept pace with the problem, or whether it was growing at a rate which exceeded the provision for it. But on the whole public concern is a matter of judgement for the local historian, though a judgement he cannot avoid.

2

It is not possible to deal, even in outline, with the whole of this subject here, nor even with the more limited theme of the poor law. But something of the background is necessary.

The size of the problem in local communities in medieval England cannot be assessed. The plagues subsequent to the Black Death (1349) may not have been matched in intensity in earlier years but 'the poor you have always with you'. Statutes from 1388 onwards indicated that vagrancy and mendicancy were already a problem, and in 1391 the responsibility of the beggar's place of birth to contribute towards his maintenance was clearly enunciated — the start of much ineffective legislation. One measure of the problem may be seen in the concern of the church over the giving of alms, in the frequent establishment of hospitals and bedehouses and in the emergence of manorial or parochial collectors of alms to maintain the poor. The reputation of the clergy, especially the friars, in treating the sick was matched by the gilds in providing self-help, including pensions and sick relief. The sale of 'deferred endowment policies' (corrodies) by medieval monasteries eventually helped to run them into financial trouble. But these on the whole applied to the middle ranks of society, those who could afford the annual dues or the initial premium. The very poor relied upon alms; the unemployed ran away.

Poor relief
It was not until the middle of the sixteenth century that compulsion came to be directly applied to the giving of alms for poor relief. By then, the size of the problem seems to have increased; at least the mobility of the needy had increased, so that more people were conscious of injustices. Secondly, the agencies relieving the poor had been reduced in number and effectiveness. The Reformation deprived most local communities of some help — a neighbouring monastery, visiting friars, a chantry priest or other religious assistant within the parish. Many local charities were lost, especially with the abolition of the chantries, despite the surveys of 1546 and 1548 which were in part designed to record 'for what purpose and dedes of charitie anye of them were founded ...' and what 'poore men ... hathe ben Relieved by the said Chauntery'. Thus it was that statutory exhortation was followed by statutory compulsion. Work was to be supplied to the unemployed and parish overseers to be appointed, subject to the local J.P.s (1572, 1598). The voluntary giving of alms was for a time positively discouraged, until in 1601 a compulsory poor rate was established within each parish. Self-help was largely nonexistent. For the sick and the aged, this was probably their leanest time, though some boroughs established (or continued) their own measures for the relief of the needy, like Holt's poor houses and Great Yarmouth's fund for orphans.

For the next two hundred years, the pattern of formal poor relief agencies was fairly stable within the local community.[2] The problem of course fluctuated at various times. Provision for the aged became more necessary as mortality rates declined and people lived longer. Peak years of sickness created major problems in most communities and resulted in special action. The pattern of poverty was related to changes in local trade or industry. But on the whole genuine unemployment does not seem to have been a significant factor in the problem of the poor until the middle of the eighteenth century; rather it was prices and rising population on limited resources which forced so many to accept the alms offered to them.[3]

The formal agencies then were at work within the community. The overseers of the poor were the king-pins in this. From 1610, local houses of correction were to be built; from 1722–3, workhouses established, sometimes for more than one parish. Local inhabitants served as overseers, by election, appointment, or by rota; how often it was by choice does not appear. Local rates were collected and expended on those who applied and qualified for relief within the parish – and as rates rose, so did discontent with the system. The system of 'settlement' (by which a pauper was to be supported by the parish of his or her birth) was codified, defined, modified and reinforced in a long series of statutes from 1662 onwards.[4]

Almost all of these statutes were concerned with the undeserving poor, those 'idle and disorderly; rogues and vagabonds; and incorrigible rogues', as the 1744 statute categorised them. But what of the bigger problem, the deserving poor? For them there was the world of charity, a booming movement during the seventeenth and eighteenth centuries. A large number and wide range of local charities were established in the towns and villages of the country; hardly any parish can be entirely free from them. Charities giving cash (including some loans to set young men up in business), food, clothes and blankets, fuel, housing and education or other community amenities (like sermons or a common bull or church bells), to free pews from rents or bridges from tolls, to maintain local roads or local pastimes, charities administered by the parson and churchwardens or by trustees, charities for the benefit of all comers or the poor and sick or certain individuals – the variety is unending, the supply seemingly inexhaustible. The government became concerned at the loss of many charities and in 1758 a Board for the Recovery of Charitable Bequests was set up. Many were the law suits over local charities. From the late eighteenth century, there began a process of reorganisation, of amalgamation, of supervision, in which the parish itself was very active; it was not unknown for the charity to pass from trustees into the control of the churchwardens or vestry, with its funds reinvested and its disbursements supervised. In this sense, what began as a matter of patronage, of endowment by landowners and prominent merchants, became a matter of common involvement.

How far this charity movement helped to deal with the needs of the deserving poor must be a matter for local calculation. But by the end of the eighteenth century the problem was so acute as to call for new and wider measures. Clearly the growing industrial nature of society, and the greater amount of poverty and un-employment (especially seasonal or cyclical) this brought with it, created a stronger demand for action, while the outbreaks of typhus, smallpox and (from the 1830s) cholera similarly provoked action. Charity was no longer enough, if indeed it ever had been enough; rather it slackened (but never failed altogether) just as the problem became most acute. Self-help began to appear once again in the form of local friendly societies. Outdoor relief for the employed poor, paid in some parishes before it was finally authorised by Parliament in 1782, became organised in many counties on the so-called Speenhamland system from 1795–6. Within the towns, specialist committees for various amenities began to appear with paid officials.

Voluntary effort also continued but in newer forms, generally a non-endowed form. Medical missions and dispensaries for the sick sprang up, while many individuals devoted themselves and their money to private programmes of inoculation. The professionalisation of poor relief spread gradually to the countryside as well, with a number of unions of parishes set up under the Gilbert's Act (1781–2), the building of a network of common workhouses and paid Poor Law overseers. But the problem grew and rates continued to increase.[5] Some landlords 'closed' their villages to new settlers to prevent the possibility of increasing the burdens on the rest of the community — an action which bore hardly on the more 'open' villages.

The nineteenth century

Such was the condition in the early nineteenth century. The size of the problem in each local community seems to have been growing at an alarming rate. Cholera was active until the late 1860s, while demographic trends increased the proportion of the older members of the community; the sick and the old were fast becoming a more costly problem than the poor. Both the size and nature of poverty in nineteenth-century towns and villages are unknown, but the fact is clear.[6] Unemployment fluctuated greatly; very high totals were recorded for very short periods, but for the whole of the century in some areas, jobs were short.[7] In any case, the problem was often not so much one of unemployment as underemployment; thus in 1844 nearly 1,700,000 paupers were in receipt of relief, of whom only 234,000 were in the workhouse.

During the century the three main types of agency continued their combined efforts to cope with the problem. From 1834 to 1848 the professionalisation of the formal organisations was taken further. Boards of Guardians, covering several parishes and elected by the ratepayers, were set up, employing paid officials, and either ran their own workhouses (usually built for the purpose) or leased them out under the general supervision of the Poor Law Commissioners. Parochial overseers lasted until 1929 but their duties were greatly reduced. The main responsibilities lay with the Guardians, save in those towns where their authority was challenged by rival bodies, like Improvement Commissioners.

The work of the formal agencies increased as the nineteenth century progressed and became more specialist in character, with schools and sickrooms and other services within the workhouse — until indeed there was some jealousy from the non-pauper of these 'free hospitals for the destitute'. Naturally there were vast local variations, and generalisations are difficult. On the whole, the northern unions were reluctant to implement the law as long as possible, but when at last they established new workhouses, these tended to be more pleasant buildings, although at the same time, they managed to support more people out of the workhouse; in the south on the other hand the workhouses were less comfortable, more forbidding final refuges for the destitute. As time went on, the cost of poor relief everywhere rose, often at an alarming rate. It is estimated that the national bill rose from £1½ million in 1776 to nearly £8 million 40 years later. There were of course many fluctuations and years of very heavy demand on the purses of the ratepayers, but on the whole the trend was upwards until the 1830s saw some temporary relief. Then it began again. The total spent by the 'formal' agencies on the poor of England and Wales rose from nearly £5½ million in 1850 to £8 million in 1880; in London, the rate doubled between 1850 and 1870. In these circumstances it is not surprising that some rethinking was done in the 1870s, associated with Goschen's Code. First, there was a reversion to what was thought to be the policy of the 1830s — to make the workhouse into a deterrent, harsher, less welcoming, more of a social stigma. Certainly this was the policy of the Local Government Board. Secondly, hand-in-hand with this, there was a greater concentration on the workhouse, resulting in more specialist institutions, better services within the workhouse and (so far as the paid staff were concerned) greater professionalism in the service. The amount of outdoor relief was cut. In the end, this meant that probably a smaller number of people in all benefited from official poor relief; certainly it cannot be denied that the percentage of the population helped in this way fell[8] – which is why contemporaries felt that despite rising costs, nothing was being achieved.

Bromley (Kent)

Something of all of this can be seen in a recent study of the poor law in Bromley (Kent) made by Dr Crowther. Bromley was a growing community in a heavily pauperised county, with agricultural workers largely dependent upon Speenhamland-type relief. The village itself was expanding from a purely rural settlement to include some very light industry and some commuting (Fig. 27). The problem of the poor in Bromley was thus different from those large, heavily populated and heavily industrialised areas in the north of England or indeed from nearer towns like Brighton or Canterbury.

The parishes in the Bromley Union contributed to the poor rate not according to the value of the property within them, but according to the amount of pauperism in each parish. Thus Bromley parish was paying 27% of the poor rate for the Union in 1842 and 30% in 1882: the percentage of paupers in that parish had been somewhat increased by the influx of men working in the building trade, who tended to be unemployed during the winter.

These figures do not show the total cost of poor relief, as the Treasury gave

Table showing the expenditure on the maintenance of the poor in Bromley parish and Bromley Poor Law Union 1834–87, compared with the population of the area.

Amount spent on the poor in the year ending 30 September				Population				
The year 1842 is taken as being 100, being the nearest available date to the census year				The year 1841 is taken as 100				
Year	Parish		Union		Year	Parish		Union	
	£	%	£	%		£	%	£	%
1834–6 av.	1,294*	112	8,101	155	1831	4,002	92	14,413	93
1837	903	78	4,664	89					
1842	1,152	100	5,229	100	1841	4,325	100	15,442	100
1847	1,393	120	6,443	123					
1852	984	85	4,846	93	1851	4,127	97	17,837	115
1857	1,067	93	5,421	104					
1862	1,217	106	6,045	116	1861	5,505	106	20,368	151
1867	2,063	179	6,507	124					
1872	2,471	214	7,802	149	1871	10,674	246	32,184	202
1877	2,395	208	8,069	154					
1882	2,930	254	10,491	201	1881	15,154	350	48,972	317
1887	3,952	343	12,616	241					

* The average expenditure for 1834–6 was calculated by the Poor Law Commissioners, and may be rather exaggeratedly high, as the Commissioners were taking great pains to prove that the new law had drastically reduced poor relief.

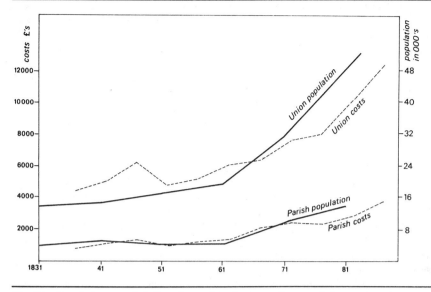

Fig. 27 Population growth in Bromley and the increase of poor relief.

grants towards the salaries of workhouse teachers and union medical officers, and pauper lunatics were maintained in asylums partially from the county rate, which was levied separately from the poor rate. But the main burden of maintaining the poor still fell on the individual parish, and the total amount granted to Bromley Union from non-parochial sources in 1877 was only £554. In addition the union might manage to claim a few pounds from the relatives of paupers who were supposed to help pay for their maintenance, but this never provided much revenue.

It will be noticed that the poor rate continued to increase, though not as fast as the population. From the 1860s the railway was turning the parishes of Bromley and Beckenham from quiet rural towns into suburbs of London. The cost of maintaining the poor rose sharply during the 1840s, which were times of national economic difficulty, and then fell in the more prosperous 1850s, after which they rose steadily. Nevertheless, there seems to have been little discontent expressed over the rates imposed on the various parishes of the Union by the Board; there were no contests for seats on the Board of Guardians until the elections of 1877, and then they were confined to the two main areas of the Board's region, the parishes of Bromley and Beckenham.

The Guardians were at first landowners (led by Lord Sydney who was both lord of the manor and active chairman of the Board for some 42 years), farmers, clergy and other professional men, but increasingly the smaller tradesmen came to be represented. An attack led by the editor of the *Bromley Telegraph* (Mr Gedney) on the grounds that the Board would not publish its business ended with his being elected to the Board and rather more liberal changes came over the Board's activities. From the 1880s, the Board's work resulted in a number of specialist committees being set up. More particularly, changes can be seen in the major officials. Their salaries rose in the 1870s; the schoolteachers appointed were better qualified persons; the relieving officers similarly rose in status. Particularly the masters and matrons of the workhouse (Plate 31) became careerists. They were no longer local

Plate 31 Bromley workhouse (now part of the Farnborough Hospital (Kent)). The main
building of the old workhouse was completed in 1845 at a cost of £8,000; it was considerably
enlarged in 1886. A separate infirmary was erected in 1870, and enlarged in 1898. The square
formation of the buildings is of the characteristic type approved by the Poor Law Commissioners, with divided courtyards in the middle where the different classes of inmates were
allowed to take the air. In the nineteenth century the workhouse was surrounded by a large
garden where the able-bodied men and boys worked to produce the vegetables for the workhouse diet. The little tower on top of this building is also characteristic of much institutional
architecture of this period, and seems to be the reason why tramps came to call the workhouse
'the spike'. The view shows one of the courtyards, which at that period would have been merely
paved, with no grass or tree.

persons; Bromley was one step on a ladder. They did not tend to stay long, for the Bromley Board was not a large one and the wages were low; in moving on to better posts they revealed their professionalism. But they carried out their work reasonably well. Until Gedney achieved his seat on the Board, the workhouse did become more unattractive, the diet harsher, and in general except for the bad winters (which particularly hit the builders) numbers in receipt of poor relief fell.

On the whole it would seem that most of the poor relief in Bromley was done by the Guardians. There were only five endowed charities recorded for the town in the Brougham Report (1837), and these were very small indeed. There was, it is true, Bromley college, a wealthy institution with an annual income of nearly £2,000 p.a., but this was for clergy widows. Apart from the school trust, with an income of £42 p.a., the rest amounted to only £6 p.a. 'for the poorest and most necessitous' with a further £3 for bread to be given to 'the industrious poor not in receipt of relief' after church on Sunday morning.[9] Further, there were only two Friendly Societies in 1851, the Bromley Philanthropic Society meeting in the Duke's Head and the Orphan's Friend Lodge.[10] A further result of the change of policy in the 1870s was thus not apparent in this town. This was an attempt to incorporate the voluntary efforts permanently into the field of social welfare, as they became so incorporated in education. The movement failed, but the attempt is significant, for it reveals the reliance of the formal agencies on the voluntary. Official poor relief could in most places be kept low because the charitable bodies relieved more of the poor.

Voluntary agencies

How much the charities spent in any town or village is not generally known. In London about 1870, probably some £5½ or £7 million was distributed each year by established charities at a time when the national Poor Law bill came to only £7½ million. Charities continued to proliferate, although they now took a rather different form.[11] In the seventeenth and eighteenth centuries, the endowed charities had taken (and kept) the form of self-perpetuating trusts. The later ones were both formal 'associated' charities, with elected boards and committees, and informal 'do-it-yourself charities' (as Professor Best calls them), involving the unpaid services of professional and educated people in philanthropic enterprises. Dr Newton's study of Exeter provides examples of this. There in the 1820s, the Dispensary was built by public subscription (Plate 32(a)): there during the 1831 cholera outbreak, doctors gave their services free. There in 1838 was founded the Exeter Relief Society, an 'associated' charity to relieve the poor and destitute. It began by aiding some 138 families, but the average over the first ten years was 531, reaching a total of 887 in 1849. At the same time (1846–7), the Exeter Union relieved out-of-doors an average of 570 families, and this was a bad year for the town with bread riots and great distress resulting in the launching of the Exeter Famine Fund. Thereafter the Poor Law relief fell, while the work of the Relief Society increased until in 1850 it 'assisted 1,131 poor families not otherwise in receipt of parochial assistance' (see Fig. 28). The two kinds of provision went hand in hand. When a public meeting in the Guildhall (1854) voted an extra 6d per head to the poor from the corporation funds, an appeal was similarly launched for further subscriptions for relief and door to door collections were made. But there were objections, which increased as time went on and the costs of the Poor Law went up – the numbers of those relieved rose from 750 (1856–7) to over 1,500 (1870). On the other hand, the Society's relief work also increased; it was at its peak with some 3,580 in 1870.

Plate 32(a)   Exeter Dispensary, established by subscription in 1818 and re-built in 1840.

This was another bad year for Exeter; the borough stepped in with 'an unemployed labour fund'. In 1871, it was estimated that about one in seven of all Exeter's population received some relief. The figures continued at a high rate, and the Society ran into financial trouble in 1879. But private effort was by no means at an end; in 1909, the Society was still able to help 2,000 families.[12]

Private charity thus in any community, whether large or small, was an essential ingredient in the handling of the poor problem in the nineteenth century. It is not

2

RULES

OF THE

PRINCE OF WALES

FRIENDS OF LABOR

LOAN SOCIETY.

1—That this Society be denominated "The PRINCE OF WALES FRIENDS OF LABOR LOAN SOCIETY," and shall consist of an unlimited number of members. Every person must be duly proposed and seconded, and shall, on admission, pay one shilling, and threepence extra for a copy of rules and card.

2—The object of this society is to raise, by equal contributions from each member, a fund for the purpose of lending the same in sums of not less than five shillings, nor more than fifteen pounds, to the industrious classes, and taking payment of the same by instalment, with interest thereon.

3—That this society shall meet every Thursday evening, between the hours of half-past eight and ten o'clock, when one of the trustees must attend to conduct the business, and shall pay over to the Treasurer, at the close of the meeting, all monies that have been received.

4—Each member to subscribe threepence per week on each share, and threepence per quarter for the payment of the Secretary. The Secretary to receive ten shillings per quarter extra if there is sufficient profits after paying ten per cent. to members' capital. Each member to be allowed to hold twelve shares, but no member to be allowed more than one vote or privilege on any occasion.

5—That the amount of Loans shall be sums of not more than fifteen pounds, nor less than five shillings, which shall be paid by weekly instalments at the rate of sixpence in the pound for every pound, and the charge for interest at the rate of one shilling in the pound. The first payment to be made on the twenty-first day after the granting of the loan, and the sum, according to the following scale, shall be paid for the form of application, expenses of making enquiry, &c. :—

		£	s.	d.		£	s.	d.		
A Loan from		0	5	0 to	3	0	0	—	3d.
"	"	3	0	0 to	5	0	0	—	6d.
"	"	5	0	0 to	7	10	0	—	9d.
"	"	7	10	0 to	10	0	0	—	1s.
"	"	10	0	0 to	12	10	0	—	1s. 3d.
"	"	12	10	0 to	15	0	0	—	1s. 6d.

6—That when a loan is granted, the borrower must provide one or more satisfactory sureties, who shall undertake by signing the note pursuant to 3 & 4 Vic., c. 110, to pay any sum or sums of money that may be unpaid at any time the borrower passes one single day on which his weekly instalments should have been paid,

---

Fig. 32(b) First two pages of the rule book of the Prince of Wales Loan Society, established in Exeter in 1863. Although not strictly speaking a Friendly Society, a Loan Society represented the element of 'self-help' in social welfare.

surprising that it should have been regarded as a permanent ingredient. But alongside this grew up the self-help element, especially in 'the newer and rawer industrial areas'. Co-operative Societies, Building Societies, Housing Associations, Savings Banks, Trade Unions often had an element of unemployed relief built into them.[13] Especially prominent were the Friendly Societies. Such societies were not new; by the end of the eighteenth century there were a large number of them in towns and villages throughout England.[14] Nottingham in 1801 had no less than 51 such societies, with more than 2,000 members in all. They had many functions, such as burial clubs, convivial meetings and trades associations. Some were national in coverage, like the Oddfellows and Foresters, with local branches; others (especially the early ones) were purely local, sometimes centred on a pub. Thus in 1870 there were two societies with a total of three lodges in Bromley, the Orphans Friend Lodge (founded in 1844 and housed at the Rising Sun) and the Court Robin Hood (established in 1854). Between them they had some 380 members and in the previous five years had paid relief for a total of 1,272 sick weeks.[15] Similarly at Exeter in 1870 there were at least 12 societies all founded between 1825 and 1867, with a total of well over 1,000 members in their various lodges. Several were designed for mariners, but there were others, some of them more widely based like the respectable Earl of Devon Lodge and the Exeter Philanthropic Benefit Society or the temperance society (St Andrew's Tent, housed in the Temperance Hall), and some for other specific groups like the Locomotive Steam Enginemen's and Firemen's Society. In addition there were at least three Exeter Loan Societies (Plate 32(b)). By 1872, it has been suggested, there were some four million people in one

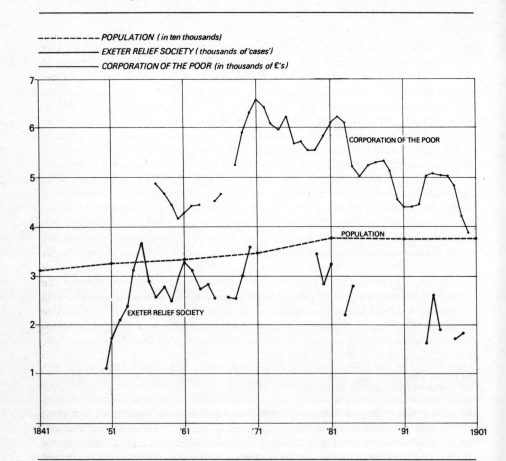

- - - - - - - - POPULATION *(in ten thousands)*
——————— EXETER RELIEF SOCIETY *(thousands of 'cases')*
——————— CORPORATION OF THE POOR *(in thousands of £'s)*

Fig. 28   Population growth in Exeter and poor relief.

Note: This graph illustrates some of the difficulties in plotting poor relief. The Exeter Relief Society figures refer (from 1850) to 'cases' helped: these do not seem to be families (as before 1850). The sums involved were small — in 1857 the help given to 2,556 cases came to only £129 6s 0d. The figures for the Corporation of the Poor are sums spent. It is possible to distinguish between indoor relief (i.e. the workhouse) and outdoor relief, but the workhouse costs were relatively steady; the major fluctuations (from £464 to £1,416 per quarter) came in regard to outdoor relief. The annual totals are calculated from the quarterly returns in the minutes of the Corporation (counting the January return with that year, not the previous year); the figures for some years are incomplete and have not been included. When the Exeter Relief Society was founded (1838) there were at least 44 other benevolent organisations in the town. This graph is based on figures supplied by Dr Newton.

or other of these benevolent societies.[16] They were able to compete with the general insurance movement, despite the travelling insurance agent, and thus they survived as a major working-class force until the legislation of 1911 placed National Insurance within the reach of everyone. And there were other, even less formal groups like the Great Yarmouth chapel which ran a small insurance scheme for its members. It is in these elements that self-help expressed itself.[17]

3

The sources for this study may be discussed quite briefly, for most of them have been mentioned in the previous chapter. They are for the most part scattered although there are some general surveys particularly of charities which are most rewarding.[18]

The source material is on the whole thin. It is most unlikely that any serious attempt can be made to assess the full extent of the problem of the poor and the sick, although the parish registers may help one to trace the incidence and severity of epidemics within the community. For the agencies at work, there are the manorial records and especially the borough records. The existence of charities may be found in scattered references in religious sources and in the surveys of chantries and gilds conducted in 1389 and in 1546–8.[19] Churchwardens' accounts begin in the fifteenth century for some places, and they become much more common after the sixteenth century; they frequently contain references to charities and alms.[20]

On the other hand the local historian may be able to trace something of the nature of poverty within the community. The various taxation returns, like the sixteenth-century lay subsidies and the seventeenth-century hearth taxes, may show proportions of the wealthy to the poor, especially where one can discover the number of persons who were exempt from the tax on the ground of poverty.[21] Inventories too may be used to illustrate the meaning of poverty, what it was like materially to be poor. A statistical approach to poverty, as to housing, will not reveal the quality of life; perhaps inventories more than most other sources can give an insight into what it felt like to be poor.

With the development of parochial organisation, there was a good deal of interest and local pride in the charities of any town or village. In 1601 a major survey was undertaken, preparatory to legislation, but its records are rare. Among the later quarter sessions papers are returns of friendly societies' rules and some information on charities as well as on the local working of the poor law, especially the level of rates. The incumbent was on occasion asked to make a return of the local charities to the diocesan office along with his other visitation material, and such notes often survive. Lists of charities were ordered to be placed in churches and many of these still remain painted on boards, often under the church tower or in the vestry. Some local descriptions by contemporaries are very revealing; a survey of Sheffield in 1615, for example, made for the lord of the manor, refers to the 725 'begging poore' who are not able to live without charity, the 100 householders 'which relieve others' and the 160 householders not able to relieve others. This is an unusually detailed survey, but others exist which at least list many of the more obvious (usually the endowed) charitable concerns of the local community. This series of records is carried on in directories and in other local surveys like Arthur Young's.

The most important source for the poor law before 1834 is, of course, the parish chest and especially the poor law and charity papers contained in it. A good series of poor law papers (and many such exist) will include some overseers' accounts indicating the rate levied and the disbursements made, and papers relating to settlement, removal and the like. Something of removal can be learned from the constable's accounts, for he was responsible for the execution of the order.[22] Miscellaneous correspondence and law suits can help to fill out the bare references, as can later newspapers.

The same location, the parish records, is almost as valuable for charity records, though these will more often be found among the papers belonging to the firms of solicitors who acted as clerk. Deeds and leases of the trust property, accounts of income and expenditure, rules and revised rules governing the charity, legal opinions and transcripts of Chancery cases (for a large number of charities were involved in law suits during the seventeenth and eighteenth centuries) are among the most useful of these records. The period ends with some major surveys. Among the earliest parliamentary papers of local significance are the returns of charitable donations of 1786–88 and the returns of poor rates for 1776–85, while in 1803 and 1818 there were detailed surveys of poor relief throughout the country covering the later years of the eighteenth century.[23] And secondly, Sir F. M. Eden's monumental survey, *The State of the Poor*, contains a good deal of local information concerning self-help.

4

With the changes in the poor law in the early nineteenth century, the local historian can hope for more light to be thrown upon his subject, though he must be prepared to look outside the immediate parish for his information. Some of the earlier sources continue, it is true. The parish records still supply much information, especially on epidemics, on the charities and even on the local overseers' work. The quarter sessions still supervised friendly societies until 1846. The records of endowed charities survive in bulk, for the work of the Charity Commissioners demanded a more rigid attention to duty, higher professional standards on the part of local trustees and administrators. And, of course, borough records are full of the problem of the poor and particulars of the means taken to overcome the problem.

Union records

There are, however, two main groups of records which the local historian must examine. First, of course, are the papers of the local Unions. These do not always survive but where they do they will provide much information (and much work) for the student of poor relief. Some of them will go back before 1834; the Union of Selling in Kent has minutes as early as 1790. But it is from 1834 that these records become formalised and bulky, and it is on these papers that studies like Dr Crowther's can be done. On the whole the papers fall into four groups. There are family and settlement papers, certificates and less formal documents relating to bastardy, maintenance, affiliation orders, removal and/or settlement (on a sort of 'knock-for-knock' basis) as well as much litigation concerning orders. Secondly, there are the Union administrative and financial records – minute books of the Guardians and Committees, draft parliamentary returns, rate books (on the whole rare), Union ledgers (Plate 33) and other accounts. Thirdly, there are the records concerning 'out-relief', the support of the destitute in their own homes. Details of disbursements, receipts and vouchers (for there was still a poor law 'truck' system), relieving officers' order books, district medical officers, details of employment like the Bromley labour yards scheme, and so on. And fourthly, there are the records of 'in-maintenance', the workhouse itself. Perhaps the most prolific of all, they are amongst the most closely studied as well. Minute books, admission and discharge registers, diet sheets, masters' reports and punishment book, and records of the school and sick room may all exist for fortunate places. Here may be found particulars of the officers, of their service and remuneration, their qualifications,

165

Common Fund Account *continued*

Date.	Folio of Minute Book.	Folio of corresponding Credit.	Corresponding Credit and Items.	TOTALS	D
			To	£ s d	£ s d
1877					
25 Mch	146	80	In Maintenance Account	1415 8 8½	
" "	148	"	Out-Relief Account	1045 2 7½	
" "	149	"	Paupers in Hospitals	3 2 .	
" "	150	"	Lunatics in Asylums	196 14 7	
" "	153	"	Salaries of Officers	353 11 2	
" "	154	"	Officers' Rations	102 19 9½	
" "	153	"	Superannuation Allowances	25 . .	
" "	155	"	Extra Medical Fees	8 10 .	
" "	156	"	Vaccination Expences	55 7 .	
" "	157	"	Registration Expences	66 10 8	
" "	161	"	Legal Expences	29 11 11	
" "	131	"	Building & Repairs	91 15 9	
" "	132	"	Farm Account	. 6 8 2	
" "	133	"	Furniture & Property	33 2 10	
" "	134	"	Printing & Stationery	19 10 5	
" "	134	"	Advertising	5 5 8	
" "	136	"	Nurses Services in Infectious & Fever Cases	2 17 4	
" "	145	"	Elections of Guardians Expences	. 15 .	
" "	149	"	Hire of Relief Rooms	2 5 .	
" "	160	"	Subscriptions to Institutions	5 5 .	
" "	161	"	Shaving & Hair Cutting	10 17 5	
" "	161	"	Porters Uniform	4 10 6	
" "	162	"	Officers Disbursements	33 11 9½	
" "	163	"	Rent Account	7 10 .	
" "	163	"	Rate Account	30 10 .	
" "	163	"	Tithes Account	1 2 5	
" "	163	"	Insurance Account	6 13 5	
				£ 3599 3 2½	

Plate 33 A page from the Bromley Union Ledger for the half year ended 25 March 1877. This document gives some idea of the expenses of poor relief, though it does not show the complete cost to the union. There were separate parochial expenses for the repayment of building loans and the salaries of certain union officials. But the Common Fund, into which each parish paid

Caption continued on p. 186

experience and how long they stayed. Here, too, are details of the paupers – how many there were and how long they stayed. The buildings themselves too – the workhouses and hospitals – and their location have a good deal to tell us about the way in which the local community treated their poor and sick in the course of the nineteenth century.

Parliamentary papers

The second main group of sources are parliamentary papers. The records of the Poor Law Commissioners are essential. Returns of rates for every place were collected for 1803 and the years before 1818 and again for 1825–34; the great Report of 1834 has much local information, and the Annual Reports of the Poor Law Board from 1835 contain many useful statistics. In 1850 a Report on the operation of the laws of settlement was presented to the Poor Law Board, with detailed information covering fourteen counties. Workhouses were regularly surveyed (Plate 35), and after the Local Government Board was set up in 1871 (a most important department for the local historian, for the records of this body contain many local returns), plans of workhouse building and improvements were deposited with it. Other major commissions or committees surveyed the Unions and collected local material in 1862, 1873 and especially in 1909, a most valuable paper. Material on the poor law may be found too in non-poor law reports, for the local Poor Law officials were regularly charged with giving evidence before other government enquiries, like that on the employment of children, young persons and women in agriculture (1867).

From this evidence, a full study of the local poor law may be possible. One may trace the extent of local support in terms of service and elections and the level of the rates. Less easy are the numbers of those who received relief. In order to get a complete picture of the maintenance of the poor, it is necessary to find out how many people were relieved by the union inside and outside the workhouse. This is surprisingly difficult, as the weekly returns sent to the central authority were condensed into largely meaningless statistics for a whole county and then destroyed. The returns printed by the Assistant Commissioners record the numbers of those who benefited each week, but they do not indicate how many came back the next week, how long individuals were in receipt of relief either within or without the workhouse.

The most useful source for this are admission and discharge books which survive for many unions. These give a good picture of the movement of paupers in and out of the workhouse and the average numbers relieved there, but it is more difficult to find records of paupers on out-relief, or to distinguish between those who received regular relief for long periods and those who received a small grant in the shape of a free visit from the doctor or a coffin for one of their family. There were always far more people receiving relief outside the workhouse than in it, mainly because it was cheaper to give a family a few shillings to keep it going during temporary distress than to give it full board and lodging in the workhouse. It is possible to find runs of

---

Caption continued from p. 185

according to its degree of pauperism, was the bulk of the expenditure. The most important items were 'in-maintenance', which was the cost of clothing, provisions and necessaries for the workhouse inmates, and the out-relief for those maintained by the union in their own homes. The 'hire of relief rooms' refers to the rooms where those on outdoor relief came to receive their maintenance, which was given mainly in the shape of loaves of bread and small sums of money.

Bromley.

Bromley College,
continued.

first part, the Archbishop of Canterbury, the Bishop of Rochester, and John Wells, esq., of the other part, the said William Makepeace and others, in consideration of 1260*l.*, conveyed to the parties of the second part and their heirs a messuage, with a piece of ground called the College Field, containing, by estimation, three acres, abutting west on Bromley College, and also a slip of ground extending from the street in Bromley to the south-east corner of the said field, subject to a right of road over the same, in trust for the college, and the charitable objects thereof, according to the trusts that existed with regard to the sum of 1200*l.* Reduced Annuities, which had been sold out of the college funds for effecting this purpose.

The 1200*l.* Stock sold for 796*l.* 10*s.*, and 350*l.*, required for completing the purchase and the payment of the expenses attendant thereon, was contributed by several subscribers.

The object of obtaining these premises was to prevent it being sold to other persons, who were in treaty for it, with the view of building thereon, which would have been a great annoyance so near the college.

The land is let to Godfrey Stidolph, as yearly tenant, as a nursery-ground, at a fair yearly rent of 36*l.*

5*l* An allotment of 1ᴿ. 20ᴾ. set out to the college on the enclosure of Bromley Common, and let to a yearly tenant at 30*s.* a-year.

6. There is standing in the names of the Archbishop of Canterbury, the Bishop of Rochester, and John Wells, esq., arising from different benefactions, 42,073*l.* 3*s.* 4*d.* Consols, and 7600*l.* Old South Sea Annuities, producing annual dividends to the amount of 1490*l.* 3*s.* 10*d.*

The annual income derived from these sources amounts to 1992*l.* 13*s.* 10*d.*

Besides the several official trustees described in the decree of the Commissioners, other persons have been elected from time to time as vacancies have occurred, according to the directions of the said decree. The elective trustees were, at the time of this inquiry, Multon Lambard, esq., since deceased, Lord Farnborough, John Wells, esq., and the Marquis Camden, there being one vacancy to be filled up at the next general meeting.

Mr. Wells is the treasurer, having accepted this office before he was elected a trustee, and the Bishop of Rochester and Lord Farnborough act as auditors.

The establishment consists of a chaplain and, at the present time, 42 widows. The chaplain is elected from Magdalen College, Oxford, according to the directions of the founder: his duties are to read prayers twice, and to preach a sermon every Sunday, which is accordingly done; also to read prayers once every other day, though in practice this duty is not performed, except on Wednesdays, Fridays, and Saints' days. He has also the general superintendence of the college, and sees that the regulations are properly observed. The present chaplain is the Rev. Thomas Scott, who is constantly resident in the college, and he receives a yearly stipend of 150*l.*

Of the widows, 40 are considered as the complement of the college, the other two having been added in 1829, to live in the treasurer's wing, with a smaller stipend, and that only to be continued so long as the funds would allow. In the appointments the widows of clergymen who had had the cure of souls in any parish in the diocese of Rochester, or in any of the peculiars of the Archbishop of Canterbury, within the ambit of that diocese, are chosen, a preference being given to the former. The merits of each are fully investigated and considered at a meeting of the trustees.

The 40 widows receive 38*l.* a-year, by quarterly payments, and the two additional widows 20*l.* a-year each.

There are also three out-pensioners of the same description, each of whom receives 30*l.* a-year, as the gift of Bishop King.

The following is a summary of the annual disbursements :—

	£.	*s.*	*d.*
To 40 widows 38*l.* a-year each	1520	0	0
To two widows 20*l.* each	40	0	0
To three out-pensioners, Bishop King's gift of 30*l.* each .	90	0	0
Rev. Thomas Scott, the chaplain, salary	150	0	0
Ditto, as secretary	5	0	0
To a porter, for work of various sorts about the college, 16*s.* a-week	41	12	0
Insurance 232*l.* 4*s.* every seven years, annual average	33	8	0
£	1880	0	0

To these, which may be considered as the whole of the regular annual disbursements, except some small payments for postage and stamps, are to be added the expenses of repair, the average of which for the last four years has amounted to about 260*l.*

As the surplus income after paying the regular expenses above mentioned amounts only to 113*l.*, these expenses could not have been defrayed unless the trustees had adopted the plan of not appointing to the vacancies until there are three vacancies, and it seems doubtful whether it will be practicable to continue the stipends to the widows in the treasurer's wing. But this will be a question for the consideration of the trustees.

On the 1st of January there was a balance of 119*l.* due to the treasurer, but in a few days the half-year's dividends on the Consols would become due, out of which, on the other hand, the quarter's pensions would be payable.

harity of Buck-
ridge Bishop of Ely.

CHARITY OF BUCKRIDGE BISHOP OF ELY.

It is stated on a table of benefactions in the church that *John Buckridge Bishop of Ely,*

Plate 34   A page from the Brougham Charity Commission Report, with details of one of the Bromley charities, Bromley College, 1839. The page also shows the start of the section dealing with the Buckridge Charity.

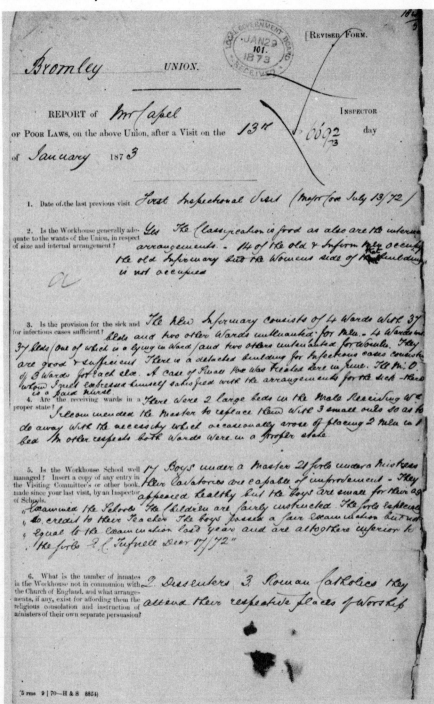

Plate 35   An example of a formal report on the condition of the Bromley union workhouse, sent to the Local Government Board by their inspector, after one of his periodic visits. The

the 'Paupers' Classification Book' for some unions: this will give a good idea of how many people were on relief and whether they were able-bodied or ill. It also gives some indication of why they needed relief, by distinguishing widows, orphans, illegitimate children, etc. But it will not always be available.

The parliamentary papers throw much light on the work of the voluntary bodies. Here, of course, the major sources are the Reports (Plate 34) and records of the Charity Commissioners.[24] Again, friendly societies are well recorded among the papers of the central authorities. Returns were made to Parliament in 1824, 1837 and 1842; two major reports containing local information appeared in 1852 and 1871—4. In 1880, each village society was surveyed in detail, while registration of the societies' rules began in 1856.[25]

Not all of these voluntary efforts and friendly societies will be found in this series, however, and to gain extra information the local historian must look elsewhere. The newspapers will bulk large — figures for unemployment, notices of hospitals, advertisements for charities, reports on annual meetings or society annual feasts, all appear here. Then there will be local directories and gazetteers. These are immensely valuable, giving dates and costs of buildings, donations, subscriptions and numbers of persons helped. But above all will be local reports — the annual reports of the Poor Law Board and the hospital or the charitable trusts, many of them containing accounts; or the more occasional reports commissioned by local authorities or produced gratuitously by local well-wishers. Many of these have vanished; the annual reports of the Exeter Relief Society can now only be traced in the local newspaper. But others still exist. Similarly there are some surviving records of Friendly Societies, especially rules (Plate 32(b)) together with annual reports and accounts. These (except the rules) are on the whole rare.[26]

It is quite clear that in a large town the bulk of this material is overwhelming. But for smaller communities a survey is still possible, for the source materials are more manageable though scattered. And it is a study which, if related to the census books, can make the community live in a way which few other such studies can do. We can learn much of the people in what they do for a living; we can see the effects on them of changes in transport. But it is surely in their religious affiliations and activities and in their attitudes to economic and social problems that we can really understand the community as a whole.

---

twice yearly inspections of the Poor Law Inspectors were the chief means by which the central authority was able to find out what was going on in the Poor Law Unions. Their reports, sometimes very detailed and informal, provide a great deal of information on local Poor Law affairs, but public opinion was so strongly against the growth of centralised bureaucracy that their numbers were kept down below the level of efficiency. Each inspector had a district so large that he could only cover it superficially, or investigate some unions more than others. He would see obvious defects in union organisation, but his visit would not be long enough to enable him to detect all possible malpractices.

This report for 1873 is taken from an extensive correspondence between Bromley Union and the central authority. The Inspectors usually tried to encourage boards of guardians to employ as many paid officers in the workhouses as possible and to do away with the system of using paupers as nurses and cooks. Mr Capel notes in this report that Bromley had a paid nurse. He is also worried about the use of double beds in the wards for the reception of new male inmates, as these might encourage unnatural practices. He had to be careful to check the religious facilities allowed to non-Anglicans, as the Dissenters were likely to raise a public outcry if there was any suspicion of non-Anglican paupers being forced to attend the Anglican services which were held in the workhouse.

Chapter 10

Education

1

Education is another example of co-operative enterprise in the management of community affairs, and on the whole it is a well recorded one. There are of course still some obscure aspects to the subject. Parts of it are considerably under-recorded. But local historians have traditionally regarded it as an important theme; it is for instance one subject regularly (although inadequately) treated in the *Victoria County Histories*. This is perhaps a reflection of modern attitudes to education which give it an importance which earlier ages have not allowed to it. The local historian must try to rid himself as far as possible of modern presuppositions, especially in this field.

Attitudes to education
How then did men and women in the past think of education? Here the local historian may be misled by the general histories of education with their necessary emphasis on the main educational theorists. Most people in his local community were entirely indifferent to education. Those who were concerned to press for some kind of educational provision did so on the whole for social reasons. Education was an answer to certain problems. It was a means of employing the idle, of harnessing the inactive. It would help to make people satisfied with their position in society. It was a form of political or social protective medicine. There was also present, it seems, an element of improvement for the few, the opening of doors for some individual children who were called by their birth or perhaps by their ability to occupy a stated position within the social hierarchy. It was not until a very late stage in the development of the local community that the inalienable right of every child to some form of education became at all commonplace.

Such were the general considerations behind the provision of educational facilities in English towns and villages up to the end of the nineteenth century. In practice however the local historian will rarely be able to start with such philosophical matters. His surest guide to the way in which a local community thought about education is through the provision actually made for its children. For these attitudes are reflected in three main ways — in the number and size of schools provided for the young, in the way in which they were provided, and in the nature of the education within them. Concepts of education have, until our own age, more often been expressed in buildings than in words.

Provision: who for?
The first set of questions the local historian must therefore ask himself relates to the amount of provision for education within his community. How many schools

were there? How many children were they intended to cope with? And what attempts were made, if any, to cater for changes in the numbers of children within the community? It will be rare until the nineteenth century for these schools to provide places for all the children within the community. Who then were they for? Were they for the children of rich parents or for the poor? Were they for boys or for girls? And whom in practice did they actually serve?

The local historian must therefore relate the numbers of children in the community with the school places available at any one time. The difficulty here is to know the ages to be taken as the determinant of a school child. Education in the past was an occasional occupation; it filled the gaps not occupied with more congenial or gainful employment. Thus it is rarely possible to be certain when a child started attending school, or how long on average he stayed, for there were often long intervals between bouts of school attendance. The age at which children started work, if it can be discovered, is of particular help here, but of course it can usually only be found out for one or two occupations and is rarely applicable throughout the whole community. Nevertheless it is an important factor in assessing the size of the possible school population.

Provision: who by?

The basic attitude to education as a not very important means of social control also expressed itself in the way in which the local schools were provided. Here the balance between the three elements of formal agencies, voluntary bodies and self-help becomes particularly significant. There were few 'formal'[1] agencies of education before the School Boards were established from 1870 onwards, but the apprenticeship schemes and 'town schools' which existed in many boroughs may be regarded as semi-formal institutions. These however tended to lack sanctions and were in the main an offering by the corporation for the benefit of the local inhabitants. They are indeed in one sense a measure of self-help. There were other forms of self-help, especially at the adult level, at most times in the past. On the whole however, educational provision was left to the voluntary effort. Most local schools were provided by charitable, religious and philanthropic enterprise, though whether from a sense of self-preservation or a sense of mission cannot always be determined. There was also an extra ingredient in the mixture, commercial interests. Men and women made a living out of teaching the young; it was in the interests of these teachers to promote the desire for education (and at times to restrict the provision available). In most local communities, this element has not been lacking in the provision of an educational service, and at times it has played a very important part.

This last element raises the question of how involved was the local community in meeting the needs of its young. If the schools and other means of tuition were left to individuals, at least the community acquiesced in that state of affairs and its members patronised their institutions. If on the other hand it was felt that this was not enough, then the community had to support greater efforts — by paying for the schools, or by giving up time to provide services freely or at least by choosing representatives to act on their behalf. The local historian thus cannot just be content with a mere statement of the number of educational establishments there were, any more than he can simply say how many children there were in the local community. He needs to go deeper. How were these schools financed? How were they staffed? How were they managed? How far was the community involved in its schools?

Nor must the local historian assume that, just because a school is situated in one place, it therefore will serve that community. Boarding schools, even in rural areas, were intended to draw from a wide area, and did in fact do so. Read's School in Corby (Lincs) had boys from as far away as Rugby among its nineteenth-century pupils. And there is of course always the question of sex differentiation in local educational provision — there were often more places for boys than for girls. These are factors which play some part in determining the kinds of provision available to the younger members of the local community.

Effectiveness

Finally, there is perhaps the most important question of all: what sort of education did the schools provide and how effective were they in meeting the need as it was defined locally? We today would include a further question. We would also ask how many children did the schools leave quite untouched? Were they adequate in terms of the size of the community? But this is perhaps to assume too much of the past. What we must really ask is what the community or rather some individual patron within the community set out to do through its schools, how many children it set out to touch and for how long, and then see whether these more limited aims were achieved.

The assessment of the effectiveness of local schools is a very difficult task indeed. There are some indications which the historian can pursue. One concerns the staff. Who were they? How well educated were they? And how long did they stay? How many children did they teach at a time? — the use of the monitor system or the pupil-teacher system is of particular relevance here. And of course there is more to a school than the teachers. There are for instance the managers or governors, and their relations to the staff will need examination. And further there is the building itself. Was it of a kind which encouraged (or at least enabled) effective work to be done? Was it in fact located in the right place? — for education too has a topography of its own.

A second group of questions concerns the curriculum. What was taught, and to what level? Clearly we today would insist on the basic means of communication and the ability to widen horizons by reading and writing, if not also numeracy. Nevertheless, this may once again be to import modern concepts into the past; a large number of schools set out to do a more limited task, such as to inculcate religious knowledge or a technique of industry rather than to provide elementary educational skills. Thus the local historian must examine what kind of schools were provided and what went on within them.

A third group concerns the pupils themselves. How many attended school and how many were regular? Seasonal attendance and high rates of absenteeism in a great many cases undermined all the efforts of well-educated, long-serving, conscientious teachers.

Finally, there can be some slight measure of assessment of the final achievements — not perhaps in terms of examinations but at least in terms of literacy. The ability of the individual to read is of course more widespread than the ability to write, but the latter can be traced more easily and it does provide some guide to the spread of educational standards within past communities. And in the end, the true assessment of effectiveness comes from the demands of adults for basic education. A high rate of adult illiteracy and a strong demand for adult elementary instruction would indicate one of two things — either the schools were not doing their jobs well or the community as a whole had misjudged the needs of its young. On the other hand, not all the demands for adult education were for elementary education; indeed, it was often the case that in those places where the schools were most effective, there was a strong call for facilities for further study. The local historian thus has to assess his adult educational movement. Was the demand for elementary education, the basic skills? If so, did it come from those who had been to school or from those who had been denied or who had refused its services? Or was the demand for other aspects of the field of learning?

The questions to be answered by the local historian of education may thus be summarised. How many schools were there and who were they for? Who were they provided by and what were their aims? And thirdly, what sort of education did they in fact provide and how effective were they, both in terms of the whole child population of the community and in terms of their own more limited objectives? The subject is a complicated one. As with so much in local history, it can most easily be dealt with in the context of a medium-sized community. The evidence for the average village is on the whole sparse; that for a large town is often overwhelming. But for whatever community the local historian may choose, if he bears in mind these sorts of questions before he tackles the very wide range of source material, his studies will be set on the right track.

2

For the background of the general developments of English education, the local historian may be referred to the large number of general studies which now exist.[2] The subject has been fully discussed often. Most clearly explored so far have been the fields concerning the provision of educational facilities and the kinds of education within the different kinds of schools. Less well examined have been the changing attitudes to the needs of the young and the demands of adults, and in particular the impact of these general trends on local provision.

The changes in age structure, which affected the numbers of children in the community, have been discussed earlier, but probably the size of the child population in any place varied according to local factors rather than more general ones. Each place will have its own structure. Some communities consisted largely of older people, others of younger ones. Closed villages on the whole tended to discourage children, open villages to attract and provide for younger parents. But even this varied from time to time. Apart from the general growth of population, when one expects the child proportion to increase, one can say little of the development of general averages. Further, there is the question of the age at which one ceased to be defined as a child, a problem closely related to the local social and economic structure of the community; the gentry kept their offspring as 'children' far longer than textile or agricultural workers.

Education, until the nineteenth century, was regarded as a means to an end, to fit a person to a required position in society. Some positions needed no education. Thus the agricultural labourer and the domestic servant did not need to be literate; they merely had to acquire the skills for their tasks. This similarly was true of many of the simpler industrial processes. But the priest and the landowner, the clerk and the merchant, needed education to varying degrees. And education can also be the social improver — which is perhaps one reason why its facilities were relatively limited during the Middle Ages when social improvement often meant disturbing the eternal harmony of society.

Early provision

Educational provision thus in the medieval community was very restricted, aimed at the bright peasant (a potential priest) and at the wealthy. It was almost entirely associated with the Church.[3] Ecclesiastical organisations founded and ran the schools. Diocesan authorities controlled the educational processes by the licensing of teachers.[4] Most of the instruction was given by clergy; the small amount of secular endowment in the later Middle Ages did not result in secular teachers, even though of course commercial rather than religious interests lay behind much of the instruction given by many of these clergy. Behind all the work of the schools lay the assumptions of the Church, even though the provision was well enough used by those who did not intend to take orders.

On the whole, as is to be expected, the towns were better off than the villages. Until the Reformation, the village child might be able to obtain some formal education from one of the local parish or chantry clergy or from a nearby cathedral, monastic or friary school. There was some opportunity for boarding in the church song schools. But in general there was much more provision in the towns where many of the monasteries and virtually all the friaries were set; where there were more clergy attached to the churches or gilds; where there were great households employing tutors. Gilds were often established, one of their aims being to provide education for the sons of members. Endowed and grammar schools developed and were well used by the laity, especially the merchant classes. So any town might expect to have at least one friary and/or monastic school, perhaps a grammar school, and some parochial provision.

It would seem that in general this type of education was efficient in what it set out to do. But it was clearly inadequate for the total community, for this was never intended. The schools were small, meeting in church rooms or porches, rarely in their own buildings. Not many of all the children were expected to receive any instruction, nor did they expect it. Literacy certainly spread throughout the Middle Ages, as wills listing books bear witness, but it was still confined in any local community to a very few individuals.

The last medieval century saw changes in attitudes. Some educational accomplishments for most people became desirable; literacy, for self-instruction in religious matters in the vernacular, came to be regarded by many as a necessity. In the end, however, such changes made little real local difference, although the changed attitudes and increasing literacy helped on the process of Reformation. And this profoundly shook the educational world.

Later provision

On the whole, the rural child lost out by the Reformation.[5] It is probable that in the late sixteenth century a good many rural communities had less educational provision than before. Some schools vanished. The local parson might still teach some children their letters but this seems to have become increasingly rare; free boarding facilities in Church song schools declined although they did not altogether disappear. Apart from this, there was very little. Those schools that remained were administered by laymen, trustees or parish officials. But their teachers were still licensed by the bishop, and most of them were still clergymen. And the schools were still aimed at a few bright poor children (given free places by philanthropy) or the merchant's child; the landowner often educated his children now as earlier within his own or someone else's household.[6]

From the late seventeenth century, however, began that charity movement which covered England with small endowed schools.[7] From village to village, landlords (and later industrialists) left rent charges or pensions to pay for a schoolmaster, to pay for free education for a certain number of poor children, or to set up establishments to teach skills like sewing or agriculture. A number of them were ephemeral, the endowment proving inadequate or being lost or stolen; several were re-endowed and re-established, sometimes after a hiatus. Most were inadequate in terms of the schoolmaster's income; almost all were inadequate in terms of the total child population in the community. But although small, they were an improvement. They were somewhat freer from the Church; their teachers were laymen and women, and the schools were sometimes held in their own buildings. How effective they were must have varied (as always) with the teacher but there was no element of compulsion in attendance (save presumably by the parents, especially the fee-paying parents). And there were some villages which had no such charitable bequest or had lost it completely. The children of these places must have depended upon neighbouring schools or the willingness of individuals to share their hard-earned literacy.

Such individuals were of course more numerous in the towns than in the rural communities. Here too provision was more lavish. Some of the religious schools (chiefly the endowed ones, not those which the corporation would have had to maintain entirely) were taken over and continued by the borough. At Morpeth (Northumberland), for instance, both the chantry building and the estate once used to maintain the bridge were later used by the borough for a school. Where they were lost or appropriated, it was not long before the corporations concerned took steps to get new ones established, generally with an endowment. In addition to this initial urge, charitable bequests were more numerous. Educated persons began to establish their own private schools from the seventeenth century, charging their pupils for the privilege of sitting at their feet — or sitting at their boards, for many of these were small boarding schools. The churches played their part in this movement, especially the dissenters who established their academies. The Church of England was on the whole reluctant; apart from the charity school movement, it was not until the late eighteenth century that it woke up to the need to establish some schools for the poorer child.

The major change, in terms of these children, came with the development of the Sunday School movement. The movement unashamedly aimed at reaching all the children in the community — except perhaps for those in the workhouse. But because the schools were the products of rivalry between the denominations, it is clear that many children were never touched in any way at all. Nevertheless a recent detailed study of schools in Nottingham has shown that in 1802, no less than 1,860 children were in some form of Sunday School, and by 1834 this had risen to at least 7,000.[8] The schools themselves aimed at inculcating attitudes and providing religious information. Some began to give elementary teaching in the basic skills of reading and writing, and it was from these that there developed day schools, on a similarly wide basis. Not all the day schools of course were provided for religious motives. Some (like the industrial schools) had a mixture of philanthropy and commercial interest behind them. But most had some religious basis. It was recognised that only a small percentage of the children of the community would in fact be able or willing to attend these schools. Universal education was not intended; what was hoped for was at least some education for all those children whose parents wanted it. For the rest, at least in the towns, there were some later opportunities for self-help — for an educational element was often involved in the more political groups like the Corresponding Societies and Hampden Clubs for those who wished to further themselves, the Working Men's Associations and the Secular or Adult Sunday Schools for those who needed the elementary essentials.

What then might one expect in any town at the end of the eighteenth century? There could well be a town grammar school, endowed and therefore partly free, often with a continuous history from the Middle Ages. On the whole it catered for the sons of the wealthier tradesmen, often from outside the town. There was a wide range of this type of school. Sometimes they were wealthy institutions with broad local support and elected boards of trustees; at other times they were simple charity schools. The larger nonconformist chapels could well run their own schools, frequently equal in repute with the town grammar school. Both of these were probably confined to boys. Then there would be the private schools, tutors giving lessons for money, local academies and dame or penny schools. It now seems clear that the commercial element in the eighteenth century has been under-rated; perhaps because it is usually impossible to determine just how many private schools there were in any locality, for they often operated without the bishop's licence. Nevertheless, there were many, often more than the voluntary schools. These, where they existed, tended to take two forms: the charity school (the endowed school run by lay trustees) and the more specifically religious school (run by and often housed in the local church or chapel). The distinction between the two is often very blurred. Free schools would consist of charity schools (though many of these also made a charge) or the church and chapel Sunday Schools.

How many of the population went to school, or if they did, how many acquired a smattering of literacy? Studies in this are just beginning. Some recent work on literacy in a group of twelve south Lincolnshire villages suggests that nearly 60% of the bridegrooms and 33% of the brides between 1760 and 1769 were literate; by 1810—19 the figures had risen to 66% and 44% respectively, though there are many local variations within these figures.[9] Such figures can be paralleled elsewhere. In two Nottinghamshire villages the figures show in fact an increase in illiteracy from 1750 to 1800 and then a decline during the nineteenth century, slow at first and rapid from 1860. The general rise in literacy in the early eighteenth century gave way to a fall, sometimes a drastic fall, from the 1780s to the 1820s, to be followed by an upward turn, slow at first but then gathering momentum as the nineteenth century progressed.[10] In almost all cases where literacy has been studied, the figures show some long-term progress in the spread of literacy, especially among women.

Nineteenth century

The nineteenth century produced considerable changes.[11] For one thing, as the population rapidly expanded, so the proportion of children in the population increased — and when this rose (as it did at Long Buckby, for instance) as high as 37%, this was something which could be seen (and heard, no doubt). Secondly, great concern was felt about children being employed — not indeed because they were thereby being denied their rights to education, but because they were being maltreated or became deformed by their employments. Those who sought to limit the employment of young children had to face an opposition query — what were these children to do when not so employed? It was in answer to this that schools were suggested. Thus the 1833 Factory Act provided for those children aged from nine to thirteen who were employed in textile mills that they should have limited working hours (only nine hours) and at least two hours schooling daily. The concern for formal education which these two factors aroused grew throughout the century, as both population growth and further legislation increased the possible school-going population. Throughout the century, the numbers of children aged under fourteen in employment fell. It is not surprising to find several employers or other philanthropic persons paying in part or in full the school fees of their poorer employees — a factor which further increased the number of potential scholars.

The increased demand for education did not only come about from these causes. There were changed attitudes over child needs, for a large number of reasons. Improvements in educational methods like the Lancasterian methods made more schools possible. Hard-headed businessmen came to believe that England needed an educated and skilled population, especially when faced with the industrial rivalry of nations like the Prussians. The propertied classes saw in education a powerful police weapon; in Nottingham the effects of Luddism were felt in the demand for schools. Religious and socialist idealists had a vision of education as the right of every child. When all these were combined in one and the same person, the combination was a very powerful one. All children needed education — and if the parents would not agree, they must be compelled. Not all persons, of course, saw it as clearly as this, especially those who most needed it: 'Drunkenness and ignorance, which latter is more a misfortune than a fault, are the present great evils of which society has to complain, for neither of these are considered a disgrace', wrote a factory inspector in 1865.[12]

With this concern came an increase in provision. Much of this was, of course, voluntary and religious in character and sprang from two main motives, a continued rivalry between the denominations and an increasing sense of mission. Sunday Schools continued to grow: in 1851, more than 9,000 of Nottingham's children were in 38 Sunday Schools. At first it was the nonconformists who led the way in that town, but from the 1830s the Anglican Church outstripped its rivals, although both sets of schools were probably equally ineffective from an academic point of view.

With the increase of Sunday Schools also came an increase in day schools. The competition of the church and chapel already seen in the towns began to spread to rural areas as the influence of the nonconformists became more widely distributed throughout the country. Here the Church of England had an advantage with its network of charity schools and the wider range of patron it could call upon: but the nonconformists and Roman Catholics were not far behind. The founding in 1808 of the non-denominational (but largely nonconformist) British and Foreign Schools Society and in 1811 of the (Anglican) National Society recognised and indeed promoted this rivalry;[13] but they did lead to the establishment of something like a national system of schools in both towns and villages. There were others; several charity schools not affiliated to one or other body were founded, although many were in fact Church of England schools. There were few completely secular schools. A number were established by the Poor Law authorities who were obliged to educate their paupers, a few by industrialists under the Factory Acts, a provision which must not be ignored by the local historian.

These latter schools are the only ones which can be called 'formal' educational provision, with an element of compulsion attached to them. All the rest were voluntary. Nor did the early nineteenth century wish to depart from the principles of voluntaryism and unrestricted commercial enterprise in education. Parliament had no agency to establish local schools and in 1853 refused Lord John Russell permission to grant such powers to the reformed town corporations. The state attempted to improve the schools which the voluntary bodies provided by making grants for building from 1833 (supervised by a special committee of the Privy Council from 1839) and for teaching purposes from 1846, by appointing inspectors for these grant-aided schools and later (1868—9) by reforming the endowed schools; but until 1870 it did not step into the field itself. Local authorities similarly encouraged endowed or voluntary schools in a number of ways but (except where they had been doing so long before 1834) were not in a position to run such schools themselves. If some towns took rates to support their schools, this was the result of old custom, not legal requirements.

Nottingham

Nottingham may be taken as a local example. Something like eight day schools had survived from earlier times or had been established by the religious bodies between 1800 and 1820. They were not on the whole well supported; they had room for more than twice the 700 children who probably attended. The size of the private contribution to the educational scene cannot be assessed but it was clearly consider-able. From the late 1820s, new schools came at an increasing rate. In a strongly nonconformist town, it is somewhat surprising that the dissenters ceased their efforts in 1835 with a school built over a sewer with the financial help of the corporation, but their concern was largely with the slum areas of the town. In 1835, there were some fourteen 'public' schools,[14] with places for some 3,000 children and attendances of over 2,000, of which one-third was Anglican. By 1851, there were 12,000 places in 37 schools; rather more than one-third of the 9,330 attendances were Anglicans (see Fig. 29). By 1870, the new School Board estimated that the existing schools had largely catered for all the children who needed educa-tion. The Church of England especially made a spurt, raising the five schools of 1835 to twenty-two in 1870. And they were large schools, an average of nearly 250 children against the dissenters' average of 150 and the Catholic average of 77. How many children attended and for how long is more difficult to assess; one school for instance with an average attendance of 154 recorded 144 leavers and 149 new pupils within one year. But at least the schools were there, provided by the churches and by private individuals; there were still no 'state' schools except in the workhouse.

It was 1870 and the subsequent legislation which changed all this.[15] In that year, Forster's Education Act allowed the establishment of a School Board in areas where the school-going population and existing provision (or rather the lack of it) warranted it. In other words, if voluntary bodies were unwilling, unable or other-wise slow in providing schools for a certain proportion of the population (estimated at one-sixth of the total community), then the local residents were compelled to set up a Board with its own elections, officers, schools and rates. Such schools were to be fee-paying, and attendance was not compulsory, though in some areas the Boards could enforce it for all those below thirteen if they thought fit. Clearly such a local decision is of particular significance to the historian. Under the Acts of 1876 and 1880, education for children under thirteen (with numerous exceptions) became compulsory, and further legislation gave the local Board of Poor Law Guardians (not the School Boards) the power to set up a School Attendance Committee and to pay fees in cases of need. From 1880 (and in some places earlier), the bar of fees in all schools supported by public funds was gradually removed, and between 1900 and 1918 the age of compulsory schooling was raised to fourteen. The whole set-up was revised in 1902 with the abolition of the School

No. of schools	1835	1870	1902
Anglican	5	22	64
Dissenters	6	8	–
R.C.	2	6	14
Board	–	–	94

No. of places	1870	1903
Anglican	5,354	13,079
Dissenters	1,197	–
R.C.	462	2,473
Board	–	28,546

Sizes of schools	1870	1903
Anglican	243	204
Dissenters	150	–
R.C.	77	176
Board	–	304

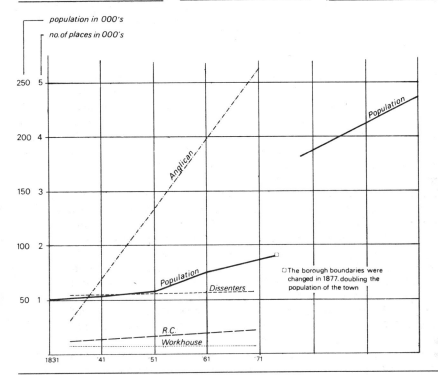

Fig. 29   Growth of Nottingham population and school places

Boards, the new Local Education Authorities taking over responsibility for both the Board's obligations to their own schools and the State's obligations to the voluntary (by now almost only Church) schools.

It was not the intention of the framers of the 1870 Act to exclude the voluntary and commercial provision. Indeed, there was a marked reluctance to establish Boards, and large numbers of places were forced to do so by order of the Department of Education. In Nottingham as in many other places, the first School Board was set up rather as a school rating and attendance committee than as a rival of the religious bodies. And this meant that in general the Board elections were uncontroversial. The major disputes at Nottingham resulting in contests for seats on the Board were over economies, especially after the 1880s. The new Board examined 105 schools and approved 65 as efficient. With some improvements all the children could be accommodated in existing schools. Three-quarters were Anglican, one-sixth were British schools; the rest were Catholic. But as the population grew, so did the need for new schools. The churches did their best; by 1882, the peak of their effort, they had nearly 20,000 places in voluntary schools against the Board's

TABLE P.—*continued.*

DESCRIPTION OF SCHOOLS.	MERTHYR-TYDFIL. (*Parliamentary Borough.*) Population, 63,080.*				NEWCASTLE-UPON-TYNE. (*Municipal Borough.*) Population, 87,784.				NORWICH. (*Municipal City.*) Population, 68,195.				NOTTINGHAM. (*Municipal Borough.*) Population, 57,407.			
	No. of Schools.	Number of Scholars belonging to the Schools.			No. of Schools.	Number of Scholars belonging to the Schools.			No. of Schools.	Number of Scholars belonging to the Schools.			No. of Schools.	Number of Scholars belonging to the Schools.		
		Total.	Sex.			Total.	Sex.			Total.	Sex.			Total.	Sex.	
			M.	F.			M.	F.			M.	F.			M.	F.
DAY SCHOOLS	59	3679	2017	1662	115	9089	5014	4075	151	7760	4243	3517	119	5925	3143	2782
PUBLIC DAY SCHOOLS	16	2544	1325	1219	26	5328	2959	2369	45	5207	3000	2207	25	3330	1883	1447
PRIVATE DAY SCHOOLS	43	1135	692	443	89	3761	2055	1706	106	2553	1243	1310	94	2595	1260	1335
Classification of Public Schools.																
CLASS I.—SUPPORTED BY GENERAL OR LOCAL TAXATION	..	..	..	..	2	307	175	132	1	40	31	9	1	104	56	48
CLASS II.—SUPPORTED BY ENDOWMENTS	1	226	102	124	5	1284	1013	271	5	534	346	188	3	364	259	105
CLASS III.—SUPPORTED BY RELIGIOUS BODIES	7	1100	541	559	13	3260	1542	1718	36	4278	2433	1845	18	2647	1402	1245
CLASS IV.—OTHER PUBLIC SCHOOLS	8	1218	682	536	6	477	229	248	3	355	190	165	3	215	166	49
CLASS I.																
Corporation School	..	..	..	..	1	146	100	46	..	..	..	..	..	..	..	..
Workhouse Schools	..	..	..	..	1	161	75	86	1	40	31	9	1	104	56	48
CLASS II.																
Collegiate and Grammar Schools	..	..	..	..	1	117	117	..	..	..	..	..	1	91	91	..
Other Endowed Schools	1	226	102	124	4	1167	896	271	5	534	346	188	2	273	168	105
CLASS III.																
Denominational.																
Ch. of England—*National*	2	579	267	312	4	1067	429	638	13	1915	987	928	4	1115	564	551
„ *Others*	2	263	118	145	4	738	515	223	10	712	363	349	6	684	366	318
Presbyterian Church in England	..	..	..	..	1	64	47	17	..	..	..	..	..	..	..	..
Independents—*British*	..	..	..	..	..	..	..	..	3	361	152	209	..	..	..	..
„ *Others*	1	36	26	10	..	..	..	..	2	185	165	20	2	162	87	75
Baptists	..	..	..	..	1	98	51	47	1	102	49	53	..	..	..	..
Unitarians	..	..	..	..	1	134	80	54	..	..	..	..	..	..	..	..
Wesleyan Methodists	..	..	..	..	..	..	..	..	..	..	..	..	2	211	136	75
Dissenters—*British*	1	72	50	22	..	..	..	..	..	..	..	..	..	..	..	..
Roman Catholics	1	150	8)	7(	1	769	420	349	1	67	43	24	2	277	94	183
Undenominational.																
British	..	..	..	..	1	390	..	390	6	936	674	262	2	198	155	43
CLASS IV.																
Ragged Schools	..	..	..	..	2	116	61	55	..	..	..	..	..	..	..	..
Blind Schools	..	..	..	.!	..	..	..	..	1	25	14	11	1	18	10	8
Deaf and Dumb School	..	..	..	..	1	27	13	14	..	..	..	..	..	..	..	..
Factory Schools	7	1115	594	521	..	..	..	..	..	..	..	..	..	..	..	..
Other Subscription Schools, of no specific character	1	103	88	15	3	334	155	179	2	330	176	154	2	197	156	41

(The CLASS III. Denominational and Undenominational rows are bracketed with the rotated label "Supported by".)

* MERTHYR-TYDFIL.—Parts only of the Parishes of Merthyr-Tydfil and Vainor are within the Borough of Merthyr-Tydfil, but the Schools and Scholars of the whole are here included. The population of the added parts is 964.

Plate 36 Part of the Report of the Census on *Education, 1851*, showing Nottingham schools in various categories.

10,000, but since they still charged, the abolition of fees in Board Schools in 1891 hit them hard. The chapels (which had given up the struggle in the 1840s) came to accept state involvement and handed over their schools to the Boards. Dame schools and places of private instruction still flourished, and how influential they were can still not be assessed. In 1851, 100 private schools of all kinds held 2,500 pupils. But this number fell; by 1898, there were only 13 with 270 pupils, a direct result of free education in the Board Schools. Clearly they were losing ground. Similarly the late nineteenth century saw the decline of many of the old-established rural grammar schools whose endowments were not adequate for the higher remuneration of the teacher and the higher costs of teaching aids to allow them to compete with the free schools. Nor was it simply a matter of finance; many of these schools were plagued with long and costly disputes which sapped their confidence and their funds.

The churches of Nottingham thus proved unable to cope with the increasing flood of children needing education, and the other kinds of voluntary and commercial schools were declining. It was left to the Board to meet the needs of the new housing areas (especially when the borough was extended in 1877), to face the problems of increasing population and the demands for children to stay at school longer.

By 1877, there was a deficiency of 4,600 places and two new Board schools had been established. From then on, till 1892, there was a continuous building programme, most of it of elementary schools. All the British schools were taken over, the last in 1892. On the whole the Board favoured large schools with specifically educational architecture (Plate 38, p. 206). By 1903, there were four times more school places in Nottingham than in 1870, but the voluntary share (which had been the whole at that time) was now under a third. Nor was the Board's work confined entirely to elementary education. It began to build Higher Grade Schools and other specialist institutions; by 1902, it was administering no less than 39 of these.

The local balance between these types of provision varied. In some places, there were only Board schools; in others, only Church schools; in still others, a rivalry. In rural areas there was often only one school, seemingly ill-attended, despite the social sanctions of the landowners and clergy. But even quite small villages might have more than one type of school. Some places saw a hostility from the Church of England to the 'godless School Boards'; but this was not strong in the 1870s. Indeed, some parsons used a Board to get a Church school on the rates. But opposition grew precisely as the Church of England lost ground. [16] Church schools were rarely able to expand like Board Schools which were often situated in slum areas and among the newer developments (partly, of course, because of the costs of building land). The topography and architecture of local schools is never more interesting than at this period, for the size and location of the various types of school can be most revealing. Thus for instance the older endowed schools began leaving the redeveloping city centres for the newer higher-class suburbs. And the composition of the schools reflected the areas in which they found themselves. [17]

In all this educational effort, the local community became more fully involved. Fund-raising now gave way largely to rates; there were elections to the Boards and for a few (farmers in rural areas, or in the town business and professional people, especially clergymen and almost always men) there was service on the Board. There was still much apathy, but on the whole local involvement had probably increased.

How effective was all this mass education? Probably it is impossible to assess this

NOTTINGHAM SCHOOL BOARD ELECTION.

Considerable interest has been manifested in the School Board election for a day or two back. On Sunday several electioneering sermons were preached, and yesterday there was a good deal of canvassing in several of the wards on behalf of the Conservative candidates, on behalf of Messrs. Mellers and Wood, and other gentlemen. We understand that Mr. W. A. Richards and the party with whom he is associated have been putting in operation the machinery of the Parliamentary elections to ensure their return. Allegations of bribery were also rife, and there is no doubt that there were many cases where "influence"—whether "undue influence" or not we are not prepared to say—was used to make the electors fetch their voting papers to be filled up by others. Up till the various offices were closed last night the number of papers applied for was about 5,600. If all these papers are deposited, with the full number of votes entered, Nottingham will, at least, be considerably ahead of Manchester in taking an interest in this matter, since in the great Lancashire city only about a third of the votes were recorded. Though the Returning Officer did not desire this to become widely known, lest it should prevent persons from applying, voters will also be able to obtain papers to-day (Tuesday). It is to be regretted that the contest should recently have assumed so much of a party character. The Five who have held meetings (under the presidency of Dr. Ransom) to protest against what they call dictation seem likely to lose votes, because an impression prevails that instead of utilizing the existing schools (which by the time-table conscience clause, that religious instruction must be given at the beginning or the end of the school hours, and that any child can be withdrawn from this instruction if its parents desire it), this party desire to erect new ones to enter into competition with these, and, if possible, bring them to a " painless extinction." As this would be a costly experiment for ratepayers, already too heavily burdened, it may be easily believed that Messrs. Rothera, Richards, and others (though well known as clever manipulators of party elections) may lose votes to which, from their former party connexions, they may think themselves fairly entitled. It is idle to speculate upon what candidates are likely to win, and seeing how complicated the question is rendered by the cumulative vote, the electors will have great cause for satisfaction if it is found on an examination of the proceedings of this day that they have not resulted in "a fortuitous concourse of atoms." It is something to be thankful for that in the earlier stage of the proceedings men of all parties were found working cordially together to promote the election of a Board that would be thoroughly representative. If by the action of a clique that can agree to nothing this harmonious action should be frustrated, the electors will have cause for regret. The only advice that we feel justified in offering to the electors is to select men who are likely to act well together for the common good, and to avoid crowding their votes upon one or two popular candidates.

Plate 37(a)   An account of the first School Board election in Nottingham, taken from the *Nottingham Journal*, for 29 November 1870. This is one of a number of newspaper notices concerning the School Board.

adequately. From the middle of the century there were steady improvements in the standing and training of teachers, which together with changes in the curriculum and the age-requirements of the pupils seem to have made for better schools. That the Norwich Baptist Night School was still admitting illiterates as late as 1907 will perhaps not surprise some of those who have taught in rural areas today. The extent of self-help in the form of adult remedial education is one guide, through Evening Schools, extension courses, religious bodies, People's Colleges, Mechanics' Institutes, Friendly and Co-operative Societies and the like. But much of this was voluntary in character.[18] So far as the schools were concerned, a school place was not the same as an attendance; all schools were grossly under-used in fact. At Nottingham again, a survey of 4,000 children in 1872 revealed that more than 500 never went to school and that a further 1,200 were away on the particular day of the survey. Nevertheless throughout the century attendance, teaching methods and the pupils' sense of purpose all seem to have improved. The average attendance rose, for the ages 5–11, from 60% to some 90% by 1902. If the schools of the later nineteenth century seem by our standards still to be odious places, it must be remembered that they were vastly more numerous and better than they had been a hundred or even fifty years earlier.

3

The sources for the study of education in the locality may be discussed briefly. On the whole the range of source material is much the same as for other aspects of local community problems.

The age structure of the community has already been discussed (Chapter 3, p. 38), and some estimates of the numbers of children can be arrived at. For the provision and its various forms of activities in the Middle Ages, the local historian must have recourse largely to ecclesiastical records, such as bishops' licences to schoolteachers, to the chantry certificates and gild records and to borough records for towns. Something of this is discussed in the relevant volumes of the *Victoria County History* but this often omits the unendowed school, the ephemeral institution associated with an individual teacher. These are the hardest to trace, and many must be totally unrecorded.

For the later period there is more which can be learned. The parish chest, especially churchwardens' accounts, may often have much to say, as will certainly borough archives for towns. These latter (together with poor law and quarter sessions records) will throw some light on apprenticeships. The local poor law records may also have a good deal on the workhouse school and child-paupers. Charity papers will on occasion contain detailed references to the school, its teachers, pupils, equipment and buildings. The buildings themselves often survive and will prove rewarding if examined carefully.[19] And then there is a large range of other sources. The local clergy were often asked at visitations to report on schools, and what they said frequently survives in the diocesan registry. The teachers may be documented from subscription books which they had to sign from 1562, or from letters testimonial that they presented to the bishop, or from the visitation papers called Call Books, and several of these records are among most diocesan archives. The local denominational schools will be mentioned in the annual reports of such central authorities as the S.P.C.K. (from the early eighteenth century) and the Methodist Conference rather later. Local newspapers may carry notices and advertisements. But still the smaller private schools will escape attention.

The problems of literacy and attendance are still more difficult. Literacy has normally been assessed by counting the signatures of brides and grooms in the

NOTTINGHAM SCHOOL BOARD.

PUPIL TEACHERS' CENTRE CLASSES.

People's College Higher Grade Board School.

LIST OF INSTRUCTORS FOR 1884-5.

	YEAR I.	YEAR II.	YEAR III.	YEAR IV.
Mathematics.	Mr. Potter.	Mr. Bowness.	Mr. Chasteney.	Mr. Francis.
Grammar.	Mr. Mitchell.	Mr. Potter.	Mr. Francis.	Mr. Jefford.
Geography.	Mr. Dickinson.	Mr. Morley.	Mr. Young.	Mr. Francis.
History.	Mr. Chasteney.	Mr. Jefford.	Mr. Young.	Mr. Francis.

| **Drawing.** | { *Freehand and Model* - - Mr. Chasteney. |
| | { *Geometry and Perspective* - Mr. Francis. |

| **Music.** | Mr. Lees. |

| **Sciences.** | { *Chemistry* - Mr. Francis. } Science Demonstrator, and |
| | { *Physiology* - Mr. Levy. } Mr. Wilkins if necessary. |

| **Language.** | *French* - Mr. Francis and Mr. Tardif. |

REGISTRAR. - Mr. FRANCIS.

N.B.—The Classes will commence on Monday, 6th October. All Stationery, Apparatus, &c., will be under the care of the Registrar. Instructors will be held responsible for the collection and delivery to Mr. FRANCIS of the Registers and Materials used in their respective Classes.

For the carrying out of the new " Work Card " System it will be necessary for all instructors to take home their students' work for correction, and endorsement with the marks assigned (1 Excellent, 3 Good, &c.) This will leave the class period free for Lecture Notes and Demonstrations, which should occupy nearly the whole of the time appointed for the various lessons.

W. PACKER,

CLERK.

19th September, 1884.

Plate 37(b)   One of the many ephemeral sources for the study of local history, this poster indicates the extending range of provision by the Nottingham School Board. Many similar, and more controversial, posters survive.

marriage registers. It is unlikely that any better method will be devised, but the local historian must remember that he will generally be dealing with very small figures (the largest total in the survey mentioned above was only 48 in the ten-year period 1760—9, an average of less than 5 per annum). Secondly, the historian can never know how many of these persons did not wish to sign personally, nor how many of those who could not write could in fact read. The subject is fraught with dangers.[20] But more can be said on this subject than on school attendance, unless perchance some diaries or school log books survive.

4

As usual, the problem with the nineteenth century is the wealth of material rather than the opposite. The local historian of this period has his difficulties but they do not include the lack of material. It is only possible to discuss the sources briefly here.

For the size of the school-age population, there is the census material. This has two main uses. It can reveal the numbers of children between given ages in the local community and the increase in their numbers. Secondly there are those children who are listed as 'scholars'. It is clear that some errors were made here; there were also a number of omissions. Further, many children both attended school and had some form of employment, and in some cases it was the latter which was recorded. Nevertheless the numbers and ages of the scholars recorded in each of the census years may reveal something of the trends.

More important than this however is the special education census taken in 1851. The school enumeration schedules (unlike those for the churches and chapels in the same year) are very rare indeed, but the printed report[21] contains a great deal of local information (Plate 36). Each place is listed, with the numbers of its private schools (i.e. those entirely supported by fees), its public schools (i.e. those with some form of local support such as government grants, local rates, endowments or voluntary subscriptions) and its Sunday Schools. The numbers of children actually in attendance on the census Sunday or the Monday following and the numbers on the roll were also recorded. Some schools have been omitted — not perhaps important to the national picture but very important to the local historian. Further, there were no sanctions and the returns were completed by the teachers or managers themselves. And there are difficulties in interpreting the returns which were made. It is impossible, for instance, to say from this material just how many children in the whole community received some form of education during their lives, for many attended schools for very short periods. Nevertheless, the results can enable us to say something about the numbers and types of schools and their sizes in the local community.

This is only one of the government reports which the educational historian must draw on; there are others. Some were specifically educational. Especially important here are the parliamentary surveys taken in 1816—18 and in 1833.[22] There are many reports of the Inspectors of Schools, and returns of elementary schools were published in 1871, 1893 and 1899. The grants lists give returns of average attendances for grant-aided schools. Similarly there are unpublished files of papers on each school from 1870 in the Public Record Office. The long series of printed papers, called first minutes (1839—57) and later reports (from 1857) of the Committee of the Privy Council on Education and later educational reports like the Taunton Commission of 1864, whose 20 volumes (10 of them full of local studies)

Plate 38   Changing patterns of school building, Nottingham

(a) Church of England School, established in Burton Street area, a new development to the north of the town largely devoted to civic offices.

Board Schools, St. Ann's Well Road, Nottingham.
Messrs. Evans & Jolley, Architects.

(b) A Board School in one of the industrial and working-class areas of the town. Note the large number of separate classrooms, typical of the use of certificated teachers by the Board.

'provide the most complete sociological information pertaining to education ever assembled in this country',[23] or the Newcastle Commission to enquire into the state of popular education in England (1861), or the report that the Endowed Schools Commissioners eventually produced in 1887 after several attempts, or the report on technical education in 1884 — all of these contain local information.[24] In 1870 the Council called for returns of all existing schools to establish whether the need for a local School Board existed or not, and returns of all 'public' schools were made in 1875 and 1894. Similarly the Boards had to report annually to the Committee of Council.

Not only are there these specifically educational reports, but other government papers, like the Charity Commissioners' Reports, contain useful information about local schools. Bromley school is fully reported, for example. Again there are incidental references; the Reports of the Children's Employment Commission, for instance, showed that some schools were in fact small domestic factories.[25] These and other reports need to be examined for they will often have something to say on education.

The 1851 census can be compared in some places with other local surveys, usually printed in the local newspapers or in directories and guide books. Nottingham had one in 1833 and Sheffield one in 1840, for instance, but as with religious censuses it is important to distinguish between places available and actual attendances of children.

But perhaps the most valuable sources here are the detailed accounts drawn up preparatory to the establishment of a School Board in 1870 or soon after. This usually gives the numbers of schools, the numbers of pupils and attendances and other information. It was generally reported on fully in the local newspapers, but in some cases the full report survives among the School Board records. These latter, where they still exist, are very full — minutes, accounts, printed reports and many other papers.[26]

Other local records will also survive. Newspapers (Plate 37) (especially for the sometimes hotly contested Board elections as well as other aspects of education) and directories throw a lot of light on the local provision, and this can often be supplemented by local memories, diaries and by visits to the buildings themselves (Plate 38). Some schools will have their own records. Log books (an immensely rich source for all sorts of local history) will say a great deal about buildings, equipment, attendance and curriculum, and will usually contain copies of the Inspectors' reports. There will often be attendance registers as well. The Poor Law records will deal with the union school and the borough itself may still have some material concerning local charity schools. The most revealing sources here however are the papers of the charity trustees which may be in the hands of local solicitors or the parish authorities.

The Church was, of course, greatly involved in education and this is reflected in the sources. Not only will the church and chapel magazine and other records discuss the schools, especially the Sunday Schools, but the visitation returns for the nineteenth century are often particularly full. From 1839, Diocesan Boards of Education spread slowly throughout the country, starting with London, and their papers (especially annual reports) may survive. Above this, there are the records of the central bodies like the British and Foreign Schools' Society and the National Society whose annual reports are full once more of local information. The local historian in search of his schools may have to go far in pursuit of his objective, but the search will be worth while: he will find much.

Chapter 11

Leisure and cultural provision

1

One of the most revealing of all the aspects of local community affairs which were jointly handled by all three agencies, the formal authorities, the charitable bodies and self-help, was the provision of facilities for leisure and cultural activities, and it would seem useful to take this as another example of the inter-action of these three interests. But as with education, other forces played their part, especially the commercial interests which saw in man's need for recreation an opportunity for profit. These categories were not, of course, mutually exclusive. Those who profited might still be philanthropic in their business projects; the formal agencies might be as concerned to aid the movement of 'self-help' as they were to regulate the ill-ordered activities of the populace. But for the sake of study, the strands may be disentangled by the local historian.

The questions which may be asked in this respect are relatively obvious and straightforward. Clearly, some assessment must be made of the *need* for leisure-time provision. The time to engage in hobbies or other non-remunerative activities was for most people for most of the past limited; it had to be taken from the rest of the working day. A preliminary question thus relates to the two forms of leisure time, the daily or weekly leisure time and the annual holidays. How long was the working day and what time was left for more enjoyable employments? And secondly, with what frequency did non-working days occur? The growth of holiday periods is one of the most remarkable features of English history during the last hundred years.

Having established the opportunities for leisure and cultural activities, a description of the type of *provision* available becomes important. Such provision varied considerably. It is not just that later communities were more well-supplied than earlier ones; indeed, in some respects this is not true. Rather, it is that the types of provision reflect the nature of the community, the interests of the persons who comprised it. Related to this is the question, who provided the facilities for leisure activity? This is immensely revealing of the balances within the community. In some places, there is evidence of 'planning', of the formal agencies of local government interesting themselves in what the residents (or some of them at least) wished to do in their spare time. In others, the element of patronage is strong; the 'do-gooders' knew exactly what other members of their community *ought* to do. Almost everywhere at certain periods, there are clear signs of the growth of 'self-culture' in two main forms, the middle-class aesthetic culture and the artisan 'pop culture' centred (for example) on drinking houses.

Not all that was provided was used, and the *preferences* of those who lived within our towns and villages are noteworthy for what they tell us of the quality of life within the communities they created. Partly of course, the use was dictated by the location of the provisions; leisure and cultural activity, like all the other aspects of our study, has a topographical aspect which needs examining. But factors other than sheer location were also involved; the Assembly Rooms were hardly designed for the gunsmith of Birmingham, the Athenaeum for the textile-worker of Manchester. It is true that these social prejudices which, for instance, usually placed the race course near the smarter end of town, were reflected in the topography of leisure; it is also true that 'pop culture' created its own topography, with its pubs on almost every corner of blocks of working-class housing. Nevertheless, the two subjects, how extensively the provisions were used and what significance might lie in their locations, may well need to be treated separately by the local historian.

2

The development of leisure and cultural provision in England is still in many places obscure. It is of course related to the extension of leisure time. During the earlier periods of English history, working hours were long, longer (as ever) in the country than in the towns, but universally long by modern standards. It is unlikely however that they were as bad as they were to become in the industrial agglomerations of the late eighteenth and early nineteenth centuries. That period certainly seems to have witnessed the low-mark of leisure time, whether regarded in terms of the length of the working day or the existence of regular breaks from labour. For the medieval peasant had those great religious feasts which lie behind the word 'holiday'. However secularised these became, they never completely lost their religious significance. In each local community, too, there was the patronal festival, in some places a date of great importance for jollification, while many persons of all walks of life (apart from Chaucer's tale-bearers) went on lengthy pilgrimages, several of them more than once.

It was the towns of course which provided more opportunities for such leisure and pleasure. Apprenticeship regulations sometimes limited industrial hours, borough rules limited shopping hours. Fairs became great occasions for holiday, being open to rural as well as urban residents. Gild feasts and the plays, civic elections and the like made for regular breaks, while the more occasional (but still quite frequent) great event, such as the passage of a royal or noble household through the town, was greeted by a freedom from work not notable in eighteenth-century Bradford or early nineteenth-century Slough. Much of the provision was of the nature of 'self-help', though the borough corporations played their part.

Such a pattern remained relatively unchanged, although the gilds and pilgrimages passed away under Henry VIII and his children, while the theatres, heirs to the traditions of borough plays, came under attack from the puritans whom the Reformation bred. In general, however, little real change can be seen until the second half of the seventeenth century or the early eighteenth century, and indeed in the countryside for even longer. For the rural dweller, there were still the religious or semi-religious activities, like the annual village feast, the Mumming Plays, the beating of the parish bounds and the great Christian festivals. All of these had become even more secularised in content, while other, more purely commercial events like the annual hiring fair (the Statis) and the estate 'rent days', might paradoxically be treated as occasions for rejoicing.

Meanwhile the towns enjoyed both greater opportunities for leisure and cultural activity and greater social amenities. For the leisured classes came together in a way not known before. Theatres, Assembly Rooms, concert halls, spa centres, race courses sprouted from the late seventeenth and early eighteenth centuries. The social round at Bath is well known but this could be paralleled (even if not equalled) in a very large number of other towns throughout the country. Even the 'uncommon dullness' of Warwick was enlivened by races (from 1707), the theatre (from at least 1792), balls, concerts, public breakfasts, card parties and other assemblies, usually held in the Shire Hall and Court House, or by wild animal shows, waxworks, cock-fights and gaming for 'less refined tastes'.[1]

Most of this provision was of course for the wealthy, the person of independent means. For the rest, in both town and country, there were the drinking houses. How far these increased in numbers is not certain but in every community there were very many. Some were purely temporary *ad hoc* pubs, others brewed regularly, though the proprietors were rarely able to make a living purely by selling conviviality. Thus we find many doubling up with farming, with brickmaking or carpentry, with some craft or other commemorated in the name of the pub. Nor did they confine their amenities entirely, within the drinking hours, to the sale of liquor. Their activities ranged from betting games like bagatelle or cock-fighting to organised sports like boxing and (from the mid-eighteenth century) cricket. The George Hotel at Grantham ran its own theatre. As drinking houses, whether socially prestigious or not, they had always been subject to some control, from the days of the manorial assize of ale in the Middle Ages. Licences had to be obtained from the J.P.s from 1552, granted (from 1729) in a special September session of the justices; when in 1835 the borough justices were stripped of most of their powers in the municipal reform movement, they retained their licensing functions for public houses. In addition, from at least 1839 for some large towns or 1848 for the rest of the country, opening hours were restricted by legislation.

Nineteenth century

It was the combination of the growth of large industrial conurbations and the spread of the evangelical conscience which brought about great changes in the nineteenth century, in both the pattern and provision of leisure activities. The huge towns deprived the inhabitants of the more proletarian countryside activities. This was particularly true of the rural workers who moved into the town. Such people found themselves able to join in few common festivities; only the great annual fairs and the pubs remained. The towns even removed the amenities of the countryside itself. The only open spaces apart from market squares were private grounds and botanic gardens occasionally opened to the public. In many of the largest towns common land ceased to be within easy access by the 1820s and 1830s. On the other hand, the town gave its workers more time for leisure. The structure of some industries, the apparently unceasing cycle of slumps and booms and the more regular seasonal fluctuations all meant that the town labourer had time on his hands — or he took it by the worship of Saint Monday.[2] During the late eighteenth and early nineteenth centuries this became particularly apparent. One answer was to provide more and regular work, which the factories certainly did. The result was probably to bring the town worker, at least for a time, closer to the rural worker. On the whole the agricultural labourer probably still worked longer hours than town workers, though even this varied from industry to industry. Nor was it long before the town workers achieved greater leisure time. Starting with the textile factories (not, however, the domestic workers), hours were gradually shortened from the 1833 Factory Act onwards, until in 1847 the first of the so-called 'Ten-hour' Acts was passed; by 1874, the week's work was fixed as lasting for 56 hours only. The textile workers led in two other changes, the Saturday half-day and the annual holiday. Bank holidays were first made general in 1871, while annual holidays, forced on the northern cotton factories in the form of Wakes' Weeks, began to become more common. Professor Best estimates that in 25 years alone, the average daily labours of the factory and skilled workers were reduced by something like an hour, and the week by half a day, although he reminds us that there were many occupations in which there were no limits to work.

The need of the nineteenth-century town worker was thus great and obvious, and all agencies rallied to make provision for it.[3] There were still of course the great events like local elections or the annual fairs — the Goose Fair in Nottingham, Newcastle Race Week, St Giles' Fair at Oxford or Manchester races in Whit Week. The funfair aspect of these events came to predominate, first with 'Wild Beast Shows' from about 1800, then with 'merry-go-rounds' from about 1810 through to the continental steam-organ of the 1880s. Some of this change necessitated in many cases a new venue for the fair, but little progress in moving the activities out of the town had been made by 1900, and it was perhaps urban trams rather than amenity which finally forced the change.

The only other regular excitement was provided by the pubs. These played a major part in the life of most townsmen and women in the nineteenth century. One recent local study, for Banbury,[4] shows the increase in pubs in that town from 1830 to 1860; they achieved their maximum population density about 1841:

Public houses in Banbury 1831—71

	Population*	Taverns/ Inns	Beerhouses	Total pubs	Number of people per pub
1831	6,427	37†	11†	48	134
1841	7,241	45	22	67	108
1851	8,793	45	35	80	110
1861	10,238	46	42	88	116
1871	11,768	46	44	90	131

Sources: Census Returns; Rusher's Banbury Directories, published annually from 1832.

* Population figures refer to the whole ecclesiastical parish, i.e. the municipal borough and the township of Neithrop with other outlying townships in Oxfordshire, and the townships of Grimsbury and Nethercot in Northamptonshire. The 1832 Reform Act made the parliamentary borough co-extensive with the ecclesiastical parish.

† Figures for 1832. No directory available for 1831.

They were not evenly spread throughout the town. The topography of pubs may reveal something of the functions that the pub performed. The most important ones, the White Lion and the Red Lion, 'were at the hub of Banbury's transport system'; but the very large numbers of smaller beerhouses and pubs which lay in Neithrop (the lower-class area of the town outside the jurisdiction of the borough authorities) help to indicate that the presence or absence of pubs also reflects the social life of the community. The respectable residents of north Oxford (Plate 39), drinking wine at home or in college, neither needed pubs nor encouraged them. For by the 1880s, the presence of a pub could lower the tone of an area; and it was for commercial as well as temperance reasons that some landlords and some Building Societies refused to allow pubs to be established on their new developments. The

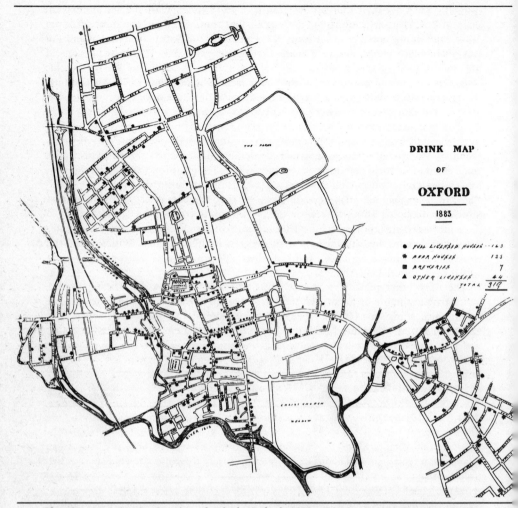

Plate 39   Map showing location of pubs in Oxford, 1883. This shows concentrations of pubs and especially beerhouses in the poorer areas of the towns; others near the Carfax and cattle market catering for suburban visitors and traders; and others along the main highways. There is a void in the more polite northern suburbs, save for some wine shops, and in the better class central streets.

pubs themselves varied, of course. Some were well placed to turn into coaching or railway hotels; some had functions of civic entertainment, while others in the town centre areas served as marts or exchanges. But most were small drinking houses with attached recreations and sports.[5] The development of large breweries helped the spread of these institutions. Some 268 existed in Oxford in 1883, a population density of 146. Nottingham's total provision of 156 in 1799 had risen by 1864 to 389, with 17 'vaults' for wine and spirits. Some 169 of these were beerhouses, given a freer licence under the Beer Houses Act of 1830 in an attempt to counteract the increasing spirit drinking which caused the reformers so much concern.

That there was a real social problem of drink in the nineteenth century cannot be doubted.[6] Legislation like the Public House Closing Act of 1864 and the Beer Houses Act of 1869 (forcing these houses to get a justices' licence like other pubs) was one answer. Reforming bodies, like the 'Central Association for Stopping the Sale of Intoxicating Liquors on Sundays,' the Band of Hope, the nonconformist Temperance Mission and the Anglican Temperance Society, were another. The temperance movement in most places was an important part of town and village life by the 1870s. It played a major role in local politics; it too had a topography but this was in general associated with the churches and chapels.[7] Certainly the temperance halls did not make the same immediate impact on the local community as the pubs did, clustered at street corners, often with two or more doors.

The temperance movement was only one answer to the problem. Local government reacted by buying up pubs and demolishing them in the name of redevelopment, a traditional local government approach to difficult problems. But they survived and in their hey-day provided considerable outlet for 'self-help' in the way of lending clubs and friendly societies, trade unions and even cultural activities like the five Nottingham pubs who employed newspaper readers or the six which established lending libraries between 1835 and 1844.[8]

Such 'self-help', however, like the adaptation of commercial fairs into pleasure holidays, was frowned on by authority. There were more approved means of self-employment during leisure hours — gardening clubs, large choral and smaller debating societies and the physical recreation groups associated with sports like cricket, football and (later) cycling, which drew large crowds of spectators. But authority was more hesitant about such bodies as Working Men's Clubs, some of which (according to the chief constable of Nottingham) 'are nothing more than places of resort, when the licensed houses are closed, where drinking and debauching goes on until any hour in the morning. . . .'

Authority was not unaware of the problem. It was rather that its answer was different. Basically, it consisted of a two-fold approach. One was the provision of parks. How important a movement this was is only now becoming apparent. There had been 'Walks' in towns from at least 1785 when Leicester established its famous New Walk,[9] but they were small and generally neglected. The public parks movement aimed to establish large open spaces. A Select Committee enquiry in 1833 had produced no results and it was left to voluntary efforts to take the first steps. Manchester gave the lead in 1846 as a gesture of public interest, and others followed suit. From the 1860s and 1870s the local authorities, under considerable pressure, used powers available to them to provide open spaces. Unenclosed commons were bought out, like Woodhouse Moor in Leeds. There was, of course, local reluctance; it was very costly. But there was pressure from above as well as from below.[10] Parliament came to insist that urban and general Enclosure Acts from 1838 should include provision for open spaces, and in 1859 there was a general Recreation Grounds Act. A major reform movement calling for allotments was under way by the early nineteenth century.[11] As usual, it began as a voluntary movement in the 1850s, and it was not until 1887 that local authorities were given powers to provide these small open spaces for cultivation. Similar groups like the Commons Preservation Society of 1865 called passionately for town parks or fought to preserve commons, while wealthy gentlemen gave open spaces to the public, until a town like Exeter could become famous for 'its delightful diversity of public walks'. Some survived but many have now gone, especially the smaller pleasure gardens.

But apart from the provision of *rus in urbe*, authority also attempted to cultivate the masses. Some local government bodies secured local Acts so as to build libraries or establish museums (usually in converted buildings, like the later Nottingham

Museum in the Duke of Newcastle's mansion on Castle Rock in 1875–8) and other centres of culture, until William Ewart in 1845–55 persuaded Parliament to give to the municipal corporations such powers if they so wished without individual recourse to legislation.[12]

Few local authorities did in fact so wish. Most libraries, art galleries and museums were provided by local philanthropy, along with Literary or Mechanics' Institutes. These were cultural and educational bodies for the masses, but largely neglected by them. Chelmsford's Literary Institute was founded in 1833 by a Quaker and contained among other things newspapers, a games room and library.[13] Philanthropy provided not only alternatives to drink in Temperance Societies' teaparties but other forms of association, including some of the most famous football clubs of the later nineteenth century, even if at the same time they limited leisure activity on Sundays.[14]

If therefore in any local community there were a tension between the 'self-help' of the artisan and the authority and patronage of the more leisured, the former found an unexpected ally during the nineteenth century. This was the commercial interest. Realising the potentialities of increasing leisure, many professional and businessmen set out to exploit it. Music halls from the 1860s are perhaps the most notable form of this activity, with most towns sporting two or three at least.[15] Theatres (Plate 40(b)) and dance halls similarly sprang up. Even the local football clubs got taken over by commercial interests, while more seriously booksellers and publishers sought to promote local books, journals and newspapers. The development of the local news media is of particular importance to the local historian.[16] Meanwhile, the railways cottoned on to the new openings and either itself or through agents like Thomas Cook promoted its passenger services with trips like 'Temperance Specials', so that the local community began to establish its own distinctive pattern of excursion and holiday.[17]

The railway made all these facilities available to a large part of the countryside. But rural communities were not devoid of their own leisure activity. The formal authorities provided nothing. Local patronage provided village halls and institutes, church fêtes and garden parties, ploughing matches, public lectures and Sunday School outings. The inhabitants of Rauceby were regaled with a lecture from Cecil Rhodes' brother.[18] Improvement, however, frowned on the traditional festivities: 'We are gratified to learn', wrote the *Colchester Gazette* in 1837, 'that the Rev. John Bramston, Vicar of Great Baddow [Essex], has been endeavouring to prevent the holding of the annual fair in that parish . . . these annual scenes of iniquity . . . remnants of bygone ages of political degradation and moral darkness.'[19] By the middle of the nineteenth century the 'attack on peasant culture', as historians have come to call it, was launched in many places on a systematic basis, and provoked much reaction, often violent. But some forms of popular self-entertainment were tolerated, such as ploughing and shearing matches, agricultural clubs (especially Pig Clubs) and flower shows and above all village bands. This most important of institutions in the industrial village is one of the least recorded of the varied leisure and cultural activities of the local community.[20]

Bristol

Dr Meller's[21] survey of the provision of leisure and cultural facilities in Bristol from 1870 to 1910 reveals something of the tensions between the various bodies engaged in what was seen as a very necessary task. In 1861 the municipal authorities bought Clifton Downs in the respectable part of the town to save it from

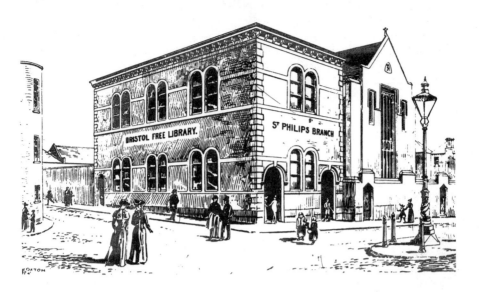

Plate 40(a) Bristol's first free library provided by the Corporation, 1876.

development, but it was pointed out by the Liberals that there were no similar open spaces in the poorer parts. Local philanthropy was not forthcoming until 1882, when the council had turned down at least one public park on the grounds of cost. In the next five years the council provided a number of very small pleasure gardens and thereafter with great reluctance some larger parks. A swimming bath was attached to the new Baths House at Mayors Paddock in 1870 as a sanitary measure for the poorer classes, at a time when there were already three middle-class private ones, making a profit; others followed in the 1880s and 1890s, and in 1897 two of the private ones were bought up. The public library was an endowed foundation run by a Library Society, and it was not until 1855 that the Council took over, raised a rate and eventually provided it with a different building. A branch lending library opened in 1876 (Plate 40(a)) in a working-class district and others followed in 1877 and 1878; it was not until 1883 that a new purpose-built branch library was set up, in the middle-class Redland. In this the Council first began with the premise that they were providing social facilities for the poor; it was later that the middle classes came to enjoy the same free services.

The voluntary bodies provided more of a philanthropic nature for the poor. Apart from the library building and Art Gallery, local benefactors provided the Museum, though this was bought up and given to the Council when the Society which ran it found itself in difficulties. The Bristol Institution from the early nineteenth century provided lectures. And then there were the 'missionaries' of many different kinds — the temperance movement from the 1830s, the Quaker Mission in the 1860s, Penny Readings, Winter Amusement Committees, Reading Rooms for the Working Classes, the Wednesday Evening Entertainments, Cocoa Meetings, the Band of Hope, the Blue Ribbon Gospel Temperance Army and the like, with music, lectures and parties — apart from the youth movements like the Y.M.C.A. and the

Plate 40(b)   Grand Theatre, Hyson Green, Nottingham: playbill, 1891. Such ephemera contain much useful information for the local historian.

Boys' Brigade, with their sports and organised games, choir and orchestra. Clifton College established a Working Men's Club in 1883 (the forerunner of a church) — not the first in Bristol, for a private benefactor had established such a Club in 1880. Before the end of the century most of the town was provided with facilities for recreation. Adult Schools sprang from Sunday Schools, starting in 1857, and by 1900 there were 45 such denominational schools as well as many purely secular Adult Clubs, Co-operative Societies, the Workers' Educational Association and the Bristol Sunday Society (which took over the Empire Theatre in the late 1890s).

Plate 40(c) The Reindeer Inn, Banbury. In its famous Globe room, the predominance of the Tory Red Lion and the Liberal Flying Horse was first challenged by Sir Charles Douglas, an independent Liberal in 1859. Later in the century the inn seems to have had fewer political pretensions.

Industrialists like Wills provided many facilities for their workers, and works-clubs developed.

Much of this secular work was done by self-help — like the working-class political clubs and trade union associations. Self-help took two forms, the middle-class search for a cultural identity, and the working-class provision. The former included the Museum and Library Society, the Fine Arts Society of 1845, Literary Institutions and the middle-class Temperance Friendly Societies like the Rechabites and the Good Templars. The working classes too were not slow to organise their own cycling and fishing clubs, copying their 'betters' in Exhibitions and Shows, and holding their own Labour Festivals, musical entertainments and sports.

The mass spectator sports like football became largely commercialised. Both Bristol City (1884) and Bristol Rovers (1883) began as working-class football teams but they soon received enough support to go professional (1897). This was only one of the commercial interests in the leisure activities of the people of Bristol. There was the Zoo, the Theatre Royal and Prince's Theatre and three music halls, all of them save the Theatre Royal established after 1860. The Colston Hall, built for concerts in 1857, was intended as a commercial enterprise as well as a town amenity. The railways provided excursions to Bath or the seaside at Weston-super-Mare, Cleveland and Avonmouth. On a smaller scale, there were circulating libraries and other similar efforts to provide what was needed. Not all of these types of provision can be clearly distinguished; the total scene at Bristol was of an integrated field of leisure and cultural provision, with all the main elements closely connected.

3

What sources may be used to trace the growth of leisure and cultural activities within any local community? Prior to 1800, the material is thin on the ground and for any given place one cannot be sure of finding very much. This is particularly true of the question of assessing the opportunities of members of the community to enjoy what facilities were available. Information relating to the working day and holidays is scarce. Borough records may throw some light on working hours in certain occupations for those places but this is on the whole rare.

There is more evidence for the sort of activities engaged in and the kind of provision made available. Once again the towns come off best. Borough records may help to indicate such things as the existence of theatres and assembly rooms. At the same time, field surveys may make it possible to record the date of the erection of these and similar buildings, as well as their location. Regulations concerning fairs are frequently mentioned in such town sources, as are on occasion medieval town plays. But most of these latter were provided by voluntary agencies, and it is from the records of gilds that most of our information concerning the medieval town plays comes. Perhaps the tradition is continued in the increasing numbers of rural Mumming plays which are being discovered. The records of charitable bodies and of the churches and chapels will reveal something of the voluntary provision made both for those within the church orbit and for those without. But in all cases, the major source of information for both town and country communities (although only available for part of the eighteenth century) must be the local newspapers. Until the nineteenth century, these contained little in the way of local news items; their main task was to retail London material to the provinces. It is rather the columns of announcements that are of particular interest to the eighteenth-century local historian.[22] Here will be found advertisements for forthcoming attractions, accounts of past events; here the sale notices will refer to pubs. Such pubs may however be noticed elsewhere — in deeds, for instance, or sale particulars and in town maps. These will enable a study of the topography of leisure to be attempted, at least to a limited extent.

Above all, there are the immensely valuable registers of alehouses to be found among the records of quarter sessions, following upon the Acts of 1552 and 1729 ordering their registration. The names, the owners and the tenants of all those inns which did not escape registration are recorded here. But it must be remembered that pubs were often of short duration; in the early years of the local community they came and went with considerable ease.

Something of the kind of leisure life can be gleaned from the records of these public houses themselves, where they exist. These can be most valuable. It is the records of the Greyhound Inn at Folkingham (Lincs) which reveal that the rent day of the extensive Heathcote estate was held there and clearly became a major event for the whole community, an event needing extra provisions.[23] Further evidence of this must lie in estate accounts. But once again the major source must be the newspapers. Here can be found evidence as to how widely supported particular events were. In addition, literary material can be immensely valuable. Charles Burney's accounts of his stay at King's Lynn as organist at St Margaret's parish church (1751—60) are even more revealing of life in that town than his daughter's novels are of life in Holborn. In a study of the social activities of the various members of the community, the historian's net must be cast widely, and he must learn to make what sense he can of the few broken fragments he may collect.

4

The period from 1800 onwards is once again more fully documented than the earlier centuries. Perhaps the main aspect of the study for which there is a distinct lack of evidence is the first, the particularly local conditions governing hours of work and regular holidays. Some evidence can be found in the various government reports on conditions of employment in specific industries; some in the records of the early trade unions. Newspapers once more may reveal annual holiday patterns. But in general, the particular must here be assumed from the general.

The types of provision available are well recorded. The facilities made by the *formal* local government bodies are of course documented in the records of those bodies, the minutes of the borough councils and corporations or of their library and museums committees (especially their annual reports with figures of attendances and loans), while a survey of such existing buildings or photographs of ones now gone can be most revealing in terms of their architectural style and location. Again there are parliamentary papers — returns of libraries from 1852 to 1891 and a Select Committee on Public Libraries in 1849.[24] These are however often less rewarding than the many private censuses into the use made of the various facilities provided, which were taken and published locally. Perhaps most revealing of the efforts of the urban local authorities is the O.S. map, with its areas of green within each town. The minutes of the Parks and Gardens Committee do not often reveal the struggles that preceded the establishment of these oases, though they may reveal subsequent threats from developers. For such early controversies, one must have recourse (as ever) to the newspapers and to locally published pamphlets, often anonymous.

The *voluntary* provision can first be seen from local directories. The records of several of these bodies survive locally and need studying. The church and chapel may retain information about their efforts to guide the straying flock into more profitable paths, while magazines and pamphlets in great quantity urge the faithful and dissident alike to support the new causes. Memories (verbal and written) are as valuable in this respect as in any, for most of those who had leisure to record their past for the benefit of others seem also to have been inspired to help the poor to fill their lives outside of working hours with brightness. But once again the surest and most profitable source must be the newspaper.

By the middle of the nineteenth century, provincial newspapers have changed from the reproduced London tabloid into a verbose local production, full of gossip and small talk.[25] And in this lies part of the trouble from the local historian's point of view. First, they are so bulky, and they do not always record things systematically. It is true that gradually they came to place particular items on particular pages. Those papers which covered large rural areas seem to have done this early, so that items of news relating to specific villages can often be traced quite quickly. But even then, most of the best information comes from the advertisements and these are not always conveniently placed for the local historian to make a quick survey of them. Secondly, there are a large number of local newspapers. Many towns had several: Bristol in 1870 had five daily papers (four calling themselves Liberal)[26] and five weeklies (three Liberal) — apart from the smaller, more temporary journals and magazines and apart from the more general Bath and Somerset papers which covered the town. Banbury's papers are more manageable, but even for that small town there were in that same year four major papers, the *Advertiser*, the *Beacon*, the *Guardian* and the *Oxfordshire Weekly News* (formerly the *Herald*). Further, a

SUBSCRIPTIONS, 1871.

	£	s.	d.		£.	s.	d.
Betts, S.	0	2	6	Johnson, W.	0	10	0
Ball, G. V.	0	10	6	Kench, K.	0	1	0
Baylis, W.	0	5	0	Kingerlee, H.	0	2	6
Benford, Isaac	0	2	6	Lake, W.	0	2	6
Brummitt, R.	0	2	0	Lamb, J. and A.	0	10	0
Bennett, E.	0	2	6	Lumbert, J.	0	2	6
Birkby, T. S.	0	5	0	Lampitt, J.	0	2	6
Bolton, H.	0	2	6	Looker, J.	0	1	0
Butcher, J.	0	1	0	Mousir, G. W.	0	2	6
Burgess, F.	0	5	0	Mewburn, W., Esq.	1	1	0
Bartlett, C.	0	1	0	Mawle, J.	0	5	0
Brazier, R.	0	1	0	Mander, R.	0	1	0
Buller and Pearse	0	5	0	Mander, C.	0	1	0
Clarke, Thos.	1	0	0	Neighbour, —	0	2	0
Cobb, T. R.	0	10	0	Norton, J.	0	2	0
Cluff, D.	0	2	6	Potts, E.	0	1	0
Carter, S.	0	2	0	Potts, J.	0	2	6
Cheney, J.	0	5	0	Pidgeon, Mrs.	0	5	0
Cubitt, W.	0	2	6	Pain, T., Esq.	0	5	0
Cadbury, Jas	0	10	0	Potts, F.	0	1	0
Cooper, S.	0	1	0	Robins, J.	0	1	0
Carey, Mr.	0	2	6	Rice, J C.	0	5	0
Coleman, W.	0	2	6	Railton, E.	0	2	6
Dalby and Son	0	2	6	Railton, T.	0	2	6
Dumbleton, Mr.	0	1	0	Rainbow, Mrs.	0	1	0
Donnelly, T.	0	1	0	Rathbone, T.	0	1	0
Eason, Miss	0	2	6	Stevens, R.	0	2	6
Edmunds, R., Jun.,	0	5	0	Stutterd, Mrs.	0	2	6
Faulkner, C.	0	5	0	Stutterd, S.	0	2	6
French, A.	0	1	0	Stone and Hartley	0	2	6
Gillett, J.	0	10	0	Samuelson, B., Esq., M.P.	2	0	0
Gillett, C.	0	10	0	Samuelson & Co.	1	0	0
Gibbs, R.	0	5	0	Shilson, W.	0	5	0
Garrett, T.	0	1	0	Shilson, C.	0	5	0
Grant, G.	0	2	6	Smith, R.	0	1	6
Hankinson, Thomas	0	2	6	Sanderson, Mrs.	0	2	6
Harrison, J. J.	0	1	0	Taplin, T.	0	1	0
Harlock, J.	1	0	0	Thomas, A.	0	1	0
Hodson, R.	0	1	0	Tearle, L.	0	2	6
Hart, J.	0	7	0	Walford, G.	0	5	0
Hodson, Mrs.	0	1	0	Walford, H.	0	2	6
Hyde, J.	0	2	0	Wall, E.	0	2	6
Hughes, S.	0	1	0	Wilkins, W.	0	2	6
Hawkins, Mr.	0	2	6	Watkins, T. J.	0	5	0
Jarvis, J.	0	5	0				

DONATIONS, 1871.

	£	s.	d.		£	s.	d.
———— A.	0	3	0	Jas. Cadbury	18	4	10
W. A. Skinner	0	2	6	Rev. R. Guinness	1	5	0
W. Mewburn, Esq.	21	0	0				

Plate 40(d) This subscription list comes from the 34th report of the Banbury Temperance and Alliance Association, 1871. Earlier lists of those who signed the pledge and registers of members sometimes give occupations. This, the second such list for Banbury, may be compared with the census books to discover just who the active supporters of the movement were.

good deal of information about the town comes from papers with a wider circulation, like the *Oxford City and County Chronicle*, the *Northampton Herald* or *Jackson's Oxford Journal*. Many were ephemeral; a Banbury *Evening News* ran for one year in 1877, and a *Telegraph* in 1893–5. Others were quickly bought out or amalgamated. Such can be traced through a number of aids. The series of Mitchell's *Directories* (first issued in 1846) records local newspapers in a way which most others do not, but the important ones are mentioned in most town directories. In 1874, F. L. May compiled his *British and Irish Press Guide*, a useful but rare hand-list, while in 1920, *The Times* issued a handlist of newspapers,[27] a comprehensive list which fully reveals the complexities of the local scene. But even this does not exhaust the smaller local press, the parish magazines, the society newsletter, the political bulletin and the like.

Leaving these latter on one side, the bulk of local newspapers in the nineteenth century makes the historian's task a very onerous one indeed. A lengthy run through even a weekly is a laborious task; to attempt to do thoroughly a decade for a place like York with its two evening and three Saturday papers may be both soul-destroying and time-consuming. There are of course some helps. Not all of these papers are of equal value and the local historian will quickly learn to concentrate upon the most useful sources. Secondly, most local history libraries have files of newspaper cuttings. Some places have employed indexers and progress is being made to simplify the work of searchers (at the same time, of course, easing the hard wear on long-suffering and ill-bound copies of the paper). But for others there is little help. Nevertheless, the rewards are great and for many aspects of the local historian's task in the nineteenth century a search through the local newspapers is absolutely essential, a chore though this may be.

To try to record the various *pubs* from this source, however, is both unwise (for the list will certainly be incomplete) and unnecessary. Licences for both pubs and dance halls survive amongst most corporation or quarter sessions papers. There are also parliamentary papers dealing with the licensing laws, inquiries in 1850, 1853 and 1855, and especially the report of the Royal Commission of 1897.[28] And from these sources, and from maps, the student can pursue the most practical task in this aspect of his subject – recording the numbers of pubs, their density per head of population, the different types of pubs, their location (for the licences enables them to be closely located) and relative density in each area of the place. Here is a limited project which can be filled out from other sources. Thus one can trace something of the use of inns, for commercial transactions or for the sessions of the justices or for middle-class social and intellectual activities and recreation. One often neglected source for the life of the public house is the series of annual reports of the chief of police, and indeed the other records of the local police force. Unfortunately these latter are not always as readily available as the printed annual reports, but the fruits of an examination of this material can be very great indeed. Again one may be able to trace something of the standing of the publican in the community, for inns came to have a hierarchy of prestige and on occasion innkeepers moved from pub to pub around the town as they became vacant.

The *temperance societies* are not so well recorded. There is some information in directories, and occasionally society records with lists of members survive (Plate 40(d)). More frequently, the local historian may find runs of local temperance journals, but material on this subject, apart from the newspapers, is thin. Nevertheless, it should be possible to analyse something of the membership, especially the officers, and to describe the activities of the various groups.

There are other sources which must not be neglected. Railway timetables and posters will indicate something of the *holiday pattern*, or at least those which the railway company sought to promote. At the same time, for rural areas, they can indicate which town facilities were easily accessible to the rural community. The numbers of *theatres* can be obtained from directories. Theatre handbills are prolific and very often contain information not available elsewhere (e.g. the price of seats, etc.); but there are in addition parliamentary reports on theatres and their licensing in 1866 and 1892.[29] Local scrapbooks are most informative, with early photographs of Sunday School outings or chapel anniversary feasts or bellringers' meetings.

How far was such provision used? Many newspapers and periodicals contain lists and figures of attendances at specific events such as art exhibitions or museums and the like; while the annual reports (where available) of many of the more formal bodies give some clue as to the use made of the facilities. But beyond this, the evidence is scanty. Not so on topography. Much still stands and can be examined; while the larger scale O.S. maps record the position of almost all of the public buildings of every community, both large and small. It is perhaps here that one should start in any examination of the leisure pursuits of the nineteenth century local community.

Conclusion

This book has set out to ask a number of questions about local communities in the past and to indicate how these might be answered by the local historian. It aims to provide a number of strictly practical tasks for the individual or group engaged in this work.

It has not of course asked all the questions which might be asked. There is nothing, for instance, on crime, nothing on public health, nothing on shipping. Nor has it by any means exhausted those topics which it has discussed. It aims to open doors, not to sweep the rooms clean.

A full study in the sense of these questions has never yet, to my knowledge, been attempted, let alone accomplished. Probably the records do not exist for such a full attempt in any one locality; the local historian has always to fill in some gaps from his knowledge of the general background. But more particularly historians do not in general work in this way. They get interested in particular problems or find an intriguing new source or pass from topic to related topic. In each of these processes, however, the historian is gradually building up to a complete picture of the past.

It is of course an enormous task, perhaps too big for one man. This is the reason many local historians merely skate over the surface. They so rarely tell us about the people; there is a great deal on the place or the buildings or on individuals or even groups, but very little about the community as a whole.

And in one sense, this is a recognition of the inevitable. For the complete picture of the past is gone. We can never know much about the quality of life of past communities, even where there are still living memories. Nevertheless the historian's task is to try to recreate the past community as far as he can. And the recent development of active and well-equipped local history groups perhaps makes the task not quite as impossible as it was when each historian worked completely on his own. The task may be attempted; and this book is offered as some help towards that task.

Note on social structure

It will be remarked that no guidance has been given above on a social analysis of the local community, although many local historians do this. The reason for the omission here is that I am not sure what such an analysis is based on. Nor am I at all certain that the modern categories of working class, middle class (divided like university degrees into division one and division two) and upper class and the criteria used to arrive at these classifications have any meaning in the past, certainly in the pre-industrial past.[1] Modern criteria are themselves very mixed — wealth, occupations, employment status, housing, education, social habits, and the like, and even these are not consistent. The wealthiest people do not always live in the largest houses, for instance. In the end, it is alleged that people belong to the classes which they or other people *think* they belong to; it is a measure of identification with a group, even though on occasions the group may not accept the individual.

When one looks at the social analyses made by local historians of past communities, one is aware of the same confusion, the same mixed bases. Some are based on wealth — i.e. a hierarchical analysis of taxation.[2] But it is clear that this has considerable limitations. Some of the wealthiest were members of more than one local community but were usually only taxed in one of them. Further, not all the native wealthy were influential within any local community; some were too involved in larger spheres to be active in smaller ones.[3] And again in many local communities, the *nouveaux riches* were not always accepted; one had to have family connections or length of tenure to secure acceptance and influence. In less mobile times and isolated communities, wealth may be an adequate measure of social status, but it is not so in other communities and other times.

Housing has similarly been used to analyse society; the Hearth Tax returns lend themselves to such an examination. But not only are these records on occasion unreliable in the facts they give about a house, but they rarely reveal *how* a house is used, although probate inventories may help a lot here. Certainly it is a long path from the numbers of rooms or hearths to one's place in local society, a path perhaps marked by too many assumptions to be worth traversing. Size of house does not necessarily equal wealth any more than wealth necessarily equals influence or prestige.

Other historians use occupations, particularly some sections of the trading interests or the leisured classes and the professions. But there are so many variables here. Not all clergy in the eighteenth century were on the same level as squires, but several were; even this limited equation is untrue for the sixteenth century, and indeed in the Middle Ages most local clergy were nearer to the peasants than to the lord of the manor. The same is true of other professions — the banker, the doctor and the teacher have all changed their position in society as time has progressed.

Others have used titles as at least some indication of social status — the nobility, gentry and those citizens, burgesses and yeomen who, as Sir Thomas Smith said in 1560, wielded power over 'the fourth sort of men who do not rule'.[4] But these are uncertain guides. An esquire who is regularly absent from the community may be of much less local consequence than a local burgess. Again titles, even when they can be traced (which is not always), were used and dropped in the fluid English society with an ease which tells us much about the individual and his pretensions but little about the social group. A merchant may or may not call himself a gentleman at whim.

The landlord—tenant relationship is sometimes held to indicate social structure; or at other times the size of estates. Thus the land tax or the enclosure award has been used for a social analysis. The three classes of landlord, owner-occupier and tenant have been classified according to the size of their holdings. Such a classification, regarded intelligently, may have more nearly universal truth for rural societies, and as such is of very great importance. For some people did regard themselves as the hereditary governors of society. But there are difficulties here. For one thing, many men were both freeholders and tenants at the same time. But more important, the analysis is based on a composition of two elements. A 200-acre tenant farmer will usually be regarded as of greater 'worth' than a 10-acre freeholder. The *legal* status in itself does not imply the level in society which the individual sought and obtained. Some tenants in communities where the landlord was non-resident might well be more socially prestigious than the freeholders farming the same sized holdings. On the other hand, the *size* of the holding alone is not enough.

In the towns, or at least in the industrial towns where the interest focuses rather upon the relations of employer and employed, the complications in the various ways of earning one's living result in no clear hierarchic structure emerging. Clearly an employer occupies a higher status in general than his worker, but if in part or wholly an absentee he may well have less 'say' in the community than the other.

Now all of these criteria have some justification. There is a 'social structure' of housing and landownership; there is a structure in employment. There are family and racial groupings within the local community. This is why several of the chapters above have a section dealing with the social structure of the subject under discussion.

But the corollary of this is that there is no one agreed basis for a social structure, no criteria which can be applied universally. And it is for this reason that there is no section in this book dealing with social structure. But I do not wish to be understood as implying that the subject did not exist, nor that it is not worth analysis. Every community had a structure, a hierarchy of deference and, with this, influence. But in each community the basis of this structure varied. In some it was wealth; in others landholding. For some communities, however, these criteria may not have applied. There may have been other groups with great influence — the tanners in one place, a gild in another. In still others, the really important individual may be the one who is merely active, whose force of personality is sufficient to impress his contemporaries. What the local historian has to do in each study, if he can, is to assess what is the structure of the community and to determine on what it is based.

Note on location of sources

Many of the sources listed in this book are widely scattered and the local historian will need to seek them out. The following note it is hoped will help him in this.

1   A start must always be made in the place studied. Not only will the student find here the material remains for his local community, the houses, churches and chapels, schools and public buildings, fields and roads, but he will also discover much of a more intangible nature – local memories, traditions and names. What is more there will be much in the way of documentation. Many parishes still keep their own records; there will be private papers, business and estate accounts, and much beside.

2   The second main port of call must be the local history section of the city, borough or county library. These will hold other local histories which often contain useful material or point the way to hidden sources. In addition, these sections collect a good deal in the way of printed material; they usually have runs of the local newspapers.

3   Some of the local documentary material has by now been collected into record offices. There is one (and sometimes more) for almost every county; most cities have one also, usually in the library. These can be found most easily in a Directory issued by HMSO.[1]

   In addition to collecting in outlying official and private records, these offices hold large local government deposits, like quarter sessions papers.

4   The records of the ecclesiastical authorities may be found in the diocesan record offices, also listed in the Directory cited above. These are often combined with county record offices. But a word of warning is needed here. Diocesan boundaries have changed rather more often than have county boundaries. Therefore the papers relating to some local communities involved in these changes may be dispersed between several diocesan repositories. The local historian must learn of these changes in order to seek out his records.

5   At some stage, especially for nineteenth century local history, he will also need a major library. Few county or city libraries hold runs of parliamentary papers; even the nearest university library may well lack the particular volumes he needs. They must be sought in the end, if necessary, in such libraries as the Guildhall Library or the British Museum Reading Room. At the British Museum too can be found the earliest O.S. maps (in the Map Department) and those local newspapers which cannot be obtained locally (at Colindale).

6   Central records are generally housed in repositories in London. The Public Record Office and its offshoots hold government records, including the census. But there are also many other centralised archive offices – for the denominations like the Baptist Union, for major industrial and commercial concerns like

the British Transport Authority, for special collections like the College of Arms, and so on. The most important of these are listed in the Directory quoted above.

7   Finally, however, some libraries and repositories hold somewhat surprising collections, of wider interest than just the area covered normally by the services of that body. The Guildhall Library in London, for instance, holds fire insurance records covering the whole of England. The only way the local historian can learn of these is by exploration, and especially by studying other local histories similar to the one he is writing, by looking at the sources used and by using intelligent guesswork. Most archivists, in my experience, answer letters courteously, provided the writer does not expect them to do his work for him.

Writing a local history is a search for the truth about the past. Those who wish to write one must be prepared to go out and look for material; if they do so, they will find a great deal.

Notes on the chapters

Introduction

1 H. P. R. Finberg, 'Local history', in *Approaches to History*, ed. H. P. R. Finberg, Routledge, 1962, pp. 120–2: 'the local community is not a mere fragment splintered off from the history of England': it 'deals with a social entity which has a perfectly good claim to be studied for its own sake'.

2 For instance, Scotland had a census some forty years earlier than England; its range of public records differs significantly from those in England, as does its legal background. For Wales there is the language problem, among other difficulties. See B. Skinner, 'Scottish local history: an introductory survey', *Local Historian*, ix.7 (1971) pp. 353–6; B. Howells, 'Local history in Wales', *Local Historian*, x.8 (1973) pp. 404–11.

3 There have been many descriptions of the census records: a recent one is J. J. Bagley, *Historical Interpretation*, vol. ii; *Sources of English History 1540 to the Present Day*, Penguin, 1971, pp. 243–8. See below, pp. 37–8.

4 For an account of the various maps, see J. B. Harley, *The Historian's Guide to Ordnance Survey Maps*, National Council for Social Service, 1964, and his *Ordnance Survey Maps: a descriptive manual*, O.S., 1975.

5 Some towns had very large-scale surveys, made either privately or by government departments; see above, p. 150.

6 The study of 'oral history' has made great strides in the last few years. The best introduction to the subject is probably through the pages of the journal *Oral History*, issued since 1972. See J. Vansina, *The Oral Tradition*, Routledge, 1965; Penguin, 1973. For two good recent studies based largely on oral tradition, see David Jenkins, *The Agricultural Community in South-west Wales at the Turn of the Twentieth Century*, Univ. of Wales Press, 1971; and Robert Moore, *Pitmen, Preachers and Politics*, Cambridge U.P., 1974. R. Samuel, *Village Life and Labour*, Routledge, 1975, also uses oral evidence.

7 One of the best ways of acquiring the social and economic context for the local study is still through the relevant chapters in the *Pelican History of England*, 8 vols, Penguin Books. For all subjects see F. G. Emmison, ed., *English Local History Handlist*, 4th edn, Historical Association, 1969.

8 There are many accounts of the sources for local history. Among the best are F. G. Emmison, *Archives and Local History*, Methuen, 1966; W. G. Hoskins, *Local History in England*, Longmans, 1959; J. J. Bagley, *Historical Interpretation* (2 vols, Penguin, 1965, 1971), only partly on local history; W. E. Tate, *The Parish Chest* (3rd edn, Cambridge U.P., 1969); W. B. Stephens, *Sources for English Local History*, Manchester U.P., 1973. The series begun and edited by G. R. Elton with his book *Sources of History, England 1200–1640*, Collins,

1969, is useful. There is a long series of Short Guides to Records published in the journal *History* from 1962, and many articles in the journal *Local Historian*. But the best descriptions of most of the sources are to be found in the introductions to published records. The introductions to the quarter sessions records in *Lincoln Record Society*, xxv (1931) and to the hearth tax records in *Warwickshire Hearth Tax Returns*, i (1957) are good examples of this. One may also refer to D. J. Steel, ed., *National Index of Parish Registers*, vol. i, Society of Genealogists, 1966, a book which has much wider relevance than its title suggests.

9 On the general background to the later nineteenth century, there is probably no better account for the local historian than Geoffrey Best, *Mid-Victorian Britain 1850–1875*, Weidenfeld and Nicolson, 1971; Panther, 1973; on pp. 287–8 he cites a number of other background books which are most useful. L. Madden, *How to Find Out About the Victorian Period*, Pergamon Press, 1970, has some useful material relating to other sources for the study of the background. For the period after 1900, see A. Marwick, *Britain in the Century of Total War: war, peace and social change, 1900–1967*, Bodley Head and Penguin, 1970.

Chapter 1   *Local history and its approaches*

1 One of the best recent discussions is in D. Thomson, *The Aims of History*, Thames and Hudson, 1969. J. H. Plumb makes the confusion worse confounded in *The Death of the Past*, Macmillan, 1969, by which he means the decline of a school of historiography of which he does not approve, to be replaced by sounder historical scholarship.

2 For Myddle, see D. G. Hey, *An English Rural Community, Myddle under the Tudors and Stuarts*, Leicester U.P., 1974; a good deal of what Dr Hey says applies to the parish as a whole rather than to the settlements within it. Mrs Joyce Young is working on Gedling parish, near Nottingham. On the general problem of the local community, more is still needed. Finberg, *Approaches to History*, p. 117, speaks of the defined territorial limits of the local community. This is of course not always true. A medieval gild for example falls within his definition of a 'social entity' without having *exclusive* territorial limits. The whole discussion here is useful.

3 Sir Francis Hill's four volumes (all Cambridge U.P.), *Medieval Lincoln*, 1948; *Tudor and Stuart Lincoln*, 1956; *Georgian Lincoln*, 1966; and *Victorian Lincoln*, 1974 reveal this progression clearly.

4 A. Rogers, 'Three early maps of the Isle of Axholme', *Midland History*, i.2 (1971).

5 On the definition of local history, see Finberg, 'Local history', in *Approaches to History*; H. P. R. Finberg, *The Local Historian and his Theme*, Simpkin Marshall, 1953; H. P. R. Finberg and V. H. T. Skipp, *Local History: objective and pursuit*, David and Charles, 1967; W. R. Powell, 'Local history in theory and practice', *Bulletin of Institute of Historical Research*, xxxi (1958) 41–8; and the various articles in the *Amateur Historian* (now the *Local Historian*), vi and vii.

6 A. Rogers, *History of Lincolnshire*, Darwen Finlayson, 1970, p. 85; J. D. Chambers, *Modern Nottingham in the Making*, 1945; A. Rogers, *The Making of Stamford*, Leicester U.P., 1965, pp. 99–100; S. Elliott, 'The Cecil family and the development of nineteenth century Stamford', *Lincolnshire History and Archaeology* iv (1969) 23–31. See generally A. Rogers and T. Rowley, ed.,

Landscapes and Documents, Bedford Sq. Press; Nat. Council Social Service, 1974, and D. P. Dymond, *Archaeology and History*, Thames and Hudson, 1974.

7 J. D. Chambers, *Nottinghamshire in the Eighteenth Century*, Nottingham Journal Ltd., 2nd edn, Cass, 1966, pp. 89—100.

8 F. Lee, The origin and early growth of Northampton, *Archaeological Journal*, cx. (1953), 164—74.

9 See the interim reports of the excavations of Wharram Percy in *Medieval Archaeology*.

10 M. Bloch, *The Historian's Craft*, Manchester U.P., 1954; see R. R. Davies, 'M. Bloch', *History*, lii (1967) 269.

11 E. Gillett, *A History of Grimsby*, Oxford U.P., 1970.

12 A. S. Mottram, 'The King's Lynn archaeological survey', *Loc. Hist.* viii.4 (1968) 139—45; for Winchester, see the interim reports of the work done there in *Medieval Archaeology*.

Chapter 2   *The size of the community*

1 It is not easy to obtain realistic figures for the medieval period. J. C. Russell, *British Medieval Population*, University of New Mexico Press, 1948, would seem to place the figures too low, M. M. Postan places them too high. See J. Z. Titow, *English Rural Society, 1200—1350*, Allen and Unwin, 1969, pp. 66—71. P. Ziegler's book, *The Black Death*, Collins, 1969, is one of the best recent summaries of the present discussion on this subject. A. R. Bridbury, *Economic Growth: England in the later Middle Ages*, Allen and Unwin, 1962; M. M. Postan, *Cambridge Economic History of Europe vol. i: The Agrarian Life of the Middle Ages* (2nd edn, Cambridge U.P., 1966), pp. 561—2; also 'Some economic evidence of declining population in the later Middle Ages', *Economic History Review*, 2nd ser., ii (1950) 221—46; and *Medieval Economy and Society: an economic history of Britain in the Middle Ages*, Weidenfeld and Nicolson, 1972. For the later period, see M. Ashley, *England in the Seventeenth Century*, Penguin Books, 1952, p. 12; G. Davies, *Oxford History of England*, vol. ix; *The Early Stuarts 1603—60*, 2nd edn, Oxford U.P., 1959, p. 261; I. Blanchard, 'Population change, enclosure and the early Tudor economy', *Econ. Hist. Rev.*, xxiii (1970) 427—9.

2 The later figures are taken from P. Deane and W. A. Cole, *British Economic Growth 1688—1959*, 2nd edn, Cambridge U.P., 1969, pp. 5—12. This is a valuable book but it has the danger of giving the impression of statistical accuracy with its precise figures. It may hide the fact that, for all its seemingly tested data, all population figures before 1801 are estimates, however thoroughly based. The same criticism may be levelled at a good deal of detailed historical demography. When all is said and done, a round approximate total is more revealing of the individual community than arguments over multipliers or formulae. See also J. D. Chambers, 'The course of population change', reprinted from *The Vale of Trent 1670—1800*, Cambridge U.P., 1957 in D. V. Glass and D. E. C. Eversley, ed., *Population in History*, Edward Arnold, 1965, pp. 221—46. The other essays in this book are useful.

3 For the late nineteenth century and the twentieth century, details may be obtained from B. R. Mitchell and P. Deane, *Abstract of British Historical Statistics*, Cambridge U.P., 1962, p. 6.

4 F. W. Maitland, *Domesday Book and Beyond*, Collins, 1960, pp. 45—6; S. P. J. Harvey, Domesday Book and Anglo-Norman Governance, *Trans. Royal Hist.*

Soc. 25 (1975) pp. 175—94; H. C. Darby, 'The economic geography of England, 1000—1250', *Historical Geography of England before A.D. 1800*, ed. Darby, Cambridge U.P., 1936, pp. 207—9, and his study in *A New Historical Geography of England*, Cambridge U.P., 1973. L. J. White, 'Enclosures and population movements in England, 1700—1830', *Explorations in Entrepreneurial History* vi (1966) 175—85, suggests that the later enclosure movement did not result in large-scale migration, but the earlier movement clearly did. See also P. E. Jones, 'Population and agrarian change in an eighteenth century Shropshire parish', *Local Population Studies* i (1968) 6—29; E. E. Rich, 'The population of Elizabethan England', *Econ. Hist. Rev.* ii (1949—50) 247—65; E. J. Buckatzch, 'Constancy of local populations and migrations in England before 1800', *Population Studies* v (1951—2) 62—9. See also C. C. Taylor, 'The Anglo-Saxon countryside', in *Anglo-Saxon Settlement and Landscape; papers presented to a symposium, Oxford, 1973,* T. Rowley, ed., *British Archaeological Report* vi (1974) 5—15.

5 For what follows, see Deane and Cole, *British Economic Growth*, pp. 99—112. J. D. Chambers, W. A. Armstrong, ed., *Population, Economy and Society in Pre-industrial England*, Oxford U.P., 1972, summarises the early period, N. L. Tranter, *Population since the Industrial Revolution: the English experience*, Croom Helm, London, 1974, the later period, as do M. Drake, ed., *Population in Industrialisation*, Methuen, 1969 and H. J. Habakkuk, *Population Growth and Economic Development since 1750*, Leicester U.P., 1974.

6 Deane and Cole, pp. 10—11.

7 H. J. Dyos, *Victorian Suburb*, Leicester U.P., 1961, p. 58.

8 Best, p. 13.

9 Bagley, *Historical Interpretation*, i, pp. 22—36; V. H. Galbraith, *The Making of Domesday Book*, Oxford U.P., 1961; Maitland, *Domesday Book and Beyond*; R. Lennard, *Rural England, 1086—1135*, Oxford U.P., 1959.

10 J. F. Willard, *Parliamentary Taxes on Personal Property, 1290—1334*, Medieval Academy of America, Mass., 1934; M. W. Beresford, *Lay Subsidies and Poll Taxes*, Canterbury, Phillimore, 1964; R. E. Glasscock, *The Lay Subsidies of 1334*, Brit. Acad.: Oxford U.P., 1975; J. C. Cornwall, 'English country towns in the 1520s', *Econ. Hist. Rev.* xxxiii (1970), and 'English population in the late sixteenth century', *Econ. Hist. Rev.* xv (1962) 54—69; J. C. Cornwall, ed., *Lay Subsidy Rolls for the County of Sussex*, Sussex Record Soc., lvi (1956); S. Dowell, *History of Taxation and Taxes*, 2nd edn, 1888.

11 Bagley, *Historical Interpretation* ii, pp. 122—8; Short Guide 7, *History* xlix (1964) 42—5; C. A. F. Meekings, ed., *Dorset Hearth Tax Assessments, 1662—4*, Dorset Natural History and Archaeological Society, 1951, and *Surrey Hearth Tax 1664*, Surrey Record Soc., xvii (1940).

12 D. V. Glass, 'Gregory King and the population of England and Wales at the end of the seventeenth century', in *Population in History*, eds Glass and Eversley, pp. 169—73; P. E. Jones and A. V. Judges, 'London population in the late seventeenth century', *Econ. Hist. Rev.* vi (1935—6) 45—63; P. H. Styles, 'A census of a Warwickshire village in 1698', *Univ. of Birmingham Hist. J.* iii (1951) 33—51.

13 Hoskins, *Local History in England* p. 146; Historical Manuscripts Commission, 5th *Report*, Appendix I; F. West, 'The Protestation Returns of 1642', *Bulletin of Local History, East Midlands Region* vi (1971) 50—4. Most of the Protestation Returns are in the House of Lords, some are in the British Museum (e.g.

Cheshire, Harl.MS.2107). See C. S. A. Dobson, ed., *Oxfordshire Protestation Returns 1641–42*, Oxf. Record Soc., xxxvi (1955).

14 D. M. Owen, *Records of the Established Church in England*, British Records Association, 1970, p. 33; Short Guide 8, *History* xlix (1964) 185–8; A. Percival, 'Gloucestershire village populations', *LPS* viii (1972) 42–6; J. C. Cornwall, 'An Elizabethan census', *Records of Buckinghamshire* xvi (1959).

15 R. Lennard, 'What is a Manorial Extent?', *English Hist. Rev.* xliv (1929) 256–63.

16 *LPS* viii (1972) 42; A. Rogers, 'Surveys of church livings, 1647–57', *Bull. Local History* vi (1971) 55–6; many of these are in Lambeth Palace Library.

17 Perhaps the earliest is for Coventry in 1520, and the most famous are those for Clayworth, Notts, in 1675 and 1688; see P. Laslett and J. Harrison, 'Clayworth and Cogenhoe', in H. E. Bell and R. L. Ollard, eds, *Historical Essays 1600–1750, presented to David Ogg*, A. and C. Black, 1963, pp. 157–84; M. D. Harris, ed., *Coventry Leet Book* iii (1913) pp. 674–5.

18 For a general survey of possible sources, see J. Thirsk, *Sources of Information on Population 1500–1760, and unexplored sources in local history*, Phillimore, 1965; Hoskins, *Local History*, pp. 142–8; D. V. Glass, 'Population and population movements in England and Wales, 1700–1850', in *Population in History* pp. 221–46; T. H. Hollingsworth, *Historical Demography* (Sources of History), Hodder and Stoughton, 1969. C. T. Smith, 'Population' in V.C.H. *Leicestershire* iii, 1955, is a useful example.

19 See an example (Wigston Magna, Leicestershire) in W. G. Hoskins, 'The population of an English village, 1086–1801', in his *Provincial England*, Macmillan, 1966, pp. 181–208.

20 Very little of value can be gained from the medieval population figures for Stamford: see Rogers, *Making of Stamford*, p. 49.

21 These figures were first published in *Tourist Stamford*, Annual Report of the Stamford Civic Society, 1967 *The sources from which they are drawn are as follows:

1563	213 families – B.M.Harl.MS.618.
1603	746 communicants – *LRS* xxiii pp. 325, 442–3
1665	283 houses* ⎱ Transcript of Kesteven hearth tax returns in L.A.O., Foster
1674	394 houses ⎰ Library.
1676	1,594 communicants – Compton return, printed (for Lincolnshire) in *LRS* xxv pp. cxxxi–viii.
1705–23	470 families – *LRS* iv pp. 114–16.
1785	3,937 heads – W. Harrod, *Antiquities of Stamford*, 1785
1788–92	856 families – L.A.O. Visitation Bks, SPE 4.

* This figure is suspect.

22 A figure of 40% below the age of fifteen is often accepted; Hoskins, *Provincial England*, p. 188, uses $33\frac{1}{3}$% below fifteen, a figure which is too low. See below, p. 32; *Agricultural Hist. Rev.* xx (1972) 7. *LPS* viii (1972), 39, suggests a multiplier of 1.65 for figures of communicants.

23 At Boston, Lincs, local counts gave two contemporary figures – 3,008 heads of whom 207 were dissenters (1709), and *c.* 650 families of which one in every fifteen or sixteen were dissenters (1705–23). The correlation of 4½ heads to the families works out for the total size of the community (3,008 gives 668 families), while an average of 4½ for 43 families (i.e. a 15th of the 650) gives

194, which is close to the figure of 207; *Lincoln Record Society* iv, p. 19; P. Thompson, *History of Boston* (1856 edn), pp. 104—6.

24 Bourne's medieval growth is clearer than Stamford's because of some fine early fourteenth-century extents for the manor, which coincided with the whole settlement.

25 Figures (with conversions in brackets, using the same formulae) and sources as follows:

	Bourne	Rauceby	Source
1563	(1,003) 223 families	(193) 43 families	B.M.Harl.MS.618
1603	(1,200) *c.* 900 communicants	(147) 110 communicants	*LRS* xxiii pp. 300—19
1665—74	(883) 175—8 houses	(230) 44—8 houses	LAO Hearth tax transcript
1676	(1,076) 807 communicants	(241) 181 communicants	*LRS* xxv pp. cxxxii—vi
1705—23	(1,077) 217 families	(243) 54 families	*LRS* iv pp. 19, 99
1788—92	(1,350) 330 families	(247) 55 families	L.A.O. SPE 4
1801	1,664 heads	287 heads	Census

26 There are many discussions of parish registers, most notably Tate, *Parish Chest*, pp. 43—79, and J. C. Cox, *The Parish Registers of England*, 1910, reprinted, 1974, E. P. Publishing.

27 J. T. Krause alleges that from 1780 registration of baptisms and burials became progressively worse, but this varies from place to place: *Econ. Hist. Rev.* xi (1958) 52—70. See D. E. C. Eversley, 'Exploration of Anglican Parish Registers by aggregative analysis', in E. A. Wrigley, ed., *Introduction to English Historical Demography*, Weidenfeld and Nicolson, 1966. This book is an essential tool for the local historian; it refers to many other studies which will prove useful to the local demographer. M. Drake, *Historical Demography: problems and projects*, Open University, 1974, is particularly helpful. D. V. Glass and R. Revelle, eds, *Population and Social Change*, Edward Arnold, 1972, contains some stimulating papers. In addition there may be mentioned *Local Population Studies*, a broadsheet appearing twice a year which deals with more recent relevant literature. See also E. A. Wrigley, 'Parish Registers and population history', *Amateur Historian* vi, 5 and 6 (1964—5) 146—51, 198—203.

28 Owen, *Records of the Established Church*, pp. 26—7.

29 Many of these registers have been collected and are now in the Public Records Office. They are listed in List and Index Society, vol. xlii, *General Register Office List of Non-parochial Registers*, 1969. See R. W. Ambler, 'Non-parochial registers and the local historian', *Loc. Hist.* x.2 (1972) 59—64.

30 Hoskins, *Provincial England*, p. 189, uses this multiplier.

31 I must thank Canon A. H. Lanham for help with these figures and below.

32 There are several well-known examples of this, such as Fledborough in Nottinghamshire. A similar distortion occurs in the neighbourhood of cathedrals. See, for example, *The Marriage Registers of Norwich Cathedral, 1697—1754*: in 1698, out of seventy-five marriages, thirty-two involved one or both parties from outside the city. Not all of these marriages were of persons in the upper occupational or social groupings. There were soldiers, mariners, journeymen weavers or carpenters, woolcombers, labourers, innholders, bakers and the like, often coming from many miles to be married at the cathedral.

33 Tate, *Parish Chest*, pp. 80—2; Hoskins, *Local History*, pp. 143—4. Boston, Lincs, had an average of 98 baptisms per annum in the early eighteenth century (this allows 1/15 for dissenters, see above); this multiplied by 31 gives 3,038,

against the careful figure of 3,008 in 1709 (figures from Rev. M. Spurrell of Boston).

34 The process is described in detail by R. S. Schofield, 'Some notes on aggregative analysis in a single parish', *LPS* v (1970) pp. 9—17; and by Eversley in *Introduction to English Historical Demography*. See, for some reservations concerning the process, M. W. Flinn, *Econ. Hist. Rev.* xx (1967) 140—4.

35 These graphs have been compiled from data gathered by a group of sixth-form history students at a course in Chester in 1971. They were obtained easily, because of the very great help of the archivists of both the county and the city record offices and their respective staffs. David Cope of the Institute of Planning Studies of Nottingham University assisted in their preparation for the press.

36 Some good examples may be seen in Chambers, *Vale of Trent*, pp. 34—5.

37 M. Drake, 'An elementary exercise in parish register demography', *Econ. Hist. Rev.* xiv (1962) 427—45.

38 For a comparison of the Nottingham maps of Speed, *c.* 1610, Badder and Peat, 1744, and Stavely and Wood, 1832, see A. Rogers, *Old Nottingham: from the Castle to St Mary's*, University of Nottingham, Department of Adult Education, 1968, p. 3. Professor J. D. Chambers's study, 'Population change in a provincial town, Nottingham 1700—1800', in L. S. Pressnell, ed., *Studies in the Industrial Revolution*, Athlone Press, 1960, shows the use of supplementary material.

39 A recent collection of nineteenth-century photographs in R. Iliffe and W. Baguley, *Victorian Nottingham* i—xiii (1970—5) has revealed incidentally that a great deal of timber-framed building was done in the town before the late seventeenth century. For prints and drawings, see M. W. Barley, *Guide to British Topographical Collections*, Council for British Archaeology, 1974.

40 See above, pp. 37—8.

41 The Enumeration Abstracts have been published for each census from 1801. The volumes may be discovered from the *Guide to Official Sources no. 2: Census Reports of Great Britain, 1801—1931*, Council for British Archaeology, HMSO, 1951. The 1851 summary gives a shortcut to all the figures from 1801, HC. 1851, vol. xliii; HC. 1852, vol. xlii.

42 Usually in the section on Economic and Social History of the county; but not always — for example, the Cheshire totals for the 1801 census are in Lysons, *Magna Britannia* II, part ii (1810) since there is as yet no V.C.H. *Cheshire*.

43 But see above, pp. 37—8.

44 Major boundary changes in urban areas took place in the 1870s in most parts of the country, as well as at other times.

45 See P. M. Tillott, *Collections for the History of Tickhill*, University of Sheffield, Department of Adult Education, 1967; R. Fieldhouse, an unpublished analysis of the 1851 census schedules for Richmond; and R. L. Greenall, *The Population of a Northamptonshire Village in 1851*, Univ. of Leicester, Dept. of Adult Education, 1971. The above graphs do not appear in these studies; they have been compiled from the printed census summaries. These works are cited hereafter as Tillott, Fieldhouse and Greenall.

Chapter 3   The structure of the community
1 These are best presented in the form of a pyramid diagram, see below, Fig. 12. See *Report of the Royal Commission on Population*, Cmd 7695, HMSO, 1949.
2 See D. Turner, 'The effective family', *LPS* ii (1969) 47—52.

3 Hey, *English Rural Community*, examines kinship groups in Myddle (Salop), but the most significant work here is Michael Anderson, *Family Structure in Nineteenth-Century Lancashire*, Cambridge U.P., 1971. On the Irish sub-groups, see T. Dillon, 'The Irish in Leeds 1851—61', *Thoresby Soc.* liv (1973) 1—28.

4 J. P. Huzel, 'Malthus, the poor law and population in early nineteenth-century England', *Econ. Hist. Rev.* xxii (1969) 430—52.

5 See for example, J. Z. Titow, 'Some differences between manors and . . . the condition of the peasant in the thirteenth century', *Agric. Hist. Rev.* x (1962) 1—13.

6 See M. W. Flinn, *British Population Growth, 1700—1850*, Macmillan, 1970, for the latest discussion of the disagreements. See also E. A. Wrigley, *Population and History*, Weidenfeld and Nicolson, 1969.

7 Except for 60—70 years, when there were 72,700 more males (figures are given to the nearest 100). It must be remembered that no age was recorded for one-ninth of the 14 million population in 1821. A substantial proportion of the missing figures would probably have been for the very young and the very old. In any case, ages were rounded off to the nearest 5. In addition of course, many children were totally unrecorded. But both of these factors would apply equally to males and females.

8 Best, p. 101.

9 P. Laslett, *The World We Have Lost*, Methuen, 1965; P. Laslett and R. Wall, eds, *Household and Family in Past Time*, Cambridge U.P., 1972.

10 Similarly, at the end of the nineteenth century, fertility fell by a half from a figure of 154 births per thousand of women aged 15—45 in 1871 to a figure of 62 in 1938; 1871 may well have been high — the net reproduction rate rose from 1.3 in 1851 to 1.5 (1871—81), falling to 1.2 (1901) and 1.1 (1911—21), finally reaching 0.8 in 1931—39. It must be noted, however, that none of these figures commands completely universal assent, except those based on the registrar-general's reports for the nineteenth and twentieth centuries.

11 First published 1854 and re-issued on many occasions; E. Royston Pike, *Human Documents of the Victorian Age*, Allen and Unwin, 1967, pp. 362—6.

12 It was some thirty years at Colyton, Devon, in the late seventeenth century.

13 For genuine purposes of comparison, these figures need to be standardised to allow for changes in the age structure; but the general trends are clear enough and it is the trends rather than the figures which concern the local historian.

14 At Colyton, the expectation of life in the Tudor period was 40—45 years; it declined during the seventeenth century.

15 T. McKeown and R. G. Brown, 'Medical evidence related to English population change in the eighteenth century', *Population Studies* ix (1955) 119—41.

16 L. J. Lamballe, 'Ironstone miners of Cleveland', *Bulletin of the Cleveland and Teesside Local History Society* vii (1969).

17 Deane and Cole, *British Economic Growth*, pp. 108—9: London:

	Natural increase/decrease	Migration	Total gain
1701—51	−568	+602	+35
1751—81	−171	+405	+234
1781—1801	+81	+285	+366
1801—31	+525	+473	+998

(Figures in thousands.)

18 V. Smith, 'The analysis of census-type documents', *LPS* ii (1969) 12–24, a most valuable study of the type of questions a local historian can ask in static analysis. See also P. Laslett, 'Study of social structure from listings of inhabitants', in *Introd. to Engl. Hist. Demog.*, pp. 160–208.
19 See above p. 15.
20 See F. West, 'Protestation Returns, 1642', *Bull. Local History* vi (1971) 53–5.
21 Some of the best, as at St Thomas, Chester, provide dates of birth and death as well as dates of baptisms and burials. These are most useful to check delays from birth to baptism, a factor which varied considerably. See D. R. Mills, 'The christening custom at Melbourn, Cambs', *LPS* xi (1973) 11–22; R. W. Ambler, 'Baptism and christening', *LPS* xii (1972) 25–7; B. M. Berry and R. S. Schofield, 'Age at baptism in pre-industrial England', *Population Studies* xxv (1971).
22 I am grateful to Dr Mills for allowing me to refer to his unpublished work. See the important articles by L. Bradley, 'An enquiry into seasonality in baptisms, marriages and burials', *LPS* iv (1970) 21–40; v (1970) 18–35.
23 St John's and St Michael's parishes, Chester, have reasonably sized samples: the figures are as follows:

	St John	St Michael
1760–4	5.0	3.0
1765–9	3.4	2.0
1770–4	3.5	3.0
1775–9	4.3	5.0
1780–4	3.8	3.0
1785–9	3.3	4.0
1790–4	3.3	3.8
1795–9	3.15	6.5

It is hard to determine just what these figures indicate.

24 This is fully described by Dr Wrigley, *Introduction to Historical Demography*, pp. 96–159; and in M. Ballard and M. T. Smith, eds, 'Population, family and household', in *New Movements in the Study and Teaching of History*, David and Charles, 1970.
25 A. C. Wood, 'A note on the population of Nottingham in the seventeenth century', *Transactions of Thoroton Society* xl (1936) 109–13.
26 It is strictly incorrect to call these 'schedules', for the original schedules rarely survive. These books contain copies of the schedules.
27 The books survive in the Public Record Office. The later books will not become available until 100 years have passed from the date of completion – i.e. 1982 for the 1881 census returns. See L. C. Hector, 'The census returns of 1841 and 1851', *Amat. Hist.* i.6 (1953) pp. 174–8; M. W. Beresford and R. L. Storey, *The Unprinted Census Returns of 1841, 1851 and 1861 for England and Wales*, Phillimore, 1966, originally in *Amat. Hist.* v.8 (1963) pp. 260–9.
28 A. J. Taylor, 'The taking of the census, 1801–1951', *British Medical Journal*, 7 April 1951: I owe this reference to Mr R. Fieldhouse.
29 The totals at the bottom of the pages were often compiled by adding up the entries in the male and female age columns respectively. Several of these entries were not completed; sometimes figures were given in both columns. This is one source of error which needs to be checked. See Plate 8(b).

30 As Alan Armstrong's analysis of York, *Introd. to Engl. Hist. Demog.*, pp. 217–20; in H. J. Dyos, ed., *The Study of Urban History*, Edward Arnold, 1968, pp. 81–2, and *Stability and Change in an English County Town: a social study of York, 1801–51*, Cambridge U.P., 1974. Other places, such as Liverpool, have been sampled; see above, p. 90.

31 *Study of Urban History* pp. 87–112; as might be expected, this is a technical discussion.

32 Census report, *Abstracts* 1821, HC. 1822, vol. xv.

33 Out of nearly 16 million, this number is not of course very great, one-third of 1%.

34 A. Rogers, *Stability and Change: Some Aspects of North and South Rauceby in the Nineteenth Century*, Univ. of Nottingham, Dept. of Adult Education, 1969, p. 13. Similar figures to those of Rauceby are recorded elsewhere — 47% at Burton Joyce, Notts, 45% at Bleasby, Notts, whereas the figures for today are only 39% under 25 years; A. Rogers, ed., *Nottingham and its Villages 1750–1850*, 1969, p. 28.

35 B. J. Biggs, ed., *Living by the Trent*, Retford and District Historical and Archaeological Society, 1971, pp. 39–43.

36 These figures have been computed from the totals in the work cited above.

37 Neither of these subjects has been treated at Long Buckby.

38 Rogers, *Stability and Change*, p. 13.

39 It is misleading to call this a family structure, for the household is not the same as a family.

40 Rogers, *Nottingham and its Villages*, p. 30.

41 These figures are not given at Tickhill or Richmond.

42 P. M. Tillott of Sheffield University devised a process using printed forms to cover this reconstitution; see 'The analysis of census returns', *Loc. Hist.* viii.1 (1968) 2–10; and 'An approach to census returns', *LPS* ii (1969) 25–8. See also W. A. Armstrong, 'The interpretation of the census enumerators' books for Victorian towns', in Dyos, ed., 1968, *Study of Urban History*, pp. 67–85, and E. A. Wrigley, ed., *Nineteenth Century Society*, Cambridge U.P., 1972.

43 The registration certificates recorded at Somerset House were the only complete successors to the parish registration of vital events; these are not readily accessible to local historians in the sense that they are filed by date first and then by location. But they may be available locally; see *LPS* xiii (1973) 5–6, and the editorials in *LPS* viii (1972) 4–9, and ix (1972) 4–7.

44 See H. J. Smith, 'Local reports to the General Board of Health', *Short Guide to Records* xxiv, *History* lvi (1971) 46–9.

45 This comes from the report, a copy of which is in Arnold Public Library. The figures were first printed in *Nottingham and its Villages*, p. 17.

46 HC. 1845, vols xvii and xviii.

47 Sir Arthur Helps, *The Claims of Labour*, 1845.

48 Recent studies on migration in the nineteenth century are drawn from these reports and those of the registrar-general and other official surveys — cf. A. Redford, *Labour Migration in England, 1800–1850*, Manchester U.P., 1964; R. Lawton, 'Rural depopulation in nineteenth century England', in D. R. Mills, ed., *English Rural Communities: the impact of a specialised economy*, Macmillan, 1974; P. S. Richards, 'The growth of towns', *Loc. Hist.* ix.4 (1970) 190–5, and the works cited there; M. Drake, *Historical Demography: problems and projects*, Open University.

49 Rogers, *Stability and Change*, p. 11.
50 *Nottingham and its Villages*, p. 29.
51 A. Rogers, 'Mid-nineteenth century village life', *The Village* xix.2 (1964) 61—4.

Chapter 4   Housing and the community

 1 For other examples, see D. Ward, 'The pre-urban cadastre of Leeds', in A. R. H. Baker, J. D. Hamshire and J. Langton, eds, *Geographical Interpretations of Historical Sources*, David and Charles, 1970, pp. 317—36; M. J. Mortimore, 'Landownership and urban growth in Bradford and its environs, 1850—1950', *Trans. Inst. British Geographers* xlvi (1969) 105—19.
 2 For a discussion of this well-known concept, see D. R. Mills, 'English villages in the eighteenth and nineteenth centuries: a sociological classification', *Amat. Hist.* vi.8 (1965) 271—8, and vii.1 (1966) 7—13; for an example of the contrast between these two types of village, see Rogers, *Stability and Change*.
 3 J. Finberg, *Exploring Villages*, Routledge, 1958; B. Roberts, 'The study of village plans', *Loc. Hist.* ix.5 (1971) 233—41.
 4 M. W. Beresford, *The Lost Villages of England*, Lutterworth Press, 1954; M. W. Beresford and J. K. St Joseph, *Medieval England: an aerial survey*, Cambridge U.P., 1958; M. W. Beresford and J. G. Hurst, *Deserted Medieval Villages*, Lutter-worth Press, 1971.
 5 M. W. Beresford, *The New Towns of the Middle Ages*, Lutterworth Press, 1967.
 6 See H. Thorpe, 'The Lord and the Landscape', and M. B. Gleave, 'Dispersed and Nucleated Settlements in the Yorkshire Wolds, 1770—1850', in Mills, *English Rural Communities*.
 7 See above, p. 135.
 8 Rogers, *Old Nottingham*, pp. 11—12.
 9 See for example, G. R. Potts, 'The development of New Walk and King Street', in A. E. Brown, ed., *The Growth of Leicester*, Leicester U.P., 1970. See gener-ally J. R. Blunden, 'Zoning in cities', *Spatial Aspects of Society*, Open University Course Book, 1971, pp. 55—86.
10 There is a good example at Toftwood Common, Dereham, Norfolk, enclosed in 1815; see N. Boston and E. Puddy, *Dereham, the Biography of a Country Town*, Dereham, Coleby, 1952.
11 M. W. Barley's books, *House and Home*, Vista Histories, Studio Vista, 1963, and *The English Farmhouse and Cottage*, Routledge, 1961, are good beginnings to an extensive literature. The town house is still neglected. See also W. G. Hoskins, 'The rebuilding of rural England, 1570—1640', in his *Provincial England*, pp. 131—48; J. Woodforde, *The Truth about Cottages*, Routledge, 1969; Peter Eden, *Small Houses in England 1520—1820*, Historical Association, 1969. The chapters on housing in H. P. R. Finberg and J. Thirsk, eds, *The Agrarian History of England*, Cambridge U.P., will, when complete, form the best introduction to the local variations in housing.
12 From a list of deeds belonging to the former owner of the house, and now among the records of the Stamford Survey Group. Mrs J. Varley of the Lincoln-shire Archives Office has given much help in elucidating the past of this property.
13 S. D. Chapman cites the example of William Felkin who in 1785 at the age of thirty-five built his own house with outbuildings on land allotted to him by the lord of the manor of Bramcote; 'Working-class housing in Nottingham', S. D. Chapman, ed., *The History of Working-Class Housing: a symposium*, David and

Charles, 1971, p. 136. There were others, especially associated with small enclosure allotments.

14 S. J. Price, *Building Societies: their origin and history*, Franey, 1958; E. J. Cleary, *The Building Society Movement*, Elek, 1965; M. Gaskell, 'Self-help and house building in the nineteenth century', *Loc. Hist.* x.2 (1972) 65—9.

15 C. W. Chalklin, *The Provincial Towns of Georgian England*, E. Arnold, 1974.

16 Professor Best has an account of the environment of most people in the mid-Victorian period which is very revealing, *Mid-Victorian Britain*, pp. 1—72.

17 See W. V. Hole, *Trends in Population, Housing and Occupancy Rates, 1861—1961*, HMSO, 1971.

18 See Chapman, *History of Working-Class Housing*; J. E. Vance, 'Housing the worker: deterministic and contingent ties in nineteenth century Birmingham', *Economic Geography* xliii.2 (1967); Vanessa Parker, *The English House in the Nineteenth Century*, Historical Association, 1970; M. W. Beresford and G. R. J. Jones, *Leeds and its Region*, British Association, 1967, pp. 186—97; J. N. Tarn, *Five Percent Philanthropy: an Account of Housing in Urban Areas between 1840 and 1914*, Cambridge U.P., 1974; E. Gauldie, *Cruel Habitations: a history of working-class housing, 1780—1914*, Allen & Unwin, 1974; A. S. Wohl, 'Unfit for human habitation', in H. J. Dyos and M. Wolff, eds, *The Victorian City: Images and Realities*, Routledge, 1973, ii, pp. 603—24; and the essays by D. J. Olsen and H. J. Dyos and D. A. Reeder, in the same work, i, pp. 333—88. M. Kaufmann's older work, *Housing of the Working Classes and the Poor* (1907) has been reprinted, 1975, E.P. Publishing, Wakefield.

19 See Chambers, *Modern Nottingham in the Making* and *A Century of Nottingham History, 1851—1951* (1951).

20 Professor Beresford has produced diagrams to show how long some developments took to complete.

21 See Fig. 16, p. 63 and Fig. 9, p. 26.

22 See, e.g., M. W. Beresford, *Time and Place*, Leeds U.P., 1961, for Prosperity Street and the university precinct area; also *Leeds and its Region*, loc. cit.

23 This material has been supplied by Professor Beresford and is based on material largely in Leeds City Library. Its use here is by permission of the City Librarian, Leeds.

24 Dyos, *Victorian Suburb*, chapter v. See also two important papers in *Victorian Studies* xi (1967) 5—40, 641—90, and D. A. Reeder, 'A theatre of suburbs: some patterns of development in West London, 1801—1911', *Study of Urban History*, pp. 253—71. On urban topography in general, see the essays by G. F. Chadwick and S. Marcus, in Dyos and Wolff, eds, *The Victorian City*, and G. H. Martin, 'The town as palimpsest', in Dyos, ed., *Study of Urban History*.

25 I am most grateful to Professor Dyos for allowing me to quote this material.

26 S. D. Chapman and J. N. Bartlett, 'The contribution of building clubs and the Freehold Land Society to working-class housing in Birmingham', *History of Working-Class Housing*, pp. 235—46.

27 Diagrams showing such changes in Leeds have been drawn by Professor Beresford.

28 M. Spufford, 'The significance of the Cambridgeshire hearth tax', *Proc. Cambridge Antiquarian Soc.* lv (1962); D. Foster, 'Hearth tax and settlement studies', *Local Hist.* xi.7 (1975) 385—9.

29 In 1801 it was almost exactly the same, 5,177 dwellings to 28,972.

30 B. Cozens-Hardy, *History of Letheringsett*, Norwich, Jarrold, 1958, pp. 145—6; taken by Rev. John Burrell, it lists all houses rather than occupants.

31 Some enclosure award plans cover village sites as well as the fields, but not all do so.

32 See D. Iredale, *This Old House*, Shire Publications, 1968; J. H. Harvey, *Sources for the History of Houses*, British Records Assoc., 1974. For deeds, see the works cited in Harvey, and the essay by G. H. Martin in D. A. Bullough and R. L. Storey, eds, *Study of Medieval Records*, Oxford U.P., 1972.

33 See for an example M. W. Barley, A. Rogers and P. Strange, 'The medieval parsonage house, Coningsby, Lincs.', *Antiquaries Journal* xlix (1969) 346—66.

34 J. West, *Village Records*, Macmillan, 1962, pp. 92—131, greatly overrates the value of probate inventories for architectural history; see A. Rogers, 'Corby Glen: three houses and their records', *Lincolnshire Historian* ii.12 (1965) 19—25, for an example of the traps these documents can lead one into. For inventories, see M. A. Havinden, ed., *Household and Farm Inventories in Oxfordshire, 1550—1590*, HMSO, 1966; F. W. Steer, 'Probate inventories', *History* xlvii (1962) 287—90.

35 R. W. Brunskill, *Illustrated Handbook of Vernacular Architecture*, Faber, 1971; J. Thompson, 'Investigating domestic buildings', *Amat. Hist.* vii (1966) 126—33.

36 See A. Rogers, 'Parish boundaries and urban history', *Journal of Brit. Archaeol. Ass.* xxxv (1972) 46—64; A. Rogers, 'The origins of Newark: the evidence of boundaries', *Thoroton Soc. Trans.* lxxix (1974) 13—26.

37 J. B. Harley, 'The re-mapping of England, 1750—1800', *Imago Mundi* xix (Amsterdam, 1965) 56—67; R. V. Tooley, *Maps and Mapmakers*, 4th edn, Batsford, 1970; R. A. Skelton, *County Atlases of the British Isles, 1579—1850 vol. I, 1579—1703* (Carta Press, 1970).

38 The survival of these is patchy; they cover only the later sixteenth and early seventeenth centuries. Those for Somerset have been published, S. W. B. Harbin, ed., *Somerset Enrolled Deeds*, Somerset Record Soc. li (1936).

39 W. G. Hoskins, *Industry, Trade and People in Exeter, 1688—1800*, Manchester U.P., 1935. In Chester, a similar study by wards showed some central areas of larger houses.

40 Vol. I, ed. M. D. Lobel, appeared in 1970; vol. II in 1975.

41 W. Urry, *Canterbury under the Angevin Kings*, Athlone Press, 1967. For other studies, see *Birmingham before 1800: six maps in the Local Studies Library, Birmingham*, Birmingham Public Libraries, 1968; J. A. Patmore, *An Atlas of Harrogate*, Harrogate Public Library, 1963; A. J. Hunt, 'The expansion of Sheffield and its boundary problem', *East Midland Geographer* xix (1963) 115—23, etc.

42 Leeds township:

	Population	Houses occupied	Density per house	Empty	In building
1801	53,162	11,258	4.7	341	–
1811	62,534	12,249	5.1	536	75
1821	83,796	17,419	4.8	1,165	114
1831	123,393	25,456	4.8	1,793	246
1841	152,054	31,626	4.8	2,276	366
1851	172,270	36,165	4.7	1,646	259
1861	207,165	44,651	4.6	1,204	319
1871	259,212	55,827	4.6	2,476	557
1881	309,119	64,981	4.7	4,597	428

Changes after 1881 make comparisons difficult.

43 The corrected figures, allowing for the Hall in South Rauceby (see above) are as follows:

	North Rauceby	South Rauceby
1841	5.7	5.2
1851	5.1	4.3
1861	5.8	4.8

Rogers, *Stability and Change* p. 10.

44 A brief guide exists in W. R. Powell, *Local History from Blue Books*, Historical Association, 1962. A useful discussion of the material in this type of report is by M. W. Flinn in the Introduction to the reprint of the Chadwick Report, published by Edinburgh University Press, 1965.

45 For these records, see H. C. Prince, 'Tithe surveys of the mid-nineteenth century', *Agric. Hist. Rev.* vii (1959) 14–26. I am grateful to Mr Henstock, Peter Fletcher and the members of the Ashbourne group for this example, so far unpublished; for a description of the work, see A. Henstock, 'House repopulation in the mid-nineteenth century', *Bull. Local History* vi (1971) 11–20.

46 See Bagley, *Historical Interpretation*, ii, pp. 217–23.

47 The historian may trace them for his area (up to 1856 only) in J. E. Norton, *Guide to the National and Provincial Directories of England and Wales (excluding London) published before 1856*, Royal Historical Society, 1952. See *Bull. Local History East Midland Region* iii (1968) for those of the counties in that region; also D. Page, 'Commercial directories and market towns', *Loc. Hist.* xi.2 (1974) 85–8.

48 By Dr Jennifer Tann and Mr Robin Chaplin, among others.

49 These plans are usually very flimsy and damaged; they may survive in almost any department of a modern local authority. Some are carefully kept in books, others loose.

50 The annual returns are printed among the parliamentary papers but are not very useful to the local historian. The monthly returns show work done, owners, builders and other details.

51 See Harley, *Historian's Guide to O.S. Maps*, an essential introduction, and two articles on town plans, *Amat. Hist.* v.8 (1963) 251–60, and vii.6 (1967) 196–208.

52 D. R. Mills, 'Main types of source material for eighteenth and nineteenth century village study', *Amat. Hist.* vii.1 (1966) 7–13. For photographs and prints, see above, p. 20, and note 39 on p. 234.

53 V.C.H. *Leicestershire*, vol. iv, pp. 260–5.

54 See note 35 on p. 254; J. Bateman, *Great Landowners of Great Britain and Ireland*, 1883 edn, repr. Leicester U.P., 1971.

Chapter 5   Earning a living

1 See note at end of chapter.

2 This underlies Alan Armstrong's work in *Introd. to Engl. Hist. Demog.*, pp. 209–37; in *Study of Urban History*, pp. 78–81, and in his more recent book *Stability and Change in an English County Town*.

3 Alan Everitt, *Ways and Means in Local History*, Council of Social Service for the Standing Conference for Local History, 1971, pp. 30–3.

4 A. Rogers, 'A Lincolnshire innkeeper', *The Village* xxii.2 (1967) 46—54.

5 James Hopkinson, *Memoirs of a Victorian Cabinet-Maker, 1819—94*, ed. J. B. Goodman, Routledge, 1968.

6 K. C. Edwards, ed., *Nottingham and its Region*, British Association, 1966, pp. 407—8.

7 A good local study is R. A. Church, *Economic and Social Change in a Midland Town: Victorian Nottingham, 1815—1900*, Cass, 1966; see also J. M. Prest, *The Industrial Revolution in Coventry*, Oxford U.P., 1960, for the ribbon-makers of that town.

8 The best current survey of agricultural history is in H. P. R. Finberg and J. Thirsk, eds, *The Agrarian History of England and Wales*, Cambridge U.P., 1967—72. For the Middle Ages, see G. Duby's short *Medieval Agriculture 900—1500* (1969); for the later periods, see Lord Ernle, *English Farming Past and Present* (6th edn, Heinemann, 1961) and works listed there. The articles in *Agricultural History Review* provide local studies. For field systems, see R. C. Russell, *The Logic of the Open-Field System* (1974) and A. R. H. Baker and R. H. Butlin, ed., *Studies of Field Systems in the British Isles*, Cambridge U.P., 1973. One of the best recent studies of field systems and land use is J. R. Ravensdale, *Liable to Floods: Village landscape on the edge of the Fens*, Cambridge U.P., 1974.

9 E. Kerridge, *The Agricultural Revolution*, 1967, and *Agrarian Problems in the Sixteenth Century and After*, Allen and Unwin, 1969; J. D. Chambers and G. E. Mingay, *The Agricultural Revolution 1750—1850*, Batsford, 1966; J. Addy, *The Agrarian Revolution*, Longman (Seminar Studies), 1972; E. L. Jones, *Agriculture and the Industrial Revolution*, Oxford, Blackwell, 1975, and *Development of English Agriculture 1815—73*, Macmillan, 1968.

10 M. Spufford, *Contrasting Communities: English villagers in the sixteenth and seventeenth centuries*, Cambridge U.P., 1974, argues that the decline of the peasantry was related to years of poor harvest, but there are other interpretations. See, e.g., R. H. Hilton, *A Medieval Society: the West Midlands at the end of the thirteenth century*, Weidenfeld and Nicolson, 1966, and *Bondmen Made Free*, Temple Smith, 1973. On the disappearance of the peasantry, see S. H. Franklin, *The European Peasantry, the last phase*, Methuen, 1969; H. A. Landsberger, ed., *A Rural Protest: peasant movements and social change*, Macmillan, 1974.

11 See A. M. Everitt, *New Avenues in English Local History*, Leicester U.P., 1970, and in the *Agrarian History of England* iv (1967) pp. 466—592.

12 Beresford, *New Towns of the Middle Ages*; G. H. Martin, *The Town*, Vista Histories, Studio Vista, 1961.

13 See J. Jean Hecht, *The Domestic Servant Class in 18th Century England*, Routledge, 1956.

14 W. H. B. Court, *Concise Economic History of Britain*, Cambridge U.P., 1954; S. D. Chapman and J. D. Chambers, *The Beginnings of Industrial Britain*, Univ. Tutorial Press, 1970; R. M. Hartwell, *Industrial Revolution in England*, Historical Association, 1964. On marketing, see G. Porter and H. C. Livesay, eds, *Merchants and Manufacturers: studies in the changing structure of 19th-century marketing*, Johns Hopkins Press, 1971. A useful study of the relations of local and national is in J. A. Schmiechen, 'State reform and the local economy', *Econ. Hist. Rev.* xxviii (1975) 413—28.

15 See, e.g., J. T. Ward and R. G. Wilson, eds, *Land and Industry: the landed estate*

and the industrial revolution, David and Charles, 1974; L. G. Mee, *Aristocratic Enterprises*, Blackie, 1975.

16 Best, pp. 100, 110—17. There was a slight national increase in women in employment in 1861 and 1871. On the other hand, the education legislation of the 1870s reduced child employment by at least a quarter in a decade, Best, p. 107.

17 Best, p. 104; see also ibid., p. 79.

18 These are domestic servants in relation to total population, not to the working population.

19 Prest, op. cit.

20 H. Pelling, *History of British Trade Unionism*, Macmillan, 1963; A. Aspinall, *Early English Trade Unions*, Batchworth Press, 1948.

21 G. J. Holyoake, *Self-Help by the People: the History of the Rochdale Pioneers*, 1857.

22 From a forthcoming book by A. J. Peacock on York in the early nineteenth century.

23 See, for example, the vivid account of the eighteenth century riots in Newcastle-upon-Tyne in J. Brand, *History of Newcastle*, 1789. M. I. Thomis, *The Town Labourer and the Industrial Revolution*, Batsford, 1974, is the most recent introduction to this subject.

24 Nottingham borough records, City Library; M. I. Thomis, *Politics and Society in Nottingham, 1785—1835*, Oxford, Blackwell, 1969.

25 Emmison, *Archives and Local History*, pp. 61—9.

26 Inquisitions post mortem, see West, *Village Records*, pp. 49—59.

27 See Short Guide to Records 16, *History* lii (1967) 283—6; D. Grigg, 'Land tax returns', *Amat. Hist.* vi.5 (1964) 152—7.

28 D. M. Barratt, 'Glebe terriers', Short Guide to Records 13, *History* li (1966) 35—8; see also D. M. Barratt, *Ecclesiastical Terriers of Warwickshire Parishes*, Dugdale Soc. 22 (1955). For inventories, see F. W. Steer, *Farm and Cottage Inventories of Mid-Essex 1635—1749*, 2nd edn, Phillimore, 1969, and note 34 on p. 240. For parish tithe papers, see Tate, *Parish Chest*, pp. 133—42.

29 G. E. Mingay, *Enclosure and the Small Farmer in the Age of the Industrial Revolution*, Macmillan, 1968; W. E. Tate, *The English Village Community and the Enclosure Movements*, Gollancz, 1967; H. G. Hunt, 'Landownership and enclosures 1750—1830', *Econ. Hist. Rev.* xi (1958) 497—505. E. C. K. Gunner's old study, *Common Land and Inclosure*, 1912, has been reprinted, M. J. Clifton, Kelley, 1972.

30 See two articles on 'Content and sources of English agrarian history before and after 1500', by R. H. Hilton and J. Thirsk in *Agric. Hist. Rev.* iii (1955).

31 W. G. Hoskins, *The Making of the English Landscape*, Hodder and Stoughton, 1955; for a good local example, see C. Taylor, *Dorset*, Hodder and Stoughton, 1971. See A. R. H. Baker and J. B. Harley, eds, *Man Made the Land*, David and Charles, 1973, for a useful summary of modern thinking.

32 Associated largely with the name Arthur Young and his *General View of Agriculture* in various counties; but there were others involved in these reports, like Thomas Stone and R. Lowe.

33 J. Thirsk, *English Peasant Farming: the agrarian history of Lincolnshire from Tudor to recent times*, Routledge, 1957; D. Grigg, *The Agricultural Revolution in South Lincolnshire*, Cambridge U.P., 1966. Probably few other counties have been surveyed in the same depth as this county, but the regional summaries in

the *Agrarian History of England* are invaluable. On the general background, see G. E. Mingay, *English Landed Society in the Eighteenth Century*, 1963, and F. M. L. Thompson, *English Landed Society in the Nineteenth Century*, both Routledge, 1963.

34 E. Moir's account of them in *The Discovery of Britain*, Routledge, 1964, is perhaps the best way into this subject. See W. Matthews, *British Diaries 1442–1942: an annotated bibliography*, Cambridge U.P., 1950.

35 J. Leland, *Itinerary*, ed. L. T. Smith, 1908, vol. ii, p. 97.

36 Hoskins, *Provincial England*, pp. 78–9; A. J. and R. H. Tawney, 'An occupational census of the seventeenth century', *Econ. Hist. Rev.* v (1934) 25–59; and J. Patten, 'Village and Town: an occupational study', *Agric. Hist. Rev.* xx (1972) 1–16, and J. C. Cornwall, 'A Tudor Domesday', *Journal of Society of Archivists* iii.1 (1965) 19–24.

37 See J. R. Vincent, *Pollbooks: how Victorians voted*, Cambridge U.P., 1967. In some places, like Northampton and Westminster, the franchise was very wide. It is necessary to check this first, the best account being T. H. B. Oldfield, *An Entire and Complete History of the Boroughs of Great Britain* (1972). It must be remembered however that on occasion, especially at fiercely contested elections, there were several persons voting who were not in fact entitled to do ·so. See M. Drake, *Introduction to Historical Psephology*, Open University, 1973, and W. A. Speck and W. A. Grey, 'Computer analysis of poll books', *Bull. Inst. Hist. Res.* xliii (1970) 105–12 and xlviii (1975) 64–90.

38 Based on work done by Priscilla Weston.

39 This view has recently been challenged by Dr R. B. Dobson in 'Admissions to the Freedom of York in the later Middle Ages', *Econ. Hist. Rev.* xxvi (1973) 1–21.

40 O. Ashmore and J. J. Bagley, 'Inventories as a source of local history', *Amat. Hist.* iv (1959) (four articles). A useful article on probate inventories and agriculture is J. A. Yelling, 'Probate inventories and the geography of livestock farming: East Worcestershire, 1540–1750', *Trans. Inst. British Geographers* li (1969) 111–26. For wills see A. J. Camp, ed., *Wills and their Whereabouts*, Phillimore, 1963, and R. S. France, 'Wills', *History* l (1965) 36–9.

41 Some are in the Public Record Office; they cover all adult males and often give occupations. See *LPS* viii (1972) 43; V. A. Hatley, ed., *Northants Militia Lists 1777*, Northamptonshire Record Society, 1973, and M. A. Faraday, ed., *Herefordshire Militia Assessments 1663*, Camden Society x (1972).

42 The figures, which I owe to Dr Chalklin, are as follows: builders 111; metal workers 1,135; professional 154; general tradesmen and craftsmen 1,529; gentry, etc., 106. *Universal British Directory* (1794) ii, pp. 207–41.

43 Mostly in Guildhall Library, London.

44 R. F. Hunnisett, *Calendar of Nottinghamshire Coroners' Inquests, 1485–1558*, Thoroton Society Record Series, xxv (1969).

45 J. P. M. Pannell, *Techniques of Industrial Archaeology*, 2nd edn, David and Charles, 1974. See M. Rix, *Industrial Archaeology*, Historical Association, 1967, and articles in the journals *Industrial Archaeology* and *Post-Medieval Archaeology*. R. A. Buchanan, *Industrial Archaeology in Britain*, Allen Lane and Penguin, 1972, and A. Raistrick, *Industrial Archaeology, an historical survey*, Eyre & Spottiswoode, 1972, are useful background books.

46 See above, p. 39.

47 Best, p. 124, etc.

48 Best, p. 102.

49 Lionel Munby informs me of one rural blacksmith's workshop which he has traced by the directories, changing through a bicycle shop into a garage; this can be done for larger concerns as well.

50 *Census Abstracts: Occupations*, 2 vols, 1844, was the first full study, HC. 1844, vol. xxvii; there were abstracts in 1831, but they only list seven broad categories.

51 *Journal of Royal Statistical Society* xlix (1886) 314—435; Professor Best draws heavily on this.

52 Rogers, *Stability and Change* pp. 29—32. A quarter of all households in North Rauceby employed servants; less than one-sixth in South Rauceby did so.

53 Some of these variations are due to different codes being used. Similar figures are not easy to deduce for Long Buckby, but there were some 100 engaged in trades, about a tenth.

54 See Armstrong, in *Introduction to English Historical Demography*, and 'The interpretation of the census enumerators' books for Victorian towns', in *Study of Urban History*.

55 H. J. Dyos and A. B. M. Baker, 'Computerising census data', in *Study of Urban History*, p. 101. The use of household heads would reduce this category.

56 Armstrong, in *Introduction to English Historical Demography*, pp. 217—20; also D. E. C. Eversley, ibid, pp. 269—71; and *Study of Urban History*, pp. 81—2. R. Lawton, 'The population of Liverpool in the mid-nineteenth century', first printed in *Trans. Historic Society of Lancashire and Cheshire* cvii (1955) 89—120, and reprinted in Baker, Hamshere and Langton, eds, *Geographical Interpretations of Historical Sources*, pp. 381—415.

57 J. T. Coppock, 'Agricultural returns', *Amat. Hist.* iv.2 (1958) 49—56. For estate records, see R. J. Colyer, 'The use of estate home farm accounts', *Local Hist.* xi.7 (1975) 406—13.

58 These in fact followed the last report of the Children's Employment Commission in 1867, which also dealt with 'gangs'.

59 Bagley, *Historical Interpretation*, ii, pp. 235—43.

60 These are now kept in the House of Lords Record Office; see M. F. Bond, *Guide to the Records of Parliament*, HMSO, 1971.

61 Pike, *Human Documents of the Victorian Golden Age* p. 87.

62 These are cited in Pike, op. cit.

63 V.C.H. *Essex*, vi.

64 V.C.H. *Essex* v, pp. 1—96.

65 A series of 'Special Properties' Ratebooks, *c.* 1900—30, came to light after the completion of the survey. They include sections on 'Mills, manufactories and warehouses' which are of great interest.

66 cf. *Census 1961, England and Wales, Occupational, Industrial and Socio-Economic Groups (Essex).*

67 There are many studies of individual firms which show the range of sources, such as S. D. Chapman, *Jesse Boot of Boots the Chemists*, Hodder and Stoughton, 1974. See the articles in the journals *Econ. Hist. Rev.* and *Business History* for further material. See also T. C. Barker, *Business History*, Historical Association, 1960.

68 Best, pp. 75, 109.

69 e.g. *The Agricultural Lockout of 1874*, written by the journalist Frederick

Clifford in 1875, published by Blackwoods, covers nine counties. For rural discontent, see J. P. D. Dunbabin, *Rural Discontent in Nineteenth-century Britain*, Faber, 1974; R. C. Russell, *The Revolt of the Field in Lincolnshire* (1956); E. J. Hobsbawm and G. Rudé, *Captain Swing*, Lawrence and Wishart; Penguin Books, 1973; R. Arnold, 'The revolt in the field in Kent 1872–9', *Past and Present* lxiv (1974) 71–95.

70 Thus Costessey (Norfolk) Baptist register records the suspension of John Reeve from membership in 1830 for machine breaking.

71 Vincent, 'Notes on the meaning of the occupational categories used in analysis', *Pollbooks*, pp. 51–4.

72 See above, n. 51.

73 Cited in Vincent, p. 53.

74 Patmore, *Atlas of Harrogate*.

75 *The Social Classification of Occupations*, HMSO, 1950.

76 See Armstrong, 'The classification of occupations', *Introd. to Engl. Hist. Demog.*, pp. 272–3; and *Studies of Urban History*, pp. 101–7 and especially pp. 147–9.

77 *Standard Classification of Industries* (1961) has twenty-seven categories, of which only nine agree even approximately with the HMSO *Schedule on Occupations*, 1960, issued by the census authorities – an indication of the difficulties of this problem.

Chapter 6   Transport and communications

1 J. K. Edwards, 'Communications and the economic development of Norwich, 1750–1850', *Journal of Transport History* vii (1965–6) 96–108. This journal is essential for all aspects of this study.

2 R. A. Pelham, 'The provisioning of the Lincoln parliament of 1301', *University of Birmingham Historical Journal* iii (1951–2) 16–32.

3 In the British Museum; see F. Stenton, 'The road system of medieval England', *Econ. Hist. Rev.* vii (1936–7) 1–21.

4 M. W. Barley, *Documents Relating to the Manor and Soke of Newark-on-Trent*, Thoroton Society Record Series, xvi (1956) p. xix; Rogers, *History of Lincolnshire*, p. 48.

5 See A. M. Everitt, *Perspectives in Urban History*, Macmillan, 1973, pp. 213–40 for a study of carriers in the nineteenth century; *Agrarian History of England*, vol. iv, *1500–1640* (1967) pp. 467–76, for an earlier period.

6 The first Turnpike Act was 1663 but it covered three counties and was vested in the justices. Local companies set up by private Acts began later. W. Albert, *The Turnpike Road System in England 1663–1840*, Cambridge U.P., 1972; S. and B. Webb, *Story of the King's Highway*, Longmans, 1932; for a local study, A. Cossons, *The Turnpike Roads of Nottinghamshire*, Historical Association, 1934. See also W. T. Jackson, *Development of Transport in Modern England*, 2 vols, 1916; R. Syme, *Story of Britain's Highways*, Pitmans, 1952; W. Rees Jeffreys, *The King's Highway*, Batchworth Press, 1949; J. Copeland, *Roads and their Traffic, 1750–1850*, David and Charles, 1968. H. J. Dyos and D. H. Aldcroft, eds, *British Transport: an economic survey from the seventeenth century to the twentieth*, Leicester U.P., 1974, is a more general survey, as is T. C. Barker and C. I. Savage, *An Economic History of Transport in Britain*, 3rd edn, Hutchinson, 1975.

7 Tate, *Parish Chest*, pp. 240–8.

8 C. Hadfield, *British Canals*, 5th edn, David and Charles, 1974.

9 T. S. Willan, *River Navigation in England, 1600–1750*, Oxford U.P., 1936.

10 W. Ashworth, *The Genesis of Modern British Town Planning*, Routledge, 1954.

11 A. Jopson, *The Felixstowe Story*, Hale, 1968, p. 103.

12 *Coventry Herald* in 1841, cited by Prest, *Industrial Revolution in Coventry* p. 20; see J. R. Kellett, *The Impact of Railways on Victorian Cities*, Routledge, 1969; J. Simmons, 'The power of the railway', in Dyos and Wolff, eds, *The Victorian City: images and realities*, i, pp. 277–310; H. Perkin, *The Age of the Railway*, David and Charles, 1971; H. Pollins, *Britain's Railways: an industrial history*, David and Charles, 1972.

13 James Hopkinson, *Memoirs of a Victorian Cabinet-Maker*.

14 *c.* 27,000 visitor weeks, 1845–8; 33,500, 1849; 36,000, 1850; see B. Jennings, ed., *A History of Harrogate and Knaresborough*, Advertiser Press, 1970, pp. 310–15.

15 H. J. Dyos, 'Railways and housing in Victorian London', *Journal of Transport History* ii (1955–6) 11–21, 90–100.

16 J. Simmons, *St. Pancras Station*, Allen and Unwin, 1968, p. 21.

17 Patmore, *Atlas of Harrogate*.

18 R. Gurnham, 'The creation of Skegness as a resort town', *Lincolnshire History and Archaeology* vii (1972) 63–76. See J. A. R. Pimlott, *The Englishman's Holiday*, Faber, 1947.

19 I. Nairn and N. Pevsner, eds, *Sussex*, Penguin Books (Buildings of England), 1965, p. 602.

20 For further information, see H. P. White, *A Regional History of the Railways of Great Britain*, vol. ii, *Southern England*, 3rd rev. edn, David and Charles, 1969, p. 84ff.

21 Copies of the plans are deposited in the East Sussex Records Office at Lewes and at the British Transport Historical Records Office, London.

22 East Sussex Records Office, Seaford Corporation Records, 391.

23 Rogers, *Making of Stamford*, p. 69.

24 D. Defoe, *A Tour Through the Whole Island of Great Britain*, introduced by G. D. H. Cole, Peter Davies, 1929, i, pp. 73–4.

25 For the ports, not discussed here, see R. C. Jarvis, 'Sources for the history of ports', and 'Sources for the history of ships and shipping', *Journal of Transport History* iii (1957–8) 76–93, 212–34.

26 B. F. Duckham, 'Turnpike records', *History* liii (1968) 217–20.

27 See Bagley, *Historical Interpretation*, ii, 159–73. The records of Parliament are fully described by M. F. Bond in 'Materials for transport history amongst the records of Parliament', *Journal of Transport History* iv (1959–60) 37–52.

28 C. Hadfield's paper, 'Sources for the history of British canals', *Journal of Transport History* ii (1955–6) 80–9, is essential here.

29 I. S. Beckwith, 'The river trade of Gainsborough 1500–1850', *Lincolnshire History and Archaeology* ii (1967) 3–20.

30 See P. and G. Ford, *A Guide to Parliamentary Papers*, Oxford, Blackwell, 1955 (this has been revised on several occasions). There are indexes to Parliamentary Papers which are listed in this book.

31 HC. 1818, vol. xvi; HC. 1840, vol. xxvii and subsequent reports; the returns are in HC. 1841, xxvii and 1849, vol. xlvi.

32 HC. 1824, vol. xx; HC. 1836, vol. xix, xlvii, etc. — a regular series lasting until 1872.

33 HC. 1873, vol. lviii; HC. 1878, vol. lxvi.

34 HC. 1883, vol. xiii; HC. 1906, vol. xxxii, etc.

35 For all these, see Powell, *Local History from Blue Books*.

36 e.g. HC. 1877, vol. lxxiii, etc.

37 See Rogers, *History of Lincolnshire*, pp. 81—2; and M. J. Dickenson, 'Short-term effects of the G.N.R. on the economy of S. W. Kesteven, 1850—52'. *Lincolnshire History and Archaeology* vi (1971) 103—11.

38 J. Simmons, 'Railway history in English local sources', *Journal of Transport History* i (1953—4) 155—69, and H. J. Dyos, Counting the cost of railways', *Amat. Hist.* iii.5 (1957) 191—7.

39 See Bond, *Guide to the Records of Parliament*.

40 Gurnham, op. cit.

41 It is relatively easy to find the minutes of the committee relating to a specific project; what is less easy is to be sure that all the material has been covered.

42 These are now in the Public Record Office.

43 See L. C. Johnson, 'Historical records of the British Transport Commission', *Journal of Transport History* i (1953—4) 82—96, and later articles in this journal, such as v (1961—2) 159—62 and vii (1965—6) 141—8.

Chapter 7   *The bond of religion*

1 It is not necessary to give an extensive bibliography here. A good general account of the early years of Christianity in England is F. F. Bruce, *Light in the West*, 1952, the third part of a trilogy on the early Church called *The Spreading Flame*, Paternoster Press, 1958. But the story is well told in most secondary histories of Anglo-Saxon England. For the recent studies in pagan survivals, see A. Macfarlane, *Witchcraft in Tudor and Stuart England*, Routledge, 1970, and Keith Thomas, *Religion and the Decline of Magic*, Penguin Books, 1973. Two earlier works, R. T. Davies, *Four Centuries of Witch Beliefs*, Methuen, 1947, and E. Hull, *Folklore of the British Isles*, Methuen, 1928, are still useful. See also C. Phythian-Adams, *Local History and Folklore*, Bedford Square Press for the Standing Conference for Local History, 1975.

2 Some of this hostility has, of course, been over-written because it made 'news' at the time. The best recent account is M. D. Knowles and D. Obolensky, *The Christian Centuries*, vol. ii, *The Middle Ages*, Darton, Longman and Todd, 1969.

3 See Rogers, 'Parish boundaries and early urban history', *Journal of British Archaeological Association* xxxv (1972).

4 D. M. Owen, *Church and Society in Medieval Lincolnshire*, History of Lincolnshire iv, History of Lincolnshire, 1971.

5 A. Rogers and J. S. Hartley, *The Medieval Religious Foundations of Stamford*, Stamford Survey Group Report II, 1974.

6 M. Deanesly, *A History of the Medieval Church 590—1500*, Methuen, 1954 edn, pp. 164—5.

7 A. G. Dickens, *The English Reformation*, Batsford, 1964; W. O. Chadwick, *The Reformation*, Penguin Books, 1964, are the best recent guides. There have been some detailed regional and local studies for Lincolnshire, York and other places — e.g. R. B. Manning, *Religion and Society in Elizabethan Sussex*, Cambridge U.P., 1969; C. Haigh, *Reformation and Resistance in Tudor Lancashire*, Cambridge U.P., 1975.

8 See R. B. Pugh, *How to Write a Parish History*, Allen and Unwin, 1954, pp. 83—6.

9 H. Davies, *The English Free Churches*, 2nd edn, Oxford U.P., 1963; R. Currie, *Methodism Divided*, Faber, 1968; R. T. Jones, *Congregationalism in England, 1662—1962*, Independent Press, 1962. On the nature of early Methodism, see J. D. Walsh, 'E. Halévy and the birth of Methodism', *Trans. Royal Hist. Soc.* xxv (1975) 1—20, and H. Perkins's important review of B. Semmel, *The Methodist Revolution* in *Econ. Hist. Rev.* xxviii (1975) 530—1.

10 This and other material comes from C. B. Jewson, *The Baptists in Norfolk*, Carey Kingsgate Press, 1957.

11 E. Mansel Sympson, *Memorials of Old Lincolnshire*, Cambridge U.P., 1911, pp. 155—6.

12 Most useful to the local historian are the works of A. Tindal Hart, especially *The Country Clergy, 1558—1660*, Phoenix House, 1958. Margaret Spufford, *Contrasting Communities*, has much to say on religion in her three Cambridgeshire villages in the seventeenth century. The Civil Wars and Interregnum have of course much more local significance than just in religious affairs, but it is here that the local community was affected most; see R. W. Ketton-Cremer, *Norfolk in the Civil War*, Faber, 1969; J. S. Morrill, *Cheshire 1630—1660*, Oxford U.P., 1974; R. N. Dore, *The Civil Wars in Cheshire*, Cheshire Community Council, 1966; Clive Holmes, *The Eastern Association*, Cambridge U.P., 1974; J. Sterling, *The Civil War in Lancashire*, Dalesman, 1971.

13 The best general survey is J. R. H. Moorman, *History of the Church in England*, 2nd edn, A. and C. Black, 1967. See W. O. Chadwick, *History of the Church: a select bibliography*, Historical Association, 2nd edn, 1966.

14 These figures are derived from the 1851 religious census and the numbers of seatings for each ten year date.

15 I owe these figures to Professor Ward. The first Waterloo churches in Leeds cost as much as £7.80 per sitting, immense, solid churches. See W. R. Ward, 'The cost of Establishment: church building in Manchester', G. J. Cumming, ed., *Studies in Church History* Nelson, 1966, iii, 277—89, and his *Religion and Society in England, 1790—1850*, Batsford, 1972.

16 See Best, pp. 170—97.

17 This omits West Lynn beyond the river.

18 E. R. Wickham, *Church and People in an Industrial City*, Lutterworth Press, 1969.

19 Total congregation here means the sum of attendances at all services on the census day.

20 W. O. Chadwick, *The Victorian Church*, 2 vols, A. and C. Black, vol. i: *1829—59*, 3rd edn, 1971; vol. ii: *1860—1901*, 2nd edn, 1972. See also R. P. Flindall, *The Church of England, 1815—1948: a documentary history*, SPCK, 1972; Alan Smith, *The Established Church and Popular Religion, 1750—1850*, Longman, 1972; P. T. Marsh, *The Victorian Church in Decline*, Routledge, 1969; Anthony Armstrong, *The Church of England, the Methodists and Society, 1700—1850*, Univ. of London Press, 1973. For the nonconformists, see A. M. Everitt, *The Pattern of Rural Dissent: the 19th century*, Leicester U.P., 1972; D. M. Thompson, ed., *Nonconformity in the Nineteenth Century*, Routledge, 1972; J. H. Briggs and I. Sellers, *Victorian Nonconformity*, E. Arnold, 1973. J. Gay, *The Geography of Religion in England*, Duckworth, 1971, has some interesting comments and maps.

21 Best, pp. 47, 183.
22 All the Lynn material must be regarded at this stage as tentative. I must acknowledge the help of Miss A. S. Mottram of King's Lynn Museum.
23 Best, pp. 174, 189—91.
24 See H. McLeod, *Class and Religion in the Late Victorian City*, London, Croom Helm, 1974; R. Moore, *Pitmen, Preachers and Politics, a study of three Durham communities*, Cambridge U.P., 1974, a book based on a good deal of 'oral history'.
25 See for example the detailed records of taxation in the Lincoln diocese in 1526, ed. by H. E. Salter, *Oxford Historical Society* lxiii (1909), a most revealing document. For what follows, see Rogers and Hartley, *Medieval Religious Foundations of Stamford* for a full list of sources for that period; cf. also D. M. Owen, *The Records of the Established Church in England*, British Records Association, 1970.
26 W. E. Lunt, *The Valuation of Norwich*, Oxford U.P., 1926; *Taxatio Ecclesiastica*, Records Commission, 1802; *Nonarum Inquisiciones*, Rec. Comm., 1807; *Valor Ecclesiasticus*, Rec. Comm., 1810—25.
27 See also D. Knowles and R. N. Hadcock, eds, *Medieval Religious Houses, England and Wales*, Longmans, 1953.
28 The survey of 1389 is summarised in J. Toulmin Smith, *English Guilds*, 1870. Many of the 1,548 certificates have been published in local record societies; they are in P.R.O. as are Inquisitions Ad Quod Dampnum. Lists to these classes exist. Other inquisitions and material survive in such records as the Close and Patent Rolls or (in original) among private collections, especially the universities' college collections.
29 The question of whether the benefice was a rectory or vicarage is of relevance to two subjects: the question of property rights within the parish, for the rectory was not extinguished by appropriation; its ownership was merely transferred: and the question of the value of the benefice. Appropriation could in some circumstances be an advantage, for a rich rectory in the Middle Ages might well have fallen to a royal clerk who served it by a stipendiary curate rather than by a reasonably educated priest, whom a perpetual vicarage might have attracted. The history of the advowson, until the societies came on the scene in the early nineteenth century, really belongs to property ownership: R. A. R. Hartridge, *A History of Vicarages in the Middle Ages*, Cambridge U.P., 1930; J. R. H. Moorman, *Church Life in England in the Thirteenth Century*, Cambridge U.P., 1946; G. W. O. Addleshaw, *Rectors, Vicars and Patrons*, York, St Anthony's Press, 1956.
30 See I. M. Kirby, *Catalogue of Records of the Bishop and Archdeacon and Dean and Chapter of Bristol*, 1970; Owen, *Records of the Established Church*; P. S. Purvis, *Introduction to Ecclesiastical Records*, St Anthony's Press, 1954; D. Baker, ed., *Materials, Sources and Methods of Ecclesiastical History*, 1974.
31 Some conventicles were listed under an Act of 1670, but the series of licences begins in 1689.
32 The volumes of the Catholic Record Society and the journal *Recusant History*, especially vol. iv, nos. 5—6 (1958) will provide an introduction to the sources for this subject. For the recusant rolls in the P.R.O., see Short Guide xi, *History* l (1965), 193—6. See A. Davidson, 'Recusant History: a bibliographical article', *Loc. Hist.* ix.6 (1971) 283—8, and (for a specimen study) J. C. H. Aveling,

Catholic Recusants in the City of York, 1558–1791, Catholic Record Society, 1970.

33 G. Lyon Turner, *Original Records of Early Nonconformity*, 3 vols, Unwin, 1911–14; A. Gordon, *Freedom After Ejection*, Longmans, 1917: a Presbyterian and Congregational Survey, 1690–92. There are statistical surveys of 1715, 1773 and others in Dr Williams's Library. The records of Methodism and Congregationalism are described in *Amat. Hist.* iii.4 and 5 (1957) 143–9, 208–12; *Loc. Hist.* ix.3 (1970); *Journal of Society of Archivists* iv.3 (April 1971); *Journal of Wesley History*; W. R. Powell, 'Sources for the history of protestant nonconformist churches in England', *Bull. Inst. Hist. Res.* xxv (1952) 213–27; B. J. Biggs, 'Nonconformist records and their uses', *Bull. Local History* ix (1974) 14–26. M. Spufford, 'Dissenting Churches in Cambs., 1660–1700', *Proc. Cambs Ant. Soc.* lxvi (1968) and other studies have shown how to relate hearth tax returns to lists of chapel members. See also A. Everitt, 'Nonconformity in country parishes', in J. Thirsk, ed., *Land, Church and People, essays presented to H. P. R. Finberg*, Brit. Agricultural Hist. Soc., 1970.

34 C. W. Foster, ed., *The State of the Church*, Lincoln Record Society, xxiii (1926); the 1649 survey is in the P.R.O., the later ones divided between there and Lambeth Palace Library. See J. Houston, *Catalogue of Ecclesiastical Records of the Commonwealth, 1643–1666*, Grigg, 1968; *Bull. Local History* vi (1971) 55–6.

35 For examples, see Rogers, *Lincolnshire Historian* ii.12 (1965); and Barley, Rogers and Strange, *Antiquaries Journal* xlix, 357–66.

36 J. Blain, *A List of Churchwardens' Accounts*, Ann Arbor, Univ. of Michigan Press, 1933.

37 The signature on the transcripts and parish terriers shows who actually was serving the cure.

38 'This church was builded of Timber, Stone & Bricks
In the year of our Lord God XV hundred and six
And lately translated from extreme Idolatry
A thousand five hundred & seven & forty.
And in the first year of our noble King Edward
The Gospel in Parliament was mightily set forward.'
There is another inscription relating to Elizabeth who 'Set up the Gospel and banished Popery'.

39 For example, E. Peacock, *English Church Furniture*, 1866, a list of ornaments destroyed up to 1566; cp. the 1552 survey of church furniture in P.R.O.

40 A. G. Matthews, *Calamy Revised*, Oxford U.P., 1933; A. G. Matthews, *Walker Revised*, Oxford U.P., 1948.

41 P.R.O./HO 129. The printed volume is full of local material: *Religious worship, England and Wales*, HC. 1853, vol. lxxxix.

42 The best accounts are K. S. Inglis in *Journal of Ecclesiastical History* xi (1960) 74–86; see more recently, W. S. F. Pickering, *British Journal of Sociology* xviii (1967) 382–407; D. M. Thompson, *Victorian Studies* xi (1967) 87–97; R. W. Ambler, 'The 1851 Census of Religious Worship', *Local Hist.* xi.7 (1975) 375–81.

43 Greenall, p. 7.

44 K. S. Inglis, *The Churches and the Working Classes in Victorian England*, Routledge, 1963; I. S. Beckwith, 'Religion in a working men's parish, 1845–93', *Lincolnshire History and Archaeology* v (1970) 29–38;

R. B. Walker, 'Religious changes in Liverpool in the nineteenth century', *Journal of Ecclesiastical History* xix (1968) 195—211; see R. Mudie-Smith, ed., *Religious Life of London*, Hodder and Stoughton, 1904; and the articles by D. E. H. Mole, S. Gilley and J. Kent in Dyos and Wolff, eds, *The Victorian City: images and realities.*

45 In *The Nonconformist*, August 1872.

46 HC. 1814—1815, vol. xii.

47 E. J. Robinson, 'Records of the Church Commissioners', *Journal of Society of Archivists* iii.7 (1968), and in *Loc. Hist.* ix.5 (1971) 215—21.

48 *Bishop Wilberforce's Visitation Returns for the Archdeaconry of Oxford, 1854*, Oxfordshire Record Society, xxxv (1954); see M. R. Austin, *The Church in Derbyshire in 1823—4*, Derbyshire Archaeological Society Record Series v (1974).

49 Copies may survive in the parish or in the diocesan record office; some 11,800 apportionments exist in P.R.O. Gaps may be filled in from HC. 1887, vol. lxiv, while surviving tithes were surveyed in 1896 by H. Grove in the rare book *Alienated Tithes* (1896).

50 BM, Harl.MS.47777, fol. 14; noted in the Newark Archaeological and Local History Society *Newsletter* for August 1971.

51 E. R. Creighton, ed., *Ellen Buxton's Journal, 1860—1864*, Bles, 1967.

Chapter 8   The concerns of the community

1 In Mrs Humphrey Ward, *Robert Elsmere*, 1888.

2 E. J. Erith, *Woodford, Essex, 1600—1836; local government in a residential parish*, Woodford Historical Society, 1950, is a good introduction.

3 Alan Harding, *A Social History of English Law*, Penguin Books, 1966, is the best general introduction to this subject.

4 A. Rogers, 'The borough council of Stamford', in Everitt, ed., *Perspectives in English Urban History*, 1973.

5 Tate, *Parish Chest* is still the best guide to this. See also S. and B. Webb, *History of English Local Government, Parish and County*, 1924.

6 E. Moir, *The Justice of the Peace*, Penguin Books, 1969; J. H. Gleason, *Justices of the Peace in England, 1558—1640*, Oxford U.P., 1969. The importance of the church courts in regulating affairs must not be forgotten; see F. G. Emmison, *Elizabethan Life; morals and the Church Courts*, Essex Record Soc., 1973. On the whole, it has been argued, these represent a major and acceptable form of local authority.

7 A. M. Everitt, *The Local Community and the Great Rebellion*, Historical Association, 1969, p. 8.

8 D. Gray, *Nottingham Through Five Hundred Years*, 2nd rev. edn, Nottingham City Council, 1960.

9 See the important essay by J. Simon, 'Town estates and schools in the sixteenth and early seventeenth centuries', in B. Simons ed., *Education in Leicestershire, 1540—1940*, Leicester U.P., 1968. J. H. Plumb's *Growth of Political Stability in England 1675—1725*, Macmillan, 1973, reveals the swing from some democratic involvement to increasing oligarchy in the constituencies.

10 For example:

In Memory of

MARY the Relict of THOMAS DEACON Esq.
Daughter of JOHN HAVEY of Spalding Gent.

To which place She was a kind and Generous Benefactor, and bestowed upwards of 400 *Pounds* in pious and useful Charities. She gave also to Fleet 250 *Pounds* for founding a Charity School in that Parish. To the Poor of this City She extended her dayly Bounty, So private as not to be told, so large as scarce to be equall'd. To which She added several publick Benefactions and gave towards augmenting the Vicaridge of St. John Bapt. 100 *Pounds*, and likewise 100 *Pounds* to add to ye Salary of the Grammar School. She died January 27 1730. Aged 77 years.

11 There were others — Burial Boards, Sewerage and Drainage Boards, Baths and Washhouse Boards as well as Registration Districts from 1836. Most of these had rates, all had their own officials. It is important to remember that some boards came before the legislation — a few boards of health were set up following a circular from the Privy Council after the first cholera outbreak of 1831—2.

12 F. H. Spencer, *Municipal Origins, 1740—1835*, 1911.

13 Best, pp. 42—54; B. Keith Lucas in J. Redlich and F. W. Hirst, *History of Local Government in England*, Macmillan, 1958; G. Sutherland, ed., *Studies in the Growth of Nineteenth Century Government*, Routledge, 1972.

14 Best, p. 37.

15 R. Newton, *Victorian Exeter*, Leicester U.P., 1968.

16 W. Richards, *The History of Lynn*, 1812, vol. ii, p. 985.

17 E. P. Hennock, 'Finance and politics in urban local government', *Historical Journal* vi (1963) 212—25, an essential study for all nineteenth-century urban local historians.

18 R. Newton, 'Society and politics in Exeter, 1837—1914', in *Study of Urban History*, pp. 301—13.

19 Newton, *Victorian Exeter*, pp. 28—9.

20 Some of these changes, of course, reflect changes in the structure of local industry; E. P. Hennock, 'The social composition of borough councils . . . 1835—1914', in *Study of Urban History*, pp. 315—40. See his *Fit and Proper Persons, Ideal and Reality in Nineteenth Century Urban Government*, E. Arnold, 1973; also D. Fraser, 'The fruits of reform, Leeds politics in the 1830s', *Northern History* vii (1972).

21 Professor Pugh gives the best guidance on how to do it; R. B. Pugh, *How to Write a Parish History*, Allen and Unwin, 1954, pp. 48—68.

22 Many, but not all, of these have been printed in the *Rotuli Hundredorum* (Rec. Comm., 1812—18). They are difficult to use.

23 The medieval inquisitions have been printed (in English) but the extents have not. See N. J. Hone, *The Manor and Manorial Records*, 1906; West, *Village Records*, pp. 30—42.

24 These have been indexed but are not printed. All these records are in the P.R.O.

25 A. Ballard and J. Tait, eds, *British Borough Charters 1042—1307*, 2 vols, Cambridge U.P., 1913—23; and M. A. Weinbaum, ed., *British Borough Charters, 1307—1660*, Cambridge U.P., 1943.

26 A good example of a study based on these sources is in F. W. Hill, *Medieval Lincoln*, Cambridge U.P., 1948.

27 See above, pp. 15, 142.

28 W. B. Willcox, *Gloucestershire: a Study in Local Government, 1590—1640*, Yale U.P., 1940.

29 For example, the current series of Leicester borough records.

30 Most of these borough records have been listed in the volumes of the Historical

Manuscripts Commission or in two parliamentary papers, the *General Report from the Commissioners on Public Records*, HC. 1837, vol. xxxiv, no. i, and the *Interim Report of the Committee on House of Commons Personnel and Politics*, HC. 1931, vol. x.

31 See below.

32 The earliest seems to be for Grimsby, see A. Rogers, 'Parliamentary elections in Grimsby in the fifteenth century', *Bull. Inst. Hist. Res.* xlii (1969) 212—20. A useful introduction for the local historian to all aspects of local elections is in Drake, *Introduction to Historical Psephology*.

33 I owe this example to Professor Temple Patterson.

34 There is a guide to these sources in Short Guides to Records 24, Local Reports to the General Board of Health, *History* lvi (1971) 46—9.

35 This important paper has been largely overlooked by local historians: *Owners of Land, England and Wales, 1872—1873*, HC. 1874, vol. lxxii, called 'The Modern Domesday Book'. See Bateman, *Great Landowners of Great Britain and Ireland*; A. J. Langdon, 'Victorian Landowners', *Amat. Hist.* ii.8 (1955) 230—1.

Chapter 9   Social welfare

1 See, e.g., J. J. Tobias, *Nineteenth Century Crime: Prevention and Punishment*, David and Charles, 1972, and *Crime and Industrial Society in the nineteenth century*, Batsford, 1967; Penguin Books, 1972.

2 J. J. and A. J. Bagley, *The English Poor Law*, Macmillan, 1966; G. W. Oxley, *Poor Relief in England and Wales, 1601—1834*, David and Charles, 1974; M. E. Rose, *The English Poor Law, 1780—1930*, David and Charles, 1971. The three volumes by S. and B. Webb on the *English Poor Law History*, repr. Cass, 1963, are still valuable for the period after 1689.

3 See W. K. Jordan, *Philanthropy in England 1480—1660* and *The Charities of Rural England, 1480—1660*, Allen and Unwin, 1959, 1960; G. Jones, *History of the Law of Charity 1532—1827*, Cambridge U.P., 1969, is useful on legal matters.

4 Tate, *Parish Chest*, pp. 188—97.

5 Dorothy Marshall, *The English Poor in the Eighteenth Century*, rev. edn, Routledge, 1969; J. D. Marshall, *The Old Poor Law, 1795—1834*, Macmillan, 1968; G. Taylor, *Problems of Poverty 1660—1834*, Longmans (Seminar Studies), 1969.

6 Best, pp. 120—33.

7 Best, p. 76.

8 Best, p. 147. There is a lengthy debate on whether the operation of the Poor Law meshed in with the economic interests of the local landowners who acted as guardians. See the discussion between A. Brundage and P. Dunkley in 'The landed interest and the new Poor Law', *English Historical Rev.* lxxxvii (1972) 27—48, lxxxviii (1973) 836—41, and xc (1975) 347—51; and A. Digby, 'The labour market and the continuity of social policy after 1834: the case of the eastern counties', *Econ. Hist. Rev.* xxviii (1975) 69—83. N. Middleton, *When Family Failed*, Gollancz, 1971, continues the argument into the early twentieth century.

9 This is taken from the Analytical Digest to the Report, HC. 1843, vols. xvi and xvii; this is probably the easiest way to find particular sections of this complicated Report. The main Bromley evidence was taken in 1837 and appears in HC. 1837, vol. xxiii, 444—7.

10 HC. 1852, vol. xxviii gives one of these; the second comes from the later survey of 1870.

11 D. Owen, *English Philanthropy, 1660–1960*, Oxford U.P., 1965.

12 Newton, *Victorian Exeter*, passim.

13 H. Pelling, *A History of British Trade Unionism*, Penguin Books, 1970; G. J. Holyoake, *History of Co-operation in England*, 2 vols, Unwin, 1906; B. Webb, *Co-operative Movement in Britain*, 1910.

14 Sir F. M. Eden, *The State of the Poor*, 3 vols (1797) new edn, Cass, 1966.

15 This information comes from returns made to the Registrar of Friendly Societies. The figures do not say how many *people* drew benefit.

16 P. H. J. H. Gosden, *The Friendly Societies of England, 1815–75*, Manchester U.P., 1960.

17 K. Fielden, 'Samuel Smiles and self-help', *Victorian Studies* xii (1968) 155–76.

18 Several counties, like Kent and Cambridgeshire, have prepared their own bibliographies on this subject.

19 For a useful local discussion, see V.C.H. *Warwickshire* ii, pp. 149–55, for the gilds of Coventry and their functions, and more recently C. Phythian-Adams, 'Ceremony and the citizen, the communal year at Coventry 1450–1550', in P. Clark and P. Slack, eds, *Crisis and Order in English Towns 1500–1700*, Routledge, 1972.

20 J. C. Cox, *Churchwardens' Accounts: from the 14th century to the close of the seventeenth century*, Methuen, 1913; Tate, *Parish Chest*, pp. 86–107.

21 R. Fieldhouse, 'Richmond hearth tax and social structure', *Cleveland and Teesside Local History Society Bulletin* xiv (1971). I am most grateful to Mr Fieldhouse for his help with this section.

22 Tate, *Parish Chest*, pp. 187–239.

23 HC. 1816, vol. xvi; HC. series 1 (1774–1802) vol. ix; 1803–4, vol. xiii; 1818, vol. xix; 1819, vol. ix; 1822, vol. v; 1825, vol. iv; 1830–1, vol. xi; 1835, vol. xlvii. These so-called 'Pauper Returns' were collected by the quarter sessions and copies often survive locally. See D. A. Baugh, 'The cost of poor relief in S.E. England 1790–1834', *Econ. Hist. Rev.* xxviii (1975) 50–68.

24 For this body and the changes in its activities, see Owen, *English Philanthropy, 1660–1960*.

25 Most of these parliamentary papers are listed in Powell, op. cit.; see also HC. 1880, vol. lxviii.

26 For the full range of sources for local friendly societies, see Gosden, op. cit.

Chapter 10   Education

1 The use of the word 'formal' in this chapter is to be read in the light of chapter 8 above. It applies to providing bodies, not to 'formal education' as used by educationalists.

2 W. H. G. Armytage, *Four Hundred Years of English Education*, Cambridge U.P., 1964; H. C. Barnard, *A History of English Education from 1760–1944*, Univ. of London Press, 1961; S. J. Curtis, *History of Education in Great Britain*, 7th edn, Univ. Tutorial Press, 1967; D. Wardle, *English Popular Education, 1780–1970*, Cambridge U.P., 1970; M. V. J. Seaborne, *Education*, Vista Histories, 1966; J. Lawson and H. Silver, *Social History of Education in England*, Methuen, 1973.

3 A. F. Leach, *The Schools of Medieval England*, Methuen, 1915, repr. 1969;

N. Orme, *English Schools in the Middle Ages*, Methuen, 1973, with a useful gazetteer.

4 Licences were often ignored or only sought when a rival teacher appeared on the scene; some requests for licences stated that the teacher had been so engaged (unlicensed) for thirty years or so.

5 J. Simon, *Education and Society in Tudor England*, Cambridge U.P., 1966.

6 For different aspects of what follows, see B. Simon, ed., *Education in Leicestershire, 1540–1940*, Leicester U.P., 1968, a most important collection of essays.

7 M. J. Jones, *The Charity School Movement*, Cass, 1938, repr. 1963. See M. Spufford, 'The schooling of the peasantry in Cambridgeshire 1575–1700', in J. Thirsk, ed., *Land, Church and People*, British Agricultural Hist. Soc., 1970.

8 The Nottingham material comes from D. Wardle, *Education and Society in Nineteenth-Century Nottingham*, Cambridge U.P., 1971.

9 Unpublished figures supplied by W. H. Hosford of Sleaford; for a critique of this method of analysis, see below.

10 *Nottingham and its Villages*, pp. 24–5; M. Sanderson, 'Literacy and social mobility in the Industrial Revolution in England', *Past and Present* lvi (1972) 75–104; F. Musgrove, 'Middle-class education and employment in the nineteenth century', *Econ. Hist. Rev.* xii (1959) 99–111.

11 See L. Stone, 'Literacy and education in England, 1640–1900', *Past and Present* xlii (1969) 69–139; W. P. Baker, *Parish Registers and illiteracy in East Yorkshire*, East Yorks Local History Society Series xiii (1961); R. C. Russell, *History of Schools and Education in Lindsey, 1800–1902*, 4 parts, Lindsey Education Comm., 1965–7. See note 20 below.

12 Pike, p. 94. See J. S. Hurt, *Education in Evolution: Church, State, Society and Popular Education, 1800–1870*, Hart-Davis, 1971; G. Sutherland, *Elementary Education in the Nineteenth Century*, Historical Association, 1971; W. B. Stephens, 'Early Victorian Coventry: education in an industrial community, 1830–51', Everitt, ed., *Perspectives in English Urban History*.

13 There were other societies, such as the Home and Colonial School Society, the Wesleyan Methodist Education Committee, the Catholic Poor School Committee, the Congregational School Society and the Baptist School Society.

14 For the terms of public and private, see above, p. 205.

15 See on this Best, pp. 156–60; M. Cruikshank, *Church and State in English Education, 1870 to Present Day*, Macmillan, 1963; P. W. Musgrave, *Society and Education in England since 1800*, Methuen, 1968.

16 A. Rogers, 'Churches and children, a study in the controversy over the 1902 Education Act', *British Journal of Educational Studies* viii (1959) 29–51.

17 Best, pp. 159–60.

18 J. F. C. Harrison, *Learning and Living 1790–1960*, Routledge, 1961.

19 M. V. J. Seaborne, *The English School, its Architecture and Organisation, 1370–1870*, Routledge, 1971. There are very useful articles on the Sources for Educational History in *British Journal of Educational Studies* i and ii (1952–4). Students should use this journal and the more recent *History of Education Society Bulletin*, issued by the University of Leicester.

20 R. S. Schofield, 'Measurement of literacy in pre-industrial England', in J. Goody, ed., *Literacy in Traditional Societies*, Cambridge U.P., 1968; T. W. Laqueur, 'Literacy and social mobility in the industrial revolution in England', *Past and Present* lxiv (1974) 96–107; R. T. Vann, 'Literacy in seventeenth century England, some hearth tax evidence', *Journal of Interdisciplinary*

History v.2 (1974) 287–94; M. Spufford, *Contrasting Communities*, Cambridge U.P., 1974, pp. 192–218.

21 *Education, England and Wales*, HC. 1852–3, vol. xc; 1854, vol. xl; see R. J. Smith, 'Education, society and literacy: Notts. in the mid-nineteenth century', *Birmingham Historical Journal* xii (1969–70) 42–56.

22 HC. 1818, vol. iv; 1819, vol. ix; 1835, vols. xli–xliii. See E. G. West, 'Resource allocation and growth in early nineteenth century British education', *Econ. Hist. Rev.* xxiii (1970) 68–95, and the reply by J. S. Hurt, xxiv (1971) 624–42.

23 B. Simon, *Studies in the History of Education, 1780–1870*, Lawrence and Wishart, 1960, p. 320.

24 The most useful are listed in Powell, *Local History from Blue Books*.

25 See Pike, pp. 120–5.

26 See B. G. Everett, 'The school board, an exercise in participation', *Loc. Hist.* ix.3 (1970) 130–3; B. V. Spence, 'School board records in Co. Durham, 1870–1904', *Archives* x (1971) 13–18. Many Board records are in the library of the Department of Education and Science, Curzon Street, London. See G. Baron, *Bibliographical Guide to the English Educational System* (1965).

Chapter 11   Leisure and cultural provision

1 V.C.H. *Warwickshire* viii, pp. 512–13. The literature is large and growing. See F. Alderson, *Inland Resorts and Spas of Britain*, David and Charles, 1973; R. W. Malcolmson, *Popular Recreations in English Society 1700–1850*, Cambridge U.P., 1973.

2 See D. George, *England in Transition*, Penguin Books, 1953, pp. 52–9.

3 Best, pp. 197–227, is important here.

4 B. Harrison and B. Trinder, *Drink and Sobriety in an Early Victorian Country Town: Banbury, 1830–1860*, Longmans, 1969.

5 See B. Harrison, 'Religion and recreation in nineteenth-century England', *Past and Present* xxxviii (1967) 98–125. See also Dr Harrison's paper, 'Pubs', in Dyos and Wolff, eds, *The Victorian City: images and realities*, i, pp. 161–90; for the earlier period, see A. M. Everitt, 'The English urban inn, 1560–1760', in Everitt, ed., *Perspectives in English Urban History*.

6 See B. H. Harrison, *Drink and the Victorians*, Faber, 1971.

7 B. H. Harrison, 'Temperance societies', *Loc. Hist.* viii.4 and 5 (1968–9) and the sources quoted there. His *Dictionary of British Temperance Biography*, published by the Society for Labour History, 1973, is a mine of information.

8 Iliffe and Baguley, *Victorian Nottingham* iv, p. 82.

9 A. E. Brown, ed., *The Growth of Leicester*, Leicester U.P., 1970, pp. 55–62.

10 G. F. Chadwick, *The Park and the Town*, Architectural Press, 1966.

11 Cf. D. C. Barrett, 'Allotments and the problem of rural poverty, 1780–1840', in E. L. Jones and G. E. Mingay, *Land, Labour and Population in the Industrial Revolution*, E. Arnold, 1967, pp. 162–83.

12 These Museums and Public Libraries Acts of 1845, 1850 and 1855 were adoptive.

13 A. F. J. Brown and A. C. Edwards, *English History from Essex Sources, 1750–1900*, Chelmsford, Essex C.C., 1953, pp. 176–7.

14 Best, p. 173.

15 Best, pp. 214–15.

16 See A. Briggs, *Mass Entertainment: Origins of a Modern Industry*, Griffin Press,

Adelaide, 1960; G. A. Cranfield, *Development of the Provincial Newspaper, 1700—1760*, Oxford U.P., 1962; D. Read, *Press and People*, E. Arnold, 1961; I. Jackson, *The Provincial Press and the Community*, Manchester U.P., 1971.

17 Pimlott, *Englishman's Holiday*; A. B. Granville, *The Spas of England and Principal Sea-bathing Places*, 2 vols (1841) reprinted Adams and Dart (Moonraker Press) Bradford-on-Avon, 1972—3.

18 Rogers, *Stability and Change*, p. 76.

19 Brown, *English History from Essex Sources*, p. 176. This attack on peasant culture is seen in many places; see Rex C. Russell's forthcoming study of the Lincolnshire peasant, and R. Samuel, ed., *Village Life and Labour*, Routledge, 1975.

20 See the calendars for Banbury in 1843 and 1858 in Harrison and Trinder, cited above.

21 H. Meller, *Leisure and the Changing City*, 1976.

22 Bagley, *Historical Interpretation* vol. ii, pp. 114—22.

23 Rogers, 'Lincolnshire innkeeper', *The Village* xxii (1967) 46—54.

24 HC. 1852—1853, vol. ci, etc.; HC. 1849, vol. xvii.

25 Bagley, *Historical Interpretation* ii, 272—9.

26 But see above, p. 169.

27 *Tercentenary Handlist of English and Welsh Newspapers, 1620—1920*, Hodder and Stoughton, 1920; the early part is easier to use in R. S. Crane and F. B. Kaye, *Census of British Newspapers, 1620—1800*, Univ. of North Carolina Press, 1927.

28 HC. 1898, vol. xxxvi.

29 HC. 1866, vol. xvi; HC. 1892, vol. xviii.

Note on social structure

1 Alan Armstrong, in Dyos, ed., *Study of Urban History*, pp. 78—9, and in his later study, *Stability and Change in an English Country Town*, uses the 1950 categories for nineteenth-century York.

2 Such analyses may be seen in D. Charman, 'Wealth and trade in Leicester in the early sixteenth century', *Trans. Leicestershire Archaeological Society* xxv (1949); Hoskins, *Provincial England*, pp. 83—5, 90—3, and *Industry, Trade and People in Exeter, 1688—1800*, pp. 111—22; V.C.H. *Leics* iv, p. 159; J. F. Pound, 'Social and trade structure of Norwich, 1525—75', *Past and Present* xxxiv (1966) 49—69; R. Fieldhouse, 'Social structure from Tudor lay subsidies and probate inventories', *LPS* xiv (1974) 9—24.

3 Rogers, 'Borough council of Stamford' in Everitt, *Perspectives in Urban History*, pp. 28—9.

4 See the discussion in P. Laslett, *The World We Have Lost*, 2nd edn, Methuen, 1971. The study by M. Drake and P. Hammerton, *Exercises in Historical Sociology* (Open University, 1974) is now the best introduction to the whole subject.

Note on location of sources

1 *Record Repositories in Great Britain*, HMSO, latest edn. See also *Directory for Local Historians*, Standing Conference for Local History N.C.S.S., 1968.

Index